The New Nature of History

History

Knowledge, Evidence, Language

Select List of Publications by Arthur Marwick

The Deluge: British Society and the First World War (1965; 2nd edn, 1991)
War and Social Change in the Twentieth Century (1974)
The Home Front: The British and the Second World War (1976)
Women at War 1914–1918 (1977)
Class: Image and Reality in Britain, France and the USA since 1930 (1980; 2nd edn, 1989)
British Society since 1945 (1981; 3rd edn, 1996)
Beauty in History: Society, Politics and Personal Appearance c.1500 to the Present (1988)
(ed.) *The Arts, Literature and Society* (1989)
Culture in Britain since 1945 (1991)
The Sixties: Cultural Revolution in Britain, France, Italy and the United States, c.1958–c.1974 (1998)
A History of the Modern British Isles, 1914–1999: Circumstances, Events, and Outcomes (2000)
(co. ed.) *Windows on the Sixties: Exploring Key Texts of Media and Culture* (2000)
The Arts in the West since 1945 (2001)

The New Nature of History
Knowledge, Evidence, Language

ARTHUR MARWICK

LYCEUM
BOOKS, INC.

5758 S. Blackstone
Chicago, IL 60637

Published by
LYCEUM BOOKS, INC.
5758 S. Blackstone Ave.
Chicago, Illinois 60637
773+643-1903 (Fax)
773+643-1902 (Phone)
lyceum@lyceumbooks.com
http://www.lyceumbooks.com

ISBN 0-925065-61-7

Printed in Great Britain

Cataloging in Publication data is available from the Library of Congress

Published in North America under license from Palgrave Publishers Ltd, Houndmills, Basingstoke, Hants RG21 6XS, United Kingdom

Contents

Preface

When I was studying history at Edinburgh University in the mid-fifties, no explicit attention was paid to the questions of 'What is history, and why and how do you do it?' As a kind of ineffectual dietary supplement, all too typical of the attitudes of those days, we were given, quite separately from the main curriculum, a short course of lectures entitled 'History: Its Nature and Methods' by a then professor of philosophy, who had written a book, *Introduction to the Philosophy of History*. I remember, at the age of 19, getting into heated debate with the professor as I argued that what he was saying bore no relationship to our actual experiences of studying history (ever since, I have felt that philosophers, because of their *a priori* attitudes, their rigid conventions, and their specialist language, as well as their lack of practical experience, have the greatest difficulty in understanding what historians actually do). In the sixties, after interludes at Oxford and Aberdeen, and during which I also spent a year in the United States, I was back at Edinburgh as a history lecturer. In common, I don't doubt, with many other colleagues I gave considerable attention to the nature of primary sources, the different types of secondary sources, and the writing of precise, directly expressed history essays; but the general orthodoxy at the time remained that one learned what history was, and how to do it, by actually doing it. A much repeated notion was that history was a 'messy' subject, and so could not be systematised.

Towards the end of the decade, we began, with Geoffrey Best as the senior and proactive member, to develop a first-year history course which aimed to be explicit about historians' methods and assumptions. But in practice, it seemed to me, we didn't really get down to introducing students to the range of different types of primary sources most historians use and to the problems inherent in them (Engels's *The Condition of the English Working Class* stimulated debate – but not about the nature of historical sources). The other problem was the lack of suitable textbooks. Historians had not thought very deeply about their own practices, and so grasped eagerly, and somewhat thoughtlessly, at whatever books seemed to do the job for them. R. G. Collingwood (a philosopher and archaeologist) was said to be brilliant, this being proved by the fact that you couldn't always follow what he was saying, and so everybody referred, and deferred, to his *The Idea of History*. E. H. Carr was recognised as being very witty, and the Penguin edition of his *What is History?* as being a bargain, though in fact this was a book which sold almost entirely on the basis of its (misleading) title alone. Pieter Geyl's *Napoleon For and Against* was said to be a shrewd exposure of the impossibility of there being any certainty in historical writing; the book, actually, was naïve drivel (see Chapter 2). *Introduction to the Philosophy of History* by W. H. Walsh at least had the merit of being easy to understand but had nothing on the basic activities of the historian. Marc Bloch's *The Historian's Craft* (an incomplete and misleading translation of the French title, as I explain in Chapter 4) was, and is, brilliant but, for the tragic reason that as a French Resistance hero he had been tortured and shot by the Germans, unfinished; it is also rather sophisticated for first-year students. Geoffrey Elton was then only just beginning to publish his magnificent exposures of the nonsense spouted by philosophers (including Collingwood) and Marxists, particularly Carr; unfortunately, Elton insisted on the primacy of political history, unhelpful to those of us who wished to demonstrate that social history was not just an important pursuit, but a very rigorous one.

There were, I felt, important things which needed saying that were not featured in any of the existing books; above all, I felt that one could systematise the practices and purposes of the historian and that one should set these out at the beginning of a history syllabus, rather than let them 'emerge' over several years of study. So, at the age of 32, having already published four books (one of them, at least, being not at all bad – it is indeed still in print), I embarked on the writing of what I modestly called *An Introduction to History*. It was while discussing this project with my agent, Michael Sissons, that I mentioned the course I had endured as a student, 'History: Its Nature and Methods', whose deficiencies I now proposed to remedy; Michael, who believes that no book should ever be called 'An Introduction' to anything, seized on the phrase 'History: Its Nature . . .'. And so the book in progress got its title: *The Nature of History*.

At that very juncture, I was appointed the first Professor of History at the newly established Open University. My overwhelming motivation in seeking that job was that it would give me the opportunity to teach history in the way I thought it ought to be taught: I began writing the 'Introduction to History' which, in a series of revised versions, has appeared in successive Open University foundation or first-level Arts courses ever since. Prior to the delivery to students of the first Open University courses in 1971, *The Nature of History* hit the bookshops in 1970. I was now 34.

The aims of the book were clear and, I think, fairly satisfactorily achieved. But there was a great deal of naïvety and cumbersome writing. In the second edition of 1981 I failed to address these problems thoroughly enough. The book remained an entirely positive one, enthusiastically expounding 'the social necessity' for history, as I put it. I was still unaware of the attacks on professional history being mounted by its postmodernist critics. For the third edition of 1989 I did come close to rewriting the entire book, expanding what I have always regarded as its most important part, 'The Historian at Work', from one chapter to two. For the first time I introduced Foucault – courteously and without engaging in any angry polemics.

As attacks on the intelligence, and sometimes even the integrity, of historians have mounted I have felt bound, as explained in Chapter 1 of this book, to take up the more aggressive stance evident in a couple of articles I published during the 1990s. Since others have commented on this 'aggressiveness' or 'intemperance' (often using less genteel epithets!), I want to make a couple of clarifications here:

(1) In the late 1980s I deliberately set out to learn more about postmodernist theory, and when commissioned by the Social History Society to organise a conference on 'The Arts, Literature and Society' I made a special point of inviting two distinguished pioneers in the application of discourse theory to literature and art, Professors John Barrell and Marcia Pointon, to give papers. It is no reflection on these two highly respected academics that I came to the conclusion that, fascinating as their approaches were, they really had nothing to offer to historical study.

(2) When, in the autumn of 1993, I gave a public performance at the Open University (no notes, but slides of various paintings and the duet 'O soave fanciulla' from *La Bohème*) with the 'intemperate' title 'Metahistory is Bunk, History is Essential', I took care to arrange a seminar for the next day in which the following leading 'metahistorians' were invited to criticise my lecture: Hayden White, Ludmilla Jordanova, John Tosh, and Stuart Hall. The subsequent published debate between myself and Hayden White, first in the *Times Higher Education Supplement* and then, more substantially, in the *Journal of Contemporary History* (January and April 1995) was entirely arranged and, indeed, *insisted on* by me. I am always eager to have weaknesses in my arguments pointed out to me, and I have never felt any need to have the last word. One should not, in my view, impose one's own assumptions on students, without giving them a proper opportunity to consider the opposition case. Perhaps I can add that I found Hayden White a delightfully civilised person and a wonderful drinking companion. I believe in uncompromising intellectual debate, and have never ever considered that intellectual disagreement must entail personal antagonism.

Anyway, I have totally recast and rewritten the book, giving it a new coherence and a new dynamic thrust deriving from the three words of the sub-title, 'Knowledge', 'Evidence', 'Language'. I stress *knowledge* first because historians do not, as too many of my colleagues keep mindlessly repeating, 'reconstruct' or even 'represent' the past. What historians do is produce *knowledge about* the past. Once that fundamental point is grasped all kinds of misconceptions fall away. History, the production of bodies of knowledge about the past, is, like the sciences, a collective enterprise. In this book, I criticise what I call the *auteur* theory of history, the theory that historians, or at least a select few of them (the rest, the assumption usually seems to be, can be ignored), should be treated as individual literary figures, akin to best-selling novelists.

The second fundamental relating to history is that it must be seen to be based on *evidence* (hence the apparatus of footnotes and bibliographies) and not on mere speculation, or *a priori* theorising. Since history is a collective enterprise, some of that evidence will be found in the works of other historians (the secondary sources). But in the last analysis, the production of new historical knowledge (as this book will demonstrate over and over again) depends on highly skilled and difficult work among the primary sources. The more ignorant among history's critics like to use sneering phrases like 'the cult of the archive'. There is no cult of the archive, just the fundamental fact that without work in the archives, which can often be grindingly boring, the supply of new history would simply terminate.

Problems of *language* are encountered by historians both during their researches in the primary sources and in writing up these researches in their articles and books. The difficulties, obscurities, and ambiguities contained within the language of the primary sources were first addressed by the *érudits* (erudite scholars) of the sixteenth and seventeenth centuries, who developed the technical – or ancillary – skills in deciphering the 'codes' different types of documents were written in, their formal qualities, their handwriting and so on, these ancillary skills being known as philology and palaeography. Only those who have actually laboured in the archives – and this excludes practically all of those who prattle on about the 'linguistic turn' – can understand the nature of these problems. Primary sources are filled with technical terms which have to be construed with the utmost care. Analysing the language and format of a primary source in order to squeeze the last drop of information out of it is a fundamental skill of the historian on which no advice is required from postmodernist theorists. When it comes to writing history, pains (literally!) have to be taken to write precisely and explicitly, avoiding the temptation to reach for ready-made metaphors and clichés, working overtime to get the words and phrases absolutely right, being conscious always of the ambiguities inherent in such words as 'state', 'liberal', 'class', 'culture', 'cultural', not to mention 'ideology', 'discourse', and 'narrative', and the vagueness of such phrases as 'public opinion' or 'the middle-class vote'.

In my original plans for *The New Nature of History* I envisaged cutting the two historiographical (that is, concerning the history of history, from Thucydides to the present) chapters to one. However, it has become clear through the national benchmarking and learning outcomes exercises that there is a strong feeling within the historical profession that those who study history should have knowledge of such past historical writers as Thucydides, Voltaire, Ranke, Namier, Braudel, and so on. What I have done is to reduce the length of the first of these chapters (now Chapter 3, not 2) and of the main part of the second (now Chapter 4), while adding a great deal of new material on the most renowned historians writing at the beginning of the new century. More important, I have restructured both chapters in order to concentrate on one composite theme: What questions arise whenever anyone attempts to write history? What positive solutions have past historians come up with, and what inadequate ones? What have been their 'errors' and misconceptions? Overall, in what ways, through setbacks as well as advances, has the discipline of history become more effective, more sophisticated, more able to cope with an ever-widening domain of topics and problems?

It is a contention of this book that historical controversies (that is, debates among historians) do serve the vital function of eventual increases in historical knowledge – few would today accept A. J. P. Taylor's views on the origins of the Second World War, but he did perform a useful service in forcing re-examination of the orthodoxies of his time. In the old book there was a whole chapter on historical controversies. But there are now masses of excellent books and pamphlets on major historical controversies, and keeping up with all the latest work in the major areas of controversy is nearly impossible for one individual. In any case, I am anxious not to put too much emphasis on historical debates, which are sometimes tainted with self-glorification and the sheer joy of battle. Thus, I have dropped that chapter, incorporating brief discussions of historical controversies elsewhere. To me, as already remarked, the most important part of the book was always that discussing – as the other books never do – the actual activities of the working historian, including that vital distinction, which I first introduced in 1970, between the 'witting testimony' and the 'unwitting testimony' of the primary sources. As a result of my further reflections on these matters, the two relevant chapters (5 and 6) have been extended. Elsewhere, and particularly in the old Chapters 1, 4 and 7, there was much which now seems of little importance, or even interest, and that has been cut ('junk cuts', you might say, if in a light-hearted mood). Even in the 1989 edition many sentences and phrases were sloppy and lacking in that precision all historians should aim at. I believe I have done a little better this time. 'Revise, revise, revise', that is the lesson for all who would write history, whether students, general readers, or professionals: not to achieve literary or rhetorical effect, but to achieve the essential exactness, and to avoid any 'slippage' of meaning.

In my case against the metaphysical critics of what historians do, and don't do, one of my strongest points is that they themselves have little or no experience of producing research-based history. It is only proper, therefore, that I should make brief reference to my own experience as a writer and a teacher of history. Almost all of my published work has concerned the late twentieth century: my *The Sixties* was based on extensive archive research in four countries. For my book on *Class* I worked in archives relating to the 1930s, 1940s and 1950s in France and America, as well as Britain. My work on *Beauty in History*, however, entailed analysing French and Italian printed sources from the sixteenth and seventeenth centuries, and using nineteenth-century American archive materials. In my earliest research I worked in a range of British archives, with reference first to the Independent Labour Party, and then principally to the domestic experience of the two world wars. Production of Open University television programmes has involved me in retracing the research of Professor Michael Thompson in the major archives relating to English landed society in the nineteenth century, in the study of seventeenth-century manuscript materials relating to the family (with the expert guidance of my colleague Professor Rosemary O'Day), and of documents relating to the French Revolution in the National Archives in Paris and two different local archives in Nantes (guided expertly by Professors William Doyle and Colin Jones). I have certainly experienced many times the sense of shock and revelation referred to by one of today's most illustrious historians, Robert Darnton, as one encounters the attitudes and mental set of a past society very different from our own. I know only too well that documents in the archives do not regularly present 'facts' or 'narratives', and how complex is the task of extracting relevant information from them. I have long had a specialist interest in non-traditional sources – the artefacts of high culture as well as popular culture – and I have a long record of using visuals in my books as genuine primary sources to be explicated, not simply as ornamentation.

The standard platitude of history's critics is that it is 'in crisis', this being part of an alleged greater crisis in capitalism or 'bourgeois society'. 'Crisis, What Crisis?' is the sub-title of my concluding chapter. Actually, history has never been more popular amongst students and general readers. History's achievements in explaining the origins of the French Revolution, the precise role of Adolf Hitler in the most horrible events of the twentieth century, or the religious beliefs of the Ancient Greeks, continue to expand. What the growing number of readers and students want, of course, is not the metaphysical nonsense of the postmodernists, but to find out (as far as is humanly possible) what actually happened. It is the purpose of this book to show how historians (as far as is humanly possible) try to meet that demand.

Two minor points with regard to the presentation of this book. It has been structured so that, ideally, it should be read through from start to finish: each chapter, I believe, follows logically from the previous one and leads logically into the next. However, I fully appreciate that certain chapters, particularly for students, may be of greater relevance than others. In order, therefore, that the chapters can be used as self-standing statements on their particular topics, there is a certain amount of repetition of key points (to avoid the necessity for referring back). Secondly, though there is a great deal about scholarly apparatus in this book (and detailed directions in Appendix C), I have, in a book which is pedagogic rather than scholarly in intention, kept my own endnotes to a minimum: where the essential information is already contained in my main text, I have not repeated it in an endnote.

Back in the late sixties a book of this sort was a very hazardous enterprise (no publisher would take it on the basis of the synopsis, which itself attracted much supercilious comment), and it was only when it was completed that the original version of this book was accepted for publication: I therefore remain deeply grateful for the support and advice I received at that time from Lord Alan Bullock and Owen Dudley Edwards. The rewritten version, appearing as the third edition of the old book in 1989, was commented on most constructively by my two colleagues Professors Clive Emsley and Tony Lentin. This completely new book has had the immense benefit of the critical comments of a new colleague, Dr Ole Grell. I also wish to thank Debbie Williams for deploying her considerable secretarial and managerial skills in seeing this complex new book through from first draft to finalised version, tracking down titles and publication dates along the way. Finally, my thanks to Katy Coutts for her excellent work as copy-editor and proofreader, and to Terka Bagley of Palgrave for her enthusiastic support throughout this enterprise.

1 Introduction: The Battle of Basic Assumptions

1 Stating my Position

This book offers answers to three questions: What (is history)?; Why (do history)?; How (does one do history)? Note that I say that the book 'offers' answers, not that it 'answers' the three questions. Note that I use the rather coarse verb 'doing' rather than the more elegant 'studying' history. I have, after much thought, chosen my words very carefully, in order that they should express what I intend as clearly as possible, or at least should not lead to misunderstandings or contain misrepresentations. That point will recur throughout the book: however language may be used in poetry, plays and novels, in historical writing it must always be explicit and precise. The answers 'I' offer are those which, I believe, would be agreed to by the vast majority of the historical profession. But I want it to be clear from the start that they are not the *only* answers that could be given: commentators with very different basic assumptions would give different answers. My questions and answers do not relate solely to those who are studying history, that is, by definition, students: they, certainly, are 'doing' history, but then so also are those who actually produce the history, historians, and my questions and answers cover them also. Beyond the question of why students should want to study history, or members of the general public read history books, lies the question of why historical research, leading to the publication of history books, goes on in the first place, and why professional historians are paid out of taxpayer's money to *do* this.

The next big, recurring point I want to make is that the answers one gives (and, often, the questions one asks) – and thus, of course, how one writes a book such as this – depend upon one's basic assumptions. I cannot stress too much this point about assumptions. I use the word 'battle' in my chapter title, and the simple fact is that today (unlike in 1970 when the first version of this book was published) we cannot make any progress at all in discussing the nature of history until we consider the arguments of the postmodernist critics, who have been denouncing the history of historians (such as myself) as merely bourgeois ideology, and the stories we tell as accounts without any claim to objectivity. Analogous 'science wars' have been going on over the same period, with the postmodernist critics claiming that the sciences, like history, are 'culturally constructed'. If you have done any reading at all in the area, you are almost bound to have come across the postmodernist case. I shall be arguing against it, and my hope is that you will be persuaded by what I am saying. But I know that I have no chance of convincing anyone who is already a confirmed postmodernist. Our basic assumptions are different. In my view, writers and teachers should always state their fundamental assumptions, and readers and students should always seek to find out what these are.

My assumptions relate to the first word in the sub-title of this book: 'knowledge'. We live in a dreadfully unequal world, in which basic human rights and freedoms are denied to millions. However, it is my belief (based, I think, on a rational assessment of the evidence) that the living standards and freedoms which most of us enjoy in the West are fundamentally due to the expansion in human knowledge over the centuries, principally, perhaps, knowledge in the sciences and technologies, but also in the humanities and social sciences. I further believe that decent living conditions, freedom, *empowerment* for the deprived millions everywhere depend on the continuing expansion and, above all, *diffusion* of knowledge. I make no arrogant claims on behalf of historical knowledge, simply the point (which I shall elaborate in Chapter 2) that what happened in the past influences what happens in the present, and, indeed, what will happen in the future, so that knowledge of the past – history – is essential to society.

This leads me to the point that, given that historical knowledge is essential to society, we have to be sure that that knowledge is as sound as we can make it. Technological knowledge which leads to bridges that fall down, television sets that explode, and bombs that do not is of no value. Human beings are not born with knowledge of how to build bridges or make television sets: they have to learn it. Similarly, human beings are not born with knowledge of the past (though it often seems to be assumed that they are): they have to learn it, and that learning, at whatever a remove, and however filtered (through school lessons, magazines, television, or whatever) comes ultimately from the researches and writings of historians. To my mind, it is an enormous tribute to historians that we already do know so much about the past: about ancient China, about the Renaissance, about poverty and ordinary life in an incredible range of different cultures, about the denial and gaining of civil rights by, for example, women, blacks, gays; about the origins of the First World War; about Russia under Stalin and Germany under Hitler; about the recent machinations of the CIA and MI5. How has all this knowledge come about? It has come about (this is one of my most crucial contentions, or assumptions) through large numbers of historians *doing* history in strict accordance with the long-established, though constantly developing, canons of the historical profession. Most of this book will be taken up with explicating these canons; there are, as I shall show, different types of history (social, diplomatic, econometric, history of science, history of women, and so on), but *all* – let there be no mis-understanding about this[1] – are governed by the need to conform to certain agreed standards and principles. If history, as I claim, is needed by human societies, and if, therefore, that history must be as reliable as it is possible to make it, the guarantee lies in the careful observance of the methods and principles of professional history: 'historians', as Eric Hobsbawm, Britain's most distinguished living historian (and a Marxist as it happens), has said, 'are professionally obliged not to get it wrong – or at least to make an effort not to'.[2] Correspondingly, there is little value to society in works which use events and developments in the past to indulge speculative fantasies, to purvey propaganda or to support *a priori* theories, which put forward subjective 'narratives' and are proud of it.

My assumptions, then, are the assumptions of the vast majority of professional historians: the 'History' in my main title is 'the History of professional historians' (my book is not on The Nature of 'The Past'). However, I have no mandate to speak on behalf of the historical profes-sion, though the claim I will vigorously make is that I have thought longer and harder about the issues implicit in my title than most other members of the profession. Many will disagree with the way I put things, and some even with the things I put. But I seek no identity other than that of 'historian', or, at the very most, 'social and cultural historian'. Others have categorised me, and the history I write, as 'posi-tivist' (a nineteenth-century term, which has no meaning today, but which is often used as a general term of abuse), 'empiricist' (I would hope that that term could be applied to all historians, as to all scientists), and 'reconstructionist' (this label, as used by Alun Munslow,[3] is asso-ciated with the notion of history as a 'craft', to which I am also alleged to subscribe: I have to say, as firmly as I can, that I do not believe that historians 'reconstruct' or 'craft' anything; what they do is contribute to historical knowledge, that is, knowledge about the past). If further identifying characteristics are required for the history which is expli-cated in this book, I would say that it is 'non-metaphysical' and 'source-based': it is not concerned with theoretical speculation about the nature of the past, or the nature of the relationships between past, present, and future; it is concerned with addressing clearly defined problems relating to what happened in the past, and it addresses these problems by meticulously examining all the sources relevant to them.

I have set out my assumptions. The most important one at this juncture is that there are strict historical methods and principles and that the
application of these has produced a great corpus of invaluable historical
knowledge. What I am saying here, and will be saying throughout this
book, is attacked by those who can, in convenient shorthand fashion, be
described as 'postmodernists' (I will name names shortly), and also, in
slightly different ways, by those who hold very firmly to traditional
Marxism and those, often followers of Max Weber, who adopt a holistic,
social sciences view of the problems of societies, past and present. I am
now going to work through the eight main battlegrounds wherein one
can perceive the clash of assumptions between non-metaphysical,
source-based historians and their postmodernist, and other, critics.

2   Eight Battlegrounds

1 Metaphysical, Nomothetic and Ontological Approaches

What a bunch of pompous polysyllabics! Let me explain. It is proper that
human beings should be concerned with questions about the purpose of
life, the fundamentals which determine the way in which societies
develop, the reasons behind the inequalities and oppressions which
exist in the world today, and so on: these are ontological questions,
and are the responsibility of that branch of philosophy known as metaphysics. 'Nomothetic' is a word which, I'm glad to say, seems to be going
out of use. In certain forms of intellectual discourse it used to be argued
(with reason, I think) that in all scholarly investigations one could make
a broad bipartite division between the nomothetic approach and
the idiographic, meaning, roughly, the distinction between, on the one
side, the theoretical and speculative approach, and, on the other, the
purely empirical one. In the nineteenth century, it was possible for
intellectuals (the central discipline was philosophy: professional history
was not yet fully established, and what was developing into professional
physics was usually referred to as 'natural philosophy') to formulate
grand-scale statements about how societies evolved from the past,
through the present and into the future. Such statements are sometimes
termed 'speculative philosophy of history'. Leading exponents were
Friedrich Hegel and Karl Marx. Self-evidently, such statements had to
be highly abstract and theoretical, and could not be based, if at all, upon
any very extensive range of sources. The desire to incorporate studies of
the past into some grand theory about human destiny, about the purpose
and direction, the 'meaning', of life, is still strong (and it does seem that
human beings have an inclination towards great holistic schemes, such

as religions, which can have the evolutionary functions of providing unity and emotional security). Many social scientists today, though they would probably define their aims more modestly, see themselves as the descendants of nineteenth-century philosophy; professional history, on the other hand, developed entirely separately from philosophy.

There are those, historians, social scientists, philosophers, critics, artists of all types, who see Karl Marx as a quite exceptional genius, to be ranked with Newton, Darwin and, perhaps (I am not sure that this is a compliment), Freud. This was the view, too, of two twentieth-century intellectuals central to the development of postmodernist criticisms of professional history: Michel Foucault (1926–84) and Hayden White (b. 1928).[4] I shall return to Marxist 'speculative philosophy of history' in point 3, but will state now my counter-assumption that, while it was possible for Newton and Einstein (in physics) and Darwin (in biology) to make decisive and authoritative interventions in their particular sciences, it is quite impossible for one person (however able) to make an analogous intervention covering all societies (or even just Western ones) and the relationships within them and between them, through the past, present, and into the future. I would regard that statement as being, anyway, about as absolute as anyone could make at the beginning of the twenty-first century; however, since I am not concerned to go out of my way to denigrate Marx, I would add that while many of his comments were sensible enough in the mid-nineteenth century, when he was writing, they are scarcely likely to have much validity after 150 years of change.

Those who take the opposite view would see Marx as having established the essential groundplan for the study of the way societies change through the past and into the future, which has subsequently been modified by such scholars as the Italian Antonio Gramsci, the German/American Herbert Marcuse, the French post-structuralists, including Michel Foucault, Roland Barthes, Louis Althusser, and Jacques Derrida, and the perfectly formed postmodernists Jean-François Lyotard and Jean Baudrillard. For the broadly Marxist outlook, much qualified and refined by later scholars, I shall use the adjective 'Marxisant', meaning 'leaning towards Marxism' or 'inflected by Marxism'. It is proper to record that many historians who are Marxist or Marxisant do subscribe to the principles set out in this book (Eric Hobsbawm being an outstanding example), but, to come to the centre of this battlefield, the main body of those taking up the metaphysical stance I have identified attack professional history on a number of grounds, which I shall be discussing throughout the rest of this chapter. Here, two big ones: that professional history is trivial and overly scholastic, in that it simply does not address the ontological issues; and that professional history is overly narrow and specialised, in that it misses the essential interconnectedness of everything, failing to adopt a holistic or interdisciplinary approach. Some critics, often strongly Marxist or Weberian, though not usually postmodernist, have called for a complete fusion between history and the social sciences (with, it is generally made clear, the social sciences as the senior partners). The responses presented in this book are: that history cannot, and does not aim, to answer the big questions about human destiny and the meaning of life, and that, on the contrary, its great value to society lies in the fact that in limiting itself to clearly defined, manageable (though never that manageable!) questions, it can offer clear and well-substantiated (though never utterly uncontested) answers; and that the very strength of history in producing these answers lies in its intensive specialisation – though historians have to be aware of other disciplines, and may well borrow from them, trying to resolve usually intractable historical problems requires the full method-ology discussed in this book; any contamination with the faith in a single holistic procedure will simply produce muddled and poorly substan-tiated results.

I want to insist on the distinction between the metaphysical approach and the genuinely historical one (professional, non-metaphysical, source-based). The aims are different and the very language used is different. It is simply not the aim of historians to produce exciting, speculative, all-embracing theories, or gigantic leaps of the imagination utterly detached from the evidence, and still less should they try to integrate their own researches into such speculations. As the distin-guished contemporary American philosopher John Searle has written: 'it is a sad fact about my profession, wonderful though it is, that the most famous and admired philosophers are often the ones with the most preposterous theories'.[5] The language and categories philosophers use firmed up in the nineteenth century, and they have been amplified by postmodernist philosophers adding jargon terms of their own. Of course, as Searle points out,[6] the way questions are posed determines the (often wrong) answers given: taken out of context, and used as if transparent tools of epistemological analysis, such words as 'positivist', 'humanist', 'idealist', 'materialist', constantly on the lips of the metaphys-icists, have no salience for historians.

2 Radical Politics – or just Nihilism?

Marx excoriated the philosophers of his day for merely seeking to under-stand the world: to him, the problem was 'to change it'. Within these three little words lies the key to a second divide between the metaphys-icists and the historians which reinforces the first. At the heart of the metaphysical view lies the fundamental Marxist belief that the society we inhabit is the bad bourgeois society, though, fortunately, this society is in a state of crisis, so that the good society which lies just around the corner can be easily attained if only we work systematically to destroy the language, the values, the culture, the ideology of 'bourgeois' society. This entails a massive radical left-wing political programme, and everything the metaphysicists write, every criticism they make, is determined by that overriding programme; the exceptions are those postmodernists, still convinced of the utter evil of 'bourgeois' society, who have become so pessimistic about any hope of change that they have fallen back into a destructive nihilism, together with some right-wingers who have taken a postmodernist stance because they see it as the height of intellectual fashion. Now, most historians have political views and loyalties; more critically perhaps, some are highly conservative by temperament, others instinctively ally themselves with reformers, and some can't help being enthusiastic about radicalism in the past. Political and personal attachments will enter into the history historians write, particularly in those frequent cases where the sources are inconclusive, thus leaving a good deal of space for personal interpretation. But historians are obliged, to quote Hobsbawm again, 'to make an effort not to' get it wrong, that is to say to make an effort to overcome any political predilections they may have. As citizens, historians should certainly act in accordance with their political principles; but in their history, they should make a conscious effort to overcome these. It is worthy of note that in Hobsbawm's collection of learned articles and journalistic pieces, *Uncommon People* (1999), the Marxism scarcely shows in the learned articles, where, indeed, at times Hobsbawm takes up positions contrary to orthodox Marxism, while the Marxism is often very evident indeed in the journalism. I don't doubt for a moment that whatever brave efforts the historian makes, vices of various kinds, including unconscious ones, will intervene.

But, with regard to the main battle, there are a number of points to be made. First of all, a very large number of the issues which historians deal with do not lend themselves to different interpretations depending upon political principle. One of the issues I have myself been concerned with is that of whether there is any link between total war and social change: I honestly do not know what a Tory view would be and what a socialist one. The second point is that no accounts given by historians will be accepted as definitive: they will be subjected within the profession to discussion and debate, qualification and correction, and, if they are affected by political bias, this will certainly be vigorously pointed out. Beyond that there is the role of the reader: a book that is, say, very strongly feminist in tone may still be a valuable contribution to knowledge, but the reader will be able to reject for himself/herself the bits which are manifestly feminist propaganda rather than reasoned conclusions. There is, in fact, all the difference in the world between the debates and discussions held among professional historians (and their readers) and the monolithic positions of the metaphysicists, most of whom, when you pay close attention to what they are saying (often a tough assignment!), are quite openly boastful of their propagandist aims, against the bourgeoisie, against patriarchy, for example. Professional historians should be absolutely clear that they are not propagandists: their job is to understand the past (or parts of it) – an extremely difficult task – not, as historians (as distinct from their role as citizens), to change the future.

In her *History in Practice* (2000) Ludmilla Jordanova (a specialist in the history and philosophy of science, an area which has long been influenced by Foucault) declares that the 'pursuit of history is, whether practitioners choose to acknowledge it or not, a political occupation'.[7] That seems to me both a straightforward misuse of words, and a dangerous statement. We all fall short of our principles, but it is important none the less that the principles be stated and restated. We must always bear in mind that history (like the sciences) is a cumulative and co-operative activity. Historians don't just write research monographs, where, granted, the personal passion may be a vital driving force; they also write textbooks, summaries of existing knowledge, where the biases inherent in difficult research works should be filtered out; and they teach. It is in teaching (certainly at pre-university level) that the obligation to present a fair distillation of differing interpretations, and to avoid any one political line, is strongest. To me a teacher who maintained that history was a 'political occupation', and who acted accordingly, would be guilty of unprofessional conduct. Nor would I want the general reader, seeking enlightenment on the crucial issues of the past, to be informed that every historical work is politically biased. The point, I think, comes over most strongly of all if one reflects on the task most professional historians have of supervising PhD students, that is, of enabling aspirant historians to go through their professional apprenticeship. To encourage such students to believe that it is unavoidable that their dissertations will be governed by their political attitudes is to provide exactly the wrong kind of training. Personally, as a supervisor, I have always had most trouble with Marxist students, who are so determined to read off predetermined Marxist lessons that they scarcely get round to analysing the evidence; the same can be true of strongly feminist students. But I have also had trouble with a student writing on the RAF in the Second World War who came in determined that his thesis was going to destroy lefty and pacifist critics of the RAF. Only when I had finally persuaded him to forget his preconceptions and get down to the hard work of wrestling with the primary sources did he begin to produce anything resembling professional history.

The metaphysicists have their own extreme left-wing political agenda; those who do not share this agenda, or at least do not allow it to influence their history (that is, most historians), they then, in effect, accuse of supporting the cause of the bourgeoisie. The metaphysical worldview does not allow for the possibility that historians regard an understanding of the past as vital to human society, and that it is this belief which provides their fundamental motivation, and the willingness to undertake the taxing and, sometimes, boring grind of serious research. Therein lies the measure of the distance between the two positions I am identifying here.

3 The Nature of Societies: Past, Present and Future

Perceptive readers will have noted that I make a firm distinction between 'history' (what historians *do*) and 'the past' (everything in its near infinitude that happened in the past, entirely regardless of any activities by historians). Not all professional historians make this distinction, and in that they are simply following normal colloquial, and perfectly respectable, practice. However, the distinction is a vital one in the sort of epistemological discussions we are having throughout this book. The metaphysicists definitely do not make the distinction. They, like Hegel, Marx, and (if you read him closely) Foucault, already have an *a priori* conception of history as the process which, proceeding through a series of stages or epochs, links past, to present, to future. To the metaphysicist, each epoch has an intrinsic materiality, and an essential character which, through the workings of 'the discursive', determines the nature of everything produced within that epoch. We currently live, allegedly, in the capitalist era, in bourgeois society, where everything produced is tainted by bourgeois ideology. The postmodernist refinement is that we are actually now in the period of late capitalism, a period of extreme crisis and uncertainty, which, in turn, has given rise to 'the condition of postmodernity'. To professional historians, on the contrary, 'periodisation', the breaking up of the past into manageable epochs or periods, is simply an analytical device: the periodisation that is useful for political history may well differ from that useful for economic history, and once again from the periodisation useful for social and cultural history. The society we live in has evolved through complex historical processes, very different from the Marxist formula of the bourgeoisie overthrowing the feudal aristocracy. It is highly complex with respect to the distribution of power, authority, and influence. Just as it was *not* formed by the simple overthrow of the aristocracy by the bourgeoisie, so, in its contemporary form, it does not consist simply of a bourgeois ruling class and a proletariat. The idea that we are now in a final period of late-capitalist crisis is simply nonsense. Marxists have been looking for the final capitalist collapse for over a century, in 1848, 1866, 1918, and 1968, to choose just a few dates, and they are forever doomed to disappointment. The notion of a current 'condition of postmodernity' may have analytical validity, particularly perhaps in the area of cultural production: but to treat it as having some ineluctable materiality is ridiculous, as it is to regard it as analogous to 'the Renaissance' or 'the Age of the French Revolution'. Here we have another vital battleground: the metaphysicists take 'history' as something given, something they already know; historians take 'history' as a set of procedures for *finding out* about the past, together with, of course, the results of their enquiries.

4 The Cultural Construction of Knowledge – and Everything Else

Knowledge, I have said, is vital to the existence of contemporary societies, and to their future advances ('advances' in the sense of decent living standards, empowerment, and basic rights being extended to all). To the metaphysicists knowledge is controlled by the bourgeoisie, and is simply a means of maintaining and exercising their power. Thus, Hayden White, in a marvellous simulation of Marxist rhetoric, claims that historical knowledge is actually a means

> by which individuals can be taught to live a distinctively 'imaginary relation to their real conditions of existence', that is to say, an unreal but meaningful relation to the social formations in which they are indentured to live out their lives and realise their destinies as social subjects.[8]

Note particularly the word 'indentured'; hardly necessary to say that professional historians would not accept that they play a part in 'indenturing' their readers.

Probably the most used – and, in my view, abused – verb in contemporary academic writing of all types is the verb 'to construct': 'identity' is 'constructed', 'sexuality' is 'constructed', 'meaning' (whatever that means) is 'constructed'. Such language is the very bedrock of 'critical' and cultural theory, both 'indentured' to the metaphysics I have been discussing. But there are historians, too, eager to demonstrate that they are up-to-date in their jargon, who make liberal use of this verb as well, though usually, it seems to me, without working out the full implications of what they are saying. Thus we are told that technology is culturally constructed, age is culturally constructed, gender is culturally constructed, and, of course, knowledge. The overuse of the phrase simply evacuates from it all significance, or operates as a barrier to teasing out in detail what is really happening. Thus an able writer tells us that the technology of the internal combustion engine was culturally constructed and that this led to its being exploited purely for private, rather than public, use. But although the Victorian age was even more oriented towards private enterprise than the early twentieth century, the technology of the steam engine was not exploited for private purposes – you simply could not have little steam locomotives running up and down country lanes. It is in fact the nature of the technology that governs the outcomes. There is a valid point that 'youth', particularly in the 1960s, has been defined in a variety of ways: sometimes, for instance, as a synonym for 'teenagers', sometimes meaning everyone under 30. But it is quite easy, and far more useful, to tease out all of these different usages, than to resort to the mindless statement that youth is 'culturally constructed'.[9] Again, we know all about the discrimination inflicted by society on women: but declaring 'gender' to be culturally constructed leads to gliding over the really interesting question of what is biologically determined and what is determined or insisted upon (surely more precise verbs than 'constructed') by society. *Who* is doing the 'constructing' is never explicitly stated, but one can only assume that the guilty party is the usual suspect, the bourgeois power structure. What we have is an assertion, not an explanation. Professional historians should prefer the more precise verbs used above, or the general phrase 'socially influenced', which then leaves scope for pinning down the exact weight of the different influences which do come to bear, such as the *development* of technology, changing perceptions of youth and age, fashion in dress, sexual mores, and so on.

So with knowledge. It is inescapable that history, like the sciences, is socially influenced. Historians, like scientists, are subject to social and career pressures, leading for instance to the slavish following of intellectual or scientific fashion, to publishing without adequate checking, to exaggerating the significance of the results of research. But then, as I have already said, there are the checks of peer-group discussion and criticism. This is a world away from knowledge being culturally constructed in the sole interests of the bourgeoisie.

5 Language: History a Branch of Literature?

On the central importance of language, I am in agreement with the postmodernists (and perhaps in disagreement with some of my fellow historians). However, against specious postmodernist claims to have instituted a 'linguistic turn', tearing the bandages from the eyes of those who naïvely saw language as a simple, uncomplicated medium of communication, I point out that historical method has its roots in philology and that questions of semantics and signification have preoccupied historians for generations, while the study of language formed the core of the empirical philosophy of the inter-war years (ironically Richard Rorty's *The Linguistic Turn* (1968) consists entirely of examples of this pre-postmodernist philosophy).[10] Anyway, the postmodernists come to precisely the wrong conclusions; language does not control us (daft, isn't it?), we *can* control language, *but only if we make the most arduous and time-consuming efforts.*

What is agreed is that language is difficult, slippery, elusive and allusive, that it is far from easy to express what we mean in a precise and conclusive way, and that, indeed, people listening to us or reading what we have written may well take away very different meanings from what we intended. Postmodernists, as it were, give up (though with great enthusiasm!). Even if historians have produced objective results from their enquiries, they will never, according to postmodernist theory, be able to convey these with absolute precision; what they write will always have more meanings for their readers than they intend. As soon as they begin writing, historians, this theory insists, are forced to 'narrativise' or 'textualise': what, through the imperatives of language, they will be forced to convey is (wait for it) bourgeois ideology. While Hayden White, at least, is prepared to concede that scientists communicate in logic, and therefore precisely, no special language or forms of communication are allowed for history.[11] Historians, he insists, necessarily employ the forms and devices – rhetoric, narratives, metaphor, and so on – of literature. Thus, history is simply a branch of literature, in which the 'narratives' of historians do not significantly differ from the novels of novelists (some historians, novelists *manqués*, or certainly aiming for review in the literary pages, agree, I regret to say).

The position taken by this book (and, I believe, accepted by professional historians when they really think about it) is that novelists, poets, and playwrights use language in a different way from historians. We expect creative writers to exploit the ambiguities and resonances of language, even, perhaps, to express directly the dictates of the unconscious, not always logical in its choice of words. Historians, on the other hand, should convey their findings as clearly and explicitly as possible. Some metaphors may be an aid to communication, others will simply contribute to confusion and obfuscation. With all the temptations to indulge in metaphor and rhetoric, cliché, sloppy phrasing and slang, getting it right is fiendishly difficult. But through constant working, and reworking, it is, contrary to the assertions of the metaphysicists, possible to write history which communicates clear, unambiguous *narrative* (in the historian's sense of chronological account, not the technical, loaded use of postmodernist linguistics), description and analysis. This book (in Chapter 6) will say a good deal about the writing of history, which, I know from personal experience, will prove of great use to students of history and to anyone embarking on the production of history – whether for personal reasons, or in pursuit of a PhD. In the eyes of the metaphysicists, such efforts are utterly futile; that is a very simple indicator of the difference between them and professional historians such as myself.

6 Textuality – the Alleged Existence Thereof

One of the oldest tricks practised by philosophers is the claim to have discovered some process or quality, hitherto unknown, which is now perceived to have great explanatory value: once a label has been clapped on this alleged process or quality, its actual existence is thereafter taken for granted. This trick is much used by the postmodernists: new words are invented, old ones are given new meanings. Thus we have: 'discourse', 'discursive', 'theorise', 'narrativise', 'deconstruction', 'textuality' and 'textualise'. For all the elaborate vocabulary, the basic ideas are very simple, not to say simplistic. They all depend on the notion of bourgeois society, and bourgeois dominance of knowledge, ideology, language. All individual artefacts of communication, according to this trick, are 'texts', and all are, in their very nature, impregnated with bourgeois ideology. Whatever he or she tries to do, the historian, in producing a piece of history, is, it is thus alleged, inevitably creating a 'text'. All complete pieces of writing in the past, whether published books, private letters and diaries, estate records, acts of parliament or whatever, are 'texts'. This theory neatly obliterates the distinction, a vital one for professional historians, between primary sources and secondary sources. In Chapters 5 and 6 of this book, I demonstrate conclusively, and at length, the ways in which these two types of sources are different, and why the difference is important. The historian's belief that historical knowledge must ultimately be founded on the primary sources is a cause for merriment among history's critics, most of whom have never read anything beyond printed books and articles, and who prefer inventing their history to doing the intensely hard work among both secondary and primary sources which is essential for the production of a new contribution to historical knowledge. That awful old Stalinist and Cambridge snob, the late E. H. Carr, wrote mockingly of the professional historian's 'fetishism of documents';[12] more recently Ludmilla Jordanova writes of 'the cult of the archive'.[13] Neither, as I shall show in Chapter 5, has much of an idea about the nature of primary sources, nor of how historians make use of them.

Works of art, utilitarian objects, articles of clothing, are also, allegedly, 'texts'. Just, then, as postmodernist theory obliterates the distinction between novels and poems and historical books and articles, so also it obliterates the distinction between works of art and works of scholarship. The postmodernists claim one universal, holistic method for dealing with everything, actually Marxism melded with post-structuralism, though they prefer not to declare this too openly: the mode word is 'deconstruction' which they claim to be able to apply to 'texts' of all types. It is claimed that 'deconstruction' is far superior to the techniques historians use in analysing and interpreting primary sources: in fact, deconstruction simply finds what the postmodernists put there in the first place, bourgeois ideology. When the deconstructionists have produced contributions to historical knowledge that can be set beside those that professional historians have been making for generations, then that might be the time to give more attention to deconstruction.

How historians write up their results and, in particular, how they structure their works is a most important topic, discussed in Chapter 6. The constant refrain of the postmodernist critics is that historians do not think about what they are doing, do not understand how they write their books and articles – thus, of course, requiring the postmodernists to come along to expose how they are simply 'narrativising', telling stories, falling victims to 'textuality'. Readers are welcome to accept their ludicrous assertions if they so wish; if they want to find out what historians really do, they should carry on reading this book.

7 Disagreements Among Historians

In this sub-section I shall, as promised, identify those whom I am referring to as history's 'postmodernist critics'; I shall also name those professional historians who have figured most prominently on the 'battlefields' listed in this chapter. Both Foucault and Barthes were critical of the history of professional historians – this can be seen most clearly in the essay by Barthes, 'Historical Discourse', where history is declared to be mere bourgeois ideology.[14] Hayden White, formerly Professor of Comparative Literature at Stanford University, has been the leading critic in recent years. White apparently started as a historian but seems not to have published any works of history. His researches in medieval and Renaissance Italian history appear not to have yielded any publications. He jointly authored an extremely pedestrian book on the history of ideas.[15] His *Metahistory: The Historical Imagination in Nineteenth-Century Europe* (1973) is undoubtedly a brilliant analysis of the rhetorical techniques of some famous early nineteenth-century 'historians', all writing in an amateurish way, well before the emergence of professional history. Unfortunately, White seems to have made very little acquaintanceship with what historians write today. His subsequent books, actually collections of essays, not carefully structured book-length studies, *Tropics of Discourse: Essays in Cultural Criticism* (1978) and *The Content of the Form: Narrative Discourse and Historical Representation* (1987), are full of references to other Marxist and post-structuralist writers, such as Fredric Jameson, Paul Ricoeur, Louis Althusser, and, of course, Foucault and Barthes; the only actual historian referred to is Harry Elmer Barnes, an American writer of textbooks. None of this is in any way to suggest that Hayden White was not a most distinguished occupant of first, the Chair of History of Consciousness at Santa Cruz, and then the Comparative

Literature one at Stanford; it is to suggest that he may not be the best qualified person to pontificate about what historians should and should not do. His acolytes in Britain are Patrick Joyce, who has written about the working class in nineteenth-century Lancashire, Alun Munslow, who has written an overtly postmodernist collection of biographical essays, *Discourse and Culture: The Creation of America* (1992), and Keith Jenkins, who has written *The Closed Door: A Christian Critique of Britain's Immigration Policies* (1984). Ludmilla Jordanova seems only now to be wavering in her allegiance to Foucault:[16] her production, in philosophy of science rather than history, has not been immense. In their critical works on professional history,[17] certain names crop up again and again: R. G. Collingwood, E. H. Carr, Geoffrey Elton, Lawrence Stone, A. J. P. Taylor, John Tosh, and (in Jenkins and Munslow, at least, and also Tosh) myself. These writers are not cited on account of any contributions to historical knowledge they may have made, but because of things they have said about the historian's tasks and activities.

I have to say that sometimes historians say very silly things about their own activities. This is particularly the case with historians who, as I have already hinted, like to see themselves as having the same status as popular novelists, fancying themselves as media personalities (exponents of *auteur* theory, I call them). A. J. P. Taylor was simply being ridiculous when he said that historians

> should not be ashamed to admit that history is at the bottom simply a form of story-telling...There is no escaping the fact that the original task of the historian is to answer the child's question: 'What happened next?'[18]

The question historians address is simply 'What happened?', followed quickly by 'Why?' and 'How?' To find out what historians really do it is necessary to analyse their scholarly works, and that is difficult to do if one has not already written scholarly works oneself. I'll be discussing the historians, and the critics, mentioned here later in the book, with a concentration on epistemological issues in Chapter 7 – where I will move well away from this exclusive concentration on British figures. Here just some very brief words about Collingwood, Carr, Elton, Stone, Tosh, and myself.

Collingwood was both an archaeologist and a philosopher; he didn't do history of the usual kind. I'll explain later in detail why I believe that what he said in *The Idea of History*, much quoted by history's enemies, is complete rubbish. Collingwood held sway, I believe, because few professional historians felt that there was any need to set down an account of their tasks and practices (one did history 'because it was there'), and so Collingwood's book was about the only one there was. Something the same, I'm afraid, is true of E. H. Carr's *What is History?*, originally given as a series of lectures at Cambridge, and full of little anti-Oxford jokes, as if no intellectual world existed outside of Oxbridge. Carr made some good points: about the value of knowing your historian before reading his/her book (knowing their assumptions, as I would prefer to put it); and about how one evaluates and orders explanatory factors. But Carr's title was a highly misleading one: what he wrote about was the kind of Marxist history that he wished to see replace the professional history which he thought too dominated by the 'fetishism of documents'. I explore Carr's misconceptions about the nature of primary sources in Chapter 5.

Within the historical profession, Lawrence Stone (whose contributions to family history will be discussed later) is most respected for his pioneer ventures into computer-based data analysis, but there has also been a touch of the would-be media star or *auteur*. At one stage, he announced the return of narrative to historical writing, but without really engaging with the technical way in which people like Hayden White were using the term. He did, however, engage vigorously with Patrick Joyce and the ultimate postmodernist contention that 'everything is constructed within language': 'historians', Stone wrote, 'play with words: words do not play with themselves'.[19] My own view, as will be clear by now, is that historians should not play with words, but should deploy them in the most straightforward and unambiguous way possible. That said, Stone has made major contributions to historical knowledge, as have Elton and, in perhaps a slightly different way, A. J. P. Taylor. I would surmise that what I am saying in this book would be broadly agreed to by Stone and Elton, and probably also by Taylor.

Because Carr was an old-style Marxist, and not at all a postmodernist, the critics sometimes lump him together with Elton, Tosh, and myself. Elton, politically, and in general outlook, very conservative, was in fact highly critical of Carr, and his *The Practice of History* (1968) was in part written as a riposte to Carr's *What is History?* If anything (and if possible!), I am even more critical of Carr than Elton was. Tosh, on the other hand, is a Marxist, and like so many other Marxists, has taken up the cause of postmodernism, as seen in the most recent editions of his *The Pursuit of History* (total obeisance in the second edition of 1991, a more reasoned approach in the third of 2000). His argument (which I take up in Chapter 7) was (Tosh now seems to be changing his mind, but it's hard to be sure) that history *must* have theory and since, according to him, Marxism and postmodernism, in their *pas-de-deux*, are the only show in town, we have to opt for them. That argument I find utterly unpersuasive: historians have to try to get it right, and false theory only gets in the way of getting it right. This leaves Elton and myself (not that I am in any way comparing my own contributions to historical knowledge with those of Sir Geoffrey; I'm simply referring to our views on historical epistemology). Following the last edition of *The Nature of History* I wrote a couple of strongly phrased ('intemperate'!) articles (1993 and 1995) striving to rebut, and perhaps even refute, Marxist and postmodernist criticisms of professional history.[20] Having inspired the respect of the historical profession with his *The Practice of History* (1968), followed by *Political History: Principles and Practice* (1970), which took on the philosophers (including Collingwood) on their own ground, triumphantly arguing that the past had had material reality, and that the surviving primary sources were very concrete evidence of this, Elton put together some old material and some pugnacious new stuff in his short book *Return to Essentials: Some Reflections on the Present State of Historical Study* (1991). Here his own political conservatism was perhaps too strongly marked and, as the second of the two earlier titles would also suggest, Elton was overly wedded to the notion that conventional political history was superior to all other kinds of history. On that point I very strongly disagreed with him. In addition, I was never fully persuaded by the rather narrowly political model of historical explanation he offered[21] (it is remarkable, though, how very few of those who write about history do engage with historical explanation beyond, in certain cases, routine invocations of Marxism). All this is simply by way of trying to give readers further insights into my own assumptions – warning you, if you like – before proceeding into the main body of this book. It is proper, also, to refer to the impressive summary of professional history's case against its postmodernist critics in Richard J. Evans, *In Defence of History* (1997), though readers should perhaps be warned that, in this book, Evans goes out of his way to be offensive to me, as if I were the only historian ever to have written a less than perfect sentence. I believe this may arise from the fact that at the beginning of the 1980s I did not shortlist him for a chair at the Open University; I should add that the historical profession, in my experience, is remarkably free of such pettiness.

My case is that history is an autonomous discipline with its own specialised methods. I believe that these methods can, to advantage, be applied to the artefacts created by artists, musicians, architects, novelists, and poets, taken along with all the other primary sources related to cultural production and consumption. As I shall demonstrate in Chapters 5 and 6, I certainly do not think historians should be narrow in their conception of what should be brought within their purview. But – and this is probably where I differ most from many of my colleagues within the historical profession – I do not believe that historical methods can be merged with other approaches. Jeffrey Richards, Professor of Cultural History at the University of Lancaster, has launched a series which explicitly aims to merge history with cultural studies. I wish him well, as I always wish the Scottish football team well when they embark upon

their World Cup campaigns. But, in fact, my view is that the epistemological basis of cultural studies, together with its aims and learning
outcomes, are very different from those of history. It is very British,
and very gentlemanly, to seek compromise, but I believe all of those
interested in history are better served by recognising the autonomy of
history and grasping the particular set of methods and principles
belonging to it.

8 What Precisely is the Danger?

That question might well follow from the uncompromising statement
I have just made. Historians, given the wide range of periods, cultures,
and topics to be covered, must always have open minds. I try, in Chapter
6, to say something of how historians finally arrive at their interpretations and explanations. Vital thoughts can often be triggered by reading
something which at first sight seems to be remote from the topic in hand.
It is very natural, therefore, for historians to talk enthusiastically about
the 'perceptions' or 'insights' offered by postmodernist writing. My
colleagues must seek inspiration where they may, and they are well
able to look after themselves. And I do believe that students should be
introduced to the different approaches to history, to the different
'assumptions', and to the criticisms that have been made of professional
history, and should be encouraged to decide for themselves which
arguments they find the most persuasive. But now, in concluding this
chapter, I am going to specify the dangers inherent in adopting the
'gentlemanly' position that the postmodernist agenda, cultural studies,
and critical and cultural theory are just other options in the historical
endeavour which can readily be incorporated into the standard programme of historical studies.

1 There is an organised historical profession, aiming, through the provision of teaching, library facilities, learned journals, and so on, to
   further the vital task of better understanding the past – not, as the
   postmodernists would maintain, to better serve as agents of the bourgeoisie. History courses are organised, at undergraduate and postgraduate level, to enable students to achieve certain specified
   learning outcomes. The whole profession has become steadily more
   reflexive, and much attention is given to methodology and the nature
   of primary sources. Postmodernist theories cut right across these
   developments. Pupils at school who are persuaded that there is no
   difference between primary and secondary sources will certainly not
   do well in their exams. PhD students encouraged to believe that there
   is a 'cult of the archive', and that hard research among the primary
   sources is not really a sensible requirement, are unlikely to complete

their degrees. It is open to all young people to adopt postmodern attitudes if they are persuaded by them. But if they are persuaded, they would be best advised to give up the study of history.

2 Where there is an attempt to incorporate postmodern attitudes into a basically historical programme, the danger is of students adopting the jargon (the fact of its being incomprehensible often increases the appeal) as a shortcut which will avoid the hard work which all historical study inevitably entails.

3 Postmodernist theory encourages the view that it is impossible to write in a clear, straightforward way (advice which is disastrous for history students). This in turn leads, as the writings of postmodernists themselves clearly demonstrate, to a turning towards exaggerated metaphor and rhetoric – the very things that are not required in historical writing.

4 If we are actually to believe what the postmodernist critics (for example White, Jenkins) say, then their ultimate objective is to wipe out all existing historical knowledge, and the ways in which that knowledge is acquired. One, inevitably, does wonder if the postmodernists really mean what they say, since their vocation seems to entail living off what historians produce. No history, and they would have nothing to criticise. However, the concentration on analysing and criticising what historians write, rather than expanding and communicating historical knowledge, is dangerous enough in itself. This book argues that historical study, conducted in accordance with the precepts set out in it, is important, as well as interesting and, sometimes, exciting. To me, anything which distracts students from studying history in that way, or limits their opportunities to do so, is unforgivable.

I know about the holistic, metaphysical, nomothetic approaches to the study of the past. I reject them because I don't think they actually do assist in furthering knowledge of the past. I reject the propagandist elements implicit within them, though it is not to left-wing propaganda as such that I object. I am equally opposed to right-wing metaphysical propaganda, as embodied most spectacularly (and disastrously) in Fukuyama's *The End of History and the Last Man* (a book based almost entirely on works of political philosophy and practically devoid of contact with historical sources, even secondary ones). It is not that I don't understand the metaphysical approaches (I am, after all, a specialist in the 1960s, when most of them originated). I understand them only too well. Thus, this book concentrates on presenting what I believe is a coherent, and consistent, account of the nature of historical knowledge and the nature of historical study, which accords with what historians actually do. I have been in the historical profession for over 40 years and have necessarily had extensive experience in analysing and interpreting the works of other scholars; I have also had a certain amount of first-hand experience in wrestling with the problems historians encounter when they try to make their own contributions to historical knowledge.

Notes

1   Keith Jenkins in his feeble *Rethinking History* (London, 1991, new edition) apparently thought it hilarious to refer to 'Marwick's twenty-five varieties', completely confusing what I was saying in the original *The Nature of History* about different philosophers of history and the different approaches of 'historians' down the ages, with my quite unambiguous account of basic historical methodology. See my 'Two Approaches to Historical Study: The Metaphysical (including "Postmodernism") and the Historical', *Journal of Contemporary History*, 30/1 (January 1995), pp. 26 and 34 (note).
2   E. J. Hobsbawm, *Nations and Nationalism Since 1780: Programme, Myth, Reality* (Cambridge, 1990), pp. 12–13.
3   Alun Munslow, *Deconstructing History* (London, 1997), p. 18. Indeed, according to Munslow I am a 'hardened' reconstructionist, whatever that may mean.
4   Foucault's Marxism comes through most strongly in the selection of his writings published in Colin Gordon (ed.), *Michel Foucault Power/Knowledge: Selected Interviews and Other Writings 1972–1977* (London, 1980), that of White in his response to my *Journal of Contemporary History* article cited in note 1 above, published in *JCH*, 30/2 (April 1995).
5   John Searle, *Mind, Language and Society: Philosophy in the Real World* (London, 1999), p. 11.
6   Ibid., pp. 47, 50–1.
7   Ludmilla Jordanova, *History in Practice* (London, 2000), p. xiv and passim.
8   Hayden White, *The Content of the Form: Narrative Discourse and Historical Representation* (Baltimore, Md., 1987), p. x.
9   Sean O'Connell, *The Car and British Society: The Car, Gender and Motoring 1896–1939* (Manchester, 1998), pp. 112ff.; Bill Osgerby, *British Youth Since 1945* (London, 1997), p. 2.
10 Richard M. Rorty (ed.), *The Linguistic Turn: Essays in Philosophical Method* (Chicago, 1967). This contains essays from the thirties to the fifties, by such distinctively non-postmodernist thinkers as Gilbert Ryle, Stuart Hampshire, and P. F. Strawson.
11 White, *Content*, p. 39.
12 E. H. Carr, *What is History?* (London, 1961; pb edn, 1964), p. 16.
13 Jordanova, *History*, p. 186.
14 The essay by Roland Barthes, 'Historical Discourse', in translation, is conveniently available in Michael Lane, *Structuralism: A Reader* (London, 1970), pp. 145–55.

15 William H. Coates, Hayden V. White, J. Selwyn Schapiro, *The Emergence of Liberal Humanism: An Intellectual History of Western Europe*, 2 vols (New York, 1966, 1970).

16 Jordanova, *History*, p. 82, where she appears to be accepting what I had said some years earlier, that Foucault, far from being a philosopher of majestic vision, was very much a product, and a prisoner, of his time. See Arthur Marwick, '"A Fetishism of Documents?" The Salience of Source-Based History', in Henry Kozicki (ed.), *Developments in Modern Historiography* (New York and London, 1993), p. 111.

17 In addition to works already cited, note Patrick Joyce, 'History and Post-Modernism', *Past and Present*, 133 (November 1991), pp. 204–9, and *Democratic Subjects: The Self and the Social in Nineteenth-Century England* (Cambridge, 1994).

18 A. J. P. Taylor, *A Personal History* (London, 1983), p. 124.

19 Lawrence Stone, 'History and Post-Modernism', *Past and Present*, 135 (1992), p. 190.

20 Marwick, ' "A Fetishism" ' and 'Two Approaches'.

21 G. R. Elton, *Political History: Principles and Practice* (London, 1970), pp. 138–42.

2 History: Essential Knowledge about the Past

1 The Past, History, and Sources

The Past

What happened in the past profoundly affects all aspects of our lives in the present and will, indeed, affect what happens in the future. In almost every city, town, village or country throughout the world, a considerable proportion of the buildings currently in existence were built in past times to meet the needs and aspirations of human beings now dead and societies now in greater or lesser degree changed, or even defunct. This is most obviously so with respect to great temples and cathedrals, fine palaces and manor houses and castles, city halls, houses of parliament and other public buildings; but it is also true of the most humdrum streets and the meanest housing. Look around at the areas of conflict across the globe which every second experience death and destruction – in the Indian sub-continent and Kashmir, in Indonesia, in Israel, Palestine and the Lebanon, in almost all parts of Africa, in Northern Ireland, in the Basque regions of Spain. Past movements of population, past oppression by the then-mighty of the then-weak, religious faiths and communal identities established in the past, often the very distant past, everywhere are the fundamental causes of tension and conflict. Systems of government (as well as the buildings which embody them), political ideas (radical as well as conservative), beliefs about art and culture, educational practices, customs and behaviour are all products of the past, recent and remote.

Put this way, the case that the past is important, the past is all-pervasive, that, indeed, we can't escape from the past, is persuasive. But what exactly is 'the past'? From the examples given, clearly it signifies 'what actually happened' – events (battles, assassinations, invasions, general elections) which have taken place, societies which have risen and fallen, ideas and institutions, eating habits, marital customs, all aspects of human behaviour in the past, matters large and small. All that is clear enough; but the big difficulty with the past is that by definition it does not actually exist now, it is 'past', it has gone for good. This is related both to that elusive but all-absorbing concept, 'time', and to the fact of human mortality. What I have been speaking of is the past of human activities, of human societies, of, in fact, 'the human past' (no doubt the cosmic past has affected human evolution, but that is another subject). Human beings die, human families, human communities, sometimes whole nations, die out. More important is the phenomenon of the passing of time, fascinating – as is shown by all the literature, weighty and trivial, about defying time, about time capsules, and travel in time – but ineluctable, as we all in the very depths of our fibre appreciate.

But can we really be sure about the passing of time, about past societies, past events, actually having had a material existence? Let us start with our own personal past. There is, I would think, little difficulty in believing in that: we are where we are now (I confine myself for the moment to the manageable short view) through choices made by our parents, through courses of study we pursued, through job applications we filed, through marital choices of our own; if we look back at old birth and marriage certificates, letters, postcards, home movies, photographs, diaries (even the ones where we just filled in appointments), lecture notes, recipes, there is no problem in connecting up the past which we remember, and mis-remember, to these sources, and in perceiving that a serious, systematic study of these sources could yield quite a rounded account of our past, full of surprises no doubt, but one which, if we were prepared to be dispassionate about it, we would recognise as 'true'. One can extend the same reasoning to parents, to grandparents, and, taking a long view, to our more distant forebears. Clearly generation succeeds generation and clearly each generation leaves sources of exactly the sort which, from our own direct experience, we can confirm as evidence of the material reality of the past.

But personal and family experience is only the start. Everywhere in our cities we can see old buildings being demolished, new ones being erected; from time to time we encounter a building which draws attention to itself through some distinction or peculiarity of style: a church, a disused warehouse, now perhaps serving as offices for architects or accountants, a row of houses, carefully preserved, or perhaps falling into decay. Perhaps we feel sad at the demolition, perhaps we tell ourselves that buildings constructed to meet the needs of earlier times have no place in our modern city; as we contemplate the church, the warehouse, the row of houses, even the most ignorant among us will be aware that they were built in an age other than our own. These are not the past, but they are surely as tangible evidence that the past did exist as the scientist receives of the chemical composition of a distant planet. It would – I now move far beyond our own direct apprehensions – take a very determined obfuscator indeed to deny that the imprisonment and freeing of Nelson Mandela, the economic, social, and ethnic problems of twenty-first-century Russia, the communal conflicts in so many parts of the world, had their origins, as I have just been saying, in past movements of population, past persecutions, past injustices. If the injustices are real, then so must have been the past in which they were perpetrated.

As soon as we start talking about the past we start talking about the relics and 'legacies' which it has left (I've brought these in twice already). We have to concentrate particularly on the relics and traces – most obviously, the buildings, the cities, the streets which are open to every gaze; less obviously, the billions upon billions of sources of all types which have to be sought out in libraries, and archives, and in archaeological digs. Traces of the past exist too in the memories, traditions and ceremonies that are relayed from generation to generation. All human societies betray a preoccupation with their own past, whether through ancestor worship, the invocation of past triumphs by 'witch doctors' or 'medicine men', the scriptures and chronicles of holy men and monks, or the regular mounting of national parades and ceremonies. Much, of course, of what is preserved, celebrated, and passed on from age to age may have only a tenuous relationship to the past as it really happened; much of it may well be 'myth' or 'fable'. But then myth believed by one generation and passed on to the next also becomes a part of this awesomely large and complex cluster of events and ideas, great systems and trivial pursuits, 'the past'.

The twofold point, at once so simple and so fraught with devilish implications, which this opening disquisition seeks to drive home, is that while the past is manifestly important, it is also impossible to apprehend *directly* (as one might apprehend the mountain and river system of Europe, the production and collection in a laboratory of H_2S gas, or the functions of the heart in pumping blood round the human body): it can only be apprehended through memories, myths, and, most important, through the relics and 'sources', archaeological, written, printed, painted, and so on, and so on – that it leaves.

Thus far in this chapter – have you noticed? – I have not used the words 'history', 'historian', or 'historical'. I have done this deliberately, in order to demonstrate that, even though at any given point in time, the past no longer exists, the phrase itself (or, more exactly, the phrase 'the human past') is meaningful and viable, with a legitimate usage signifying not only 'that which actually happened', but, by extension, 'that which has entailed the pre-conditions for so many bloody problems in the world of the present, as well as the political systems, cultural standards and modern conveniences which today we – according to taste and, obviously, geographical location – enjoy or don't enjoy'; and, further, to demonstrate that this usage 'the past' or 'the human past' is a clearer and more precise one than 'history'. True, in the rather loose usage of every-day speech, or perhaps when we are making some rhetorical or meta-phorical point, we do sometimes use the word 'history' when what is really meant is 'the human past'. There is nothing we can do about ordinary usage, but in serious discussion and in serious study it is best always to use words in the most rigorous way possible. Indeed, one of the most important lessons to be learnt from academic study is that most of the really important words have several meanings, so that it is always important to be absolutely clear about how *we* are using such words. If you are unhappy about my ruling here on 'history' and 'the past' just reflect for a moment that while we can talk about 'taking a course in history', we would be unlikely to say 'taking a course in the past'.

The distinction, just in case there is still any ambiguity, is that between, on the one hand, what actually happened in the (human) past (whether or not historians have written about it), which is what we mean when we say 'the past', and, on the other hand, the accounts of the past provided by historians, that is (contenting ourselves with a rather broad definition for the moment), 'history'. It is a distinction fundamental to our study in this book of what history is, and why and how you do it. Approaching the matter metaphorically, or in the rather loose jargon which historians, like others, are all too ready to reach for when confronted with quite difficult problems, it is not helpful to say that there is a past 'out there'. The past can't be 'out there', it has gone for good. The phrase arises from the central debate over whether academics (scientists, geographers, psychologists, historians, and so on) study a corpus of material which is separate from their own activities, procedures, and thought processes. It may be appropriate to say that scientists study something 'out there', that is to say, the natural world and the physical universe. And as I shall be stressing shortly, I do believe that the activities of historians are analo-gous to those of scientists, and very different from those of novelists, poets or artists. But we do also have to be aware of the peculiar difficulties of the historian's tasks. The past *was* there (it is not 'out' anywhere), and – the vital point here – it existed entirely independently of the activities of historians. No doubt human and personal factors come into play when historians begin to engage in the past, as they do when scientists begin to engage with their corpus of material, but that is a different issue, to be explored later. Self-evidently, 'what actually happened in the past' is almost infinite. Inevitably historians select which topics and problems they wish to study (as do scientists). No doubt topics which 'ought' to have been addressed have sometimes been ignored. On the whole, the range has expanded remarkably over the years since the end of the nine-teenth century, when history as a scholarly discipline became firmly established. Historians really do want to *find out*, and that desire con-stantly leads to new topics and new areas being opened up.

Primary and Secondary Sources

Opening his novel *The Go-Between* (1955), L. P. Hartley wrote: 'The past is a foreign country, they do things differently there'. This is a good example of a sentence permissible for a novelist – it does contain one important truth arrestingly expressed – but in its entirety too imprecise for a historian, though the first part did become the title of a rather fanciful book of only distant relevance to what historians actually do; in particular the American author got hopelessly confused between 'the past' and 'history'.[1] Manifestly, one cannot travel to the past by ship or plane, or even through e-mail or the internet. This is a very serious point: the only way we can have knowledge of the past is through studying the relics and traces left by past societies, which I have already mentioned. Primary sources, as it were, form the basic 'raw material' of history; they are sources which came into existence within the period being investigated. The articles and books written up later by historians, drawing upon these primary sources, converting the raw material into history, are secondary sources (pedants insist on pointing out that secondary sources *may* become primary sources for still later historians, but this is a matter of such triviality as scarcely to be worth bothering about). The distinction between primary and secondary sources is a critical one, though no historian has ever pretended that it offers a magic key to the nature of historical study, or that primary sources have a necromantic potency denied to secondary ones. There is always some excitement about being in contact with a genuine primary source, but one will not learn very much from a single source. Reading through an edited selection of excerpts from primary sources will have the salutary effect of bringing one in contact with the thinking and language of past generations, but it will not amount to research. If the ordinary reader, or history student, wants to learn quickly about the role and status of women during the Renaissance, or about the causes of the First World War, they will be well advised to go to the secondary authorities, a knowledge of the principles of history being useful in separating out the more reliable from the less.

But if you are planning to make an original contribution to historical knowledge, you are unlikely to make much of a stir if you stick strictly to other people's work, that is, the secondary sources – to which, it should be stressed, the research historian will frequently return throughout all stages of research and writing. The difference is critical in that strategy which all historians, in one way or another, devise in embarking on a new research project. It is through the secondary sources that one becomes aware of the gaps in knowledge, problems unsolved, suspect explanations. It is with the aid of these secondary sources, and all the other resources of the profession, that one begins to identify the archives in which one will commence one's researches.

Primary sources, numbingly copious in some areas, are scarce and fragmentary in others. Much has to be garnered indirectly and by inference. Historians do not rely on single sources, but are always seeking corroboration, qualification, correction; the production of history is very much a matter of accumulating details, refining nuances. The technical skills of the historian lie in sorting these matters out, in understanding how and why a particular source came into existence, how relevant it is to the topic under investigation, and, obviously, the particular codes or language in accordance with which the particular source came into being as a concrete artefact.[2]

Before I bring all of this together in a clear, concise, but comprehensive answer to the question 'What is history?', I need to make some clarifying points about primary and secondary sources. With regard to the latter there is a further broad distinction to be made between, on the one hand, research-based specialist work, which will usually appear in the form of articles in learned historical journals or specialist monographs, and, on the other, general works or textbooks, which have the function of summarising and synthesising the specialist work. In other words, we need to understand not just the distinction between primary and secondary sources, but also that there are different types and levels of secondary source. These range from the most highly specialised research-based work, through high-quality textbooks which incorporate some personal research as well as summarise the work of others, to the simpler textbooks, and then on to the many types of popular and non-academic history.

Because a source comes in the form of a printed book, that does not necessarily mean it is secondary. A book which originates within the period being studied is a primary source – it might be a legal textbook describing the law as it existed at the time of publication, a work of political philosophy, an analysis of popular music or a 'conduct book', a guide to etiquette. *Rule number one: look at the date!* Primary sources in their original form are usually only to be found in specialist libraries or record offices ('archives' is not always as simple a term as it is made to seem, though the term always carries the implication of being the location in which primary sources are kept; organisations and businesses keep their own archives, that is to say, the ever-accumulating collection of documentation relating to their own activities; what are called 'public records' in Britain are known in most countries as 'national archives'). However, as I have just hinted, it is usual to provide students with specially edited (and, if necessary, translated) collections of primary sources, and I should stress the value of selected primary sources in the teaching and learning of history. While students and general readers will always need the textbooks, and other secondary works, they will also find that actually reading the words of, or looking at the artefacts created by, the people of the past society being studied can give a more direct and vivid understanding of that society than any secondary account. To sum up: primary sources are indispensable for research and the production of historical knowledge, but selected and edited (and, if necessary, translated) they are also vital in the teaching and learning of history.

Defining 'History' and 'Historiography'

In setting out a definition of history, it is useful to consider again the analogy of the sciences. I don't want to overdo this analogy, since there are enormous differences between history and the natural sciences, as, of course, there are lesser, but still considerable, differences between the individual sciences. Still, just as the sciences are the bodies of knowledge about the natural world and the physical universe produced by scientists, applying their systematic methods of devising experiments, observing natural phenomena, recording and analysing data, and developing and applying concepts and theories, so history is the bodies of knowledge about the past produced by historians applying the rigorous methods of professional history, and deploying secondary sources in the analysis and interpretation of primary sources. The human past enfolds so many periods and cultures that history can no more form one unified body of knowledge than can the natural sciences. The search for universal meaning or universal explanations is a futile one. History is about finding things out, and solving problems, rather than about spinning narratives or telling stories. History is a human activity carried out by an organised corps of fallible human beings, acting, however, in accordance with strict methods and principles, empowered to make choices in the language they use (as between the precise and the imprecise, for example), that 'corps of fallible human beings' being known as historians.

Precise use of language is essential in historical writing. So also is precise quantification. In all historical writing we constantly encounter phrases such as 'the amount of land under cultivation drastically declined', 'there was a huge increase in the amount invested in education', 'most people rejected Protestant extremism': in every case, precise quantification is to be preferred to general statements. Statistical tables and statistical series, where they can be found or compiled, are of immense value. But whereas in the sciences many critical relationships can be expressed in mathematical terms, this is not the case in history. Regularities and predictable outcomes can be perceived in the sciences and expressed in the form of 'laws', 'theory', and, as just suggested, 'equations' (I discuss the sciences in Chapter 7). Theories and concepts are important in history (and I shall discuss these in Chapters 6 and 7) but there really is, in this sphere, no analogy with the sciences.

What I am asserting, above all, in this chapter, is that there is a vital distinction between 'history' and 'the past', and that it is certainly unacceptable to use the word 'history' to signify some *a priori*, unsubstantiated conception along the lines of 'the material process by which the past itself becomes the present and, indeed, the future, unfolding in a series of stages (or epochs or periods), according to some pattern or meaning (as decreed by Marx, or the younger Toynbee, or Foucault, or Fukuyama), involving conflicts or accommodations in the exercise of power'. Those who claim to 'know' what that meaning is, and what the stages are, would limit all empirical research to being conducted within these pre-set parameters. Historians do not believe in 'the meaning of history'; all the knowledge we have has to be worked for.

The message is that when we use the words 'history' and 'historical' we have to be very self-conscious, very reflexive. In ordinary language, which is after all intended for ease of communication, we sometimes aim for economy and elision in order to avoid the full pedantic spelling-out of distinctions. We can legitimately use 'history' to signify 'the past as we know it from the work of historians' – there really isn't any other way of knowing it. If by 'history' we mean 'the past as I have just made it up, or the past as I have learned it from films and comics', people will not pay much attention to our pronouncements.

Let us be absolutely clear that historians do not 'construct' or 'reconstruct' the past. If one thinks about the metaphor, it simply dissolves. Scientists do not 'construct' or 'reconstruct' nuclear fusion, or development in muscles. They provide knowledge about the workings of these phenomena. So, once again, it is knowledge (open to discussion and debate as all knowledge is) about the past that historians produce.

Intellectuals who use the word 'history' to signify 'the past' then have to introduce the word 'historiography' to signify the writings of historians. But if one makes the firm distinction, then that word is not needed, since what historians write *is* history. The word 'historiography', accordingly, can be reserved for the specialist study of the writings of historians (*not* the content of these writings), that is to say, the history of history: by that definition my Chapters 3 and 4 are historiography. There are minor uses of the word 'history' which we can quickly dismiss before spending some moments on the adjective 'historical'. In medicine, or psychology, or social work, it is customary to speak of a patient's or client's 'case history'. This is history in its most rudimentary sense of a present record of what actually belongs to the past – in this case the relevant (or what are thought to be the relevant) parts of the past experiences of the particular patient or client. 'Historical' is often used in this general way, to mean 'pertaining to a present record of the past' (there is no way an adjective can be shaped out of the word 'past'). To say that some statement is based on 'historical rather than contemporary' truth is to mean that while the statement was true in the past it is now no longer true. 'Historical', equally, can mean 'to do with the study of (or an interest in) history as a discipline and as bodies of knowledge': many universities have student 'historical societies', though some (the meaning here is the same) are called 'history societies'.

As I am anxious not to be too authoritarian, and to try to create some elements of reader participation in this book, I am now going to list a number of sentences involving the sorts of problems of meaning that I have been discussing. As you go through my list, you are invited to make your own comments on each phrase, indicating whether any clarification is needed, perhaps writing your answers down; my own comments follow immediately.

1. War is the locomotive of history.
2. The past is a fertile source of myth.
3. Geography is an important influence on history.
4. We have had too much drum-and-trumpet history.
5. That TV programme was very good as history.

1 An obvious implied meaning would be: 'From the knowledge of the past provided by historians we can see that war is the most powerful agent of change.' However, the phrase is Trotsky's, and as a Marxist, he meant history as the (alleged) material process converting past into present into future. It is worth noting that it is in metaphorical and rhetorical statements that one most usually encounters the more debatable uses of the word 'history'.

2 The pedantic rephrasing would be: 'from what we know about the past we know that it is a fertile source of myth'. By my own rules it would be correct to substitute 'history' for 'the past', but, such are the difficulties of the word, it might seem that we were saying that historians themselves are fertile sources of myth (which *could* always be true, of course!).

3 I think the meaning is completely unambiguous, though a pedantic gloss would have to take the following cumbersome form: 'Geography is an influence on what, according to the interpretations of historians, actually happened.'

4 The usage here (whatever the sentiment) is absolutely correct. The 'history' here can only be the writings of, or bodies of knowledge created by, historians. The view was that of the nineteenth-century English historian J. R. Green, who was criticising his colleagues for neglecting social history.

5 Again the usage is absolutely correct. The only comparison that could be intended is with the history of the historians. In its fullest gloss the

sentence would read: 'That TV programme was very good as an interpretation of the past conforming to the appropriate body of knowledge produced by historians and showing elements of the historian's own methods of enquiry.'

To conclude: even when we make a rigorous distinction between 'the past' and 'history', the latter word still continues to cover a range of processes, activities, directed at different specific purposes. 'History' embraces: the writings of historians; the research activities which lie behind these writings; the teaching and learning of both methods, on the one side, and ideas and information, on the other; the communication of historical knowledge by various means; all the activities associated with the learning outcomes inherent in the discipline of history. Often the context will make clear what precisely is intended when the word 'history' is used. If we reserve the word 'historiography' for 'the history of historical writing', as I have suggested, then there are times when the phrase 'historical writing' will be indispensable, even if it might sound tautologous ('history', after all, as we must never forget, is 'the bodies of knowledge produced by historians' which in the end equates very closely to 'the writings of historians'). An important point here is that, as is brought out in Chapters 3 (particularly) and 4, much 'historical writing' ceases to qualify as reliable knowledge, as the scope and methods of history develop and become more sophisticated.

2   The Necessity for History

History: A Social Necessity

After that disquisition, it might well be thought that the actual study of history must be a somewhat rarefied luxury. On the contrary, history is a *necessity*. Individuals, communities, societies could scarcely exist if all knowledge of the past was wiped out. As memory is to the individual, so history is to the community or society. Without memory, individuals find great difficulty in relating to others, in finding their bearings, in taking intelligent decisions – they lose their sense of identity. A society without history would be in a similar condition (every society, naturally, has a 'past', even if a totally unknown one – this points up very neatly the difference between the two words). Here, it should be noted, I am using the figure of speech known as the simile. I do not say that history *is* memory. Indeed, I think the whole notion of 'collective' or 'popular' memory is a highly dubious one; at best, that notion is metaphorical, since 'memory', properly defined, is a faculty possessed by *individual* human beings. What I am saying is that a society without knowledge of its past would be *like* an individual without memory. The simplest answer to the questions 'Why do history?' or 'What is the use of history?' is: 'Try to imagine what it would be like living in a society in which there was absolutely no knowledge of the past.' The mind boggles. It is only through a sense of history that communities establish their identity, orientate themselves, understand their relationship to the past and to other communities and societies. Without history (*knowledge* of the past), we, and our communities, would be utterly adrift on an endless and featureless sea of time.

It is indeed the case that as societies have developed in stability and organisation, so they have made greater efforts to preserve and perpetuate some account of their past: the songs, sagas, scriptures and chronicles become the increasingly systematic histories of classical, medieval, and modern times. As societies have become more complex, as the different areas of the world have become more closely interconnected, so more rigorous accounts of the past have become more necessary. Every advanced nation has, apart from its historical profession and related institutes and associations, museums and archives and libraries devoted to the preservation of these sources and relics from the past out of which history is written. Cut into the neo-classical architecture of the National Archives in Washington are the following inscriptions: 'What is *Past* is *Prologue*'; 'Study the Past'; 'The glory and romance of our history are here preserved in the chronicles of those who conceived and builded the structure of our nation'; 'The ties which bind the lives of our people in one indissoluble union are perpetuated in the archives of our government and to their custody this building is dedicated'; 'This building holds in trust the records of our national life and symbolizes our faith in the permanency of our national institutions'. The tone may seem excessively nationalistic (but then, as I have said, all nations are deeply preoccupied with their own past); it is also one of participation and sharing – history, the inscriptions suggest, is important to the whole nation, not just to a handful of scholars or the ruling elite. This is an important element in the argument that history is a necessity. In the past, history was often thought of in a functional way as a necessary education for princes and rulers. In a world of – if not democracy – what we may call mass society, an awareness of history must be diffused throughout that society; the closer the contact between the history of the historians and the history that is widely diffused, the greater the awareness of how history actually comes to be written, the better. It is necessary that new research should be constantly undertaken; it is also necessary that what is already known should be widely known.

This case is based on the importance and all-pervasiveness of the past to which I have already alluded. We cannot, as I put it, escape from the past; wherever we go we keep stubbing our toes on the past (a metaphor; but, I hope, an expressive one). The human past has determined much of the built environment, the political boundaries which divide country from country, their forms of government, the precise character of social and economic distinctions, the sources of tension within and between nations: deep in the past lie beliefs and prejudices, modes of thought, the rise, spread and fission of religious faiths, conquests and atrocities, all still exercising potent sway today.

It is a commonplace that we live in a time of rapid and far-reaching cultural change. If we are to make a rational assessment of the extent and significance of this change we have no other recourse than to look to the past: how does present change compare with previous periods of change? If we wish to discuss contemporary morality, we can only do so effectively by making comparisons with past moralities. The very stuff of so many pub conversations is in fact drawn from the past. To understand contemporary problems, to take part in contemporary debate, we *need* history.

Actually, much of the stuff of pub conversations is likely to be mythical rather than historical. Let us look more closely at myth. The characteristic of myth is that, while containing some element, often highly attenuated, of fidelity to what actually happened in the past, it is also distorted or exaggerated or simplified, almost invariably with a view to glorifying or asserting the special powers of one particular individual, or family, or community, or nation, or religious faith, or to blackening the character of some perceived enemy. Myths in this sense (the word, in a different usage, also applies to the great primordial stories emerging out of the distant past, for example the Oedipus myth) exploit the past in order to serve some current national, political, personal or religious purpose. In earlier eras it was often genuinely impossible for chroniclers and 'historians' to distinguish between what was reasonably accurate and what was entirely mythical. Myths, obviously, can be highly damaging, as, for instance, in the myths held by the Serbs or by Northern Ireland Protestants about ethnic superiority, about great victories or persecutions, in the past. Part of the necessary function of history is that, in advancing understanding of the past, it challenges and deflates myths, while at the same time explaining their origins and significance.

There is a conclusive way of rounding out the argument, one derived from the studies by Marc Ferro, a distinguished French historian associated with the *Annales* school, of the way in which history is taught around the world, published in English as *The Use and Abuse of History: or, How the Past is Taught* (the French title, less glamorously, *Comment on raconte l'histoire aux enfants*, has 'history' not 'the past'). Such is the necessity for history that all societies do indeed teach a form of history. But the 'history' taught in very many countries is in fact a 'history' designed to meet national needs, or serve the interests of the ruling regime: history is liberally mixed with myth. The history that used to be taught in white South Africa glamourised the struggles and sufferings of the Dutch settlers, attributed great qualities of tolerance to them while insisting on the primitive nature of Black Africans, and claimed that as the settlers moved north the land they occupied was empty and own-erless.[3] But decolonised Black Africa has its own self-serving history. As Ferro points out, to take one example, the long record of the Arab slave trade and the appalling atrocities it involved is practically obliterated while all attention is focused on the evils of the subsequent European slave trade.[4] Ferro shows how in the West Indies the myth is propagated of a long-established, naturally cohesive, multiracial society.[5] Indian history underplays the extent of hostility and conflict between the different nationalities, and overplays the extent of a persistent national resistance to British rule.[6] Thus, Ferro concludes,

> History in India, through its desire to legitimise the country's unity and – as we know – the dream of re-unification, finally deprives history of much of its substance. India and its people lose, thereby, a part of their identity.[7]

In Islamic countries, history sub-serves theology: the history of Islam that is taught depends upon which branch of that faith is espoused by the country's rulers.[8] How history was written and rewritten in the former Soviet Union is well known. Of incidental significance was the actual recognition of the potency of proper history and proper historical method. Not only was Trotsky eliminated from historical accounts, but the very document of October 1917 in which Lenin praised Trotsky was removed from the archives.[9] As Khrushchev said in 1956: 'Historians are dangerous and capable of turning everything topsy-turvy. They have to be watched.'[10] Ferro does not ignore the fact that much European history has been written to serve the interests of the dominant classes, and to perpetuate national myths.[11] None the less, there can be no doubt that in open, pluralist societies one can perceive the practice of history being conducted as a challenge to, rather than a perpetuation of, myths.

So, have we here a justification for history or simply confirmation of what some critics have long been saying: that much history is no better than self-serving myth? Two points emerge from Ferro's discoveries. First of all, it would not be possible for Ferro to expose the mythical quality of the history he discusses, nor to explain why particular societies foster the myths they do, if there was not already in existence bodies of historical knowledge which give us a more accurate picture of those societies against which to assess what is, or was, taught there. That these bodies of knowledge exist is a tribute to generations of professional historians. Their value is immediately clear: if they did not exist, it would not be possible to expose and explain the versions of history taught in so many countries. More than this, though: as long as countries go on teaching their biased versions of history, so long will conflicts and tensions exist between different countries. Accurate, professional history is a *necessity* if tensions and suspicions are ever to be removed. And, without it, the nations themselves, as Ferro puts it, are denied their true identities.

Other Justifications for History

All of that is in support of my contention that history is necessary to society. But that is a justification essentially for the activities of professional historians, and for their being supported by taxpayers' money. Those who study history, or who read history books, usually have more immediate reasons. For them there is a strong urge to find out about the past, which is in itself fascinating. The appeal may well be practical – learning about others different from ourselves, understanding our origins – but for many there is a kind of poetic or romantic attraction about the past. This certainly seems to be demonstrated by the enormous appeal exercised by physical manifestations of the past. Consider some of the most famous tourist traps: the Tower of London, the Conciergerie in Paris, the Gold-Rush towns of California, the late medieval village of San Gimignano in Tuscany, Ephesus in present-day Turkey (to choose but five from the thousands recorded on picture postcards around the world). One English historian, G. M. Trevelyan, spoke of the sensations aroused by the 'quasi miraculous fact that once, on this earth . . . walked other men and women as actual as we are today, thinking their own thoughts, swayed by their own passions, but now all gone, one generation vanishing after another, gone as utterly as we ourselves shall shortly be gone like ghosts at cock-crow'.[12] Another, May MacKisack, declared that there exists in the human imagination 'an instinctive wish to break down the barriers of time and mortality and so to extend the limits of human consciousness beyond the span of a single life'.[13] The Dutch historian Gustav Renier believed that feelings for the past were akin to instincts aroused on those autumnal days when there is wood smoke on the air and a strange disordered nostalgia pervades the mind.[14] We have to be careful: it may be that the poetic desires being talked of here are best catered to through historical novels; and, of course, amateur historians sometimes prefer to tempt this audience with books which are colourful and romantic, and unreliable, not rigorous and analytical, and firmly based in the sources, as genuine historical works should be.

No criticism at all is intended of tourists seeking out historical sites. Amplifying what has been gleaned from books by examining what can loosely and imperfectly be described as 'history on the ground' is a most rewarding activity. And most tourists will turn to their guidebooks to fill out contextual historical detail. Whence comes the historical information contained in the guidebooks? From, at whatever remove, the history of the professional historians. So, we see here another value in the study of history. It can provide, even when we are on holiday, the very contextual information that we crave. A rather similar, and much more weighty, point can be made in connection with the arts: usually the appreciation of a painting, or of a poem or novel or play written some time in the past, is enhanced if we have some historical knowledge of the society in which the cultural artefact was produced.

Some historians today still seem to perceive historians (usually themselves) as great literary and media figures, as individual intellectual and moral giants giving leadership to ordinary readers. I have just mentioned G. M. Trevelyan, a very popular historical writer around the middle of the twentieth century: in his biography of Trevelyan, David Cannadine, currently Director of the Institute of Historical Research in London, seems keen to reassert the role of the historian as great communicator, as played by Trevelyan; he approvingly quotes the 1957 words of another individualistic historian, Hugh Trevor-Roper, that the 'ultimate purpose of history' is to 'edify and educate' a non-professional audience.[15] The notion of historians purveying lofty moral ideas is a very old-fashioned one, and reeks of the unfortunate notion of history as a branch of literature, rather than a systematic discipline communicating well-substantiated knowledge. Upholders of this notion I refer to as adherents of the *'auteur* theory of history' (see next section).

Having dismissed that line of argument as a justification for the study of history, I now turn to the major utilitarian learning outcomes from the study of history. A training in history is a training in analysing, evaluating, and interpreting both secondary and primary sources. It develops an understanding that everything written pertaining to history, secondary or primary, must be approached with scepticism and caution. It develops the ability to distinguish between pieces of writing which are well-substantiated and logical, and those which simply express theory, hypothesis, or opinion. Primary sources by their very nature are intractable, too profuse in some areas, gravely inadequate in others, frequently confusing and contradictory, often obscure. The skills and learning outcomes[16] arising from historical study are invaluable in a contemporary world which is dominated by information and communication systems. We have newspapers, magazines, television, the web and the internet, advertisements, political statements, expert announcements, graphs, histograms, graphic visual imagery: in short, a torrent of persuasion, propaganda and pap; information, disinformation and misinformation. The methods and skills required of the historian, and, more important, the attitudes of mind transmitted in the teaching of history, are of vital importance in assessing and filtering the messages constantly battering against us. History also provides a training in the writing up of the results of one's researches, in the form of essays, reports, dissertations. The essential, as I keep stressing, is clear and effective communication, well structured, and written in precise and explicit language. That is a most important learning outcome.

Other practical justifications for the study of history can be advanced: that history familiarises us with customs, thought processes and standards different from our own, tells us about humanity and its various activities and environments, and helps us to develop an understanding of, and empathy with, attitudes and ideas different from our own; that it helps us to appreciate that present attitudes and values may themselves be ephemeral; and that it provides an understanding of the nature of historical change which should help to stimulate a personal adaptability to change and flexibility of response. But these are secondary to, or corollaries of, the central argument: the past determines and pervades the present – we'd better understand it. But now, having introduced analogies with the sciences, I have to recognise that immediate, practical pay-offs are even less than those in the sciences, as distinct from the technologies. Examples of politicians or administrators, for instance, directly and correctly acting upon their knowledge of history are not easy to identify. I certainly do not argue that history provides solutions to the problems of the present, still less does it enable us to predict the future. What I do say is that a knowledge of history helps people to behave as intelligent citizens. Without history, we shall not begin to understand the problems of the present and will be without the basic knowledge essential for grappling intelligently with the future.

To conclude this section I set out diagrammatically the relationships between history, the past, sources, and myths.

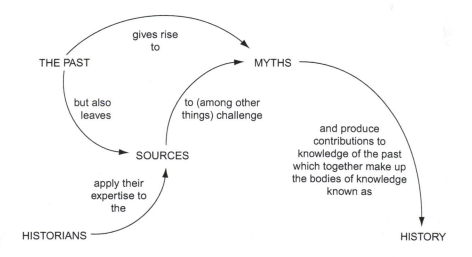

3   The *auteur* Theory of History and the Question of Subjectivity

The Historian as *auteur*

Auteur theory is the usual English translation of the French '*la politique des auteurs*', the phrase used by the early film-makers in the French 'New Wave' of the late 1950s in expressing their conviction that a film should be created by one single all-controlling genius, an 'author'. Some such notion underpins the traditional conception of history as a literary activity, of history being produced by coruscating individual figures who dazzle with the brilliance of their prose and the power of their sentiments, a view evidently espoused by G. M. Trevelyan and A. J. P. Taylor, and apparently by David Cannadine, Simon Schama, Norman Davies, Niall Ferguson, Le Roy Ladurie,[17] by many reviewers (it makes things simple) and by some publishers; giving the annual *History Today* lecture in April 2000, the respected former history publisher from Longman, Andrew MacLennan, spoke 'passionately' (his word) about the idiosyncrasies and individualistic and unconventional quirks of his authors. In introducing *The Isles: A History* (London, 1999) Norman Davies is an unabashed upholder of *auteur* theory, associating himself with Trevelyan in wanting to show 'that history is an art as well as a science' (that hoary one again!), and in the sentiment 'that history is there to enthuse the millions, not just to provide employment for academics'. This sentiment ('sentiment', not 'thought') really is cringe-makingly soppy, as well as sloppy, nonsense; history is not '*there*' – it only comes into existence through the 'employment of academics'. Richard Evans, distinguished historian of aspects of nineteenth-century Germany, has spoken of himself as exercising the talents of a novelist.[18]

My own position, to repeat, is that while historians are certainly fallible, and subject to many kinds of career and social pressures, and disagree with each other in their interpretations, as do scientists, history, for reasons which I shall continue to develop throughout this book, is an 'objective' discipline, in so far as that is possible at all. To adhere to the *auteur* theory of history is to imply, or, indeed, explicitly state, that history is in essence subjective, since the theory postulates that: the individual author, and the views expressed by that author, are paramount; the joys and benefits of reading his/her books are in nature similar to the joys and benefits of reading novels (it may be noted here that many novelists carry out very serious researches in order to provide 'authentic background' for their stories); the intellectual excitement lies in the clash of ideas, opinions, and interpretations between the various authors. This perception of history is encapsulated in the phrase 'the varieties of history', the title of an influential collection of readings from the works of 'great' historians by the American historian Fritz Stern,[19] and in the titles of two books by the Anglophile Dutch historian Pieter Geyl, *Debates with Historians* (1955) and *Napoleon: For and Against* (1949). It was given a kind of philosophical credibility by the writings of R. G. Collingwood.

Geyl (1887–1966) began his *Debates with Historians* with a reference to one of Britain's best-loved if least literate authors of detective fiction:

> Agatha Christie, in one of her books, *The Moving Finger*, introduces a girl fresh from school and lets her run on about what she thinks of it. 'Such a lot of things seem to me such rot. History, for instance. Why, it's quite different out of different books!' to which the sensible elderly confidante replies: That is its real interest.[20]

Obviously, if history does have the importance for society that I have been claiming, *that* is certainly *not* its real interest. However, Geyl is still cited as the supreme debunker of naïve misconceptions about the monolithic nature of historical knowledge. Here, now, are two passages from the introductory chapter, 'Argument Without End', from his *Napoleon: For and Against*:

> My aim in this book is to set forth and compare a number of representations of Napoleon as given by leading French historians. Striking differences will emerge, but this is hardly surprising. History can reach no unchallengeable conclusions on so many-sided a character, on a life so dominated, so profoundly affected, by the circumstances of the time. For that I bear history no grudge. To expect from history those final conclusions which may perhaps be obtained in other disciplines is in my opinion to misunderstand its nature...

> ...the scientific method is certainly not to blame. The scientific method seems above all to establish facts; there is a great deal about which we can reach agreement by its use. But as soon as there is a question of explanation, of interpretation, of appreciation, though the special method of the historian remains valuable, the personal element can no longer be ruled out, that point of view which is determined by the circumstances of his time and by his own preconceptions. Every historical narrative is dependent upon explanation, interpretation, appreciation. In other words, we cannot see the past in a single communicable picture except from a point of view, which implies a choice, a personal perspective. It is impossible that two historians, especially two historians living in different periods, should see any historical personality in the same light.[21]

Serious source-based history is certainly 'argument without end'. Historians, like scientists, build upon the discoveries of their predecessors, bring new evidence, new techniques, and new approaches to bear in refining, correcting, and, sometimes, rejecting existing interpretations. But what Geyl suggests is that each argument (one apparently as good as another) is totally replaced by a new argument; thus, unwittingly, he makes the postmodernist case. The implied sequence of discrete stages – (1) sources provide 'facts'; (2) 'facts', combined with the 'personal perspective' of the historian, yield interpretation and explanation – is a false one; of course, historians do present differing interpretations and explanations, but they do not do so in a manner detached from the sources, which at all times they must cite in showing how they have developed their train of reasoning. The concentration on a single political figure is outdated and misleading. Historians are seldom concerned solely with biographical topics: with Napoleon, as with any other single individual, there will remain aspects of his psyche which can never be penetrated, but, with respect to his actions and their impact, the evidence exists, and has been used to present interpretations which in essentials do not radically differ from each other. The disabling weakness of Geyl's book is that it does not, in fact, study serious source-based, monographic work on Napoleon, but offers no more than a series of extremely short and schematic chapters based on the writings of political propagandists whom no one would ever mistake for historians, or on the brief treatments provided in textbooks of general European history. *Napoleon: For and Against* retains some credibility as what might loosely be described as a history of changes in broad popular conceptions about Napoleon; as a study of scholarly practice, it is valueless – a stricture which I would invite readers to apply to the many books on historical epistemology which never discuss in any detail the serious research-based works which form the real stuff of history. Geyl's phrase 'we cannot see the past in a single communicable picture except from a point of view' alerts us to another couple of misconceptions in the traditional literary view of history. Historians do not attempt to 'show' us the past (just as they do not attempt to reconstruct it); what they present is 'knowledge about the past' and it is never, naturally, the whole past, but always just some limited aspect which the historian has chosen to investigate – that is where the choice lies: historians choose, or are directed towards, particular, manageable topics, as is the case in all scientific disciplines.

Relativism: R. G. Collingwood

The traditional (rather amateurish, I would say) position that history depends upon the subjective attitudes of the individual historian as *auteur* merges into the second, slightly more sophisticated position, best described as 'relativist'. This has been expressed, in rather different ways, by three much-cited 'authorities' on historical epistemology, Collingwood, Carr, and Peter Novick, who attracted much attention with his *That Noble Dream: The 'Objectivity Question' and the American Historical Profession* (1988).

Beware, I keep saying, books about history by those who have done little history themselves, nor, apparently, read any of the really serious stuff. Beware also books which turn out to be collections of lectures put together after the lecturer's death. That is the status of Saussure's *Cours de linguistique générale* (*Course in General Linguistics*, 1916), treated as a kind of bible by the postmodernists in advancing their theories about language, and which I will attack in Chapter 7. So also is it the status of *The Idea of History* (1946) by R. G. Collingwood (1889–1943), who had actually given the lectures on which the book is based in 1935 and 1936. Many of those who refer glibly to *The Idea of History* seem unaware that it consists very largely (over 200 pages) of a history of history (like my Chapters 3 and 4), with the analysis of what Collingwood thought history is contained in a 100–page 'Epilogomena' and the ten-page Introduction. We need also to consider his Historical Association pamphlet *The Philosophy of History* (1930) and his *Autobiography* (1939). His ideas were liked by his Oxford chums because they made out history to be more important, and more difficult, than the sciences, and because they made out individual historians to be very important people – *auteurs*, in effect.

Collingwood was greatly influenced by the Italian Benedetto Croce, always categorised as an 'Idealist' philosopher. With Croce and Collingwood we are back in the world of the metaphysicians, and the world in which inappropriate philosophical terms are applied to history. Practising historians do not divide into 'idealists' (those who see ideas as primary factors) and 'materialists' (those who see economic factors as primary): what happened in the past – as far as we know it – was a product of ideas, material circumstances, and other factors as well (see Chapter 6) – historians are not 'idealist' or 'materialist', just historians (or, categorised according to their specialisations, political historians, social historians, economic historians, and so on).

At the end of the nineteenth century, certain philosophers with a strong interest in history were concerned to show that methodologies in history were not just different from those of the apparently all-conquering sciences, but superior – a characteristic of today's *auteurs* (*I* think historians should settle for parity of status with physicists and biologists and earth scientists and chemists). The most important figure here was the German philosopher Wilhelm Dilthey (1833–1911) – see Chapter 3. Croce followed Dilthey in arguing that the thought processes and intellectual debates of history were superior to those of science, which was (merely!) concerned with material evidence and (he thought!) certainties. He understood that the past has no material existence ('out there'!) in the present, but fell into the intellectual's common confusion of not understanding that the absence of a present existence did not mean that past societies had not had a past existence. Scorning the arguments, which I constantly stress, that there is much material evidence of the previous existence of past societies, Collingwood adopted one of Croce's most famous slogans, 'all history is contemporary history'. Since Collingwood (and Croce) did not make a rigorous analytical distinction between 'history' and 'the past' (demonstrating, I believe, that I am right to do this), it is not usually clear what exactly they mean. Even if Croce meant 'history' in the sense in which I use the term ('knowledge produced by historians'), what he is saying is still not true: historical knowledge now still depends to a considerable extent (as does scientific knowledge) on what was produced by our predecessors in our discipline. A similar comment can be applied to Collingwood's insistence that all history 'is the re-enactment of past thought in the historian's own mind'.[22] As will become clear from the extracts that I shall quote in a moment, Collingwood, like the literary traditionalists, meant the individual historian, the historian as *auteur*. What all this ignores is that history, actually, is a collaborative enterprise: historians argue and discuss with each other, alter and refine their views. History does not emerge perfectly formed from the mind of the historian as genius; and it is certainly not confined to past *thought*.

Collingwood ran together two slightly different arguments (which does not mean to say that they cannot both, separately, be true), the full-blooded relativist argument that historians in different ages are captives of their own age, and therefore produce different historical interpretations, and the every-individual-is-different argument that, even when belonging to the same age, historians have different personalities, different personal histories, and so forth, and therefore produce different historical interpretations. He ludicrously overrated the importance of the single individual historian; he exaggerated the power of sheer thought, at the expense of ignoring the controlling significance of the primary sources; and he displayed the routine confusion over the existence of past societies (as *we* know, they don't exist *now* but they did exist *then*), incidentally mixing up 'facts' with 'sources'. Here is Collingwood running together the relativist and the purely personal argument:

Everyone brings his own mind to the study of history, and approaches it from the point of view which is characteristic of himself and his generation: naturally, therefore, one age, one man, sees in a particular historical event things which another does not, and vice versa. The attempt to eliminate this 'subjective element' from history is always insincere – it means keeping your own point of view while asking other people to give up theirs – and always unsuccessful. If it succeeded, history itself would vanish.[23]

Difficult to see how one can ask someone in a different 'age', and therefore presumably dead, to give up their point of view. More critically, what this is really saying is that history is just a matter of opinion, and that if you don't have a lot of different opinions you don't have history. The ultimate in personalisation, historians as great men, comes in his comparison between himself and the famous German historian Theodor Mommsen (1817–1903):

> My historical thought is about my own past, not about Mommsen's past. Mommsen and I share in a great many things, and in many respects we share a common past, but in so far as we are different people and representatives of different cultures and different generations we have behind us different pasts, and everything in his past has to undergo a slight alteration before it can enter into mine...[24]

I don't deny all validity to that point. Assumptions and values, which inevitably have some influence on the questions we ask and the interpretations we produce, do change from generation to generation. But the far more critical point, which Collingwood ignores, is that historical knowledge (like scientific knowledge) itself expands and becomes more sophisticated. That is the real and important reason why more recent history books are generally to be preferred to older ones. *Rule number one: look at the date*, apart from being used to distinguish between primary sources and secondary ones, should also be used for a quick judgement on the value of a particular secondary source.

I return to Collingwood's fundamental assertion, quite erroneous in the way it ignores primary sources, and the way in which historians can use them to derive accounts of the materiality of past circumstances and the reality of past events, that there 'is nothing else except thought that can be the object of historical knowledge':

> Political history is the history of political thought: not 'political theory', but the thought which occupies the mind of a man engaged in political work ... Military history, again, is not a description of weary marches in heat or cold, or the thrills and chills of battle or the long agony of wounded men. It is a description of plans and counter-plans; of thinking about strategy and thinking about tactics, and in the last resort of what the men in the ranks thought about the battle.[25]

With regard to the history that is actually produced by working historians, the truth is pretty well the exact opposite of this rubbish. Surviving sources are very unlikely to tell us 'what the men in the ranks thought about the battle' – though we are no doubt all familiar with that form of third-rate popular history where the 'historian' tells us what people were thinking (in other words, he or she invents it – see Chapter 6). On the other hand, there is a reasonable expectation that the primary sources might exist to enable one to give a reasonably well-substantiated 'description of weary marches' or of 'the long agony of wounded men'. Finally, Collingwood surmised in 1939 that we might well be standing on the 'threshold of an age in which history would be as important for the world as natural science had been between 1600 and 1900'.[26] Would you buy a book of lectures from this man? The lectures do, however, contain further unwitting testimony to the importance of detective novels to intellectuals in the 1930s (remember Geyl and Agatha Christie). Collingwood produces the stunning (but nonsensical) observation that Christie's Hercule Poirot represented the best of the current historical method (use of 'the little grey cells') whereas Sherlock Holmes represented the outdated methods (mere collection of evidence) of 40 years previously.[27] Beware the silly chatter of Oxford dons!

The Subjectivity Question

In delivering to his Cambridge audience in the early 1960s the series of sparkling and urbane lectures to which he gave the title 'What is History?', E. H. Carr did a valuable service in driving home in memorable language that history is not disembodied knowledge existing on library shelves, entirely detached from human activities. Carr's advice that one should know the historian before going on to read the history was wise enough, though he made no attempt to analyse how different kinds of history are produced. He usually managed to end each lecture with the sort of phrase that sticks. History, he said at the end of the first lecture, 'is an unending dialogue between past and present'.[28] This is simply a restatement of the familiar (and hackneyed) point made by Collingwood (and many others): 'each age writes its own history', 'each age must reinterpret the past in the light of its own preoccupations'. The metaphor, and the anthropomorphosis (turning 'past' and 'present' into humans who can communicate with each other), are far-fetched. There are much better, and more compelling, ways of putting the point that books which depend on the most up-to-date research are likely to be of more value than books whose research is outdated. But, of course, the point Carr was really trying to get over is that history in our own age is governed by the preoccupations and prejudices of that age and is therefore, in its own way, just as subjective as the history written in past ages.

The argument is not entirely without foundation, but as I shall also demonstrate, it is not sufficient to establish the case that history is inevitably subjective.

What I am doing, therefore, is challenging the arguments that history cannot achieve a reasonable degree of objectivity, while fully recognising that history, probably in common with all other scholarly activities, cannot achieve total objectivity. It is the constant fantasy of those who write critically about history that it is in a state of 'crisis'. So, Novick invented a crisis over the issue of objectivity. After taking up a great deal of space elaborating on the obvious fact that historians (again, like scientists) are frequently engaged in disputation with each other, he came to the conclusion that:

> At least for the foreseeable future, there appeared no hope that historians' work would converge to produce the sort of integrated synthesis which had long been the discipline's aspiration.[29]

This is a classic case of denigrating history through setting up an utterly unrealistic target which historians have never had, and could not possibly have. Historians concentrate on limited, manageable (but difficult enough!) topics; they add to, modify and correct what has been discovered by other historians. It is impossible to imagine what any 'integrated synthesis' could possibly look like: if it were presented in the form that any single person could actually read, then it would completely lack the detail we need when we seek information on a specific problem. Novick's is a massive statement of the obvious which does not in any way challenge the case I am making that history is reasonably objective, and certainly is not entirely subjective.

I don't for a moment refuse to acknowledge that the distinguished contemporary historians I mentioned earlier have made significant contributions to historical knowledge. It is their *perceptions* of history as a literary, and therefore subjective, activity that I reject. The trouble for me is that their views, taken along with those of such as Collingwood, Carr and Novick, only give support and comfort to the postmodernists, to whom I must now once again return.

Is it really, really true that we are all irredeemably products of the culture, or society (in this particular argument the words are used interchangeably), in which we live? Is it really, really true that everything we think and say is determined by the inescapable language of that culture or society? Is it really, really true that in our culture, or society, there is a dominant ideology and a ruling discourse which governs everything we do, whether it is reacting to a member of the opposite sex, applying paint to canvas, writing a piece of history, or, indeed, designing a scientific experiment? We are back to the point made at the beginning of Chapter

1, that we are in the realm of fundamental assumptions. For myself, I can see no good reasons for assuming that these statements are true, and many good reasons for assuming that they are not. They depend upon unsubstantiated assertions by Marx, Foucault and a few others: that Marx and Foucault were exceptional geniuses with access to truths denied to the rest of us seems to me extremely unlikely. And the cluster of assumptions just set out is integrally related to other assumptions, about the unfolding of 'history' as a series of epochs, with one class wholly triumphing over another, with the victorious class then exercising hegemony over all aspects of society or culture. The detailed work of historians indicates that these 'other assumptions' simply are not valid.[30] To maintain the assumptions, you have to assume that the work of historians is valueless, mere bourgeois ideology. The argument, then, is clearly political, about the need to overthrow (or for the more nihilistic postmodernists, reject) bad bourgeois society – the assumption being that there is some complete alternative ready and waiting, though the experiments of Mao Zedun, Pol Pot, and the Soviets would suggest that this assumption is also false. Opposing authoritarianism, conventional dogma and appeals to the status quo has contributed to the growth of freedoms in contemporary societies, and the notion of cultural or social construction when applied to allegedly immutable laws or customs can be fruitful, provided it is not made a literal absolute. But, as the philosopher of science Ian Hacking has pointed out, it soon becomes merely a mindless piece of political correctness:

> Social construction has in many contexts been a truly liberating idea, but that which on first hearing had liberated some has made all too many others smug, comfortable and trendy in ways which have become merely orthodox. The phrase has become code. If you use it favourably, you deem yourself rather radical. If you trash the phrase, you declare that you are rational, reasonable, and respectable.[31]

Which is superior: revelation or rational enquiry? In the end, it is for each individual reader to make his/her decision.

Historians recognise that we are all culturally, or socially, *influenced* but deny that their work (that is, history) is culturally, or socially, *determined* or *constructed*. Historians argue that far from being prisoners of their own culture, they are, by the very nature of what they study, particularly well qualified to understand the influences operating on them, and, therefore, to escape from them. Their claim is that, in the nature of what they do, historians are studying past societies and the way in which people in these societies were affected by the culture in which they lived. Historians, in other words, are experts on cultural influences. Accordingly, they are very aware of the danger of becoming prisoners of the dominant ideas of their own society. Historians recognise that they can never escape from these entirely, but believe that they are well equipped to make a good try.

Sometimes I think that historians themselves stress the notion of 'each age having to rewrite its own history' because they are afraid that otherwise they might find themselves out of a job. In fact, the task is not to supply a root-and-branch new version of history every 10, 25, or 50 years, but to continue refining and revising what has gone before, while also opening up totally new areas. It's a commonplace that nineteenth-century historians (in western Europe and North America) dealt largely with governments and great men, and with the developments of national consciousness and the growth of political liberalism; twentieth-century historians, more interested in economic and social democracy, turned towards economic and social history, towards peoples and away from individuals. Traditionally, historians in the Western countries were interested only in their own civilisation, seeing the rest of the world, if at all, in terms of interaction with Western culture. Now that many new nationalities compete for attention on the world's stage there has been a boom in African history, in Latin American history, in Chinese, Japanese and East Asian history. As colonisation fell into disrepute the attempt was made to study the various civilisations involved from the standpoint of their indigenous development, rather than from that of their contact and conflict with the West.

The shape and content of history, too, has varied according to the methods and materials available to different generations. The explosion of historical studies (of a sort) at the beginning of the nineteenth century was in part touched off by the opening at that time of the major European archives. Heavy emphasis today is placed on those problems, such as population growth or the social stratification of small communities, which are amenable to today's sophisticated techniques of quantification. Developments in the feminist movement at the end of the 1960s were paralleled in the production of 'women's history' and 'feminist history'. History had only begun to become a fully developed, reflexive discipline in the twentieth century, and, like the sciences, it has continued to develop. Furthermore, history is not a formation dance, in which all march in one direction at one particular moment, then turn and prance off in another. When most historians were writing political history, there were always others attempting economic and social history. Recently there has been quite a strong movement to re-emphasise the importance of politics and events, even as social and cultural history have been continuing to grow. All of this is rather obvious and scarcely merits pompous phrases about history as 'discursive practice' or 'unending dialogue between present and past'.

Arguments about subjectivity in history tend to focus far too much on individual, isolated historians, and not enough on the profession as a whole; and they tend to focus on the wrong aspects of the individual historian's work. The standard line from Carr, to White, to Jordanova is that the subjectivity lies in the way in which the historian (whether freely choosing, or compelled by the imperatives of ideology and discursivity) selects and arranges (or 'narrativises') the facts. The presumption is that the facts are easy to access and unproblematic (it is to uphold this presumption that White ignores altogether the importance of sources, and Carr and Jordanova denigrate them). Actually, the facts can only be accessed through the complex and difficult process of analysing and interpreting fragmentary and opaque primary sources. The subjectivity, or, as I would prefer to say, the 'fallibility', of history lies as much in the establishing of the facts as in writing them up. Frequently the sources are inconclusive, obscure, or contradictory. It is *this* which *forces* historians to bring in elements of conjecture and interpretation. It used to be said over and over again that given the same set of facts, historians would still produce different interpretations. A much truer statement would be that given the same sets of sources historians could still come up with different views as to what exactly the facts were.

The second point with regard to the subjectivity, or fallibility, of the historian certainly does involve selection and writing up as much as research. This is that, in a manner very different from the sciences, the topics historians investigate, being concerned with the actions and attitudes of human beings within communities and societies, are intimately bound up with values, and where there are values it is almost impossible to avoid value judgements. Here, undoubtedly, the political or moral outlook, the mental set, of the individual historian is likely to influence the contributions to historical knowledge he/she makes. Finally, there is the point I have already made, that history is a profession, a career, that there may be special rewards in supporting a particular school or approach, or alternatively in exaggerating the originality of a particular approach or set of conclusions. For historians, the temptation to play to the gallery is greater than that faced by most scientists.

Having said all that, I want to bring in two considerations traditionally ignored by both historians and their critics. The first is that we should focus on history as the bodies of knowledge produced by the labour of many thousands of members of the historical profession, not as the isolated products of *auteurs*. In history, there are no Rembrandts, no Shakespeares, no Beethovens. The work of historians is constantly being revised, modified, updated: on the whole we don't go in for revising Rembrandts or updating Beethoven. The articles and books of historians, even the most famous, are merely contributions to knowledge, and are subject to debate among professional colleagues, and to qualification and correction. Even the most original research-based monographs depend upon a whole support system of supervisors, learned journals, conferences and seminars, libraries and archives, which often provide specialist support of their own. These are the vital and exciting books which take knowledge forward. But there are also always works of synthesis and textbooks which set out honestly to summarise for us what is securely known, and which spread knowledge outwards.

The second matter for consideration is that of the role of the reader. Carr's 'unending dialogue between present and past' is exaggerated and overly rhetorical. My contention that history is, or should be, 'a dialogue between historian and reader' inevitably contains all the deficiencies of a metaphor, but does, I think, have a clear signification. Its truth depends upon the efforts both historian and reader are prepared to make. The *auteurs* often aim at a kind of authoritarianism (*I* know what I'm doing, all *you* have to do is sit back and believe me), or even illusionism (I *know* the answers, and I'm not going to *show* you how I arrived at them). But the whole point of a full scholarly apparatus of footnotes referring to the sources on which a work is based is to enable the reader to participate in the enquiry, to judge for himself/herself how well substantiated the historian's contentions are – though many readers, obviously, are not prepared to be active in this way. My argument is that the need for the historian to convince the reader (apart altogether from the whole cohort of professional peers) is a limitation upon the historian's opportunity to indulge in personal prejudice or fantasy. But let me advance the Marwick 20 per cent rule: at least 80 per cent of what a scholarly historian writes is likely to be soundly based – but the reader should always be ready to reject up to 20 per cent, which can be due to bees in the bonnet, sycophancy towards a patron, the desire to be in fashion, humble error, or various other reasons already identified. If prepared to read four or five books on the same subject, then the reader may well be able to work out for himself/herself a pretty objective account of that particular subject.

Society has always had historians (of a sort). In the next two chapters I do no more than offer a simple account of the manner in which the modern specialist discipline of history has developed. The history of historical writing cannot be chopped up into neat compartments: on the one hand there is a continuity of purpose which it will be the main task of these chapters to identify; on the other, there has often been vociferous opposition to whatever orthodoxy has, in conventional historiography, been regarded as the prevailing one of the time.

Notes

1 David Lowenthal, *The Past is a Foreign Country* (Cambridge, 1985).
2 I have discussed these issues more fully in my article 'Two Approaches to Historical Study: The Metaphysical (including "Postmodernism") and the Historical', *Journal of Contemporary History*, 30/1 (January 1995), pp. 5–34. I return to them in Chapter 5.
3 Marc Ferro, *The Use and Abuse of History: or, How the Past is Taught* (London, 1984), pp. 5–11.
4 Ibid., p. 27.
5 Ibid., p. 28.
6 Ibid., pp. 37, 45, 51–2.
7 Ibid., p. 52.
8 Ibid., pp. 50, 79–88.
9 Ibid., p. 117.
10 Ibid., p. 114.
11 This comes out most strongly in his subsequent book *L'Histoire sous surveillance* (Paris, 1985).
12 G. M. Trevelyan, *An Autobiography and Other Essays* (London, 1949), p. 13.
13 May MacKisack, *History as Education* (London, 1956), p. 10.
14 G. J. Renier, *History: Its Purpose and Method* (London, 1950), p. 29.
15 David Cannadine, *G. M. Trevelyan: A Life in History* (London, 1992), p. 226.
16 For learning outcomes, see Appendix A.
17 Apart from Trevelyan (even I am not *that* old!) I have had personal contact with all of those mentioned here, for whom I have the greatest admiration. Their sense of themselves appears in their journalism, and in books by them, some mentioned in the course of this book.
18 Richard J. Evans, *In Defence of History* (London, 1997), pp. 142–8.
19 Fritz Stern (ed.), *The Varieties of History: Voltaire to the Present* (Cleveland, Ohio, 1956; 2nd edn, London, 1971).
20 Pieter Geyl, *Debates with Historians* (London, 1955), p. 1.
21 Pieter Geyl, *Napoleon: For and Against* (London, 1949), p. 15.
22 R. G. Collingwood, *The Idea of History* (London, 1946), p. 215. Also pp. 282 and 302.
23 R. G. Collingwood, *The Philosophy of History* (London, 1930), p. 15.
24 Ibid.
25 R. G. Collingwood, *An Autobiography* (London, 1939), p. 110.
26 Ibid., p. 118.
27 Collingwood, *The Idea of History*, p. 281.
28 E. H. Carr, *What is History?* (London, 1961; pb edn, 1964), p. 30.
29 Peter Novick, *That Noble Dream: The "Objectivity Question" and the American Historical Profession* (Cambridge, 1988), p. 590.
30 The brilliant summary of the extensive literature by William M. Reddy in *Money and Liberty in Modern Europe: A Critique of Historical Understanding* (New York, 1986) is the more impressive since the author is a Marxist.
31 Ian Hacking, *The Social Construction of What?* (Cambridge, Mass., 1999), p. vii.

3

How the Discipline of History Evolved: From Thucydides to Langlois and Seignobos

1   From Ancient Athens to the Enlightenment

The Exemplar History of the Ancients

Curiosity killed the human being. No, of course not, curiosity led to the freedoms and living standards enjoyed by human beings today, though still in disgracefully few parts of the world. The British Association for the Advancement of Science was founded in 1831, the concept of 'the scientist', and the word to go with it, only beginning to come into currency at that time. The concept of 'the historian' goes back to the Ancient Greeks, but the professionalisation of history came rather more slowly than that of science. The first of the professional historical journals, 'learned journals' as they are called, *Historische Zeitschrift*, was founded in 1859. Instruction in research techniques in history was initiated at the new École Pratique des Hautes Études in Paris in 1868. The American Historical Association with its own learned journal modelled on the German one, *The American Historical Review*, was founded in 1884. The first true predecessor of this present book of mine, *Introduction to the Study of History* by C. V. Langlois (1863–1929) and Charles Seignobos (1854–1942), was published simultaneously in Paris and London in 1898.

Is it really worthwhile going all the way back to Thucydides? Is it really appropriate to call Thucydides, Bede, Gibbon and the others 'historians'? Yes, certainly we must call them historians, but we must also recognise that they were not practitioners of the professional history which is the subject matter of this book. It is utterly ridiculous, therefore, for those claiming to write about what historians do to base their assumptions on the works of these early historians (as, for example, Hayden White does – in his case Hegel, Michelet, Ranke, de Tocqueville and Burckhardt). For students and general readers with little time to spare, it is always best to go to the most recent historians whose work incorporates the most recent research. Still, there are three reasons why

51

those interested in history might want to read historians who lived and died in long-past societies. First, their works serve as primary sources for the time in which they lived, putting us directly into contact with ideas and values not generally our own, though there is often the shock of recognising attitudes remarkably similar to those still current today. Secondly – the main point of this chapter – it is interesting to see how the methods and concepts deployed by historians in the past have evolved. Thirdly, some of the great classical historical works of the past can still serve as a starting point for researchers today; or, if that is overstated, as in many cases it is, works of the past can offer insights that might be missed if we concentrated solely on the most recent publications. There is an important general point here: wide reading, even reading in the less obvious and more obscure books, can often be beneficial, provided our critical awareness of what little hints might be useful for our own immediate purpose is switched full on. That, indeed, is perhaps the major lesson of my previous chapter. There is subjectivity in pretty well all historical writing, so we should always be ready not to believe everything we read; but we can pick out the ideas and bits of information useful to our own work or interests.

Concentrating now on the second of the reasons given for bothering about past historians, we should ask of these past historians our three central questions: why did they write history anyway? (and, linked to that, who did they think they were writing for?); what did they think history was? – and linked to that, what sort of matters (military, cultural, and so on) did they think should be the concern of the historian?; and how did they do history, or, at least, how did they think it should be done? Obviously historians in the past faced the same sorts of difficult problems historians writing in the present face. What solutions did they come up with? Now, I do not for one moment intend to criticise historians of the past for not producing the kind of work we would expect of a professional historian today: but it is important, if we are to move towards establishing best practice for the twenty-first century, to be aware of where past solutions were unsatisfactory. Where there are evident advances, we shall want to note them: I'm thinking particularly of advances in method, and advances in the scope of history (going beyond mere narratives of events, for example). I'm not too keen on biological metaphors, but what I'm really hoping to demonstrate is an evolution in methods and scope until we reach 'critical mass' (a metaphor from physics) in the twentieth century, the moment when history becomes a fully autonomous professional discipline.

With regard to methodology, the two areas I want to focus on are those of (surprise, surprise!) primary sources and periodisation – that is, the attempt, analytically, to divide the past up in a way that seems logical and in conformity with the evidence. Historians who recognise the importance of primary sources, and of periodisation, are in advance of those who do not. But, we are here speaking only of first steps. The second steps are to recognise how difficult primary sources are to handle, how fragmentary, opaque and ambiguous, and to recognise that periodisation is merely an analytical device, not something which has an inherent reality of its own. The early historians did, in particular, tend to greatly overrate (often newly discovered) primary sources as fountains of transparent truth. The thing with postmodernist critics is that they are utterly out of date: daft remarks about 'a fetishism of documents' and 'the cult of the archive' may apply to historians of a hundred and more years ago, but certainly not to historians today. It is that kind of transformation that I hope to demonstrate in this and the next chapter. One other transformation, apart from the formulation and then abandonment of naïve ideas about periodisation, is that over 'meaning' in history. From the end of the classical age right through to the eighteenth-century Enlightenment, and in some cases beyond, historians believed that what they were writing about was governed by the will, or the thoughts, of God; there are those since who have believed that what a historian writes is, or should be, governed by the thoughts of Marx, or Foucault, or some other demi-god. Even within this chapter we shall see some magnificent examples of historians emancipating themselves from superstition. However, my aim of demonstrating that history is today a systematic discipline with strong claims to objectivity, though it only became so relatively recently, must always be balanced against that of showing that societies have always felt the need for some kind of awareness, even if largely mythical, of their past. However imperfectly, the historians I am now going to discuss were responding to that need. The same need, I believe, was felt in non-Western societies – in China, Africa, Persia, for instance – but not having the knowledge or space to go into that, I concentrate on the tradition which led most directly to the professional history practised all over the world, the Western tradition.

That tradition goes back to Herodotus (c. 484 BC–c. 425 BC) and Thucydides (c. 455 BC–c. 400 BC), writing towards the end of the great classical age in Ancient Greece; Polybius (c. 198 BC–117 BC), writing when Greece was falling under the dominion of Rome; and to Livy (59 BC–AD 17), Tacitus (c. AD 55–AD 120) and Plutarch (AD 50–AD 120), the great historians of Imperial Rome (Plutarch was himself actually a Greek). For the Greek and Roman writers history was quite unabashedly 'exemplar history', educational in purpose, a preparation for life, especially political and military life. Essentially, it was a narration of memorable events designed to preserve the memory and propagate the knowledge of glorious deeds, or of events which were important to a man, a family, or a people. The Peloponnesian War was still being fought among the Greek states when Thucydides was writing his *History of the Peloponnesian War*, so that famous work is, in part, what we would now call 'contemporary history'. Still, Thucydides, and the other writers mentioned, did make some effort to indicate the sources on which they were relying for their information. Thucydides tried to give a precise sense of chronology, essential to historical writing if it is to be more than just a vague celebration of past achievements.

The History of the Church (completed around 324/5) by the Greek Christian writer Eusebius (*c.* 260–339), who lived most of his life in Caesarea in Palestine, forms both a culmination of the ancient tradition and a link to medieval Christian Europe. Mainly derived from other accounts ('secondary sources', we would call their analogues today), this book is the only surviving account of the Church from the time of Christ to the conversion of the Emperor Constantine, and has earned its author the title 'Father of Ecclesiastical History'.[1]

The Medieval Chronicles

In the post-classical period, the tradition was left almost exclusively in the hands of monkish chroniclers, whose annalistic accounts have little in the way of reflection or analysis. Occasionally a chronicler would pause in his headlong flight through the years for a judgement (or is it simply politic obsequiousness?), such as this by the Anglo-Saxon Chronicler on William the Conqueror (*d.* 1087):

> King William, of whom we speak, was a man of great wisdom and power, and surpassed in honour and in strength all those who had gone before him. Though stern beyond measure to those who opposed his will, he was kind to those good men who loved God ... Among other things we must not forget the good order he kept in the land, so that a man of substance could travel unmolested throughout the country with his bosom full of gold ... If a man lay with a woman against her will, he was forthwith condemned to forfeit those members with which he disported himself ...[2]

The English monk the Venerable Bede (*d.* 735) was careful in his chronology, and does give some indication of the sources he was relying on. His premises and assumptions are vastly different from ours – the insight we get into these being one of the most important uses of his *A History of the English Church and People*, as a primary source for us today studying the early Middle Ages.

Medieval historians often did not distinguish clearly between sacred and profane matters: events, from time to time, are expressed as judgements of God, and miracles are accepted. Such writers as Otto of Freising (1111/1115–58), a member of the German Imperial Hohen-staufen family, Matthew Paris (*d. c.* 1259), a monastic chronicler based at St Albans, and the Burgundian historian of the Hundred Years War Jean Froissart (*c.* 1337–*c.* 1410), provided fairly reliable accounts of their own times, but had not found it easy to shake off the all-pervasive influence of St Augustine's *City of God* (426), a work of Christian apologetics portraying the history of the world as the long unfolding of God's will. Though often themselves expert forgers, medieval chroniclers were quite uncritical in their treatment of documentary evidence. They accepted in full the sanctions of tradition, and, since they believed in divine intervention, were inhibited in their analysis of historical causation.

Renaissance Histories and Ancillary Techniques

With the beginnings of the Renaissance, and a new enthusiasm for the works of the classical historians, we get the development of the ancillary techniques, so important to the development of scholarly history, the history of the *érudits* (I shall use this French word, coined at the time, to contrast with the other French word I have already introduced, *auteurs*). First we have the 'gloss', the explanatory note attached to a document and illuminating some of its imperfections as a primary source. The first great scholarly triumph (and one with an immense practical pay-off) was that of Lorenzo Valla (*c.* 1407–57), who exposed the document known as the Donation of Constantine, allegedly that emperor's bequest to the medieval church, as the forgery that it was. Only in the seventeenth century did the interlinked ancillary techniques of philology, palaeography, and diplomatics begin to be systematised. Diplomatics, originating from the practical need to distinguish between genuine charters and forged ones, concerns the formal qualities which distinguish one type of document from another, originals from drafts, and drafts from copies. It involves specialist knowledge of the characteristics of the offices issuing documents (royal households, or chanceries, for instance), and of the particular formulas they used, as well as of the signatures and seals intended to confirm authenticity. For the detailed analysis of seals the techniques of sigillography, which specialised in the distinctive iconographies associated respectively with royal seals, official seals, religious seals, town seals, commercial seals and personal seals, are required.

Diplomatics overlaps with palaeography when it comes to questions of the material out of which the document is composed, the ink and implements used, the style of writing, the elucidation of abbreviations, the significance of decorative elements, the conventions governing bindings, and so on. The primary task of palaeography is to ensure that the historian is correctly reading what it is the document was intended to convey. Diplomatics and palaeography together assist with establishing dates and provenance, and, of course, with distinguishing the authentic from the forgery. Philology, always of central importance to those working on Latin, Greek, and Hebrew texts, takes us in the direction of linguistics and exact translation. Deciphering inscriptions in stone is the specialist province of epigraphy.

Well before these ancillary techniques were fully developed, the events of the Renaissance provided a stimulus to historical study. Geographical exploration created a demand for exact information, historical as well as geographical. The invention of printing created an obvious incentive to the production of history books. In the scientific and intellectual revolution which culminated in the work of Sir Isaac Newton (1642–1727) history, along with all other scholarly pursuits, played a part. Everywhere among the intelligent and articulate there was an awareness of, and interest in, the processes of change. The battles of the Protestant and Catholic Reformations provided further stimulus to historical study, as each side endeavoured to demonstrate the historical validity of its position: Luther's associate Melancthon (1497–1560) brought to the German universities at which he taught an enthusiasm for the erudite study of history, and Flacius Illyricus (1520–75) directed the publication of the 'Magdeburg Centuries', an ecclesiastical history (to 1200 or thereabouts) which, though strongly biased in the Lutheran cause, did contain masses of primary source material.

The first great vernacular historians (that is to say, they wrote in Italian, or strictly speaking, Florentine, rather than Latin, and thus aimed at audiences wider than just clerics and intellectuals) were Leonardo Bruni (1347?–1444), whose *Florentine History* (1415–29) serves today as a valuable primary source for historians studying civic humanism in the Renaissance, Niccolò Machiavelli (1469–1527), and Francesco Guicciardini (1483–1540). Apart from his famous work, *The Prince* (completed in 1513, published in 1532), Machiavelli, significantly in demonstrating the influence of the classical historians, also published a series of *Discourses* (1516) on Livy; his *History of Florence* was published in 1522. *The Prince* is a work of political philosophy as well as history, for there is no sense of the complete autonomy of history until the nineteenth century (and even in the twentieth century it was common for political science and history to be taught in the same university departments); yet essentially *The Prince* is a realistic presentation of the nature of Italian government, politics and diplomacy at the beginning of the sixteenth century, rather than, as often popularly thought, a guide to the worst techniques of *Realpolitik*. Guicciardini's *History of Italy* (uncompleted on his death in 1540) offers analysis of political motivation. Its answer to my 'why?' question was in keeping with a long tradition: to give the reader 'wholesome instructions'.[3]

The Italians had no immediate disciples. In England, Sir Walter Raleigh's *History of the World* (1614) falls into the *auteur* rather than the *érudit* class. William Camden's *Britannia* (six editions, 1586–1607), however, was based on deep learning and extensive research; in his preface Camden (1551–1623) gave an answer to the 'why?' question which is essentially the one that I, too, am pressing on readers: 'If there are any who desire to be strangers in their own country, foreigners in their own cities and always children in knowledge, let them please themselves: I write not for such humours.'[4] Camden's essay in contemporary history, his *History of Elizabeth* (1615), was based on the great mass of records made available to him. In writing his *Survey of London* (1598), John Stow took it for granted that his historical treatment would be of intrinsic interest to his readers. History was but one of many interests for Sir Francis Bacon (1561–1626), the proponent of rational, or let us even say 'scientific', method in all things – detailed examination of evidence and rigorous enquiry into causal relationships are apparent in his only complete historical work, *History of Henry VII*. Most noteworthy of all English historians before the Enlightenment was Edward Hyde, Earl of Clarendon, a statesman who played a leading part in the Royalist cause during the revolutionary period. Accordingly his *History of the Rebellion and Civil Wars in England*, begun in the year 1641, leans more to *auteur* than *érudit* style: dealing with matters of great complexity, it is a masterpiece of organisation, so that the nearest parallels in modern times are Winston Churchill's histories of the two world wars.

In tandem with the elaboration of the ancillary techniques already mentioned, great efforts were made in Europe throughout the sixteenth and seventeenth centuries to bring together precious collections of primary sources. In part, this was a response to the unfortunate dispersal of valuable documents during the periods of religious strife: after the dissolution of the monasteries in sixteenth-century England, complained a contemporary with pardonable exaggeration, the new owners used the contents of their libraries for profitable sale overseas, 'to rub their boots' or to 'serve their jakes'.[5] The most significant advances in historical scholarship were made in seventeenth-century France, where such *érudits* as Duchesne, Baluze, Mabillon and Montfaucon were great exponents of the ancillary techniques, moving also into the realm of archaeology. The greatest work in the scholarly compilation of collected primary sources was carried through by the French Benedictines at St Maur. Among other large enterprises were those of certain Belgian Jesuits, followers of John Bolland (1596–1665), who initiated the *Acta Sanctorum*, and the collection of German documents *Monarchia romani Imperii*, associated with Melchior Goldast (*d*. 1635). The leading theorist of historical study was Jean Bodin (*c*. 1530–96), French author of *Method for the Easy Understanding of History*, in which he declared the subject to be of both intellectual interest and of pragmatic value for morals and politics.[6] Jacques Bénigne Bossuet (1627–1704), Bishop of Meaux in France, quite explicitly wrote his *Discourse on Universal History* for the education of the heir to the throne, the Dauphin. This book also exemplifies the notion of history as the revelation of God's will, which if anything had been strengthened by the controversies over the Protestant and Catholic Reformations.

The Enlightenment

During the eighteenth-century Enlightenment, there were both distinguished *érudits* and distinguished *auteurs*: inevitably, the latter have had more attention. Certainly, in bringing prestige to historical study they did, in that sense, help to prepare a readership for the more scholarly works of the nineteenth century. But that scholarship owed a more direct debt to the technical advances achieved by the eighteenth-century *érudits*. Particularly important was the work being carried out at the University of Göttingen (founded 1737) where, in addition to the compilation of economic, demographic, and geographic 'statistics' (data relating to states), attempts were made to write histories which incorporated analysis rather than majestic narrative: Johann Christoph Gatterer (1729–99), especially, has been seen as an eighteenth-century precursor of Ranke. The names everyone knows are those of François-Marie Arouet de Voltaire (1694–1778), Edward Gibbon (1737–94), and Charles Louis, sieur de Montesquieu (1689–1755). All four participated in the (almost) final destruction of the theological basis of historical writing. Gibbon treated Christianity, not only irreverently and empirically, but with the utmost disenchantment. 'The theologian', he remarked in a famous sentence, 'may indulge in the pleasing task of describing Religion as she descended from Heaven arrayed in her native purity';[7] he, as a historian, was content to explain the successes of early Christianity in terms of 'exclusive zeal, the immediate expectation of another world, the claim of miracles, the practice of rigid virtue, and the constitution of the primitive church'.[8] He accepted, in another famous phrase, the 'melancholy truth . . . that the Christians in the course of their intestine dissensions have inflicted far greater severities on each other than they experienced from the zeal of the infidels'.[9]

For Gibbon, the scope of history did not greatly extend beyond that envisaged by Thucydides: 'Wars, and the administration of public affairs', he wrote in the preface to his *Decline and Fall of the Roman Empire* (1776–88), 'are the principal subjects of history.' Montesquieu, whose *The Spirit of the Laws* (1748) stressed the importance of physical environment and of tradition, and, above all, Voltaire expanded the scope of history in the direction of cultural and social matters. Save for the efficiency and elegance of the narrative, there was nothing outstandingly original about Voltaire's *History of Charles XII* (1731): it was while working on *The Century of Louis XIV* (published in 1751) that he began to develop the broader cultural and social approach which characterised his *Essay on the Manners and Character of the Nations* (first complete edition published in 1756). Voltaire, in what is always recognised as an important manifesto for a more ambitious history, declared that the historian must give due attention to the civilisations of India and China, and that economic, social and cultural matters were as much the concern of the historian as the doings of popes and kings.[10]

While not quite having the vision of Voltaire, the eighteenth-century Scottish school of historical writing was characterised by a broad view of history's scope. David Hume (1711–76) is best known as a philosopher (as indeed was Voltaire), the lines between the two disciplines not yet being firmly drawn; writing rather as Tory historian than general philosopher, Hume demonstrated the absurdity of the idea that human society had originated in a 'social contract' (the fancy of contemporary French philosopher Jean-Jacques Rousseau). Hume's *History of England* was published in six volumes between 1754 and 1762. Largely a work of synthesis rather than exhaustive original scholarship (Hume once referred to research as the 'dark industry'), the *History* made its author a very wealthy man. The main text was straight political narrative, but details of wages, prices, dress and other matters, what we would now call social history, were included in the form of appendices. To my mind, Hume scores badly for his reference to the subject as an 'agreeable entertainment' more interesting than fiction. However, he scores highly for his declaration that 'a man acquainted with history may, in some respect, be said to have lived from the beginning of the world'.[11]

Adam Smith (1723–90) is renowned as the founder of the classical school of political economy, but his *The Wealth of Nations* (1776) is essentially historical in its approach to the study of humanity's economic activities. Smith, perhaps more than any of his contemporaries, brought out the importance of the economic imperatives underpinning human society, and he had already, in the *Theory of Moral Sentiments* (1759), made the point that human beings can 'subsist only in society'. Although a minister of the Scottish Presbyterian Church, William Robertson (1721–93) was the complete Enlightenment historian: he shared some of the breadth of Voltaire, some of the skills and preoccupations of the *érudits*, and he was concerned with the question of periodisation. Dividing his *History of Scotland* (1759) into four periods, he remarked of the first that it 'is the region of pure fable and conjecture, and ought to be totally neglected, or abandoned to the industry and credulity of antiquarians'. His *The History of the Reign of the Emperor Charles V* (1769) had an extensive scholarly apparatus: Robertson provided bare references in the text, then an appendix of Proofs and Illustrations as long as the text itself. His *The History of America* (1774–94) demonstrated an almost Voltairian conception of history as embracing the development of human society and civilisation.

Most interesting of all the Scottish historians was John Millar (1735–1801), Professor of Civil Law at the University of Glasgow. Two of his central ideas both anticipated and influenced Marx. In *The Origin of the Distinction of Ranks* (1771) he endeavoured to explain the changes in the power structure of society and of groups within society by associating these with changes in property relations. His *An Historical View of the English Government* (1787) divided English history into three periods, each based on the predominant system of property-holding in place at the time: the 'feudal aristocracy' to 1066, the 'feudal monarchy' to 1603, and 'the commercial government' thereafter.[12]

The Enlightenment historians were certainly great protagonists of the *auteur* theory of history, of history as a means towards making money and achieving high social status. Gibbon quite consciously reckoned history the most popular form of literature, the novel not yet having established its ascendancy. History was still far from being a rigorous discipline. The Scottish historians, particularly Millar and Robertson, with their schemes of periodisation, did show some sense of change over time, and of the need to treat each period, as it were, on its own terms, rather than judging it from the standpoint of the eighteenth century, though Robertson was contemptuous of the most remote period. Both Gibbon and Voltaire exercised their magnificent wit on the obvious fact that human beings in past ages had not always disported themselves in a fashion considered suitable in the eighteenth-century 'Age of Reason'. The medieval period was usually treated scrappily and with little respect; Gibbon seriously underrated the achievements of the Byzantine Empire. Secondly, while Robertson did make substantial gestures towards scholarship, and while Gibbon was scrupulous in his search of the available evidence, there was a tendency towards synthesis, dependence on the works of others, and a disjunction from the genuine world of *érudition*. 'Confound details', exclaimed Voltaire, 'they are a vermin which destroy books.'[13] The third weakness was that nowhere was there any efficient teaching of history, save in the palaces of princes and statesmen. True, the Camden chair had been established at Oxford in the Elizabethan period: but Camden professors confined themselves to Roman history. In the 1720s George I instituted Regius chairs of modern history (professorships appointed by the King, or, rather, by his government) at Oxford and Cambridge, but this was a political not an educational move, designed to bring Whig nominees into these centres of Toryism. The early incumbents were completely without distinction: the second Oxford professor, his more recent successor, Hugh Trevor-Roper, once informed us, was remembered only for bringing 'one Handel, a foreigner... with his "lousy crew" of "fiddlers" to play in the Sheldonian Theatre'.[14] Systematic history teaching was offered at the University of Göttingen from 1757; and in 1768 a Chair of History and Morals was established at the Collège de France, in Paris. But history as a modern discipline belongs neither to *auteurs*, nor to a few elite institutions: it is a subject researched by thousands and taught to millions.

2   Ranke: His Disciples and his Critics

Vico and Herder

It was from the simultaneous attack on these three weaknesses that the movement towards the establishment of history as an academic discipline emerged. After the great revolutionary upheavals at the end of the eighteenth century it was no longer possible to believe in the unchanging character of human behaviour, nor in the immutable nature of social institutions; as never before, intellectuals became preoccupied with the carefully documented study of historical origins and historical change. There was an *érudit* strand, but also a romantic one, most strongly represented in the novels of Sir Walter Scott, who set out with the explicit purpose of portraying the manners and morals of past ages, but also by the French historians Augustin Thierry (1795–1856) and Jules Michelet (1798–1874). The *érudit* strand is most notably represented by Barthold Georg Niebuhr (1776–1831) and Leopold von Ranke (1795–1886), though in fact Ranke, like many other historians of the time, was greatly influenced by Scott, and it was Niebuhr who neatly expressed the impact of the immediate historical context:

> It was a time when we were experiencing the most incredible and exceptional events, when we were reminded of many forgotten and decayed institutions by the sound of their downfall.[15]

But Niebuhr it was who intensified the power of philology as a vital ancillary skill.

There is no rigid division between the eighteenth-century classicism of the Enlightenment and the romanticism of the early nineteenth century. Already, in the latter half of the eighteenth century there had appeared some manifestations of what would later be recognised as the romantic sensibility, while the French revolutionaries were resolutely classicist (as seen, for example, in the paintings of David). If we look at the dates of two philosophical writers, often bracketed together, Giambattista Vico (1668–1744) and Johann Gottfried von Herder (1744–1803), we can see that they belonged to two different eras, the one dying in the same year the other was born. Vico's *New Science*, published in 1725, attracted little attention, though he presented the kind of periodisation that became familiar 50 years later: human civilisation, he claimed, had unfolded in three stages, 'divine', 'heroic' and 'human'. More significantly, he recognised the cultural differences between different ages and different nations: unlike the main Enlightenment historians, he was aware of the danger of importing ideas, or judgements, from a later age into an earlier one. Herder, whose short *Philosophy of History* of 1774 was followed by a four-volume *Philosophy of History*, published between 1784 and 1791, presented similar ideas in a much more sophisticated and coherent form, though, of course, his conception of history (that is, the past as process) as an onward march now seems very naïve. More important, he stressed (as Montesquieu had done) the importance of geography, and he developed for the first time the concept of 'national character' which he believed greatly influenced the history of any nation (an idea on which it is now fashionable to pour scorn, but I am personally far from sure that the notion is entirely without its uses). Herder coined the verb *einfühlen* ('to feel into'), as used in his injunction to historians, which, if a little simplistically expressed, really is not a bad one: 'First sympathise with the nation, go into the era, into the geography, into the entire history, *feel* yourself into it.' Against the confident contempt of the Enlightenment historians, Herder posed the notion that everything *relatively* is right *in its own historical context*.

Ranke and Niebuhr

The ideas of Vico and Herder, neglected in the eighteenth century, were welcomed by the intellectuals, novelists, and poets of the early nineteenth century who shared this desire to see past societies 'from the inside' as it were, to see the past 'as it really was' in the celebrated (and notorious) words of Ranke. Overstatement is the venial sin of all mighty innovators, and Ranke was undoubtedly guilty of it when, in the modest and self-deprecating preface to his first book, *Histories of the Latin and Teutonic Nations 1494–1514* (1824), he permitted himself the following, much-quoted and much-traduced pontification:

> To history has been assigned the office of judging the past, of instructing the present for the benefit of future ages. To such high offices this work does not aspire: it wants only to show how it actually was (*wie es eigentlich gewesen*).[16]

Those familiar with these lapidary words are often taken aback by the passion, and indeed political commitment, which they find when they come actually to read Ranke's works. Historians had still to learn that there is a big gap between stating intentions and actually carrying them out (and, no doubt, even now have some way to go). That said, a grasp of the fact that past societies are very different from our own, and – this is the real force of the point – very difficult to get to know is a fundamental one; anachronism is still one of the most obvious faults when the unqualified (those expert in other disciplines, perhaps) attempt to do history. Along with the desire to understand past societies 'as they really were' went an understanding that this could only be achieved by very meticulous study of the primary sources (popular writers are sometimes praised by reviewers for the imaginative way in which they evoke the past; but imagination, if it is not founded in evidence, really isn't much use). The ancillary skills, particularly in philology, were, as we have seen, already being developed: the first of the new, more reflexive, more determinedly rigorous scholars was Niebuhr, a native of Denmark, who from 1806 worked in the service of the Prussian government, and was closely associated with the Prussian reform movement, itself a response to the challenge of Napoleon. In 1810 he was appointed to give lectures at the newly founded University of Berlin, itself a product of the reform movement. These lectures, published in two volumes in 1811–12 as *The History of Rome* (with a completely revised three-volume edition in 1827–32), were an embodiment of the most advanced methods of philology and textual criticism applied to the primary sources relating to the historical origins of the Roman state. A certain amount of historical production in our own day takes the form of challenging, and sometimes even 'exposing', the failings in the accounts of other historians. Niebuhr exposed grave errors in the long-accepted accounts by Livy, and thus discredited a whole school of authors whose own accounts had simply been repetitions of Livy. Here, really, was the first trumpet-blast in the campaign to establish that an elevated style and hallowed modes of presentation are no substitute for getting it right. Niebuhr, as it happened, wrote clumsily, believing that you couldn't have both historical accuracy and a persuasive style (my own view is that the obligation for *all* historians is to combine getting it as nearly right as possible with communicating in a clear, precise, and appropriately uncluttered style – there is no way that serious history can be easy reading, a point, I believe, which gives rise to much misunderstanding).

Ranke was explicitly following the advanced methodology of Niebuhr when he described the sources for his *Histories of the Latin and Teutonic Nations* as:

Memoirs, diaries, letters, diplomatic reports, and original narratives of eye-witnesses; other writings were used only if they were immediately derived from the above-mentioned or seemed to equal them because of some original information.[17]

Ranke added that these sources would be identified on every page, and, in the form used by Robertson, 'a second volume, to be published concurrently, will present the method of investigation and the critical conclusions'.[18] Actually, if we reflect on comments I have already made about primary and secondary sources, the first of these statements by Ranke is not quite fully in accord with the best contemporary practice, and might suggest some weakness in Ranke's methods. You, the reader, might care to pause for a moment and reflect what that weakness might be.

Well, what I have in mind is that Ranke does not make an explicit difference between primary and secondary sources; it is not clear whether the 'other writings' are actually secondary sources, or just other sorts of primary sources. The key word for Ranke is 'original' (he uses it twice), and the implication seems to be that if a source is 'original' that makes it transparent and truthful. Of course, as we know, finding the sources is only a beginning (though an essential one, Ranke was absolutely right there); even with his 'method of investigation' and 'critical conclusions' Ranke underestimated the biases and imperfections inherent in all primary sources. The new scholarship in its most austere form was seen in the inauguration of the collection of German historical texts, the *Monumenta Germaniae Historica*, initiated by the nationalist politician Karl Freiherr von Stein and edited (from 1823) by the Hanoverian scholar Georg Heinrich Pertz. Other countries followed: nationalism was a major impulse, but scholarship was a main beneficiary.

In France, under the direction of the historian–statesman François Guizot, author of *History of Civilisation in Europe* (1828) and *History of Civilisation in France* (1829–32), and dominant minister during the constitutional (though far from democratic) monarchy (1830–48), committees were established for the publication in hundreds of volumes of thousands of manuscripts, charts, memoirs, and correspondence. Thierry explained how in writing his *History of the Norman Conquest of England* (1825) he had to 'devour long folio pages, in order to extract a single sentence, or even a word, among a thousand'.[19] In 1821 the École des Chartes was founded for the purpose of providing a training in the handling of charters and other primary sources. In scholarship, then, Germany led, but France was not far behind. Ranke himself, as I have suggested, was no cold, unemotional scholar. Not for him the scepticism of the Enlightenment. Sharing in the religiosity of the nineteenth century and seeking to show that behind the human past lay God's plan, and above human activities 'God's hand', he falls short of the calculus I have set; states he called 'thoughts of God'.[20] But Ranke undoubtedly did produce a substantial corpus of work; my constant refrain is that if we are to find out what history is we should give most attention to those who actually write the stuff. In fact Ranke produced well over a dozen substantial (usually multi-volume) books, including *The Ottoman and the Spanish Empires in the Sixteenth and Seventeenth Centuries* (1827), using an invaluable source, the reports of the Venetian ambassadors, *The Popes of Rome, their Church and State, in the Sixteenth and Seventeenth Centuries* (1834–6), and *History of the Reformation in Germany* (1845–7); these books, particularly the latter two, remain, for reasons given at the beginning of this chapter, of interest to historians today.

Ranke did little to cast off the prejudices and assumptions of his nation and class (while historians today are obliged to make a conscious effort to do this). With the influential German Idealist philosopher of the early nineteenth-century Georg Wilhelm Friedrich Hegel (1770–1831), author, *inter alia*, of *The Philosophy of World History* (1825), he shared in the belief that the national political state was vital to the progress of human society. Ranke was an extreme conservative, supporting the repressive Press Law passed in the German Confederation after the 1830 upheavals, and rejoicing in the events of 1870–1 'as the victory of Conservative Europe over the revolution'. Yet Ranke did not abuse his methods and his sources as was the case with some of his younger extreme nationalist compatriots. In the works of Heinrich von Treitschke (1834–96), author of *German History in the Nineteenth Century* (1877), history became the servant of militant chauvinism: the German state was glorified, and so was war. Partly because of his belief in the crucial importance of the nation state, and partly because the archives which were being opened up at the time were necessarily the archives of princes and prelates (the poor do not leave much in the way of primary sources), Ranke gave history a firm orientation towards 'past politics' and the relations between states ('diplomatic history'), together known as *Staatengeschichte* or political history. Even so, he did seek a rather wider scope in his final work, a massive *Universal History*, completed after his death by his students. Universal history, he had written, 'comprehends the past life of mankind, not in its particular relations and trends, but in its fullness and totality'. Although dedicated to the necessity for specialised research, he was aware of 'the danger of losing sight of the universal', of losing sight of 'the type of knowledge everyone desires'. Again, you the reader might like to reflect critically on this statement of Ranke's:

> history is not simply an academic subject: the knowledge of the history of mankind should be a common property of humanity and should above all benefit our nation, without which our work could not have been accomplished.[21]

In large part, it seems to me, this is in tune with the central theme of this book about history being a social necessity, the fundamental answer to the 'why do we study it?' question. But the less welcome nationalism, not just seeing his history as designed to benefit Germany, but saying that without Germany it could not have been written, is also very apparent. I do not wish to overdo that criticism since it does seem to me that the first need of human beings is to understand the past of their own country, before moving outwards from that. With regard to the quotation, there is always the point about the likely gap in such pronouncements between aspiration and achievement. In assessing Ranke's place in the development of the modern discipline of history it is not helpful, I think, to use such words as 'founder'. We can, if we like, use two rather pompous words to define the positive aspects of the course upon which Ranke and his disciples set the discipline. The Rankean approach is *hermeneutic* in its insistence on the supreme importance of primary sources (hermeneutics being the science of correctly understanding texts, or, more accurately, of *endeavouring* to correctly understand texts) and it is *historicist* in the insistence that the past is different from the present, that there are processes of change linking past with present, and that (this is the central idea in the original meaning of the German *Historismus*) what goes before determines what comes after; that, in fact, to understand any society, or institution, or topic, we have to understand its historical origins. The point is not to judge Ranke as some great *auteur* making unique contributions to the discipline of history, but rather to see his achievements and his failures as illuminating the problems of historical study, and the ways in which they can, and cannot, be overcome.

But we must give credit to Ranke for playing a central part in a third important development, the establishment of the teaching of history at university level. At Berlin he instituted seminars on research techniques. Other countries lagged far behind: France, where the universities had been abolished in the Revolution, lacked system and standards, there being various chairs of history in different institutions of different types, such as the Collège de France, the Faculties of Letters, and in some of the *grandes écoles* (schools of advanced study), notably the École Normale Supérieure (for training teachers in higher education) and the École des Chartes. Largely owing to the efforts of Frenchmen, impressed by their experiences in Germany, instruction in research techniques, as we noted at the beginning of the chapter, began to be provided in Paris from 1868. As a consequence there was a general improvement in the teaching of history. The German example spread more slowly to Britain and the United States. At the beginning of the chapter I mentioned the landmark founding of the *Historische Zeitschrift* in1859. Its first task, its founders declared, should be 'to represent the true method of historical research and to point out the deviations therefrom'.[22]

Mommsen and Burckhardt

Inevitably, and appropriately, Ranke had critics as well as disciples. Theodor Mommsen (1817–1903), in his multi-volume *Roman History*, was, in his meticulous scholarship, almost more Rankean than Ranke, but his instincts, revealed in his studies of numismatics, classical philology, and Roman epigraphy, were towards a history that was more widely cultural than that actually practised by Ranke. Mommsen is of particular importance for illuminating the vexed issue of the involvement of historians in politics. Unlike Ranke, he was a liberal nationalist, and fairly quickly turned against the policies of Bismarck. Mommsen believed that it was perfectly proper for him to let his liberal politics affect his historical writing: it is, he said, 'the worst of all mistakes to suspend being a citizen, so as not to compromise one's scholarly work'.[23] No need, indeed, I would echo, to suspend one's work as a citizen, but, I would add, historians today must keep their activities as citizens *separate* from their scholarly work, and, indeed, their teaching. Johann Gustav Droysen (1808–84), Professor of History at Berlin from 1859 to 1884, author of the highly pro-Prussian *History of Prussian Politics* and of a *Methodology of History* (see below), was responsible for the famous remark that the objectivity of Ranke was 'the objectivity of a eunuch'[24] – rather a good testimonial, actually, to Ranke's genuine attempts at objectivity.

The most powerful alternative to Rankean approaches was provided by Jacob Burckhardt (1818–97), Professor of History at Basle from 1845. Descendant of a patrician Swiss family, he studied under Ranke at Berlin, but reacted against what he believed to be Ranke's suppression of the poetry in history, and later showed his hostility to the Rankean tradition by refusing to become the great man's successor in the Berlin chair in 1872. Burckhardt established his reputation with *The Era of Constantine the Great* (1853) and, above all, *The Civilisation of the Renaissance in Italy* (1860) and the *History of the Renaissance in Italy* (1867). Here was the first great revival of Voltaire's vision of history as embracing culture and civilisation in all its manifold aspects. Burckhardt, most notably, presented a conception of the Renaissance, almost a theory of the Renaissance. Earlier historians, we have noted, had divided the past up into periods, placing on them rather vague or fanciful labels. There is no higher knowledge, or hot-line to the gods, which tells us that the Renaissance, or for that matter the Enlightenment, actually took place. Still, these two labels do have a particular salience in that, unlike labels invented subsequently by historians, these ones were actually coined by people living, respectively, in the periods of 'the Renaissance' and 'the Enlightenment'. Italian intellectuals used the word *rinascita* to refer to the 'rebirth' of classical learning, which they saw as recreating a 'golden age' (this phrase was also used) after what they perceived as the dark, or 'leaden', age after the fall of Rome; eighteenth-century commentators used the word 'Enlightenment' to refer to the brilliant and rational intellectual culture created by the works of Voltaire, Rousseau, Montesquieu and others and to the rational and (up to a point) liberal policies promoted by the 'Enlightened despots' – Frederick the Great, Catherine the Great, and so on. Burckhardt represented the Renaissance as marking a distinct break from the attitudes and values of the Middle Ages; he claimed to detect a new individualism, a turning away from monasticism and the consolations of religion towards life in the world outside, in the cities, towards civic humanism; what he thought he saw was no less than the birth of the modern world, the nineteenth-century world in which he lived. This conception of the Renaissance is one which has remained with us ever since, and remains the starting-point for all Renaissance research (it is, of course, a conception which has been much qualified).

Now, I have been at great pains to play down the notion of the historian as *auteur*. The names I have been singling out so far in this chapter have been lighted on because of their roles in clarifying the nature of the historical enterprise. Burckhardt stands out because of the contribution (however contested) he made to historical knowledge. As we move, in the next chapter, into the twentieth century, and as the discipline of history, though always being further refined, becomes stabilised, my intention, in so far as it is focused on individual historians, will move more to those who made contributions of that sort. If there are any 'great' historians (and, on the whole, I think the epithet is an inappropriate one), or (perhaps a better phrase) 'standard authorities', they are those who have contributed some important new (and lasting!) interpretation, explanation, or concept to historical knowledge itself. The reality, however, is that as history has developed and become ever more complex, the opportunities for such great individualistic successes have greatly diminished; it becomes much more a case of 'schools' or 'groups' jointly producing and sustaining new discoveries and interpretations.

What a lot of important reflections on the nature of history arise from simply mentioning the name of Burckhardt! – the fundamental purpose of this chapter, and the next, as I explained in introducing the chapter. With that purpose in mind, there are important critical comments to be made on Burckhardt. Strangely (as it seems to us now) he did not discuss the great paintings of the Renaissance; in fact, he depended entirely upon written sources. There were no illustrations in *The Civilisation of the Renaissance in Italy* as originally published; those in the editions most of us are familiar with were added half a century later, and actually have little or no relevance to what is said in the book. The careful and scholarly use of visual materials, with appropriate explications, is a characteristic of some of today's most striking historical work (though, with some distinguished exceptions, historians are still generally reluctant to engage with the elite arts, including music as well as painting – perhaps that will be the growth area in the first decades of the twenty-first century). In attempting to express the immense significance that he attached to the Renaissance period, Burckhardt used a naïve anthropomorphism of a sort which really obfuscates meaning rather than clarifying it, and which one would not expect historians to use today. The period, he said, 'must be called the leader of modern ages', explaining that he was 'treating of a civilisation which is the mother of our own, and whose influence is still at work among us'.[25] Burckhardt, incidentally, was even more conservative in general political outlook than Ranke: where Ranke could retain a proud nineteenth-century optimism about the development of human society, Burckhardt was deeply pessimistic.

Thierry, Michelet and de Tocqueville

Of the two Frenchmen I mentioned earlier, Thierry was the more romantic and undisciplined, whereas Michelet, though a romantic and a political partisan, was involved in the three developments I associated with Ranke. Thierry said that the essential object of his *History of the Norman Conquest of England* was to 'envisage the destiny of peoples and not of certain famous men, to present the adventures of social life and not those of the individual': but as his attack on 'writers without imagination who have not known how to paint', and his aspiration that he might produce 'art at the same time as science' suggest, he was given to over-dramatisation, and emotionalism. Michelet shared the hermeneutic impulse, being appointed in 1831 as Chief of the Historical Section of the National Archives. He was a historicist in that he spoke of the need to 'resurrect' (not a good metaphor) the past; and it was indeed Michelet who brought the neglected work of Vico to the attention of other scholars. Third, he did much for the teaching of history in France, publishing two textbooks, the *Précis of Modern History* (1827) and *An Introduction to Universal History* (1831), as well as lecturing at the École Normale, the Sorbonne and the Collège de France (where he was awarded the history chair in 1838).

Michelet's published works are substantial achievements, but certainly not models of how a historian today should go about his/her business. His *History of the French Revolution* (1846–53) is marked by romantic exaggeration, and after the first six volumes his seventeen-volume *History of France* (1833–67) is increasingly spoilt by his growing anticlericalism. Best known today of the French writers of the mid-nineteenth century is Alexis de Tocqueville (1805–59). De Tocqueville was an aristocrat, a practising politician, and a political thinker, deeply concerned with the problems of liberty and democracy. His *Democracy in America* (whose two volumes appeared in 1835 and 1840), product of his visit to that country in 1831, is still cited today for its grasp of some of the enduring features of American society. His reputation as a historian depends upon his *The Ancien Régime and the Revolution* (1856), part only of what was projected as a much larger work covering the whole course of the Revolution. What de Tocqueville provides is a thorough analysis of the nature of the *ancien régime* based on an imaginatively wide range of sources: he was one of the first to make use of that wonderful class of primary materials, the *cahiers de doléances*, the statements of grievances which, in the very early days of the Revolution, the provinces were invited to send in; he also used land registers, deeds of sale, and a great range of administrative documents both national and local. De Tocqueville, then, was 'scientific' in the sense in which Ranke and the editors of *Historische Zeitschrift* were scientific. There were others who wished to make history 'scientific' in the sense of having general laws.

3   Positivism and Marxism

Comte

The objective of Auguste Comte (1798–1857) was to study society in the same way that the natural world was studied by, as he put it, the 'positive' sciences. Comte, in effect, was seeking the laws governing history conceived of as *process*, laws which would, he believed, enable humanity to predict the future course of events; among these, the 'law of the three states' was really yet another periodisation, stating that all societies must pass through three states, which he called the Theological, the Metaphysical and the Scientific. Comte is important for his stated aims and (regrettably) for giving the confusing word 'positivism' to the language. His two major works, *Course of Positivist Philosophy* (1830–42) and *System of Positivist Politics* (1851–4), are ponderous and ill-written.

Marx

Infinitely greater importance, obviously, attaches to the theory of history which originated with Karl Marx. Marx was born in 1818, son of a lawyer in the German Rhineland, but he lived much of his writing life in England, where he died in 1883. He never presented a full and rounded account of his theory, elements of which can be found in writings spread over the period from the 1840s to the 1880s. The fullest early statement is to be found in the *German Ideology*, written in collaboration with Friedrich Engels and completed in 1846, though only a part was published during Marx's lifetime; no complete edition appeared until 1932. There is a lively sketch in the rousing *Communist Manifesto* (1848), in which Engels again collaborated, and a brief summary in the preface (first published posthumously in 1897) which Marx wrote for his *A Contribution to the Critique of Political Economy* (first published in 1859). His major work, *Capital* (1867–94), which, like Adam Smith's *Wealth of Nations*, is historical in approach, concentrates on the development of the capitalist economy, which Marx saw as the dynamic factor in modern history. Other writings by Marx, and by his close associate Engels, provide further glosses; to these have been added the explanations and extrapolations of admirers and disciples, both scholarly and polemical. Here I briefly set out the basic tenets of Marxism as it applies to the study of the past.

First, a fundamental distinction is made between the basic economic structure of any society, determined by the conditions under which wealth is produced in that society, and the 'superstructure', by which Marx meant the laws, institutions, ideas, literature, art, and so on. Second, 'history', in the nineteenth-century, metaphysical, sense of the *process* by which past, present and future are linked, has unfolded through a series of stages, Asiatic, antique, feudal, and modern bourgeois, each of these stages being determined by the prevailing conditions under which wealth is produced (for example, in the feudal stage wealth is derived from ownership of land, in the bourgeois period it is derived from the ownership of capital, particularly capital which is used for the setting up of factories). Third, the motor for this development from stage to stage is provided by the 'class struggle', classes themselves being determined by their relationship to the conditions under which wealth is produced: the bourgeoisie, for example, own the means of capitalist production. Previously, according to Marx, the bourgeoisie had led the class struggle against the dominant class in the feudal stage, the aristocracy. Now, in the modern bourgeois, or capitalist, period, the period in which Marx himself was writing, it finds itself engaged in a struggle with the class below, the proletariat or working class. The first section of the *Communist Manifesto* begins with the challenging (though extremely dubious) statement: 'the history of all hitherto existing society is the history of class struggles'. Fourth, Marx argued, the ending of each stage is signalled as new productive forces come into conflict with existing relations of production thus inaugurating 'an epoch of social revolution'. There was 'social revolution' when feudalism was overthrown by capitalism: there will be further 'social revolution' when capitalism, as its own inherent contradictions become apparent, begins to collapse and the proletariat are successful in their struggles against it.

Behind this view of the unfolding of 'history' (which, of course, has similarities with the ideas of Millar, Vico, and Comte) is the philosophical notion of the dialectic, originally put forward by the Idealist philosopher Hegel (Hegel was an Idealist in that he saw ideas as the prime factors in historical change; Marx, of course, with his emphasis on the basic economic structure, was a Materialist). The notion is the simple one that each age contains a dominant Idea, the *thesis*, but also holds within it an oppositional Idea, the *antithesis*: out of the clash of these two (hence *dialectic*) is produced a *synthesis*, the dominant Idea of the new age. (It may be noted that this apparently impressive theory, derived from the method of Plato's dialogues, is simply conjured out of thin air, there being absolutely no empirical evidence to support it.) Marx, as he put it himself, 'stood Hegel on his head', applying the dialectic to material development, not ideas: each historical stage, according to Marx, though based on one economic system, contained within itself the elements of a new economic system. Eventually, as noted above, there is a clash, 'an epoch of social revolution'. The theory of the dialectic can be used to account for the (alleged) English revolution of the seventeenth century which, John Tosh explains:

> occurred because the forces of production characteristic of capitalism, had reached the point where their further development was held back by the feudal property relations sanctioned by the early Stuart monarchy; the outcome of the revolution was a re-modelling of the relations of production which cleared the way for the Industrial Revolution a hundred years later.[26]

It is important to note that this view gets little support from the empirical studies of present-day experts in the field. However, given that the period in which Marx was writing was one of harsh conditions and frequent economic crises, his overall analysis was quite a rational one at the time; his also was a period in which grand-scale 'speculative philosophy of history' in the manner of Hegel, the search for patterns and meaning in 'history', was in fashion. But the fact is, the immediate influence of Marxism on the development of the discipline of history was not great. In the twentieth century, certainly, Marxism did assume great importance as the revolutionary doctrine which took hold in many parts of the world and which was at the heart of the Russian and Chinese revolutions (though not all revolutions are Marxist – those of Kemal Ataturk and of the Ayatollahs are cases in point). Many of Marx's ideas were taken up (and transformed) by Max Weber (1864–1920), Professor of Economics at Freiburg in the 1890s. Eventually Marxism made important contributions in drawing attention to the importance of economic, material, or (as I would prefer to say) structural factors in historical change, of social classes, of technology, of work and the workplace, and of the possible interrelationships between art, literature, ideas, and politics and economics. Approaches derived from Marx (though not necessarily from Marx alone) can act as a useful corrective to the nominalism that can result from the routine unimaginative application of what are thought to be Rankean methods ('nominalism' is that view which holds that universals or abstractions are simply names without corresponding realities, a view, in effect, which shuns all generalisation or explanatory interconnections). Given the various metaphysical schemas which were being put forward in the eighteenth and nineteenth centuries (and there were still some to come), Marx's is undoubtedly the most persuasive. Certainly more persuasive than that of Thomas Henry Buckle (1821–62), the self-taught English historian who, without knowing anything of Marx, sought to follow the positivists in their search for the general laws of human development.

Fustel de Coulanges

'Positivism' is an awkward word. The French scholar Numa Denis Fustel de Coulanges (1830–89) advocated a 'positivism of the document', which in effect was an extreme statement of the Rankean hermeneutic position. He declared (in his *History of the Political Institutions of Ancient France*) that what was not in the documents did not *exist*. That is the sort of silly belief that history's postmodernist critics like to try to pin on historians today – what is maintained in contemporary historical thinking is that what is not in some way indicated, however indirectly, in the primary sources so far discovered and analysed (which extend far beyond mere 'documents') cannot be *known*. When postmodernists use 'positivist' they are thinking (if they are thinking at all, which is open to question) of Fustel rather than Comte or Buckle (the better word would be hermeneutic, but then certain Marxists, led by Jürgen Habermas (*b.* 1929), developed a hermeneutics of their own on the basis that only they knew the correct method of interpreting texts). If we can stomach further elaborate language we may, as I indicated in Chapter 1, define those who look for general laws (like Marx and Buckle) as *nomothetic* in their approach and those who seek the detailed and the unique (like Ranke or Fustel) as *idiographic* in theirs; the distinction originates with the German philosopher Wilhelm Windelband (1848–1915) who in his *German History* (1891–8) insisted that there were general laws in history, which he took to be based on what he saw as the collective psychologies of different nations. In what is sometimes known as 'the Lamprecht Controversy' the German historical profession made it clear that it was totally behind the Rankean tradition and totally opposed to the search for general laws.

4   Anglo-Saxon Attitudes

Macaulay and the Whig Historians

In Britain, it seemed, the purpose behind writing history was to edify and entertain, and to emulate Gibbon in achieving fame and fortune. 'I shall not be satisfied', wrote Thomas Babington Macaulay, 'unless I produce something which shall for a few days supersede the latest fashionable novel on the tables of the young ladies.' His *History of England* (four volumes, 1848–55, the fifth volume being incomplete at his death) enjoyed an unrivalled success in both Britain and America: according to the American historiographer Westfall Thompson, sales in the USA exceeded those of any book ever printed, save the Bible and some school texts.[27] Macaulay did show immense energy in seeking out primary sources of many kinds: broadsheets and songs, as well as maps, political documents, ambassadors' dispatches, and private papers. But in his search after effect he sometimes cheated, so that his rendering of the past was less 'truthful' than it could have been. One notorious example is the passage in the first volume of the *History* describing the speech in which William III bade farewell to the States of Holland before setting out for Britain. Macaulay wrote:

> In all that grave senate there was none who could refrain from shedding tears. But the iron stoicism of William never gave way; and he stood among his weeping friends calm and austere, as if he had been about to leave them only for a short visit to his hunting-grounds at Loo.

Macaulay had no reliable source for this fanciful description. In fact it is a direct plagiarism (conscious or unconscious) from the *Odes* of Horace, the description of Regulus making his farewell to the Senate.[28]

More significant is Macaulay's contribution to what has become famous and notorious as the 'Whig interpretation of history', that is to say of British history, conceiving of it as a steady evolution of British parliamentary institutions, benevolently watched over by Whig aristocrats, and steadily spreading social progress and prosperity. In the first chapter of his *History* Macaulay confidently stated:

> The history of our country during the last hundred and sixty years is eminently the history of physical, of moral and of intellectual development.

The first Whig historian was Henry Hallam (1777–1859), whose *Constitutional History of England from the Accession of Henry VII to the Death of*

George II was published in 1827, and the tradition was continued throughout the nineteenth century by historians who shared with Hallam a spoken or unspoken assumption that the central theme in English history was the development of liberal institutions. Thus, in the study of remote ages they greatly exaggerated the importance of 'parliaments' or of bodies that they thought were parliaments; and they tended to interpret all political struggles in terms of the parliamentary situation in Britain in the nineteenth century, in terms, that is, of Whig reformers fighting the good fight against Tory defenders of the *status quo*.

Given that none of the historians I have been writing about observed the precepts of professional history today, is it fair to exclude Thomas Carlyle, whom I would rather describe as poet, sage, prophet? – but then there are historians today who seem to want to represent themselves or others as sages, if not prophets. There was, obviously, a strong source-based element in Carlyle's *Letters and Speeches of Oliver Cromwell* (1845), which also made a contribution to historical interpretation: for two centuries the Puritan dictator had been described as one of the most evil villains in England's past; Carlyle treated him as a 'great man'. Carlyle in fact seemed to regard 'history' as synonymous with 'biography', greatly exaggerating the significance of 'great men', as in his *Frederick the Great* (1858–65).

Bishop Stubbs

The amateurish attitudes, and literary aspirations, of the historians were reflected in the absence of any efficient provision for the systematic teaching of history at university level. There were changes at Oxford in the 1850s, when a Professorship of International Law and Diplomacy and the Chichele Professorship of Modern History ('Modern' as distinct from 'Ancient') were established. History was seen as a useful subject for lawyers, while a Regius Professor (Augustus Freeman) openly boasted that history's purpose was 'the better education of the gentry', so that they could, in these changing times, continue to run the country.[29] Only with the appointment in 1866 of William Stubbs (1825–1901) to the Regius Chair was the basis laid for the serious study of history at Oxford. Much later than in the leading European countries, the British government had initiated a redirection of energies towards the publication of basic primary sources in British history; Stubbs had for many years been working on editions of the twelfth-century chroniclers for the Rolls Series, begun in 1857. He had produced nearly 20 volumes of texts, all fine works of critical scholarship, when in 1870 he produced his volume of *Select Charters* which long remained a basic source book in university constitutional history classes (I myself studied them at

Edinburgh University in the 1950s). Between 1874 and 1878 he published his *Constitutional History of England*, based – as no other work of an English historian had been – on meticulous scholarship and exhaustive study of all primary sources so far discovered. For all that, Stubbs could not, any more than Ranke, escape the prejudices and received attitudes of his times. As the political scientist Sir Ernest Barker once remarked, 'he wrote his *Constitutional History of England* in spectacles – the spectacles of Victorian Liberalism, which are all the more curious on his nose when one remembers that he was a natural Tory',[30] the Whig interpretation of history was no narrow party matter. Stubbs began with high hopes of teaching history based 'not upon Hallam and Palgrave and Kemble and Froude and Macaulay, but on the abundant collected and arranged materials now in course of publication'.[31] Perhaps you, the reader, would like to rephrase that sentiment in simple terms – I'll do so at the end of this paragraph. While Ranke had stressed diplomatic history, Stubbs, a child of an era when British parliamentary institutions still seemed one of humanity's great inventions, saw constitutional history as the rigorous core upon which to base his teaching, that teaching, of course, to be based on primary sources not secondary ones.

Stubbs retired from his chair in 1884 (to become Bishop of Chester and, later, Oxford), a disappointed man. Despite the founding of the Historical Manuscripts Commission in 1870, publication of primary sources in Britain was lagging far behind the achievements in this respect of Germany. And although in the long term Stubbs had as profound an effect on historical scholarship and teaching in Britain as Ranke had in Germany, resistance at Oxford to any complete adoption of German methods was too strong for Stubbs to overcome. As in so many other aspects, postmodernist thought had its precursors among nineteenth-century fuddy-duddies.

From Freeman to Tout and Acton

Stubbs's successor in the Regius chair, Edward Augustus Freeman (1823–92), expressed many of the basic features of the Oxford attitude in his brief but memorable aphorism: 'History is past politics, and politics is present history.'[32] To John Richard Green (1837–83) is often given the credit for mounting the challenge to the assumption behind the first part of this aphorism. In his *Short History of the English People* (1874) Green deliberately turned away from what in a fine phrase he called 'drum-and-trumpet history'. He declared:

> I have devoted more space to Chaucer than to Cressy, to Caxton than to the petty strife of Yorkist and Lancastrian, to the poor of Elizabeth

than to her victory at Cadiz, to the Methodist revival than to the escape of the Young Pretender.[33]

For all that, Green was very much in the Whig tradition, entertaining then widely prevalent notions about the essentially democratic character of the English 'people': in his history, the men of the Middle Ages speak with the accents of Victorian reformers. The most persuasive investigations into life as it really was in the distant past were carried out by the man now universally recognised as the first practitioner of the modern discipline of history, F. W. Maitland (1850–96): 'working backwards from the known to the unknown, from the certain to the uncertain' (as he himself put it), and (as G. M. Trevelyan put it) using medieval law 'as the tool to prise open the mind of Medieval men', he produced a work of social and legal history, Domesday Book and Beyond (1897), which can still be read critically (as all history should be read) today, without any of that discomfort almost immediately induced as one embarks on Hallam, Stubbs or Green.

The best rejoinder to the implications of the second part of Freeman's aphorism was that of Samuel Rawson Gardiner (1829–1902), an Oxford historian in the style of Ranke and Stubbs, who was for a time Professor of History at King's College, London. Gardiner declared:

He who studies the society of the past will be of greater service to the society of the present in proportion as he leaves it out of account.[34]

Gardiner is recognising the necessary service to present society of history, but stresses that the quality of the history, that is to say the value of that service, will be higher the more the historian disabuses his mind of the preoccupations and values of present society.

At Cambridge, historical study began to glimmer into life after the appointment (in 1869) of Sir John Seeley (1834–95) to the Regius chair in immediate succession to Charles Kingsley, who as a novelist and Christian socialist has some claims to historical eminence, though none to eminence as a historian. The true founder of the Cambridge school of history was Lord Acton (1834–1902), of whom more in the next section. Seeley was an active politician, and one of the group of intellectuals who played a part in the development of the ideals of British imperialism at the end of the century: his most important book, The Expansion of England (1883), one of the earliest ventures into the realm of imperial history, is remembered for the classic remark (almost universally misquoted) about English imperialism: 'We seem, as it were, to have conquered and peopled half the world in a fit of absence of mind.'[35] In 1890 Thomas Frederick Tout (1855–1929), a pupil of Stubbs, became Professor at Manchester University, building it into one of the best history schools in the United Kingdom. At the beginning of the new century, the Edinburgh history school, followed by those of the other Scottish universities, was remodelled on the Oxford pattern round a solid core of constitutional history, involving some study of primary sources.

The United States

As has been the case in other spheres, the United States of America proved more receptive to the best continental European ideas about the study of history than did Britain, though for much of the nineteenth century the literary approach to history, informed by noble liberal sentiments, predominated. George Bancroft (1800–91) was as much a nationalist as a democrat: his ten-volume *History of the United States from the Discovery of America* (1834–87) established the myth of the glories of the American Revolution carried through entirely by disinterested patriots on behalf of the liberties of mankind. But American literary historians were not parochial: while John Motley (1814–77) turned to the study of the Dutch Republic, William H. Prescott (1796–1859) wrote his colourful pioneering studies of the Spanish expansion in South America. As history in America on a formal basis was developed in the last quarter of the nineteenth century the influence of Ranke was undoubtedly very strong; at the same time, positivism, in the sense of a desire for synthesis and a search for patterns and tendencies, was accorded more respect by some American scholars than was the case in Britain.

The Rankean seminar method was imported into America in the 1870s by Herbert Baxter Adams of Johns Hopkins University; and Ranke himself was made the first and only honorary member of the American Historical Association (AHA) on its foundation in 1884. Justin Winsor, president in 1887, was a strong Rankean, and the German 'scientific' approach was developed by Henry Adams (1838–1918), who inaugurated graduate studies in history at Harvard. First president of the AHA was Andrew D. White, Professor of History at the University of Michigan: on the whole White, an influential educator (he became president of Cornell University), concentrated on the exemplar function of history and was rather impatient of detailed research. He did do something to combat the view, sponsored by Bancroft and fostered by the disciples of Ranke, that the main concern of history was politics. Alfred T. Mahan (1840–1914), like White, was interested in the 'lessons' afforded by history, rather than in deep primary research: he was thus led to his important and creative idea of the vital importance in warfare of control of the sea, expressed in two books, *The Influence of Sea Power on History, 1660–1783* and *The Influence of Sea Power on the French Revolution and Empire, 1793–1812*. On the whole it can be said that American historical study only began its phenomenal expansion in the twentieth century.

5   The End of the Century

Five Major Issues

The purpose of this potted historiography ('history of history') is to bring out the way in which the problems inherent in doing history were steadily exposed, though not necessarily solved. At the end of the nineteenth century, five major issues were being discussed.

1   Is the central concern of history the political state and relationships between states, as Ranke thought? Or are there other particular 'sub-histories' which ought to be given primacy: economic history (this was the strongest candidate at the beginning of the new century, supported by those who, whether they knew it or not, shared with Marx a belief in the determining influence of economic factors); intellectual history (reasserting the supremacy of 'ideal' factors over 'material' ones)? Or should not the 'sub-histories' be reintegrated together into a 'total history', a cultural history as aspired to by Voltaire or Burckhardt, but based on the most rigorous new methods?

2   Should history seek to emulate the sciences, or should it retain its affiliations (and the readership that went with them) with literature? An important figure here, as we shall see in a moment, was the German philosopher Wilhelm Dilthey (1833–1911), who suggested that history, having modes and insights of its own, should not seek to be a science.

3   Could history be 'objective' or was it always subject to the assumptions and prejudices of the historian? Could knowledge of universal validity be established, or was it always culturally (or socially) circumscribed? Rankeans believed that the rigorous use of primary sources would entail objectivity; Marx in effect argued that such methods merely revealed the outer husk, the bourgeois view of society – what was thought of as knowledge in bourgeois society was merely part of the superstructure, it was 'constructed' in order to preserve bourgeois dominance (and thus, of course, only those possessed of the 'scientific' – in a different sense from that of the Rankeans – perceptions of Marxism could penetrate through to the reality). In fact it was again Dilthey who argued that historians are inevitably part of their own researches, inevitably shaping their

results one way or another, but that this was no totally disabling condition.

4 As new techniques were developed (psychological, statistical, and so on) were they to be: (a) treated with suspicion; (b) embraced and trumpeted as superseding all older techniques; or (c) considered as merely a further addition to the growing range of methods and approaches at the disposal of historians?

5 How legitimate, and how important, were the new areas for study which from time to time were proposed – such as the masses, economic motives and interests, religious superstition, urbanisation, demography, women? Did such new areas simply extend the scope of existing history or did they turn history into something different? (For example, did the study of the masses and of economic interests entail the creation of a 'New History'; or, much later, did the study of urbanisation, or of women, replace old history by, respectively, 'urban history' or 'feminist history'?)

Scientific History? Langlois and Seignobos

The leading figures in non-Marxist German economic history were Wilhelm Roscher (1817–94), Karl Wilhelm Nitzsch (1818–80), Gustav Schmoller (1838–1917), and, when young, Karl Lamprecht (1856–1915). The intensity of the hostility they aroused among those who held to Rankean *Staatensgeschichte* can be seen in the riposte of one Rankean, Dietrich Schäfer: 'history is not a feeding trough'.[36] This school then came to a somewhat sudden end as its protagonists became involved either in controversies over contemporary German social policy, or in the debate over nomothetic approaches to history. The scholar who bridged the gulf between this group and later economic historians was Werner Sombart (1863–1914), author of many important works, including *War and Capitalism* (1913), which drew attention to the part played by war in stimulating eighteenth-century industrialisation. In Britain there was no intellectual battle, and indeed there was only one real piece of solid economic history, though a massive one at that: between 1866 and 1902 there appeared seven volumes of *A History of Agriculture and Prices in England* by J. E. Thorold Rogers (1823–90). On the fringes of the academic world, Arnold Toynbee (1852–1903, uncle of Arnold J. Toynbee, the author of the metaphysical *A Study of History*, published between 1934 and 1954) had begun the debate on what was then as much a current social and political as a historical topic with his book *The Industrial Revolution in England* (1884). More of that later.

The big issue of whether or not history was a science was addressed by the philosopher Dilthey in his *Introduction to Historical Knowledge*

(1883) and subsequent essays. Dilthey maintained that there was a fundamental distinction between scientific knowledge and cultural knowledge, and that, as part of the latter, history had no need to attempt to conform to the norms of science. Dilthey and his followers also claimed that historians did not stand apart from, and observe, an objective reality; they observe, the argument was, a reality at least partly constructed in the process of observing. Now, whether or not the historian can remain sufficiently self-aware to counteract this tendency (as I claim in this book), or whether in fact all historical knowledge is 'constructed', eventually, as all readers will be thoroughly aware by this stage, became a matter of serious contention. For the moment, the lesson that most working historians were content to draw was that history need not feel ashamed for not conforming to scientific norms. This was the essential message contained in the *Encyclopaedia and Methodology of History* (1868) by Johann Gustav Droysen (1808–84). Droysen asserted the validity of Rankean methodology, but many historians drew from Dilthey confirmation that they were right to approach history as a literary subject.

Already I have mentioned the influential textbook of methodology published at the turn of the century, *Introduction to the Study of History* (Paris and London, 1898) by C. W. Langlois (1863–1929) and Charles Seignobos (1854–1942). Langlois and Seignobos dismissed as 'idle questions' unworthy of consideration 'whether history is a science or an art; what are the duties of history?; what is the use of history?' My own book, obviously, does not entirely follow in their footsteps. I certainly think that the unreflexive answer given in the early twentieth century that history is 'both art and science' is valueless, and that while historians should always communicate clearly, effectively, and, if possible, elegantly, they should at the same time be profoundly conscious that they should not be trying to emulate novelists or poets. Duties, of course, pertain to the historian, not history. While history has no direct, uncomplicated 'use', it is extremely important that all historians should be constantly asking themselves why they are doing what they are doing. The aim of history, Langlois and Seignobos continued, 'is not to please, nor to give practical maxims of conduct, nor to arouse the emotions, but knowledge pure and simple'. On the whole, I would say, one does want people to enjoy history, and its emotional excitements: but then that is surely also true of the sciences. The point these two earnest Frenchmen missed is that of the crucial importance to society of historical knowledge. Langlois and Seignobos did regard history as a science, save that they said it was a science whose methods differ from those of all other sciences! There is a truth there which has to be kept in mind, as long as it does not lead to a full adoption of the position put forward by Dilthey. Langlois and Seignobos seem to move in that direction but then state that, from around 1850, history had ceased, both for the historians and the public, to be a branch of literature. Previously, they continue, historians republished their works from time to time without feeling any necessity to revise them:

> Now every scientific work needs to be continually recast, revised, brought up to date. Scientific workers do not claim to give their work an immutable form, they do not expect to be read by posterity or to achieve personal immortality; it is enough for them if the results of their researches, corrected, it may be, and possibly transformed by subsequent researches, should be incorporated in the fund of knowledge which forms the scientific heritage of mankind. No one reads Newton or Lavoisier; it is enough for their glory that their labours should have contributed to the production of works by which their own have been superseded and which will be, sooner or later, superseded in their turn.[37]

I would have today's upholders of the *auteur* theory of history recite these words three times each day before breakfast. It gets better. Only works of art, Langlois and Seignobos declare, 'enjoy perpetual youth'. This is the definitive rebuttal of the strange idea that works of history can be equated with novels. No one would dream of updating the novels of Henry Fielding; but one would get a very limited and inaccurate view of the decline and fall of the Roman Empire if one relied on Gibbon alone without recourse to the historical works which have been published since.

Most famous of all turn-of-the-century pronouncements is that of J. B. Bury in his inaugural address (1902) as successor to Lord Acton in the Regius chair at Cambridge.

> If, year by year, history is to become a more and more powerful force for stripping the bandages of error from the eyes of men, for shaping public opinion and advancing the cause of intellectual and political liberty, she will best prepare her disciples for the performance of that task, not by considering the immediate utility of next week or next year or next century, not by accommodating her ideal or limiting her range, but by remembering always that, though she may supply material for literary art or philosophical speculation, she is herself simply a science, no less and no more.[38]

This kind of naïve rhetoric is as dated as that of Burckhardt, and my strong warning to all readers is to distrust any work on historical epistemology written in this vein (there is a recent one by a group of Americans which I shall discuss in Chapter 7). 'Simply a science, no less and no more' is simply as silly as 'both art and science'. Concepts of science have changed since the turn of the century when the absolutes of Newtonian physics still held sway: certainties have given way to probabilities, the absolute to the relative. In fact the whole concept of the nature of human understanding and knowledge has become more complex and more subtle. Science has changed and so has history: they have, indeed, changed in parallel. Bury was a man of wide culture and he is important with respect to the points I posed at the beginning of this chapter, in maintaining that history had increased in scope since the time of Ranke:

> The exclusive idea of political history, *Staatensgeschichte*...has been gradually yielding to a more comprehensive definition which embraces as its material all records, whatever their nature may be, of the material and spiritual development, of the culture and the works, of man in society, from the stone age onwards.[39]

Among the most impressive memorials to the 'scientific' concept of history to which Bury subscribed are the multi-volume *History of France* (1900–11) edited by Ernest Lavisse (1842–1922) and the *Cambridge Modern History*, launched by Bury's predecessor in the Regius chair at Cambridge, Lord Acton (1834–1902). Aiming to 'meet the scientific demand for completeness and certainty', the *Cambridge Modern History* was to be, as are most important advances in the natural sciences, the work of many hands. 'Contributors will understand', Lord Acton wrote,

> that our Waterloo must be one that satisfies French and English, German and Dutch alike; that nobody can tell, without examining the list of authors, where the Bishop of Oxford laid down the pen and whether Fairbairn or Gasquet, Liebermann or Harrison took it up.[40]

One can write clearly, explicitly, and elegantly, and yet have a personal 'signature' to one's writing which need not in any way obscure or slant the analysis and conclusions one wishes to present; the extirpation of that is the last thing *I* am arguing for. But Acton was right in indicating that the French historian should strive very consciously not to be jingoistically French, as the English one should strive not to be jingoistically English. But there was a very revealing weakness in this new *Cambridge Modern History*: although there would be extensive bibliographies, there were to be no footnotes. As historians have lost confidence in the possibility of the complete and certain history which the *Cambridge Modern* was supposed to provide, footnotes have come to be seen as an absolutely essential part of the historical enterprise: they are not, as critics sometimes suggest, the last word in complacent pedantry; they imply in fact an admission of fallibility on the part of historians, who are indicating their premises to their readers so that their readers may, if they wish, work out different conclusions of their own; they are, indeed, a sign of that dialogue between historians and readers of which I have already spoken, and which 'scientific' history in Acton's sense sought, in authoritarian fashion, to deny, a denial often also practised by the *auteurs*.

History as Literature

In the Anglo-Saxon world attempts continued to be made to appeal to the older literary tradition whose supercession by the disciples of Ranke had been so thoroughly welcomed by Langlois and Seignobos. The discourses of George Macaulay Trevelyan, grand-nephew of Macaulay, and Theodore Roosevelt, President of the United States, sound quite familiar. In choosing to attack the conception of history as 'scientific' they were in fact attacking scholarly history, and identifying history as amateurish and literary, as in Trevelyan's well-known essay 'Clio, a Muse' (the public-schoolboy title is almost self-condemnation enough) in the *Independent Review* in December 1903, the essay being republished in 1913 in slightly less polemical form. Trevelyan was not wrong in saying that 'no one...can ever give a completely or wholly true account of the French Revolution'. But his conclusion from that simply offered licence to the worst amateurism: 'he will give the best interpretation who, having discovered and weighed all the important evidence obtainable, has the largest grasp of intellect, the warmest human sympathy, the highest imaginative powers'.[41] If my strictures seem unfair, consider that Trevelyan then went on to declare that his last two conditions had been fulfilled by Carlyle, whose 'psychology of the mob' and 'portraits of individual characters'

> are in the most important sense more true than the cold analysis of the same events and the conventional summings up of the same person by scientific historians who, with more knowledge of facts, have less understanding of Man.

'Knowledge of facts', as we now know, is less the issue than 'knowledge and understanding of the sources'. Note also the deployment of the words 'cold' and 'conventional' to load the dice against the scholars. Trevelyan concluded that,

> in the most important part of its business, history is not a scientific deduction, but an imaginative guess at the most likely generalisations.

Yet, characteristic of the rather muddled thinking which continued to characterise the expanding historical profession and is still apparent today, Trevelyan could combine this kind of assertion with another one, that the study of history provided a basic training in citizenship. Just doing history, even if you were merely 'guessing', not really striving systematically to get it right, was, he was claiming, in itself beneficial. Trevelyan chose one of my own favourite examples in making the case that history is essential, the matter of Ireland and Britain's relations with Ireland; but I also see that example as a strong part of the case that historians must try to get it right ('scientific deduction') not indulge in 'imaginative guesses'. The brave historian of the day who had attempted to write about Ireland was William Edward Lecky (1838–1903). The value, Trevelyan said, of Lecky's Irish history was not that Lecky proves Irish Home Rule to be 'right or wrong but he trains the mind of Unionists and Home Rulers to think sensibly about that and other problems'. History, Trevelyan claimed, should not only remove prejudice, it should provide the ideals which inspire the life of the ordinary citizen. There are, unfortunately, some aspects of the past which if uncontentiously recounted are not particularly inspiring. However, I do not depart totally from Trevelyan's general tenor, save that to have these benefits the history has in the first place to be reliable, that is, 'scientific' in the sense Trevelyan detested. I concur with Trevelyan in believing that a knowledge of history (if it is serious knowledge of serious history) enhances the understanding of literature, and doubles the pleasures of travel. The remainder of 'Clio, a Muse' took the form of a lament that since the 'scientists' had taken over, the intelligent layman had ceased to read history:

> The *Cambridge Modern History* is indeed bought by the yard to dec-orate bookshelves, but it is regarded like the *Encyclopaedia Britannica* as a work of reference: its mere presence in the library is enough.

The point was witty and well taken, but we must always be careful over this ready invocation of 'the layman'. History should involve the general public; but much of the fundamental work of historians, as with scien-tists, has, in the first instance, to be for their professional peers.

Theodore Roosevelt weighed in with a letter to Trevelyan's father, George Otto Trevelyan:

> I am sorry to say that I think the Burys are doing much damage to the cause of historic [sic] writing...We have a preposterous organisation called I think the American Historical Association...they represent what is in itself the excellent revolt against superficiality and lack of research, but they have grown into the opposite and equally noxious belief that research is all, that accumulation of facts is everything, and the ideal history of the future will consist not even of the work of one

huge pedant but of a multitude of small pedants. They are honestly unconscious that... whether their work will... amount to anything really worthy depends on whether or not some great master builder hereafter arrives who will be able to go over their material... to fashion some edifice of majesty and beauty instinct with the truth that both charms and teaches. A thousand Burys, and two thousand of the corresponding Germans whom he reverentially admires, would not in the aggregate begin to add to the wisdom of mankind what another Macaulay, should one arise, would add. The great historian must of course have scientific spirit which gives the power of research, which enables one to marshal and weigh the facts; but unless his finished work is literature of a very high type small will be his claim to greatness.[42]

Readers should reflect for themselves on this piece of rhetoric. Do we really need historians who aspire to 'greatness'; isn't truthfulness to what actually happened (as far as that is possible) the more important quality? Are we really expecting historians 'to fashion some edifice of majesty and beauty instinct with the truth that both charms and teaches'? Some of those historians of today that I have described as *auteurs* may aspire to something like that. Anyway, the day of 'preposterous organisations' had definitely dawned, these organisations being absolutely integral to the pursuit of professional history.

Notes

1 See Eusebius, *The History of the Church*, trans. G. A. Williamson, rev. and ed. with a new introduction by Andrew Louth (London, 1989).
2 *The Anglo-Saxon Chronicle*, ed. G. N. Garmonsway (London, 1953), pp. 219–20.
3 Francesco Guicciardini, *L'Historia d'Italia* (Florence, 1561), p. 1.
4 William Camden, *Britain, Written first in Latin by William Camden Translated newly into English by Philémon Holland* (London, 1610), vol. 2.
5 Quoted by F. Smith Fussner, *The Historical Revolution: English Historical Writing and Thought, 1580–1640* (London and New York, 1962), p. 23.
6 Ernest Breisach, *Historiography: Ancient, Medieval, and Modern* (Chicago, 1983), pp. 180–3.
7 E. Gibbon, *The Decline and Fall of the Roman Empire* (Everyman's Library, Dent, London, 1910), vol. 1, p. 438.
8 Ibid., p. 484.
9 Ibid., vol. 2, p. 68.
10 Voltaire, *Essay sur l'Histoire générale, et sur les moeurs et l'espirit des nations depuis Charlemagne jusqu'à nos jours*, vol. 1 (Paris, 1756), pp. 1–9.

11 David Hume, *Two Short Essays, On the Study of History, and On General Reading* (Edinburgh, 1836), pp. 13–15.

12 For Millar, see S. W. F. Holloway, 'Sociology and History', *History*, 48 (1963), pp. 157–61.

13 Voltaire to l'abbé Dubos, Feb. 1738, quoted by J. B. Black, *The Art of History* (London, 1926), p. 55, and (in a slightly different translation) by Fritz Stern (ed.), *The Varieties of History: Voltaire to the Present* (New York, 1956; London, 1970), 1970 edn, p. 39.

14 H. R. Trevor-Roper, *History, Professional and Lay* (Oxford, 1957), p. 5.

15 Quoted by Stern, *The Varieties of History*, p. 51.

16 Translation in G. P. Gooch, *History and Historians in the Nineteenth Century* (London, 1952), p. 74.

17 Translation in Stern, *The Varieties of History*, p. 57.

18 Ibid.

19 Quoted in J. Westfall Thompson, *A History of Historical Writing*, vol. 2 (New York, 1942), p. 231.

20 Breisach, *Historiography*, p. 233; Gooch, *History and Historians*, p. 80.

21 Quoted in Stern, *The Varieties of History*, pp. 61–2.

22 Quoted in ibid., p. 171.

23 Cited by Breisach, *Historiography*, p. 237.

24 J. G. Droysen, *Historik* (Jena, 1858), 1937 edn, p. 287.

25 Jacob Burckhardt, *The Civilization of the Renaissance in Italy* (London, 1955 edn), pp. 1, 341.

26 John Tosh, *The Pursuit of History: Aims, Methods and New Directions in the Study of Modern History* (London, 1984), pp. 139–40.

27 Westfall Thompson, *Historical Writing*, vol. 2, pp. 297, 298.

28 See C. G. Crump, *History and Historical Research* (London, 1928), pp. 151–2.

29 R. W. Southern, *The Shape and Substance of Academic History* (Oxford, 1961), p. 11.

30 Quoted by Westfall Thompson, *Historical Writing*, p. 300.

31 Southern, *Shape and Substance*, p. 15.

32 See Westfall Thompson, *Historical Writing*, p. 317.

33 J. R. Green, *Short History of the English People* (London, 1874), p. v.

34 Quoted by Westfall Thompson, *Historical Writing*, p. 322.

35 Sir John Seeley, *The Expansion of England: Two Courses of Lectures* (London, 1883), p. 10.

36 Cited in Westfall Thompson, *Historical Writing*, p. 423.

37 C. V. Langlois and Charles Seignobos, *Introduction to the Study of History* (Paris and London, 1898), pp. 302–3.

38 Quoted in Stern, *The Varieties of History*, p. 223.

39 Quoted in ibid., p. 221.

40 Quoted in ibid., p. 249.

41 Quoted in ibid., p. 231.

42 Letter of 25 January 1904, quoted by Howard K. Beale in *Pacific History Review*, 22 (1953), p. 228.

4 How the Discipline of History Evolved: Through the Twentieth into the Twenty-First Century

1 'New' History

The Three 'New Histories'

Three groups in the twentieth century claimed to be, or were credited with, producing 'new' history: the Americans were first; then the French, after nearly two generations, from the twenties to the sixties, of what is known as the '*Annales* school', applied the label to the second and third *Annales* generations; meantime, from the sixties onwards in Britain there was talk of 'the new social history', new because it was social, and because it was open to the ideas of the *Annales* school and to those of post-structuralism and postmodernism.

I do not believe that one approach to, or school of, history is inherently better than another. I do not believe that 'new' historians are necessarily better than 'old' historians (apart from the general point that works incorporating the most recent research will almost certainly be better than works which date from before that research was available). Good political history is just as important as good social and cultural history. In detail, the approaches used will differ: one set of approaches is not inherently better than another; the point is that the approaches used should be appropriate to the nature of the particular investigation. I believe that, in common with other disciplines, the discipline of history has become more sophisticated, more self-aware, more ambitious in the subject matter it addresses ('scope') and more *effective* in coming up with answers to the problems that need to be addressed.

American 'New History'

The immediate precursor of the American New Historians was Frederick Jackson Turner (1861–1932), whose essay on 'The Significance of the Frontier in American History', the classical instance of a historical thesis in the first sense of the term, was presented to a meeting of the American Historical Association (AHA) in 1893. In one form or another, the 'Turner thesis' (not completely unique to Turner, but he was the one who expressed it most vividly) has affected American historical thinking ever since; it soon – in the manner through which disciplines always advance – provoked a violent reaction. Turner published *The Rise of the New West* in 1906, and the most important of only 30 or so articles were grouped in two volumes, *The Frontier in American History* (1920) and *The Significance of Sections in American History* (1932). The main thesis, as Turner had put it to the AHA, was that:

> The peculiarity of American institutions is the fact that they have been compelled to adapt themselves to the changes of an expanding people – to the changes involved in crossing a continent, in winning a wilderness, and in developing at each area of this progress out of the primitive economic and political conditions of the frontier into the complexity of city life.

The frontier to the Americans, said Turner, was what the Mediterranean had been to the Greeks. The second Turner thesis concerned the significance, once the frontier had disappeared, of a geographically determined 'sectionalism' in the American nation: the 'physical map' of America, he argued, may be regarded as a map of potential nations and empires. Turner was attacked for fostering isolationism and nationalism, and denying the European roots of American civilisation.[1]

First to pin the label 'The New History' on himself publicly was James Harvey Robinson (1863–1936). The New History was deliberately 'present-minded' in that it sought to use history to help in dealing with the social problems of the present; indeed it merged into that widely based school of historical writing which held sway in America until after the Second World War, always known as 'progressive history' – that is, a history informed by liberal–reformist sentiments.[2] The New History claimed that it would give special attention to economic forces, as to intellectual and any other forces relevant to social problems; in so doing it would make use of the discoveries of social scientists. Robinson himself was not much given to scholarly research and the best practical example of the New History is the work produced in collaboration with Charles A. Beard, *The Development of Modern Europe* (1907–8). Turner had given a certain primacy to geographical circumstances; Beard gave a similar primacy to economic factors and interests. His *An Economic Interpretation of the Constitution* (1913) presents the framers of the American constitution as realistic appraisers of humanity's economic instincts, rather than as liberal-minded idealists. The title of his next book, *The Economic Origins of Jeffersonian Democracy* (1915), is equally explicit.

The bridge from New History to progressive history was well represented by Arthur M. Schlesinger Sr (1888–1965).[3] His dissertation, finally published in 1918 under the title *The Colonial Merchants and the American Revolution, 1763–1776*, gave him, he wrote, 'an opportunity to examine the interrelation of economics and politics, something which Beard had so deeply interested me in'. While teaching at the State University of Iowa, Schlesinger in 1922 instituted a course on the 'Social and Cultural History of the United States', the first of its kind. This led naturally to his sponsorship of a multi-volume, co-operative *History of American Life* (first four volumes, 1927). However, his famous dictum that 'Great Men' are 'merely the mechanism through which the Great Many have spoken' now seems no more than one of those slickly punning metaphors which, if they say anything at all, say something trivial (beware that vague term 'mechanism'). The progressive tradition was continued after the Second World War by Arthur Schlesinger Jnr, whose *The Age of Jackson* was published in 1945. However, the central notion of conflict between big business and an allegedly non-capitalistic common people was beginning, as many critics pointed out, to seem rather too simplistic. Indeed, American political historians in the post-war years tended to stress the absence of social conflict in the American past and have, in contrast with the previous 'progressive historians', been dubbed the 'consensus historians'. The leading figures were Richard J. Hofstadter (1916–70), with his *Age of Reform* (1955) on the period before the First World War known as 'the progressive era', Louis Hartz (*b.* 1919), with his *The Liberal Tradition in America* (1955), and Daniel J. Boorstin, with his *The Genius of American Politics* (1953) and *The Americans: The Colonial Experience* (1958).

Founders of the *Annales* School; Febvre and Bloch

The 'New History' pioneered in France, and better described by the term '*Annales* history', demands serious attention in a way that the American New History simply does not – not, as commentators from outside with little experience of actually writing history sometimes claim, because it supplanted all other history and provided a model to which everyone today aspires, but because (a) it showed that you could, as many from Voltaire to Schlesinger Sr had postulated, open up the scope of history and genuinely produce detailed and substantiated knowledge on topics about which others had merely prated, and (b) it raised important questions about the nature of the historical discipline itself, its relationships with the social sciences and the sciences, and also questions (this pertains more to the second, postwar, generation rather than the first) about how change does and (*nota bene*) does *not* come about in past societies. In theory, the three generations of *Annales* history are bound together by a readiness to incorporate the social sciences and, as relevant, the sciences in historical study. There are limited instances (incorporating, say, social psychology or climatology) where interdisciplinary work was very successful: but it has to be recognised that a real and lasting fusion of history with the other disciplines was never achieved (and was probably never achievable).

It is because of the interdisciplinary, universalist aspiration that the name Henri Berr (1863–1954) is always mentioned at the head of any potted account of the *Annales* school. Through the journal he founded in 1900, the *Revue de synthèse historique*, and through his projected 100-volume *L'Évolution de l'humanité*, Berr sought to bring together in one great synthesis all the activities of human beings in society, calling to his aid the methods and insights of sociology and the other social sciences. Announcing such a grand project, as we know only too well today, is very different from achieving (almost certainly impossible, in any case) it. The two great achievers, realists, empiricists, men of enormous vision, historians first and last, were Lucien Febvre (1878–1956) and Marc Bloch (1886–1944).

Lucien Febvre, born into a cultivated upper-class family, received a traditional French historical training, in which a certain emphasis had always been placed on geography. His first book, in fact, was predominantly geographical: *The Regions of France: Franche-Comté* (1905). His long apprenticeship was completed with the publication in 1911 of his dissertation *Philippe II and the Franche-Comté*. Dissatisfied with the political explanations of earlier French historians, Febvre was concerned to demonstrate what he called 'the multiple action of profound causes'.[4] This work was followed immediately by a *History of Franche-Comté*, then, after an interval spent in the French army during the First World War, Febvre swung to something much more general, a volume on *The Earth and Human Evolution* for Henri Berr's multi-volume series: among the large number of points Febvre made which have now become platitudes was the rebuttal of the idea that rivers make 'natural frontiers' – in fact they serve to link the human groups on both sides together in common activities. From a special interest in geography, Febvre, in a manner typical of many twentieth-century intellectuals, moved to an interest in group psychology. The new interest was revealed first in a study of *Martin Luther: un destin* (*Martin Luther: A Destiny*) published in 1928; but his most impressive venture into what he himself called 'historical psychology' was his *Le problème de l'incroyance au XVI siècle: la religion de Rabelais* (*The Problem of Unbelief in the Sixteenth Century: The Religion of Rabelais*) published just after the Second World War (1947). This is a highly significant work in extending history into the area that was later to be known as 'mentalities', that is to say, the attitudes and values of a particular people or group of people. By illuminating the mental attitudes of people in sixteenth-century France, Febvre showed that it was quite impossible for Rabelais to be an atheist or unbeliever in any modern sense, and that to regard him as such was utterly unhistorical. Although highly original, this book was actually volume 53 in the projected *Library of Historical Synthesis: The Evolution of Humanity*, directed by Henri Berr, which envisaged a total of 96 volumes. Febvre's book carried a foreword by Berr entitled 'Collective Psychology and Individual Reason', which in the patronising manner typical of senior French academics offered a summary of Febvre's main conclusions.

Marc Bloch also came from an upper-class family, his father being Professor of Ancient History at the Sorbonne. He graduated in both history and geography, and his earliest publication, paralleling that of Febvre, was a geographical study of medieval society in the Île de France (*L'Île de France*, 1913). His historical apprenticeship was served in searching the archives of northern France for materials for this study. At the end of the First World War (through which he served with distinction) he was appointed to a chair at Strasbourg, to which university Febvre had already been summoned. With Febvre, Bloch shared an interest both in geography and in collective psychology. Beyond that he sought to borrow from sociology what he perceived as an exactness of method and precision of language, too often lacking in traditional historical writing; he was right about the latter, less certainly so about the former. He also studied archaeology, agronomy, cartography, folklore and linguistics – the last with particular reference to place names and the genealogy of language. Bloch was an early believer in both the *comparative* and the *regressive* methods. Comparative study involving comparisons within a single country or between different countries is of immense value, since in highlighting both similarities and differences it can be a source of new synthesis, new questions, and, sometimes, convincing answers. The regressive method (previously most successfully used by Maitland) involves using evidence drawn from a later age of, say, customs, traditions, place names, field patterns, which may well have endured from an earlier age, in order to cast light on that earlier age. Bloch himself tramped around the French countryside talking to the men who in the twentieth century still tilled the soil in a manner not too far different from that of their medieval predecessors.

Bloch's interest in collective psychology was seen most strongly in his book on *Les Rois thaumaturges* (1924; literally, 'The Thaumaturgic Kings' – an English translation, *The Royal Touch*, was published in 1973): in this Bloch showed that although the belief that both French and English kings were endowed with healing powers (to cure the skin disease scrofula) grew up almost by accident, that belief became a fundamental part of the concept of royalty and an important element in maintaining its strength. Peter Burke, a British historian and an expert on *Annales* history, argues that this book 'has a strong claim to be regarded as one of the great historical works of the [twentieth] century'. Burke explains:

> The study was centrally concerned with the history of miracles, and it concluded with an explicit discussion of the problem of explaining how people could possibly believe in such 'collective illusions'. Bloch noted that some sufferers came back to be touched a second time, which suggests that they knew the treatment had not worked, but that this had not undermined their faith. 'It was the expectation of the miracle which created faith in it.'[5]

Burke also draws attention to the fact that Bloch, as he himself explicitly stated, was writing 'comparative history', principally between France and England. This, if you are persuaded by the contention I will make later that the advance of comparative history is one of the most import-ant developments of the last decades of the twentieth century, is of immense significance.

But Bloch's main contributions to historical knowledge were his inves-tigations into the nature of feudal society. *Rois et Serfs: un chapitre d'his-toire capétienne* (*Kings and Serfs: A Chapter in Capetian History*, 1920) is quite a brief work, but it shows clearly the manner in which Bloch viewed feudal society from the standpoint of the peasants rather than that of the lords and kings. *Les Caractères originaux de l'histoire rurale française* (*The Original Characteristics of French Rural History*, 1931) turned firmly away from preoccupations with legal and administrative institu-tions: Bloch endeavoured to show that the forms of French agricultural life depended less on such matters than upon the persistence of the forms of tenure and organisation established in the early Middle Ages. For some of the medieval village communities Bloch investigated, there actually existed no written sources. He was right in insisting that his-torians must establish the questions that need answering, and then try to develop techniques which will help towards producing answers, even where written sources don't exist. But of course there always does come a point where, if there really isn't any evidence, then there really isn't much to say. The fact is that his *Feudal Society* (1940) is a sketch rather than a fully rounded and substantiated work.

The great vehicle for the broader history desired by Bloch and Febvre was the famous journal which they jointly launched in January 1929, *Annales d'Histoire Économique et Sociale*, generally known thereafter sim-ply as *Annales* (when the journal was revived by the post-war second generation, the sub-title was slightly different).

Pirenne, Labrousse, Lefebvre

Febvre and Bloch had wanted the Belgian historian Henri Pirenne (1862–1935) to take on the editorship of their journal, so it is worthwhile considering here what kind of work Pirenne had been doing. Belgium's best-known historian, he taught throughout his life at the University of Ghent, save for the untoward interruption while he was the defiant prisoner of the Germans during the First World War. I would, of course, resist any suggestion that his history was 'culturally constructed', but would certainly recognise that contextual influences are very obvious. Pirenne belonged to a country which had had an independent political existence only since the 1830s; since there were no early Belgian political institutions, he was more or less forced to turn to the study of economic and cultural forces in Belgium's more distant past. Along with his contemporaries in the later nineteenth century Pirenne was very conscious of the fact that urbanisation was one of the major features which distinguished the society in which he lived from that of earlier ages: hence he shared in a lively controversy over the origins of medieval towns. Belgium itself, at the end of the nineteenth century, was an urban society: and in the length of their continuous history, the towns of Belgium rivalled those of Italy.

From 1893 onwards, Pirenne began publishing articles, based mainly on the Belgian evidence, presenting his views on the origins of medieval towns, which he associated with a revival of trade in the eleventh and twelfth centuries: the final statement appeared in *Medieval Cities: Their Origins and the Revival of Trade*, published in America in 1925. Meantime Pirenne became involved in the bigger controversy of how and why the classical age gave way to what, since the Renaissance, had been dubbed 'the Middle Ages'. The famous 'Pirenne Thesis' on the issue probably emerged in his lectures at Ghent in 1910, though it appeared in print only in 1922 and 1923, and then in the form of two learned articles in the professional journals. A brief statement followed in the opening pages of *Medieval Cities*; the full statement was published posthumously in *Mohammed and Charlemagne* (1937). Through the study of economic rather than political institutions, Pirenne reached the conclusion that a Roman civilisation based on the Mediterranean survived the Barbarian invasions, and did not collapse until the Muslim expansion of the seventh century. Medieval civilisation began only with the Carolingians: 'Without Mohammed, Charlemagne would have been inconceivable.'[6] Pirenne had an article (on the education of medieval merchants) in the first issue of *Annales*, which also contained a declaration of intent.[7] The key ideas were of collaboration between disciplines and between different kinds of historical expertise, and of exact and dedicated scholarship.

If the emphasis, at first, seemed to be on economic history, *Annales* quickly claimed that, apart from bringing in the social sciences, it was going to establish itself 'on the badly cultivated terrain of social history'.[8]

Although they had some enthusiastic younger disciples, Bloch and Febvre were not, prior to the end of the Second World War, particularly influential. When we move on to the post-war second generation, and what came to be called the new French history, we find that two other figures, not directly associated with *Annales*, and strongly Marxist in a way that Bloch and Febvre were not, are very important: Georges Lefebvre (1874–1959) and C. Ernest Labrousse (1895–1986). The former is important as a protagonist of the study both of mentalities and of quantitative history; the latter is usually seen as the French progenitor of the quantitative approaches that were so important in the post-war years. Lefebvre's early training was extremely austere. His first major labour (while a teacher at the Lycée of Lille) was to translate for his patron, Charles Petit-Dutaillis, disciple of Stubbs, the famous constitutional history by the Victorian bishop. Volumes I and II of *Histoire constitutionelle de l'Angleterre: son origine et son développement par William Stubbs* appeared in 1907 and 1913 respectively, Volume III in 1927, by which time 'G. Lefebvre', now a professor at Clermont-Ferrand, had become 'Georges Lefebvre' and was ranked above Dutaillis on the title-page. Lefebvre published his own first book in 1924, *Les paysans du Nord pendant la Révolution française* (*The Peasants of the North during the French Revolution*), which established his primary interest and his primary virtue: studies in depth of the French peasantry during the Revolution, a meticulous attempt to establish the concrete realities of the social structure. Lefebvre was never a member of the French Communist Party, but he believed in the reality of the class struggle as defined by Marx; to the end he vehemently insisted, in classical Marxist fashion, that the Revolution was caused by the rise of the bourgeoisie. Yet he insisted on the need for meticulous quantification, his most famous statement being 'Il faut compter' ('one must count'). He was also responsible for one of the great pioneering works in collective psychology, or mentalities: his *La Grande Peur de 1789* (*The Great Fear*, 1932), a study of the peasant hysteria in face of an imagined aristocratic conspiracy, put a new, and widely accepted, concept into the study of the French Revolution.[9] Just at this time there appeared the most fundamental economic analysis yet of the preconditions for revolution, and one which laid the basis for many post-war studies. *Esquisse des mouvements des prix et des revenus en France au XVIII siècle* (*Sketch of the Movements of Prices and Revenues in France in the Eighteenth Century*) by the young Labrousse appeared in 1933; it was followed in 1944 by the first volume of *La crise de l'économie française à la fin de l'Ancien régime et au début de la Révolution*

(*The Crisis of the French Economy at the End of the Ancien Régime and the Beginning of the Revolution*).

Bloch's *The Historian's Craft*

The new French history was far from perfect. It incorporated holistic assumptions about entire populations, classes, and groups that seem naïve today. A certain unreflective Marxism sometimes showed through in the works of Lefebvre and Labrousse. Febvre, as Burke points out, wrote 'confidently about "the men of the sixteenth century" ... as if there were no significant differences between the assumptions of men and women, rich and poor, and so on'.[10] Bloch was a Resistance hero, shot by the Germans in 1944. He had been gathering together his thoughts on history, and these were published in 1949 as *Apologie pour l'histoire: ou, Métier d'historian* – a good translation would be *A Vindication of History: The Historian's Profession*, but unfortunately when the English version came out in 1954, only the sub-title was translated, and then inaccurately: hence *The Historian's Craft*. Translation from one language to another can often cause problems in historical study. In the current climate of postmodernist criticism, we have to be particularly precise in how we define what historians do. The notion of history as a craft is not a helpful one (the point is perhaps illuminated if I mention that if the English title were translated back into French one would have *L'art d'historien*). To be fair to translator and publisher, Bloch does at one point seem to be suggesting that the historian is a 'lute maker' rather than a 'drill operator';[11] for myself, I just say that such metaphors are seldom very useful. In all the circumstances, Bloch's book is a profoundly inspiring one, but (so fair-minded is the author) it is not really the guide from the inside to *Annales* history as it existed at that time which one might expect, nor is it a comprehensive guide to the what, why, and how of history. Of course, Bloch says many important things: after first dwelling on the poetry of history, on its 'unquestionable fascination', he goes on to say that to entertain is not enough, the use of history being that it aids understanding – 'to act reasonably, it is first necessary to understand'; history is 'but a fragment of the universal march towards knowledge', and it is only 'a science in infancy ... it is still very young as a rational attempt at analysis' (the advances, I would say, in the half-century since Bloch wrote have been immense); there is excellent technical material on the problems of forgery, reliability of records, and the like; finally, Bloch's treatment of the historian's use of words like 'serfs', 'bourgeoisie', 'Middle Ages' demonstrates that major historians have indeed long been interested in the problems of language (which the postmodernists claim to have discovered).

2   The Rise of the Sub-Histories

As history became more professionalised (and, as Bloch said, history was a new profession), various separate specialisms, 'sub-histories', began to emerge: intellectual history, economic history, political history, constitutional history, diplomatic history, urban history, labour history, historical demography, women's history, social history, cultural history, history of science, imperial and colonial history. Along with the sub-histories there developed specialist methodologies: for example, prosopography (multiple biography) in the kind of political/constitutional history developed by Lewis Namier (1888–1960), or quantitative and econometric analysis in economic history. There were also the obvious period divisions: ancient history, medieval history, early modern history, late modern history, contemporary history. Other categories were created as well, cutting across sub-histories and periods: the leading American historians after the Second World War, for instance, were generally referred to as 'consensus historians'. Career aspirations and rivalries also contributed to the flaunting of labels, with attempts being made from time to time to declare one sub-history more fashionable, more relevant, more something than the others: the Americans, as we shall see, became particularly eager to assert the superiority of certain types of history over others. The creation of new specialisms generally entailed advances in historical knowledge, but rigid compartmentalisation also led to over-reliance on particular methods, and blindness to the advantages to be obtained through varying the approach.

Meinecke, Chabod and Ritter

In creating intellectual history, or history of ideas, Friedrich Meinecke (1862–1954) sought to fuse the teachings of the two German masters who had seemed to stand at opposite poles in historical study: Ranke, who had glorified the might of the political state, and Burckhardt, who had contemplated (somewhat pessimistically) the development of human civilisation and its intellectual products. Clearly the stronger pull was that of Ranke, and Meinecke's essential interest proved to be the history of *political* ideas. His first book (two volumes, 1895 and 1899) was a biography of General Hermann von Boyen, an activist in the early nineteenth-century Prussian reform movement. In 1906 and 1907 there followed two further studies of Prussian liberalism; and in 1908 he published a book on the origins of the German nation state. His most famous work was *The Doctrine of Raison d'État and its Place in Modern History* (Munich and Berlin, 1924).

One Italian historian of ideas I have already mentioned is Benedetto Croce (1866–1952). Another was Federico Chabod (1902–60), who studied under Meinecke in Berlin and published work on Machiavelli and the Renaissance in the 1920s. His aim in regard to Machiavelli was, as he put it, to present him 'as the expression, almost the synthesis of Italian life throughout the fourteenth and fifteenth centuries; and see reflected and clarified in his thought, as it were in essential outline, the age-long process of development which led from the downfall of the old, Communal freedom, to the triumph of the princely, the absolute State'.[12] The faith in the absolute state was greatly shaken by the advent and activities of the absolute state as constructed by Adolf Hitler. Friedrich Meinecke's *German Catastrophe* (1946) voiced a repentance for his own concentration on political ideas; he argued that Germany had taken a wrong road in the nineteenth century when, instead of developing and extending her justly celebrated cultural tradition, she had turned towards the glorification of the political state. Gerhard Ritter, a younger compatriot of Meinecke's, an authority on the German Reformation and the author of an astonishingly wide range of books, commented on the imprint left by events in the later editions of his short biography, *Luther: His Life and Work*. In the preface to the 1959 edition he remarked that although the central sections of the book had not been much altered since the first edition of 1928–9, the introduction and conclusion had to be more extensively rewritten:

> The original plan of this book, made shortly after the end of the First World War, emphasised Luther's importance as a national hero, as the central figure of German culture, with vigour which I today feel to have been exaggerated. The catchword which was coined at that time – 'the Eternal German' – has been cut from this edition...

Ritter then explained how his theological understanding of Luther had been deepened by his participation in the struggle of the German Lutheran Church against the Nazi regime in the thirties:

> In retrospect I feel that my book reached full maturity in the third and extensively revised edition which appeared in 1943. The world catastrophe which we had already sensed then and which broke on us in 1945 brought Luther's ideas of the hidden God and the twilight of world history home to us Germans with remarkable actuality. This led me to re-write the introduction almost completely in the fourth edition (1947).

Early Labour and Economic Histories in Britain

In the late nineteenth and early twentieth centuries in Britain, a growing interest among the intellectual classes in the working-class movement and in socialism generally was undoubtedly a motive in spreading an interest in economic history, and in what, after the Second World War, came to be recognised as the separate sub-discipline of labour history. Arnold Toynbee the elder was an upper-class pioneer of the university settlement movement which brought concerned university men and women into deprived areas, and he is generally given the credit for popularising the concept of an Industrial Revolution: his major theme was the harsh effects industrialisation had had on the lower classes. A similar interest lay at the heart of the pioneering studies by J. L. and Barbara Hammond: *The Village Labourer* (1911), *The Town Labourer* (1917) and *The Skilled Labourer* (1919). The primary concern of the two great intellectuals and founder-members of the moderate socialist reform group the Fabian Society, Sidney (1859–1947) and Beatrice (1858–1943) Webb, was to establish the social facts upon which to predicate social reform, so that they produced a number of historical works, which for many years remained standard authorities: *History of Trade Unionism* (1894) and *English Local Government* (nine volumes, 1906–29). When it did begin to develop a separate identity, labour history was for too long preoccupied with institutions, trade unions and socialist parties, failing to recognise that the large majority of the working class were not interested in political activism. Only recently has labour history become a genuine history of the working class, rather than just a history of the working-class movement.

R. H. Tawney (1880–1962) was an Oxford graduate and lecturer at the London School of Economics, who became directly involved with the working-class movement through his activities in adult education and the Labour Party. His first book, *The Agrarian Problem in the Sixteenth Century* (1912), was concerned with the decline of the English peasantry – the former 'yeoman of England' – in face of what he saw as the unscrupulous 'rise of the gentry', an interpretation sometimes termed 'The Tawney Thesis'. Much influenced by two famous articles on 'The Protestant Ethic and the Rise of Capitalism' published in 1904 and 1905 by the German sociologist Max Weber, Tawney in 1926 published his own best-known work, *Religion and the Rise of Capitalism*. Here was another elegant 'thesis', but the jumps in argument and logic, and the lack of convincing supporting evidence, are such as to be unacceptable in the history of today.

The major figure among early twentieth-century economic historians, certainly in Britain, perhaps in the whole English-speaking world, is J. H. Clapham (1873–1946). At Cambridge, Clapham came into contact with the economist Alfred Marshall (1842–1924), who in 1897 sent the following important and revealing letter to Lord Acton:

I feel that the absence of any tolerable account of the economic development of England in the last century and a half is a disgrace to the
land, and a grievous hindrance to the right understanding of the
economic problems of our time. London and Cambridge are the
only places where the work is likely to be done well; but till recently
the man for the work had not appeared. But now I think the man is in
sight. Clapham has more analytic faculty than any thorough historian
whom I have ever taught. His future work is I think still uncertain; a
little force would I think turn him this way or that. If you could turn
him towards XVIII or XIX century economic history economists
would ever be grateful to you . . . [13]

In 1902 Clapham accepted appointment as Professor of Economics at the
college which was shortly to become the University of Leeds. While
based in this centre of the textile trade, he seized the opportunity to
make full acquaintance with the world of business: in 1907 he published
his first book, *The Woollen and Worsted Industries*. It was not until after the
First World War that Clapham revealed his talent for sustained economic narrative in areas formerly illumined only by the occasional
monograph: *The Economic Development of France and Germany 1815–1914*
was published in 1921. Clapham now devoted himself to his major life's
work, *An Economic History of Modern Britain*, published in three large
volumes between 1926 and 1938.

In the original preface to the first volume Clapham offered three
justifications for his labours. First, that the story had never previously
been handled on this scale. Clapham's second justification was that he
intended to challenge certain widely accepted 'legends' (remember my
remarks about 'myths' in Chapter 2):

Until very recently, historians' accounts of the dominant element of
the nineteenth century, the great and rapid growth of population,
were nearly all semi-legendary; sometimes they still are. Statisticians
had always known the approximate truth; but historians had often
followed a familiar literary tradition.

Actually, Clapham's explanation of population increase as due to a falling death rate has long been rejected by historians employing today's
sophisticated statistical techniques, so that there is a slightly hollow ring
about Clapham's complacent reference to 'historians who neglect quantities'. Clapham also cited 'the legend that everything was getting worse
for the working man, down to some unspecified date between the
drafting of the People's Charter and the Great Exhibition'. This 'legend'
– which had featured strongly in the work of the Hammonds – he

attributed to the way in which 'the work of statisticians on wages and prices' had been 'constantly ignored by social historians'. Against the psychological intuitions and emotional sympathies of the Hammonds, Clapham placed the quantities of the economist and a faith in the virtues of economic growth. This marked the beginning of one of the great debates in British economic and labour history, the 'standard of living controversy' – did the Industrial Revolution push living standards down or up? Third, Clapham claimed that it was possible to be much more precisely quantitative than earlier historians had assumed.

McIlwain, Namier and Elton

However, most professional historians throughout Europe and North America continued to be preoccupied with constitutional and political history. One central problem which was attacked with vigour was that of the origins of the English parliament, pride of the Whig historians. While American New Historians sought to stress the importance of the present in the study of the past, political historians were able to show how deep misconceptions about the medieval 'parliament' had grown up because of the present-minded character of Stubbs and his like. Some of the most important work in this area was done by American scholars, traditionally attracted either to medieval institutions as the forebears of American concepts of law, or to the late-colonial origins of American independence. In his 1936 presidential address to the AHA, the Harvard historian C. H. McIlwain explained how professional revisions of standard myths come about:

> They have usually come piecemeal because someone has been steeping himself in the thought and motives of some past epoch by extensive and careful reading of the records or writings of the time, and one day wakes up to find – usually to his utter amazement – that this thought or these motives and institutions are not at all the ones he has been reading about all these years in the standard modern books. Then he gets to work.

McIlwain described his own personal feeling of shock when he 'suddenly realised that men like Lambarde or Fitzherbert in Elizabeth's time, when they spoke of a parliament, were thinking of something in many ways very different from what I had learned'.

Perhaps the name of Lewis Namier (1888–1960) does not quite have the resonance today it had when A. J. P. Taylor likened the publication of *The Structure of Politics at the Accession of George III* (two volumes, 1929) to the publication of Darwin's *The Origin of the Species* (a gross exaggeration even then, of course).[14] None the less, the story of how (sideways on, as it were) he came to tackle the problems he did, and the approaches and results he came up with, are important in the expanding scope and sophistication of history as a discipline. Lewis Namier was a Polish Jew, born near the town of Lukow which was then in the Austro-Hungarian Empire, who read history at Balliol in the years before the First World War. He originally planned to do research into the British Empire at the time of the American Revolution. An American historian gently guided him away from the overcrowded American end to the British. Soon after he started on this assignment, Namier became aware of how little was really known of the nature of English politics in the later eighteenth century: under the all-pervading influence of the Whig school it had been too readily accepted that eighteenth-century political assumptions were the same as those of the nineteenth century: the works of contemporary polemicists like Edmund Burke were taken at their face value. What was really intended by Namier as a preliminary clearing-up operation became the major part of his life's work. The fashionable Whig view of eighteenth-century political history postulated that the Glorious Revolution of 1688 had created a constitutional monarchy, to which the Hanoverian accession in 1714 had added cabinet government; however, in 1760, so the story went, the misguided George III had attempted, through a vast central machinery of corruption, and in face of the heroic resistance of the Whigs, to put the clock back and restore a personal monarchy.

The essential basis of Namier's approach was the carrying out of a huge series of detailed studies of individual personages which could then be welded together into a composite portrayal of the age (*prosopography* being the elaborate name for this methodology): instead of generalisations (that is, guesses) about what 'the people', the parties or groups did or thought, Namier got down to the individual person and worked up from there. In *The Structure of Politics at the Accession of George III* he studied the separate members of parliament and the motives for their being there, showing how small was the part played by the lofty political ideals on which the Whig historians loved to expatiate. Above all Namier brought out the extent of local political influence, and showed how insignificant in fact was the reputed power of corruption held by the central government. Namier's credo was that of the professional historian of today: 'One has to steep oneself in the political life of a period before one can safely speak, or be sure of understanding, its language.'[15] Namier was the first researcher to work through the 500 volumes of the Newcastle papers in the British Museum. No 'cult of the archive' here – without the pain, there was no hope of gain.

England in the Age of the American Revolution (1930) was only the first volume of a projected multi-volume series under this general title. However, it contained enough meat in itself to force a revision of accepted views of the eighteenth century. Namier had already shown the limits to eighteenth-century corruption; now, seeing the system, not in terms of latter-day moralising, but as people saw it at the time, he justified such corruption as did exist as necessary to the smooth running of government. More than this, he demonstrated how unreal it was to see eighteenth-century Whigs and Tories as analogous to nineteenth-century Liberals and Conservatives. At the national level much of the meaning had gone out of the terms 'Whig' and 'Tory', though at the local level it was still possible to distinguish between a Whig and a Tory 'mentality'. National politics were the politics of faction and connection rather than of party and principle in any nineteenth-century sense. Finally, Namier showed that the powers of George I and II were much greater than the Whig historians had allowed for: correspondingly there was a good deal less in the contemporary and later accusations that George III was in some way 'unconstitutional' in his actions. Ministers under the two Georges, as Richard Pares, the most brilliant of the Namierites, put it, were the King's servants: but they were servants who had had 'the run of the place'.[16]

Apart from his eighteenth-century interests, Namier wrote on the diplomatic origins of the Second World War (permitting his work here to be marked by some of the passion which he strove to exclude from the eighteenth-century books) and on the 1848 revolutions. But it is the books discussed here, along with the *History of Parliament* (on which many pairs of hands were set to work) that exemplify the Namierite approach. These are works of analysis, lacking the narrative element that is so cherished by the proponents of *auteur* history. As often happens, Namier became something of a prisoner of his own successes: later writers have shown, for instance, that belief and principle did play more of a part in eighteenth-century politics than Namier allowed. In a much later work, Namier consciously adopted the concepts of modern psychology. His study of Charles Townshend, the brilliant English politician whose erratic political behaviour has sometimes been regarded as a contributory cause of the American Revolution, was not published until 1964. This work was based on a mass of unsorted manuscript material, but it also openly employed the categories of Freudian psychology and suggested that conflicts between Townshend and his father 'produced a mental attitude towards authority which he carried over into the field of politics'.[17]

G. R. Elton (1921–94), though he wrote on European as well as on British history, is irrevocably identified with a thesis, the 'Elton thesis' on the 'Tudor revolution in government'. In discussing the question of subjectivity in history, I remarked that what historians write can be influenced by their own mental set. It has been said that some historians tend naturally to stress continuities in the past, while others identify

'discontinuities', sharp breaks. It has further been argued that the cataclysmic experiences of two twentieth-century wars have tended to
encourage the notion of discontinuity. Just what exactly were the roots
of the discontinuous view of Tudor administrative history espoused by
Elton can only be a matter for speculation. It seems that it was only after
he had completed his postgraduate researches on the 1530s that Elton
became aware of the novelty of the things he thought he had discovered,
and that he hit upon the dramatic title *The Tudor Revolution in Government* for the book eventually published in 1953, in order to draw attention to the novelty of what he was saying.

According to a tradition established by Victorian historians, 1485 was
a key date in English history, marking a sharp discontinuity when,
following upon a century of civil war and social disintegration, Henry
VII, succeeding to the throne by right of conquest, proceeded to establish
what J. R. Green called the 'New Monarchy', which developed quickly
into the 'Tudor despotism' of Henry VIII. The political historians of the
earlier twentieth century, led by A. F. Pollard (1869–1948) – founder of
both the [English] Historical Association (1906) and the Institute of
Historical Research – had endeavoured to replace this by a more continuous view, stressing on the one side that many of the characteristics of
the 'New Monarchy' were in fact inherited from Henry VII's immediate
predecessors, Edward IV and Richard III, and on the other that medieval
methods persisted far into the Tudor period. For this perhaps rather
bland interpretation, Elton substituted a version which accepted
continuity between Henry VII and his predecessors, but postulated a
'Tudor revolution in government' in the 1530s: a revolution which
equipped England with a modern, national bureaucracy which could
function, and provide political stability, irrespective of the personal
qualities of the king or his deputies – medieval government, of course,
was subject to breakdown whenever a weak king succeeded to the
throne. Elton was a belligerent champion of political history, and openly
contemptuous of social history and of attempts to direct attention away
from the action of individuals to the deeper forces and structures that
historians of a different type identify. He echoed Ranke in declaring that
what counts for most is

> the condition, reconstruction, and gradual moulding of a state – the
> history of a nation and its leaders in political action and therefore the
> history of government in the widest sense.[18]

The words are taken from the preface to his textbook *England under the
Tudors* (1955). Elton gave immense weight to the actions of one particular
individual, Henry VII's secretary, Thomas Cromwell, whom he
described as 'the most remarkable revolutionary in English history'.

While much of Elton's analysis of the Tudor monarchy still stands, his praises of Cromwell are hard to sustain, and his over-concentration on politics is very open to criticism.[19]

In the main Western universities, where the study of history had been formalised, history was held to end some time in the nineteenth century, or even earlier, and there was no study of contemporary history. However, the preoccupation in the inter-war years with the origins of the First World War gave a tremendous stimulus to the study of recent diplomatic history. Before the war Bernadotte Schmitt was being highly adventurous when he prepared a doctoral dissertation on Franco-German relations in the period after 1870. An American, Schmitt studied history at Oxford, then later became one of the leading historians of the origins of the First World War. In the years after that war the various nations published volume upon volume of their diplomatic correspondence, hoping to justify their own actions, but also providing a plentiful supply of source material for this particular historical specialisation. Western liberals tended to want to exonerate Germany from the extreme charges of war-guilt which had been laid upon her at the time of Versailles, and the works of G. P. Gooch (1873–1968) and S. B. Fay were very much congruent with this, tending, if anything, to place most blame on the Austro-Hungarian Empire, which, conveniently, now no longer existed. A harsher approach towards Germany, and one which, it must be said, was more in keeping with the evidence, was taken by the distinguished French diplomatic historian Pierre Renouvin (1893–1974), and after the Second World War by the equally distinguished Italian scholar Luigi Albertini.

Arguments over the causes of the First World War suddenly sprang into life again after 1961, the year in which Fritz Fischer (*b.* 1908) published his *Griff nach der Weltmacht* (*Grasp after World Power*, though the English translation published in 1967 was given the title *Germany's Aims in the First World War*). Fischer stressed both the technological–industrial developments in Wilhelmine Germany which, he argued, made her naturally an aggressive expansionist power, and the detailed annexationist policies set out very clearly in an indisputably authentic document written by the German chancellor Bethmann-Hollweg, once regarded as a relatively liberal and pacifist politician whose true gentle nature was subverted by the belligerent Kaiser and his generals. The 'Fischer thesis', which, in effect, revivified the idea of Germany's prime responsibility for the war, aroused violent hostility in Fischer's native Germany. It was pointed out that the Bethmann-Hollweg document, having been written during, not before, the war, was scarcely evidence of German pre-war plans; if similar expressions of war aims from the other powers were to be studied, they too might appear aggressive and annexationist. However, whatever comments in detail might be made on Fischer's epochal work, it became impossible thereafter to wish away all notions of a special responsibility attaching to Germany as Europe's trouble-maker in the first half of the twentieth century.

One British historian who had no intention of wishing away such notions was A. J. P. Taylor (1906–88). Taylor, a top journalist and television star, was the epitome of the historian as *auteur*. He had a clipped, economical, modern style, full of wit and paradoxes; yet he was also essentially a diplomatic and political historian. Though he didn't boast about it, Taylor was a very able linguist, an important attribute for any historian who wishes not to be confined to working purely on his/her own country. Taylor's first two books were highly traditional diplomatic history: *The Italian Problem in European Diplomacy* (1934) and *Germany's First Bid for Colonies, 1884–1885* (1938). Like Elton, Taylor stressed the importance of the actions of individuals, though he saw even the most brilliant politicians as opportunists, and never planners. Taylor worked mainly from printed collections of diplomatic documents and from secondary sources: in his mischievous way, he expressed a certain contempt for the elaborate apparatus of scholarship. A brilliant lecturer, Taylor was seen at his best in his top-of-the-range textbooks, particularly *The Struggle for Mastery in Europe, 1848–1918* (1954) and *English History 1914–1945* (1965). These are brilliant books, but one would have to counsel students today that they would be unwise to rely on either of them as their fundamental textbooks for the areas covered. The book for which Taylor is most famous is *The Origins of the Second World War* (1961, reprinted with a new introduction, 'Second Thoughts', in 1963). Again, one has to say that anyone looking for a reliable discussion of the causes of the Second World War should not settle for this book. Its significance really lies in the part it played in generating a new, and much more thorough, analysis of the causes of that war (in this sense, though it is an entirely different kind of book, it is analogous to Fischer's work which inspired a whole new debate over the origins of the First World War).

Until 1961, the accepted versions of events in regard to the Second World War conflated the idea of a war carefully planned in advance by Hitler with that of a blind and craven policy on the part of British politicians which failed to prevent this plan from running its course: the fundamental point was repeated again and again that the Second World War was, in Churchill's phrase, an 'unnecessary' war, that by perceiving Hitler's unmitigated evil and by simply following an obvious set of alternative choices, the British government could have averted the war. Taylor's *Origins* cuts across both controversies. In the opening chapter of the first edition he explained his intention of re-examining the simple explanation that Hitler's will alone caused the war; but in the 'Second Thoughts' of the new edition he explained that the 'vital question' concerned Great Britain and France – the 'appeasing nations'. To me it has always been clear that in planning and writing the *Origins* Taylor was in the process of changing his own mind, and that this explains certain unsatisfactory features of his book (it is an indication of Taylor's warmly delightful personality that when I put this to him he responded, in that inimitable accent which still rings in my ears today, 'Quite right'). At one stage Taylor seems to have wished to defend the appeasers against the fashionable denunciations; yet in the end the arguments of the book, while removing from Hitler a peculiar and special responsibility for the war, seemed to rivet responsibility all the more heavily on them.

Taylor insisted that his work was rooted in the diplomatic sources, though his referencing was rather casual. He claimed that the Hossbach Memorandum of 1937, which contains clear evidence that Hitler was planning a war, could not be taken as authentic; he declared that Hitler's apparently clear statements of intention in *Mein Kampf* (1923) were simply ramblings and ravings not to be taken seriously. Generally, historians have not supported Taylor's attempts to deny the significance of important primary sources. Most of all, they have criticised him for relying so exclusively on diplomatic and political materials, when one really needs to understand the dynamic force of Nazism and its tremendous will towards war.

3   Latter-day Marxism and *Past and Present*

British Marxist Historiographers: Tosh and Carr

There is a form of 'Marxist history' which distorts the evidence simply to uphold Marxist theory – or, more likely, ignores the evidence altogether. This sort of stuff, produced sporadically in the West in the 1930s, and by the ton in the Soviet Union, we can ignore. However, all those at risk of succumbing to the emotional lure of Marxism should be constantly referred to the sad case of the young American scholar David Abraham, whose faith in Marxist theory, and, in particular, the simplistic thesis that German capitalists conspired to bring Hitler to power, blinded him to his own dreadful blunders in transcribing the sources and in confusing his own opinions with statements contained within them. Those who seek answers tend to anxious caution; those who think they know the answers in advance are prone to a complacent carelessness. In my experience of research supervision, Marxism is a handicap, not a help. The scholarly failings in Abraham's *The Collapse of the Weimar Republic: Political Economy and Crisis* (Princeton, NJ, 1981) were exposed and he was refused employment in the American historical profession – he became a lawyer instead! But I do recognise the major contributions made to historical knowledge by Marxists rigorously applying historical methodology; I also recognise that Marxist commitment can take historians into areas which those of a more conservative outlook would tend to ignore. Still, let us be clear that Marxist history is quite definitely *not* a superior form of history. John Tosh (*b*. 1945), in the first edition of his appealing and deeply felt *The Pursuit of History* (1984), declared that history must have a theory, and that the best theory going was Marxism; he modified his position slightly in the second edition (1991), and again in the third edition (2000), while restating his deep faith in Marxism (pp. 141–59). But there is no 'must' about it; history's achievements are already considerable – there is certainly no point in imposing a theory which demonstrably gets so many things wrong. What is needed – rather than the purchase of theory second-hand – is that historians should be reflexive and articulate about their assumptions and methods, opening their confidence to readers, rather than battering them with authoritarian pronouncements. E. H. Carr (1892–1982) claimed that Marxist history was best, because it had 'a long-term vision over the past and over the future'.[20] Demand of your historians that they show a detailed understanding of the past, 'from the inside' as it were; distrust them if they claim to have an understanding of the future.

The Frankfurt School and Structuralism: The Cross-Fertilisation of Marxism

There were three phases of cross-fertilisation which made Marxism more flexible and intellectually appealing. The first began in the interwar years with the establishment at Frankfurt in 1923 of the Institute for Social Theory, whose most notable figures were Max Horkheimer (1895–1973), Theodor W. Adorno (1903–69) and Herbert Marcuse (1898–1979), whose main work, after the advent of Hitler, was accomplished in the United States. The Frankfurt school abandoned the rigid economic determinism of what they referred to as 'vulgar Marxism': recognising the weaknesses in the notion of a mere superstructure determined by the economic structure, they granted greater autonomy to laws, ideas, modes of cultural expression. Reactions against economic determinism also came from two other imaginative Marxist scholars, the Italian Antonio Gramsci (1891–1937) and the Hungarian Georg Lukács (1885–1971), who presented much more subtle views of how patterns of cultural domination are established. Recognising that the working class rather obviously did not oppose a culture of its own to that of the bourgeoisie, Gramsci sponsored the notion of the cultural 'hegemony' established by the dominant class and unwittingly consented to by the working class. The Frankfurt scholars, too, were responsible for the second phase, bringing in ideas from Freudian psychology, ideas which, propagated by Marcuse, became very influential in the 1960s, and which gave rise to much historical writing about the family, and about 'bourgeois' sexual practices as 'instruments of domination'.

The third era of cross-fertilisation was that of the late 1950s, 1960s and early 1970s, the era of structuralism and post-structuralism, and of Marxism blending with these to create postmodernism. The French structuralists and post-structuralists were, it cannot be stressed too strongly, Marxist in their fundamental assumptions, as were practically all French intellectuals of the time. Indeed, we have to understand that many postmodernist utterances form part of a debate within Marxism, rather than having much relevance to the activities and beliefs of non-Marxists. Most French Marxist intellectuals were highly critical of the French Communist Party, which they saw as a lackey of the Soviet Union and a traitor to true Marxist ideals. In the immediate post-war years France's leading intellectual was Jean-Paul Sartre (1905–80), who managed to combine his existentialism (a philosophy which demands that individuals take responsibility for their own actions) with Marxism (which insists on the importance of collective action) into a very humanist political stance – he believed that human beings of goodwill could change the system. Party hacks poured scorn on Sartre and so did the structuralists, starting off with the anthropologist Claude Lévi-Strauss (b. 1908). According to the structuralists and post-structuralists human societies and human activities, including language, are governed by structures operating in accordance with their own self-contained codes, all, in the contemporary period, expressions of bourgeois power. Within these structures human actions, whether co-operative or not, are of no significance; the attempts of historians to evaluate different factors, including human ones, are pointless; all one can do is study the 'codes' that control us.

Louis Althusser (1918–86), a loyal, and obsequious, member of the French Communist party, analysed the Marxist scriptures in order to come up with an utterly deterministic, nihilistic version of Marxism which granted absolutely no significance to human actions. Post-structuralist theories of language, as I've already noted (and I will return to the issue again in Chapter 7), were hostile to historical study: the very forms of language, it was maintained, meant that history could not avoid being bourgeois ideology.

However, the writings of Michel Foucault (1926–84) did cover topics of interest to historians, and have provided them with perceptions and new ways of looking at things which many have felt it worthwhile to explore, even if only to come up with adverse responses.[21] Foucault was not a historian, though in many ways he did have the historian's sensitivity to the notion that the practices and institutions of any particular era have to be seen within the context of the prevailing ideas of that era, and certainly not to be seen as something absolute, or to be judged by the standards of the present day. But he was overly rigid in his concept of period, overly confident that the French Revolution had brought one period to an end and had instituted the 'modern', 'bourgeois' period, while he was impressionistic in his use of evidence, all drawn from printed sources. He was more concerned to advance his theories than to establish precisely what had happened. Foucault wrote about crime, discipline and punishment, madness, medicine, and sexuality. The general tenor of his work was that what was treated as 'crime', 'madness', or 'proper sexual behaviour' was determined by the power structure of the time, and that hospitals and asylums, as much as prisons, existed, not in the interests of their inmates, but as institutions expressly designed to preserve the *status quo*. There remains a fundamental difficulty for those following in the footsteps of Foucault: even if the historical points made by Foucault are correct, how can these be expressed if the very nature of language itself makes objective statements impossible?

Many Marxist historians remained resolutely opposed to postmodernist ideas – one, E. P. Thompson (1924–93), wrote, in 'The Poverty of Theory', a devastating attack on the Marxism of Althusser.[22] Others readily absorbed them (John Tosh is an obvious example), as did certain intellectuals who had not previously been notably Marxist (Simon Schama is a notable example); supporters of feminist and gay liberation causes were attracted by what Foucault (himself gay) said about the cultural construction of sexuality, or 'gender'. For the next few pages I shall be concentrating on Marxist historians uninfluenced by postmodernist developments, returning to postmodernist influences at the end of the chapter. It is important to record that the writings of both Marxists and postmodernists have been salutary, not just for historians but for all scholars, in drawing attention to the need to scrutinise all institutions and practices to see what influences and purposes may lie below the surface, and to take the greatest care with language. Unfortunately Marxists, and still more postmodernists, have erected alternative absolute systems of their own which they claim to be beyond scrutiny.

'Western Marxism' and the Study of the French Revolution

Probably if there had been no French Revolution, there would have been no Marxism. One of the best ways of approaching the strengths and weaknesses of some of the more important Marxist historians is by examining what they, and their opponents, have written about that cataclysmic event. The topic, heuristically, is indeed a magnificent one, since the French Revolution not only had great significance for the future development of humankind (the precise nature of that significance, social, political, cultural – probably not economic – being itself the subject of intense debate), but provides an excellent focus for historiographical and epistemological discussion. It is a topic which will run, intermittently, through the remainder of this chapter.

The more flexible, open Marxism that developed after the Second World War is sometimes referred to as 'Western Marxism'. Its course was fostered by disillusionment with Stalinism and hastened by a revulsion against the post-Stalinist repression (1956) of the Hungarian attempt to establish a more liberal regime, and then (1968) the crushing by Soviet tanks of the 'Prague Spring', the brief liberalisation of life in Czechoslovakia; among serious professional historians respect for evidence and the need, wherever possible, to quantify also played a part in drastically qualifying traditional Marxist assumptions. The collapse of the Soviet Empire in 1989 did not mean the end of Marxism as a set of intellectual beliefs, but in an obvious way it continued the dismantling of the faith that Marxists had access to truths unavailable to others.

Georges Lefebvre had formulated his own, fairly flexible, Marxism in the 1920s and 1930s, when through his seeking out of provincial archives and application of the rule 'one must count', he made enormous contributions to knowledge about the French Revolution. But, for all the complexity and detail of his arguments, he continued, as a committed Marxist, to insist that the ultimate cause of the Revolution was the rise of the bourgeoisie, 1789 being the moment when it took power after several centuries of growing in numbers and wealth. In 1939 Lefebvre published a general synthesis, *Quatre-vingt-neuf* (Eighty-Nine), which appeared in English translation after the war as *The Coming of the French Revolution* (1947). This was the fundamental text for those who continued to follow Marxist approaches. But it is quite wrong, here as elsewhere, to envisage historical interpretations as unfolding in a series of discrete, and usually contradictory, stages (the naïve error at the core of Geyl's *Napoleon: For and Against*). French historical writing at this time may have been dominated by Marxist views, but British and American certainly were not. The names of Alfred Goodwin, J. M. Thompson and R. R. Palmer have tended to disappear from recent textbooks on the Revolution, but at the time they were strong and influential proponents of the view that the French Revolution was primarily about politics, about new ideas of liberalism and democracy, not about the replacement of one class by another.

The most direct challenge to French Marxist orthodoxy came from the English historian Alfred Cobban, in his 1955 lecture 'The Myth of the French Revolution', subsequently widely available in his important book *The Social Interpretation of the French Revolution* (1964). With wit, and a wealth of detail, Cobban remorselessly challenged the whole Marxist apparatus of one rising class overthrowing the existing ruling class:

successful members of one class, he pointed out, move into the class above, but they do not overthrow it. Meantime the newest generation of *Annales* historians were moving strongly against Marxism. François Furet had already embarked on the study of changing eighteenth-century ideas, and their transmission through books, which helped to make the Revolution possible (as distinct from the Revolution being explicable in terms of a rising bourgeoisie) when, with Denis Richet, he published *La Révolution* (Paris, 1955–6), which stressed long-term changes in values and attitudes (see next section). In 1971 Furet was able to use the prestige of *Annales* to publish in its pages a devastating attack on what he called the 'revolutionary catechism', that is to say the simplistic Marxist formulations.

It is now clearly perceived that there was not in eighteenth-century France, on the one side, a distinctive aristocracy, and on the other a distinctive bourgeoisie. The upper bourgeoisie was to a considerable extent intermingled with the aristocracy; within both there were squabbles over status. The immediate circumstances leading to crisis were the financial needs of the Crown. That the crisis became intense was due to the incompetence of the Crown and the manoeuvrings within elite groups; that the crisis became revolutionary was due to the pressure of the enormous and scarcely suppressed grievances of the ordinary people (particularly in Paris) suffering from a long trend of declining real incomes and frequently near starvation. Much emphasis is now being placed on the ideas in circulation over a long period before the Revolution, and on mentalities across society. The obvious fact that there was no complete assumption of power by 'the bourgeoisie' was recognised, and the emphasis, as I have suggested, placed rather on a revolution in political ideas.

In Britain, the best account of the French Revolution is provided by William Doyle (*b.* 1942), though he does exaggerate the hegemony of the Marxist version prior to the 1960s: his *The Oxford History of the French Revolution* (1989) is an immaculate example of that 'scientific' history which presents a balanced and objective account and which, though brilliantly written, is quite simply not just the mere narrative of one single *auteur*. The Welsh Marxist Gwynne Lewis has valiantly continued to try to fly the somewhat bedraggled Marxist flag. In his brief textbook *The French Revolution: Re-thinking the Debate* (1993), he identifies two distinct approaches: what he calls 'the revisionist approach' (which includes Doyle) and what he calls, not the Marxist approach, but, in full recognition that that approach no longer carries credibility, the 'marxisant' approach (French, pronounced 'marx-eez-ong' and meaning 'inclining towards Marxism'). The use of the label 'revisionist' is not to be recommended: practically every thesis that has ever been advanced on any important historical topic has been subject to 'revisionism', 're-revisionism' and, probably, 're-re-revisionism'. The account presented so ably by Doyle would probably be better described as 'widely accepted'. As I see it, Lewis is implicitly recognising that differences are of emphasis rather than kind, though he clearly enjoys an adversarial atmosphere in which he rejoices in his own strong left-wing political commitment and makes jokes about those who don't share it. Of Cobban's critically important *Social Interpretation* he writes that it 'asks the right questions about the Marxist interpretation of the Revolution and offers wrong answers', which sounds witty, but doesn't mean much. Most revealingly he describes Doyle's *Oxford History* as 'revisionist in tone rather than content':[23] this would seem to suggest that he himself doesn't find much to disagree with in the content, but objects to Doyle drawing attention to the errors in Marxist interpretations.

Probably the best-known book on the French Revolution by a British historian is that by Simon Schama (Professor of History and Art History at Columbia University and author of a major television series on British history broadcast in 2000). Schama did his earliest work, much of it intricately statistical, on the Dutch Republic at the time of the French Revolution. Later, making detailed use of paintings as sources, he published an original study of the Dutch Republic in the seventeenth century, *The Embarrassment of Riches: An Interpretation of Dutch Culture in the Golden Age* (1987) – though one much criticised by leading Dutch experts. His *Citizens: A Chronicle of the French Revolution* (1989) is long and lavishly illustrated because his publishers saw it as a prime commercial investment in celebration of the 200th anniversary of 1789 (nothing wrong with this: historians, I have said, cater to vital social needs; they are normal human beings with normal appetites for fame and fortune). Again Schama did very interesting work in using paintings, drawings, designs and so on as basic source materials. He also made particularly extensive use of the many memoirs, autobiographies, and published letters from the time – anything yielding personal detail and anecdote. He set out deliberately to give the reader a sense of immediacy, a sense of precisely what it was like to live through the Revolution; accordingly, the reader is taken in and out through the lives of lesser people and greater ones. Given these aims, Schama, with great skill, devised a structure for his book which would communicate them with maximum effect. He called his book a 'chronicle', partly to distance himself from those (Marxists in particular) who had sought to analyse the deeper origins and nature of the Revolution, and partly to show that he was in touch with fashionable postmodernist ideas about history being 'narrative' in much the same sense that novels are 'narrative'. But he did in fact draw heavily and knowledgeably on the most recent specialist works by professional historians. He differs from Doyle, and very obviously from Lewis, in expressing anti-Marxist views in very positive terms. He maintains that France was moving towards capitalism anyway and that the Revolution was an interruption of that development. He finds the massacres and bloodshed inexcusable. He argues that the one significant outcome of the Revolution was a new phase of more intensive war based on national citizen armies.

Despite all the recent critiques, the achievements of Lefebvre and his fellow Marxists continue to deserve recognition (remember that one can accept the 80 per cent or so of well-substantiated detail, even if one rejects the 20 per cent or so of ideology). Much of the detail that undermined the old Marxist certainties was provided by two avowed Marxists, the British historian George Rudé with his *The Crowd in History: A Study of Popular Disturbances in France and England, 1730–1848* (1981) and the French scholar Albert Soboul with his *Les Sans-culottes parisiens en l'an II* (1958, *The Parisian Sans-culottes in the Year II* – the 'sans-culottes' were the ultra-radical revolutionaries, who, in theory at least, wore working mens' trousers rather than fashionable breeches) and his *Paysans, Sans-culottes et Jacobins* (*Peasants, Sans-culottes and Jacobins* – the Jacobins being an organised group of radical revolutionaries – 1966). Soboul admitted that the Revolution could not be accurately represented as a legitimisation of the maturing power of the bourgeoisie.

The British Marxists

In recent years, there have been some strong attacks on the reputation of the British Marxist historian Christopher Hill (*b.* 1912). Partly these have been based on the fact that while Hill has an unrivalled knowledge of the published polemical literature of the seventeenth century, he has never done any work in the manuscript sources. Still, he has shared in what is the main distinguishing characteristic of the post-1945 British school of Marxist historians, an interest in ordinary people as such, rather than just in their political organisations or roles as agents of revolution. *The World Turned Up-Side-Down* (1972) is an exhilarating examination of the less well-known, 'unsuccessful', movements and experiments of the seventeenth century. There followed a major biography of Milton (1977), this venture in the direction of literature being another characteristic of this particular Marxist school.

E. P. Thompson, the major figure in Britain's 'New Left', and in the various anti-nuclear campaigns, achieved world fame with his *The Making of the English Working Class* (1963). The book, 800 pages long, is a treasure-house of fascinating information, informed by Thompson's immense erudition in all aspects of the creative literature of the early nineteenth century, and indeed of many other periods. Societies are, of course, riddled with conflicts: Thompson, like most Marxists, tends to read any example of violent confrontation, or even of dissent, as entailing class conflict. His central thesis is of the growth of a specifically 'working-class consciousness' at the beginning of the nineteenth century. On the whole, though, what he shows is the appearance of 'working-class awareness' rather than 'working-class consciousness', in the technical Marxist sense which entails class conflict. Since he was arguing that the working class was only 'made' in the early nineteenth century, he has difficulties in describing the social structure of the eighteenth century. He produced the formula that in the eighteenth century there was 'class struggle without class'; David Cannadine has wisely pointed out that it would be more accurate to say that in the eighteenth century there was 'class without class struggle'.[24] Through launching the Centre for the Study of Social History at the University of Warwick, Thompson encouraged the study 'from below' of the hidden complexities of earlier British society, particularly in the realm of 'crime' and law enforcement, seen at its best in his own *Whigs and Hunters: The Origin of the Black Act* (1975), which provides an account of the world of the foresters of Windsor and East Hampshire in the early eighteenth century, and expounds the significance of the Black Act against 'poaching'.

As will already be abundantly apparent, I do not favour the identification of 'great' historians. However, it would seem grudging indeed to withhold that accolade from Eric Hobsbawm (*b.* 1917). Belonging to a central European Jewish family, he was actually born in Egypt, and was subsequently educated at Cambridge University: his command of world cultures, languages, and the imperatives of colonialism is immense. He was the principal force behind the founding, in 1952, of the Oxford historical journal *Past and Present* which, though less publicised, can stand comparison any time with *Annales*. *Past and Present* announced itself as 'a journal of scientific [meaning Marxist] history', Marx having claimed to have invented 'scientific socialism'. In practice the journal proved to be 'scientific' in a much more desirable sense: it published articles on a wide range of subjects not conventionally featured in historical journals, and it focused from time to time on major historical controversies; above all, it insisted on the very highest standards of properly substantiated archive research. Reality was acknowledged when, in the 1970s, *Past and Present* dropped the 'scientific history' and simply announced itself as 'a journal of historical studies'.

Hobsbawm's publications clearly show his ability to deal with the distinction between the strongly held political convictions of the activist citizen and the attitudes appropriate to the scholarly historian. His journalism is very strongly coloured by Marxism, but his learned articles, as well as his books, never go further than scrupulous attention to what the evidence will allow.[25] Hobsbawm has performed a fine service to the historical profession in using his great prestige (not least with those on the left) in insisting on the paramount importance of professional integrity, and in distancing himself from those Marxists who have gone down the postmodernist track. Hobsbawm has been to the fore in separating genuine working-class history from the mere history of working-class political organisations. His interest in 'history from below' can be seen in *Primitive Rebels: Studies of Archaic Forms of Social Movement in the Nineteenth and Twentieth Centuries* (1959), *Labouring Men* (1964), and *Captain Swing* (1969), written in collaboration with George Rudé and providing a record of England's last agrarian rising, that of 1830. Over a period of almost 30 years, Hobsbawm produced three complex, superior and well-illustrated textbooks of total history covering the origins of the contemporary world: *The Age of Revolution, 1789–1848* (1962), *The Age of Capital, 1848–1875* (1975) and *The Age of Empire, 1875–1914* (1987). Then, in 1997, these were topped off with *The Age of Extremes: The Long Twentieth Century, 1914–1990.* This is *the* book on the twentieth century to which all researchers of the next generation will have to refer.

The American Marxists

To the general reader it may be surprising that some of the most committed (and also most sophisticated) Marxist history is written in the United States. Eugene Genovese (*b.* 1930) was a leading figure in the American New Left of the 1960s. The preface to his collection of essays *In Red and Black: Marxian Explorations in Southern and Afro-American History* affords a nice example of Genovese's agreeably disrespectful style:

> Ironically, it was only a few years ago that a distinguished clown, who happened to be delivering the presidential address to the American Historical Association, bemoaned the influx of the non-WASP into the historical profession. After all, how could Jews, Italians, and Irishmen possibly understand an American culture that was so profoundly Anglo-Saxon and Teutonic? Putting the two arguments together, I have concluded that I am qualified only on the history of Italian immigration – a subject I know nothing about.

Genovese attempted to address the issues of political commitment and objectivity in history. He was absolutely genuine in insisting that, whatever one's beliefs, one should always strive for objectivity; the trouble was he also genuinely believed that objective history would inevitably serve the cause of socialism – this certainly cannot be regarded as a truth universally to be acknowledged. Like so many of history's critics from the left, he also insisted that writing history was 'unavoidably political intervention'[26] when again there is no reason why this should be so, unless one takes an *a priori* Marxist or Foucauldian position.

Genovese's impressive *magnum opus* (all 800 pages of it) is *Roll Jordan Roll: The World the Slaves Made* (New York, 1974). Just as E. P. Thompson had argued that the British working class was not simply an inert mass, but active human beings reacting to their situation and their experiences, so Genovese was portraying the world of the slaves in all its fullness. Genovese was able to reject both the view (that of many black activists) that the black world was an entirely separate one from the rest of American society, and the view (that of American liberals) that blacks were destined for steady integration into multi-racial American society. Genovese was clear that the black experience was distinctively American: 'In this book I refer to the "black nation" and argue that the slaves, as an objective social class, laid the foundations for a separate black national culture while enormously enriching American culture as a whole.'[27] Throughout, Genovese uses broadly Marxist categories, implicitly arguing with the crudities of vulgar Marxism, but accepting the notions of bourgeoisie, class rule, and so on; central to his writing is the Gramscian concept of hegemony.

Genovese's compatriot Herbert Gutmann (1928–85) also left an important statement on the contemporary Marxist approach to history – I disagree with it, but it expresses a point of view worthy of attention:

What is left when you clear away the determinist and teleological elements are good questions that direct your attention to critical ways of looking at on-going historical processes. A fundamental contribution of nineteenth and twentieth-century Marxist thinking is a set of questions having to do with the way in which one examines class relations and how they change, the way in which one examines the institutionalization of power, the way in which one examines popular oppositional movements, the way in which one examines the integration of subordinate or exploited groups into a social system.[28]

Gutmann's major work was his massive *The Black Family in Slavery and Freedom, 1750–1825* (New York, 1976), stimulated, Gutmann said, by the bitter public and academic controversy touched off by Daniel P. Moynihan's *The Negro Family in America* (1965), which claimed that life in white America had destroyed the Negro family and created a 'tangle of pathology'. Gutmann's work, in fact, persuasively demonstrates the stability of black families. Genovese and Gutmann were pioneers in what quickly became a major research area: black history.

A slightly different strand of Marxism is represented in the writings of Gabriel Kolko (*b.* 1932) which, in a much more rounded and a much more quantitatively substantiated way, revealed elements of the progressive tradition. *The Triumph of Conservatism: A Re-interpretation of American History, 1900–1916* (1963) debunks the notion of the high ideals and working-class sympathies of the progressive politicians of the so-called progressive era, but states explicitly that Marxism is inadequate as an explanation of developments in America. However, the book is shaped by a general Marxist frame of reference, as was another that appeared the previous year, *Wealth and Power in America*. Kolko, at a time when there was still much faith in the classlessness of American society, brought out clearly that, just like unregenerate Europe, America did have classes, and indeed a ruling class. Subsequently, studies along these lines were pursued in proto-Marxist manner by W. William Domhoff.

Jurgen Kocka

Generally, Marxist writers (in the West) had strong political commitments, and a belief in the broad philosophy of history and social development associated with Marxism. However, the German historian Jurgen Kocka (*b.* 1941), an authority on the white-collar, lower middle class in both Germany and the United States in the late nineteenth and early twentieth centuries, avowedly distanced himself from Marxist philosophy of history while adopting a Marxist model of class for the study published in English as *Facing Total War* (Göttingen, 1973 – English translation, 1984). Kocka used a strictly Marxist definition of 'objective class position', that is to say class position as defined by relationship to the dominant mode of production. He wrote:

> their objective class position was not the defining condition for the life-styles, expectations, organisation and political behaviour of either white-collar employees or of *Handwerker* [craftsmen] and *Kleinhändler* [small tradesmen]. Both groups organised themselves predominantly against those whose class position they shared; the *Kleinhändler* disassociated themselves from large-scale capital and industry, white-collar employees from the working class. Together they formed a significant factor by which Wilhelmine society was distinguished from a clearly marked, dichotomous class society. Encouraged by the state, they acted as a sort of padding, which somewhat muffled the growing class conflict. During the War, this padding was ripped apart.

Kocka set up his classical Marxist dichotomous model, showing how it diverged from reality in 1914, then arguing that the effect of the war was to bring Germany much closer to this model. His basic contention was that the Marxist model is the most effective one available for his purposes, that the model 'served as an instrument for historical understanding by permitting the description and explanation of the variable "distance" between model and reality'. Kocka's experiment in the use of theory was much praised, and also much criticised. In the 'Afterword' to the English translation, Kocka dealt very fairly (though to me, unpersuasively) with some of the main criticisms.

4 *Annales*: The Second and Third Generations

Braudel

At the end of the Second World War there was in France a determination to break with many of the aspects of the old France. The history of Bloch and Febvre now had a special appeal, an appeal recognised in the creation of a new institutional framework. *Annales*, the journal, was revived in 1946 as *Annales: Économies, Sociétés, Civilisations* (usually abbreviated to *Annales E.S.C.*); a new Sixth Section of the École Pratique des Hautes Études was established, with Febvre as first president – here research of the sort favoured by *Annales* could be carried out. The protagonists of the approaches favoured in *Annales* had thus gained the prestige, and the material assets, of an institutional base. A variety of new approaches were developed, but the irreducible essence remained an openness to, and a co-operation with, other disciplines, particularly in the social sciences.

The dominant figure in the second generation of *Annales* (and some would say the dominant figure in contemporary historical writing) was Fernand Braudel (1902–83). Braudel did not start out in the profession as a pioneer and innovator, fully formed. Indeed, the doctoral topic he took up following his undergraduate studies at the Sorbonne was a very conventional one in diplomatic history, concerning the foreign policy of the Spanish king Philip II who ruled from 1556 to 1598, when the Spanish Empire, though beginning to be undermined, was at its peak, with possessions not just in South America but in Italy, the Low Countries, and North Africa. Braudel's working title was 'Philip II and the Mediterranean'. As is the custom in France he took a job as a schoolteacher, though, rather crucially in his case, at a school in Algeria. The first learned article he wrote, a substantial one published in two parts, showed that he was already moving far from traditional diplomatic history: indeed, he criticised his predecessors for their conventional concerns and instead concentrated on the nature of the lives lived by Spanish soldiers in their Algerian garrisons, and on how their deployment in North African campaigns depended upon there being no war in Europe. Following this Braudel took absolutely crucial steps towards his eventual fame by working in a great range of archives: in Simancas in Spain, and in Genoa, Florence, Palermo, Venice, Marseilles, and Dubrovnik. There was no escaping the immense legwork, but Braudel did ingeniously bring technology to his aid by sometimes taking photocopies of the documents using an American cine-camera.[29] He spent two years teaching in Brazil, then on the way back met Lucien Febvre. Febvre's advice completed the process whereby Braudel switched from working on 'Philip II and the Mediterranean' to working on 'the Mediterranean and Philip II'.[30] The whole approach of the first *Annales* school, including the emphasis on geography, was a strong influence; another, according to Peter Burke, was Henri Pirenne, who had drawn attention to the importance of the earlier confrontation of Muslims and Christians across the Mediterranean.

Braudel had accumulated a fantastic amount of new raw material, but he had not yet written it up when war broke out. Serving in the French army, he was taken prisoner by the Germans, and spent the rest of the war in a prisoner-of-war camp. Blessed with powers of memory which most of us can only envy, and, it should be said, complete mastery of his subject, he wrote up his thesis in exercise books which he posted to Febvre. The thesis, 'La Méditerranée et le monde méditerranéen à l' époque de Philippe II', was (successfully!) presented for examination in 1947, and published in 1949, in which same year Braudel was appointed to a chair at the Collège de France. He was effectively sole head of *Annales* from 1957 to 1975.

The Mediterranean is a massive work of 600,000 words. It is, accordingly, a very comprehensive, detailed, thoroughly source-based coverage of its stated subject: it seeks not just to ask the 'what actually happened?' of the original rather conventional thesis subject, but still more 'what was it actually like to live in that large and variegated "region" at that time?'; and, most of all, 'what were the deeper geographical imperatives, ways of doing things, structures and constraints within which events and individual human actions took place?' The book itself is structured into three distinct parts, this structure, as it always must in an acceptable piece of historical writing, reflecting how Braudel believed the developments in, and aspects of, the past he was interested in came about and were related to each other. Braudel's illustrious predecessors Febvre and Bloch had always insisted that history must be oriented towards the solving of problems (as distinct, say, from the mere narrating of events). Peter Burke questioned Braudel about the problem posed in *The Mediterranean*: 'My great problem, the only problem I had to resolve, was to show that time moves at different speeds' was the reply.[31] Each part of the tripartite structure coincides with a different 'speed': the use of 'time' is metaphorical – what Braudel really meant was the different speeds of different kinds of change, or lack of it. It is best to quote from Braudel's own words from the preface to the book, where, actually, he speaks of three kinds of 'history':

The first part is devoted to a history whose passage is almost imperceptible, that of man in his relationship to the environment, a history in which all change is slow, a history of constant repetition, ever-recurring cycles. I could not neglect this almost timeless history, the story of man's contact with the inanimate, neither could I be satisfied with the traditional geographical introduction to history that often figures to little purpose at the beginning of so many books, with the descriptions of the mineral deposits, types of agriculture, and typical flora, briefly listed and never mentioned again, as if the flowers did not come back every spring, the flocks of sheep migrate every year, or the ships sail on a real sea that changes with the seasons.

On a different level from the first there can be distinguished another history, this time with slow but perceptible rhythms. If the expression had not been diverted from its full meaning, one could call it *social history*, the history of groups and groupings. How did these swelling currents affect Mediterranean life in general – this was the question I asked myself in the second part of the book, studying in turn economic systems, states, societies, civilisations, and finally, in order to convey more clearly my conception of history, attempting to show how all these deep-seated forces were at work in the complex arena of warfare. For war, as we know, is not an arena governed purely by individual responsibilities.

Lastly, the third part gives a hearing to traditional history – history, one might say, on the scale not of man, but of individual men, what Paul Lacombe and François Simiand called *'l'histoire évènementielle'*, that is, the history of events: surface disturbances, crests of foam that the tides of history carry on their strong backs. A history of brief, rapid, nervous fluctuations, by definition ultra-sensitive; the least tremor sets all its antennae quivering. But as such also the most dangerous. We must learn to distrust this history with its still burning passions, as it was felt, described, and lived by contemporaries whose lives were as short and short-sighted as ours.[32]

The first kind of history, with its own pace of change, or rather absence of it, became known to Braudel and the *Annales* school as *la longue durée* (always rendered in French since the literal translation, 'the long duration', does not quite capture the spirit of the original). Two other famous concepts lie at the heart of the kind of slow change dealt with in Part Two: *structure* – economic systems, states, societies, civilisations, and the changing forms of war – and *conjoncture* (the English 'conjuncture' with an 'o' instead of a 'u') – trade cycles, population trends, and so on (Part Two is entitled 'Collective Destinies and General Trends'). As well as being fundamentally deterministic, Braudel was enough of a Marxist to use the word 'treason' in referring to those successful members of the bourgeoisie who joined the nobility – in reality joining the nobility (not overthrowing it) is the eternal proclivity of successful members of the bourgeoisie. Yet, for the heir to Febvre, he said remarkably little on mentalities. More, perhaps, than many lesser historians, Braudel was well aware that, like all historians, he had simply made a contribution to knowledge (even if a massive one), not a total and unassailable statement completely replacing everything that had gone before. In 1966 he published a second edition with many revisions and extensions, including new material on the rural sector, and a discussion, headed 'Can a Model be Made of the Mediterranean Economy?', of the relationships between production, consumption, exchange and distribution. Even so he *complained* that while the original edition had been much praised it had been too little criticised.[33]

Braudel's three 'kinds of history' has not become a universal template for historians, but his elegant and daring exposition certainly drove home as never before the different levels of change and of causation historians must deal with. In practice, it very much depends upon the particular topic a historian is investigating. A topic confined to a few months or years will not usually require quite the same approach as one spreading over a century or more. What it is perhaps too easy to forget is that Braudel did deal with events and political leaders. Historians must always continue to write relatively short and relatively highly specialised works, but if I were to make an attempt at defining the finest work of today, I would say that it follows Braudel in trying to integrate events and politics with accounts both of how life is lived by the majority of people and of the deeper constraints upon, and forces making for, change. Braudel's *The Mediterranean* runs across political units and local cultures (whose characteristics he recognises, though perhaps insufficiently): in this sense he has that comparative quality which, again, is often a characteristic of the best work being done today.

Braudel's immediate contemporaries were noted for their work in quantitative history: Labrousse, whom I have already discussed, was probably instrumental in persuading Braudel to strengthen the quantitative elements in the second edition of *The Mediterranean*, represented by a plethora of tables and graphs. *Seville et l'Atlantique* (*Seville and the Atlantic*, 1955–60) by Pierre Chaunu (*b.* 1923) bore some resemblances to Braudel's famous work, but essentially it concentrated on economic aspects, the ones which can most easily be quantified. Much the same could be said about *Beauvais et les Beauvaisis de 1600 à 1730* (*Beauvais and its Inhabitants*, 1960) by Pierre Goubert (*b.* 1915) – both books were divided into two parts, 'Structure' and 'Conjoncture'. Robert Mandrou (1921–84), author of *De la culture populaire aux 17e et 18e siècles* (*On Popular Culture in the 17th and 18th Centuries*, 1964), insisted on maintaining the tradition of concentrating on mentalities: in 1962 there was a bitter parting of the ways from Braudel. The quantitative trend showed itself in the development of historical demography, but since that sub-history was not specifically an *Annales* initiative, I shall take it separately.

Braudel's second major work was much more strongly quantitative than the first. The original idea had actually come from Febvre, for a two-volume history of that critical period in which the world had moved from bare subsistence and constant economic insecurity to a time when the way was clear for industrialisation and economic progress, roughly from 1400 to 1800. Febvre was to do a volume (never written) on 'thought and belief' while Braudel was to concentrate on the history of material life. His *Civilisation matérielle et capitalisme* appeared in three volumes between 1967 and 1979; the first volume, translated as *Capitalism and Material Life 1400–1800* came out in 1973, just a year after the translation of *The Mediterranean* – this was the point at which Braudel achieved world-wide fame. A revised edition of the entire book, retitled *Les structures du quotidien*, was published in 1979, with the English translation, *The Structures of Everyday Life*, coming out in 1981.

With respect to the future development of the discipline of history, three points need to be made. First, Braudel had genuinely written a work of *global history*, touching on Africa, and going into some detail on Asia and the Americas. In his original title, Braudel had introduced the concept of '*civilisation matérielle*', always rendered in English as 'material *culture*' – most regrettably given the overload that weary word is already subjected to. Braudel's basic definition was 'repeated actions, empirical processes, old methods and solutions handed down from time immemorial', but he placed an emphasis too on physical artefacts, furniture, tools, and so forth. As we have seen, this concept was then overlaid with that of 'the structures of everyday life', Braudel declaring in his new introduction that his aim was 'the introduction of everyday life into the domain of history': Braudel was not the first to attempt this, but he was the first to do it so comprehensively, and in so doing effectively established a further new sub-history, sometimes going under the title of 'history of private life'. Braudel still gave little attention to mentalities, but he was now keen to stress quantities. The first chapter of his first volume is 'The Weight of Numbers'. The chapters which follow indicate what he meant by everyday life: 'Daily Bread', 'Food and Drink', 'Houses, Clothes and Fashion', 'The Spread of Technology', 'Money', 'Towns'. No doubt that, for all the rich detail, for all the fascinating by-ways explored, Braudel was addressing a central problem. The three conditions necessary for the successful development of capitalism, he said, were:

(1) A developing market economy (a necessary, but not sufficient, condition);

(2) The development over a long period of societies favourable to continuous wealth accumulation and to some social mobility with secure hierarchies;

(3) The impetus of world trade.[34]

Great works of art, I have noted, are not revised or 'updated'. History is different. Braudel invited criticism, and produced revised versions (and even revised titles!) of his massive works. Just to be clear: *Civilisation matérielle et capitalisme*, published in French in 1967, was published in English in 1973 as *Capitalism and Material Life 1400–1800*; the revised version, *Les structures du quotidien*, came in 1979, with the English translation, *The Structures of Everyday Life*, in 1981; *Les jeux de l'échange* and *Le temps du monde* were published in 1979, followed in 1982 and 1983 respectively by English versions whose titles, though not precise, got the sense well enough: *The Wheels of Commerce* and *The Perspective of the World*.

Annales: The Third Generation

As we move to the third generation of *Annales* historians, it is much more difficult to separate developments that were specific to that school from developments that were common to the most advanced historical writing everywhere. The general developments I shall pick up in the final section of this chapter, here simply identifying the leading figures institutionally affiliated to *Annales*. The exploration of mentalities, slighted by Braudel, was resumed and extended by Georges Duby (*b*. 1919), whose *Les trois ordres* (1978; English translation, *The Three Orders*, Chicago, 1980) examines perceptions of medieval society as being divided into three 'orders', priests, knights and peasants, and Jacques Le Goff (*b*. 1924), whose *La naissance du purgatoire* (1981; *The Birth of Purgatory*, 1984) analysed the part played in 'the medieval imagination' of changing representations of the afterlife. Emmanuel Le Roy Ladurie (*b*. 1929), with his *Les paysans de Languedoc* (1966; American abbreviated version, *The Peasants of Languedoc*, 1974), evoked comparisons, and contrasts, with his teacher, Braudel. This attempt at 'total history' over a period of more than 200 years, roughly (1500–1700), is not structured into different 'layers' depending on pace of change, but into three chronological periods, dependent on fundamental economic movements. In a manner which is again distinctive of many historians today, Le Roy Ladurie neatly integrated striking accounts of events and of everyday life and belief into his basically quantitative history.

Le Roy Ladurie achieved international best-sellerdom with *Montaillou Village Occitan* (1975; translated into English as *Montaillou: Cathars and Catholics in a French Village 1294–1324*, 1978). Given my running commentary on the importance of archive research, I should point out that the Inquisition Register of Jacques Fournière, Bishop of Pamiers, on which the book was based, had actually been published by another scholar in 1965.[35] Le Roy Ladurie's contribution was, first, to see the possibility of producing a work of historical significance, and, secondly, to apply the skills of a historian open to the influences of social psychology and anthropology to producing a book which first studied the material culture of the village, and then the mentalities of the villagers. Although the success was not quite repeated by *Le Carnaval de Romans* (1979; *Carnival: A People's Uprising at Romans 1579–1580*, 1980), Le Roy Ladurie's celebrity status was assured. This does not automatically make him a faultless historian; but the media attention accorded to him, as well as to Braudel and to some of their associates, does demonstrate what nonsense it is to talk of history being in a 'state of crisis'. With regard to an important development in the discipline of history, we could record Le Roy Ladurie as an important proponent of 'micro-history' – using one episode in one place to draw out wider conclusions. He is also, of course, very much an *auteur*.

Apart from his work relating to the French Revolution (already mentioned), François Furet is important for his work, with which several people were involved, in applying quantitative methods (viable computers were now widely available) to cultural, as distinct from economic, matters and, in particular, to book publication. Furet directed the research team which produced the rigorously quantitative study *Book and Society in Eighteenth-Century France* (Paris, 1965–70). From English political philosophers and American historians has come the notion of 'political culture', while an older third-generation *Annales* figure, Maurice Agulhon (b. 1926), has introduced the now fashionable concept of *sociabilité* – referring to the networks and circles which produce clusters of shared political ideas.

It is through the history of the book, and what he calls 'the culture of print', that Roger Chartier (b. 1945) has emerged as the brightest young star as the *Annales* firmament merges into that of the wider historical universe. Chartier represents this merging in that he is as much part of what the Americans call the 'New Cultural History' as he is a member of the *Annales* school. The proponents of the New Cultural History variously acknowledged the influence of, in addition to Foucault, the American anthropologist Clifford Geertz, the German-born sociologist Norbert Elias, and the American critic of non-metaphysical history Hayden White. Before coming to them, I must mention another way in which the greater world outside impinged on *Annales*: for the first time female historians were encouraged and acknowledged. After a slightly traditional study of French workers on strike, *Les Ouvriers en grève – France 1871–1890* (*Workers on Strike*, Paris, 1974), Michelle Perrot has collaborated with Duby on a massive general history of women from antiquity to the present, *Histoire des femmes, de l'Antiquité à nos jours* (5 volumes,

Paris, 1991). Mona Ozouf did a fine, and characteristically *Annales*, study of festivals during the Revolution, *La Fête révolutionnaire, 1789–1799* (Paris, 1976), and Arlette Farge produced an excellent study of everyday life in the streets of Paris in the eighteenth century, *Vivre dans la rue à Paris au XVIIIe siècle* (Paris, 1979).

5   New Economic History, New Social History, History of Science, New Cultural History

In 1980 the press of one of the American Ivy League universities, Cornell, published a book rather characteristic of the fads and fancies of the American historical profession, *The Past Before Us: Contemporary Historical Writing in the United States*.[36] This offered a kind of Super League, feverishly assessing the current standing of the different sub-histories: intellectual history 'dethroned'; both the 'new' and 'cultural' history and the 'new' political history riding high; with, no doubt, both 'old' political history and 'old' cultural history up for sale; in other words, masses of information on *what* historians were doing in the previous decade (together with their anxieties over sub-histories in decline and hysterical triumphalism over 'new' ones on the way up) but nothing on *why* or *how* they were doing it. Of course, there are always hopes of improving one's career prospects by allying oneself with what is alleged to be the new dynamic, even revolutionary, approach to history, and one can always manufacture books with titles like *The New Cultural History*, or *Beyond the Cultural Turn: New Directions in the Study of Society and Culture*.[37] The scope of history is very wide (and the *Annales* school, and the 'new' social historians, cultural historians, and, indeed, economic historians, have played a laudable part in extending that scope): the specific approach to be followed must, provided always that it falls within the established, though constantly developing, canons of the profession, be determined by the topics addressed, whether they be political, diplomatic, military, social, or all-embracing. As I conclude this chapter with a survey of the sorts of history being done at the beginning of a new century, I want to stress variety and scope, as well as rigour, sophistication, reflexiveness, emphasis on congruence between structural and quantitative circumstances and lived personal experiences, sensitivity to the significance of events and awareness of the importance of comparative approaches.

New Economic History

Two new forms of economic history, deeply rooted in the methods of economic science, developed in the post-war years. The first was a form which had already gained wide acceptance and which was concerned with concepts of economic growth and the study of national economic statistics in the aggregate. This kind of economic history was pioneered in the United States by Simon Kuznets: it was due to his initiative that in 1950 the International Association for Research in Income and Wealth decided to embark on a series of analyses of the evolutions in national income, national wealth, and their components for various countries, and that in 1956 the Social Science Research Council (of the USA) created a fund to finance research on economic growth in the various countries in the nineteenth and twentieth centuries. These initiatives were developed in France by Jean Marczewski (b. 1908), by Phyllis Deane (b. 1918) in Britain, and by W. G. Hoffmann and G. H. Muller in Germany. More controversial is the form of economic history called, boringly, the 'new economic history', or, pretentiously, 'cliometrics', or, most sensibly, 'econometric' history.

In a model exposition for British historians entitled 'The New Economic History' (1968), E. H. Hunt suggested that econometric history has three aspects.[38] The first actually differs only in degree from the approach long pursued by most economic historians: much greater emphasis is placed on statistical method and upon precision of definition and categorisation, and computers are enlisted to carry out calculations which formerly would have been impossible. We may note here, incidentally, that the extensive computerisation of historical study came in the 1960s and 1970s: spectacular recent developments in IT have really been very largely to do with the accessing and storing of information, and with *communicating* new mixes of printed information, imagery, and sound (as with CD-Roms). The second aspect of econometric history, the enlistment of economic and statistical theory in order to reconstruct 'measurements which might have existed in the past but are no longer extant' – to use the words of a leading econometric historian, R. W. Fogel (b. 1926) – is again a matter of degree rather than a complete break with older methods. Indirect quantification of a rather unsophisticated sort had been used, for example, in the standard of living controversy centring on the British Industrial Revolution (in which two leading protagonists were Eric Hobsbawm and R. M. Hartwell), or in tracing the expansion of a money economy in nineteenth-century Ireland through sales of Guinness beer. The indirect quantification of the econometric historians draws upon a much more sophisticated armoury: regression analysis, rent, input–output and location theory, hyper-geometric distribution, and the von Neumann-Morgenstern utility index. 'The third aspect of economic history', Hunt explained,

the most distinctive and ambitious is the use of the counter-factual conditional concept, starting with the premise that we can understand the significance of what did happen only if we contrast it with what might have happened, and going on to quantify 'what might have happened'.[39]

The most famous exponent of the counter-factual conditional concept is R. W. Fogel, who, in challenging the long-standing thesis about the central importance of American railroads in the expansion of the American economy, constructed a model of the American economy as it would have been *without* railroads: the American gross national product in 1890 would, he reckoned, have been only 6.3 per cent lower than it actually was. The sophisticated quantitative methods of the econometric historians spread first to social history and then to what some practitioners called 'cultural history'. Most recently, the young British historian Niall Ferguson (*b.* 1964) has argued, not altogether persuasively, that counter-factual techniques should be applied to political and diplomatic history.[40]

The potential of econometric techniques is immense, as it is for getting things wrong. That point was brought out with pyrotechnic effect in one of the most colourful historical controversies of the 1970s, that over *Time on the Cross: The Economics of American Negro Slavery* (1974) by R. W. Fogel and Stanley L. Engerman. Fogel and Engerman claimed that over the previous 15 years or so 'the cliometricians' had been able to amass, and make use of, a more complete body of information on the operation of the slave system than had ever been available previously: this showed, they claimed, that slavery was a rational and economically viable institution and, more controversially, that conditions among slaves were no worse than those of poor white workers, with family life among slaves being stable and healthy. Paul A. David, Herbert G. Gutmann, Richard Sutch, Peter Temin and Gavin Wright devoted a whole volume, *Reckoning with Slavery: A Critical Study in the Quantitative History of American Negro Slavery* (1976), to a line-by-line criticism of *Time on the Cross*:

> The authors of this volume have sought to judge *Time on the Cross* on its own merits, according to the standards of the discipline from which it claims to derive. Toward this end we have attempted, collaboratively, to reproduce every important statistical manipulation, check every significant citation, re-examine every striking quotation, re-think every critical chain of inference and question every major conclusion in Fogel and Engerman's book. To our surprise and dismay, we have found that *Time on the Cross* is full of errors. The book embraces errors of mathematics, disregards standard principles of statistical inference, mis-cites sources, takes quotations out of context, distorts the views and findings of other historians and economists, and relies upon dubious and largely unexplicated models of market

behaviour, economic dynamics, socialization, sexual behaviour, fertility determination, and genetics (to name some).

... When the faults are corrected and the evidence is re-examined, every striking assertion made in *Time on the Cross* is cast into doubt. The effect in many instances is to restore and reinforce more orthodox conclusions hitherto shared by conventional and quantitatively orientated students of the peculiar institution [i.e. slavery].[41]

In history, it is not good enough (for any length of time at any rate!) to produce some highly personal, attention-gathering, apparently revolutionary thesis; everything, as I keep saying, is subject to scrutiny by professional colleagues.

Historical Demography, Urban History, History of the Family, of Childhood and of Death

Quantification lies at the heart of the most important single development in the immediate post-war years, that in historical demography – covering births, deaths, fertility rates, family composition, population growth and movements. The critical advance was the development in the mid-1950s of the technique known as family reconstitution. Instead of using the aggregate figures of the census reports, which only exist for the modern era, information was built up from sources, such as parish registers, in which individuals are named. The first study was carried through by Louis Henry (1911–91), of the French Institut National d'Études Démographiques, into the bourgeois families of Geneva, and published in 1956 as *Anciennes Familles Genevoises*. Independently there emerged a group of English historians, E. A. Wrigley, D. E. C. Eversley, R. S. Schofield, and Peter Laslett, who in 1962 founded the Cambridge Group for the History of Population and Social Structure. The methods and operations involved in, and the fruitful possibilities of, family reconstitution using English parish registers were explained in the book edited by Wrigley, *An Introduction to English Historical Demography* (1966); some of the more dramatic aspects of the work, including the discovery that despite 'evidence' drawn, say, from the plays of Shakespeare, marriage ages for ordinary people in the pre-industrial world were very high (late 20s), were publicised in *The World We Have Lost* (1965) by Laslett.

Historical demography was central to many important topics, some, such as the family, only just coming to be fully recognised, some, such as the 'population explosion' of the late eighteenth century, long a matter of contention. A considerable body of precise work threw into disrepute the thesis which had associated rising population with a falling death rate which in turn was associated with alleged improvements in medicine, environment, and so on. It is now as well established as such matters can be that, whatever was happening to the death rate, there was in the middle and later eighteenth century a very definite rise in the birth rate; not to put too fine a point upon it, people were copulating earlier and more often. Developments in historical demography made possible a new 'urban history', fulfilling what Asa Briggs, a pioneer urban historian in Britain, called 'the need to examine in detail social structure and change in the most meaningful units that historians can discover', and providing 'knowledge of local relationships and pressures'.[42] In France the demographic stimulus to the study of urban history came from the Institut National d'Études Démographiques: important figures are Adeline Daumard, Pierre Goubert and Louis Chevalier. In America the Chicago School of Urban Sociology was a strong influence. From his work on immigrant groups (*Boston's Immigrants* (1941); *The Uprooted* (1951)) Oscar Handlin moved into urban history, and in 1963 he, with John Burchard, edited the important collection of studies *The Historian and the City* (1963). An important work in showing how the extent of, and limitations upon, social mobility could be accurately traced was *Poverty and Progress: Social Mobility in a Nineteenth-Century City* (1964) by Stephen Thernstrom, in which ordinary families in Newbury Port, Massachusetts, were followed across three generations.

From historical demography, to urban history, to the family, showing along the way that such categories interrelate and overlap; probably the best label a historian can pin on himself/herself is 'historian', proudly celebrating the achievements of the entire profession, rather than identifying with one sect, and endorsing the implication that everyone else has got it wrong. As a historical topic, the family is a good one for demonstrating the way in which, as I explained in Chapter 2, historians challenge myths; and also the way in which historians come up with new concepts and theses, which are themselves then challenged and qualified. Within, or related to, the family we can identify such further sub-specialisms as 'History of Childhood', 'History of Sexuality', and 'History of Death'. It is worth noting the full and correct title of the famous work published in 1960 by Philippe Ariès (1914–82): *L'Enfant et la vie familiale sous l'ancien régime*, which means *The Child and Family Life under the Ancien Régime* (the title of the English revision, which, revealingly, did not appear for another dozen years, was the vacuous *Centuries of Childhood*). Ariès was an amateur historian (a 'Sunday' historian, he called himself) – though he very quickly got caught up within the French historical profession, *and* he had had a training as a historical demographer. More important, he came from a right-wing Monarchist family (his parents always made sure to be well clear of Paris on Bastille day!); it is a complete myth that all innovation in history comes from those with left-wing leanings. Ariès made great use of visual evidence in arguing that the concept of 'childhood' only came into existence in the seventeenth century: previously, he argued, children were treated more or less like domestic pets up to the age of seven, and then as miniature adults. Almost single-handedly, Ariès had created a rich new sub-history, 'History of Childhood'. This is the way it goes: later researchers used a great wealth of archive material to show that Ariès's deductions drawn from visual representations were unjustified and that there was much written evidence of parents showing great affection for and understanding of their children well before the seventeenth century; Ariès was also faulted for drawing general conclusions from purely French evidence (a common French vice!). Ariès had partly created, partly reinforced, a myth about the treatment of children.

More generally, myths had developed about the existence of a 'traditional' family, highly stable and undisturbed by such disruptions as divorce – in fact, it could very readily be disrupted by the death of either the husband or the wife. A lesser myth was that for much of the past the family was a purely economic unit; linked to that was the myth that families were concerned only about the eldest son – charged, according to the myth, with perpetuating the family's fortunes. The most complicated myth was the one that there has been a universal change from the large 'extended' family of the past to the smaller 'nuclear' one of the present, partly based on a confusion between 'family' (consisting of close blood relatives) and 'household' (including servants, retainers, young house-guests from other families, usually in some kind of 'apprenticeship' relationship or such like). While extended *households* were common among the very wealthy, they were non-existent among the poor.

In his *The Family, Sex and Marriage in England from 1500–1800* (1977), Lawrence Stone (1919–99), an important British protagonist of quantitative methods in social history, and then, subsequently, of the study of mentalities, rather echoed Ariès in 'discovering' the emergence of what he called 'Affective Individualism' from the 1640s onwards. This, he claimed, led to the family being based on love and affection, rather than being a purely economic unit. Stone had set up a framework for others to operate within, and, as so often, found sharp criticisms being made of his central thesis. Changing sexual attitudes and sexual behaviour was a central theme in *Familles: Parentée, maison, sexualité dans l'ancienne société* (*Families: Kinship, Home, Sexuality in Former Times*) (Paris, 1976) by Jean-Louis Flandrin. Sex had become a subject which historians could treat openly. The taboo in contemporary society was over the discussion of death. Again, Ariès was something of a pioneer: his *L'Homme devant la mort* (*Man in Front of Death*) of 1977 appeared in English, again in a silly translation, as *The Hour of Our Death* in 1981. Death is now a very lively industry.

Feminist History: History of Women

There was a tendency in historical works to treat women largely with respect to their role within the family, though there had been studies of their role in industry, such as Ivy Pinchbeck's *Women Workers and the Industrial Revolution* (1930). Then writing about women in the past became very strongly influenced by the new feminist movement which came into existence around 1969, women now being treated as independent individuals, but subject to the unjust domination of men. Many of the new generation of feminist historians were strongly Marxist, representing women, and the family, as simply cogs in the capitalist system of exploitation. Some adopted the concept of 'patriarchy' – allegedly the system in which men dominate and exploit women, in the way in which, Marxists claimed, capitalists dominate and exploit the workers. The strongest individual influences were those of Simone de Beauvoir, whose *Le Deuxième Sexe* (1948; *The Second Sex*, 1954) had been the first book powerfully to present the case that femininity is not biologically based, but is socially constructed, and Michel Foucault with his notion of discursive practices shaped by the general culture of the age, and his assertion that the human (and, specifically, the female) body itself forms a valuable site for revealing the prejudices and preoccupations within that culture. Much of the earliest work originated in the United States, often, characteristically, in the form of collaborative ventures, collections of essays, as with *Suffer and Be Still: Women in the Victorian Age* (Indiana, 1972), edited by Martha Vicinus, *Becoming Visible: Women in European History* (Boston, 1977), edited by Renata Bridenthal and Claudia Koonz – containing, among other things, the interesting question posed by Joan Kelly-Gadol, 'Did Women have a Renaissance?' – and *Women, War and Revolution* (New York, 1980), edited by Carol R. Burkin and Clara M. Lovett. Judith C. Brown, *Immodest Acts: The Life of a Lesbian Nun in Renaissance Italy* (New York, 1985) is a most original scholarly monograph. The diligent scrutiny of new and difficult archive materials has yielded invaluable new knowledge and understanding. One sometimes wonders whether the deliberate resort to the opacities and unsubstantiated assertions of Foucauldian postmodernism really adds anything apart from career credibility in certain narrow circles; but then no historical work is perfect and the 20 per cent rule must always be kept in mind. Volume I (covering 1500–1800) of *The Prospect Before Her: A History of Women in Western Europe* (1995), by Olwen Hufton, author of *The Poor of Eighteenth-Century France* (Oxford, 1974), is of such force and interest that one eagerly awaits Volume II. On page 3, Hufton gives a persuasive account (it does not quite persuade me!) of the influence of Foucault, Lévi-Strauss, and other non-historians: I shall quote this shortly when I come to the 'New Cultural History'.

The History of Science, Medicine and Technology

There was a time when history of science tended to be written by scientists themselves, which meant that the history was rather naïve. Understanding the most recent developments in science is beyond the understanding of most scholars, whether historians or not, scientists within their own specialist fields apart. The subject, furthermore, has become embroiled in the 'science wars', a very virulent form of the arguments already mentioned, over the epistemological status of science rather than history. Much effort has been directed towards attempting to establish that science is culturally constructed. When Foucault came to submit his first major work for his doctorate, it was unacceptable both to historians and to philosophers, and was thus presented as a work in history of science. Ever since, therefore, one branch of the subject has been strongly influenced by Foucauldian relativism. One of those arresting-sounding works, seeming to offer answers to everything, which are read too uncritically, and accepted too readily, was *The Structure of Scientific Revolutions* (Chicago, 1962) by Thomas S. Kuhn (1922–96). This purported to explain why scientists concentrate on certain problems at certain times, and how 'paradigm shifts' come about, leading to a concentration on different problems. To put the matter politely, the book was received more enthusiastically by sociologists than by scientists. Historians certainly are not obliged to accept its formulaic and broadly relativist approach.

Only in the late 1950s and during the 1960s did the fully professional sub-history emerge which is best comprehended within the title 'The History of Science, Medicine, and Technology'. The pioneers at that time were: in America, G. C. Gillispie, author of *Genesis and Geology* (1951), Henry Guerlac, and David Landes, author of *The Unbound Prometheus* (1966), a study of technological innovation and industrial change; in Britain, A. C. Crombie; and in France, Alexandre Koyré, author of *From the Closed World to the Infinite Universe* (1957).

Recently, as in general history, there have been discussions over the function and status of biography[43] – in science history, perhaps even more than in political history, it is difficult to avoid recognising the outstanding significance of certain individuals such as Isaac Newton, William Harvey, Robert Boyle, Charles Darwin, Thomas Edison, Albert Einstein. Few historians get to write what can absolutely be termed indispensable works, but that label does seem applicable to, say, *Never at Rest: A Biography of Isaac Newton* (1980) by Richard S. Westfall (an American) and *Albert Einstein: A Biography* by Albrecht Fölsing (a German), the English translation of which, by Ewald Osers, was published in New York in 1997. Both of these books run to around 900 pages, and each is the product of about two decades' work. Both authors insist on the need to put a very full (and therefore very difficult) treatment of their subject's scientific achievements at the centre of their works; at the same time, they are very self-conscious about their tasks *as historians*. Westfall points out that before 1945 biographers of Newton (of the traditional scientific orientation) made use simply of Newton's published works; historians now have to go to the original manuscripts, tracing out the evolution of ideas, noting the false starts and the wrong turnings. Biographers today also have an invaluable aid to research in that the Royal Society has published Newton's *Correspondence in Seven Volumes*. There are also massive printed editions of the letters and other incidental writings of Einstein. Using these and the enormous range of scientific works, Fölsing did not actually need to work among manuscripts in the archives, but produced a full and sensitively human biography, though:

> The most important aspect to me, always, was Einstein's physics. Physics was at the core of his identity, and only through physics can we get close to him as a seeker after truth.[44]

Fölsing mentions the names Marx and Foucault – but both are genuine scientists, Wilhelm Marx and Jean-Bernard Foucault.
Westfall tells us that he set out

> to avoid composing an essay on Newtonian science. At the same time I have sought to make Newton the scientist the central character of my drama. While he devoted himself extensively to other activities which a biography cannot ignore, from theology on one hand to administration of the Mint on the other, Newton holds our attention only because he was a scientist of transcendent importance.[45]

Hence, Westfall explains, he thinks of his work as a 'scientific biography', which he then goes on very neatly to distinguish from both a work of science or a work of philosophy. His is

> a biography in which Newton's scientific career furnishes the central theme. My goal has been to present his science, not as the finished product which has done so much to shape the whole of the modern intellect, but as the developing endeavour of a living man confronting it as problems still to be solved. Scientists and philosophers can probe the finished product. My interest in this biography centers exactly on what was not yet complete, the object of Newton's own activity, the substance of a life devoted to probing the unknown. I have tried to present his scientific endeavours in the context of his life, first in Woolsthorpe and Grantham, then in Cambridge, and finally in London.[46]

With regard to the question of addressing the general reader, it may be noted that Westfall subsequently published a brief *The Life of Isaac Newton*, leaving out the mathematics. Biographies of Darwin, both 'specialist' and 'popular', are legion. *Darwin* (1991) by Adrian Desmond and James Moore was unashamedly designed to be a best-seller: it is an example of *auteur* theory with a strong infusion of postmodernist relativism.

There has been important work on scientific institutions and scientific communities, often making use of the prosopographic approaches I mentioned in connection with Namier: Arnold Thackray has been a notable figure in this context. Science outside of the West has still not been greatly written about, though it has not been entirely neglected: as I've said, I am not keen on the word 'great' where works of history are concerned, but one can scarcely withhold it from the multi-volume *Science and Civilisation in China*, very much the product of the massive pioneering work of Joseph Needham, and published from 1954 onwards.

New Social History

Behind the declaration of the advent in Britain of 'The New Social History' lay strong political motivations; in many respects it was in effect 'The New Socialist History'. It was inclined towards a trendy denim-suit jargon, talking about individuals and groups 'finding space', and favouring such concepts as 'ideology', 'hegemony', 'moral panics' (almost always a gross hyperbole), and, above all 'social control'. All this was particularly true of the British journals *Social History* (1975) and *History Workshop Journal* (1976, avowedly a journal of socialist history); less so of the *Journal of Social History* (1967, USA) and the Social History Society (UK, 1977). There was a distinctive new social history in Germany, going under the general title of *Strukturgeschichte* (structural history). At Heidelberg, Werner Conze (*b*. 1910) set up a 'Working Circle for Modern Social History' and edited a series entitled 'The Industrial World'. Reinhart Koselleck, whose *Prussia between Reform and Revolution* was published in Stuttgart in 1967, shared with Conze a belief that social history must essentially be concerned with the concepts which, as they saw it, predominate in a particular epoch. Conze and his collaborators organised a major dictionary of 'basic historical concepts', as an aid to understanding the industrial world through its language. We should also note the sparkling feminist writings of Karin Hausen (*b*. 1938), and the work on family and kinship by Hans Medick.

In Britain there was an almost evangelical enthusiasm for 'oral history' – recording people's memories before they die. Oral history – but for the very recent past only – can give us access to information we could not obtain in any other way. All primary sources are inadequate and imperfect; oral accounts are particularly subject to the fallibility of the human memory. Paul Thompson, who has interviewed financiers as well as working men, has been the acclaimed pioneer in Britain, while Lutz Niethammer, with his work on industrial workers in the Ruhr, has been a leading German figure. It is not politically correct to point out the severe limitations upon what can be learned from 'oral history' (more correctly, 'oral testimony') alone, nor to note that to give this sub-history, or rather approach, *gravitas* some of its protagonists have (in common with those trying to create a specialist sub-history out of the study of memoirs and autobiographies) been importing from post-modernism notions of 'narrative' and 'emplotment'. To aver that oral testimony, memoirs and autobiographies, as distinct from all other pri-mary sources (which also require historians to understand their imper-fections, codes, conventions and formal devices), need unique specialist treatment is specious nonsense.[47] Geoff Eley (*b.* 1949) is a British ex-ponent of new social history who has specialised in Germany, as in his *Reshaping the German Right: Radical Nationalism and Political Change after Bismarck* (New Haven, Conn., 1980).

The 'Historikerstreit'

The historians' 'controversy' over the recent German past broke out in the 1980s. On the whole academics such as Eberhard Jäckel took a left/liberal line. Thus much attention, and opprobrium, was attracted by Ernst Nolte's *Three Faces of Fascism* (1998), which argued that Nazism was essentially a response to, and variant on, Soviet Communism.

New Cultural History

In the phrase 'The New Cultural History' the word 'new' is probably as fully justified as that banal and over-used word ever can be. The problem lies with the 'cultural' bit. This word, along with its associated noun, 'culture', is used in such a confused, and confusing, variety of ways that one almost feels it should be struck from the serious historian's vocabu-lary. Robert Darnton, certainly the most reflexive of the American pro-tagonists of 'the new cultural history', comes near to suggesting that better terms would be 'anthropological history' or 'ethnographic his-tory'.[48] The chief publicist, Lynn Hunt, and her associates offer a name and a definition so encompassing that they become imploding:

> The editors hope to encourage the publication of books that combine social and cultural modes of analysis in an empirically concrete yet theoretically informed fashion . . . The concept of culture is understood here in the broadest sense, to encompass the study of mentalities, ideology, symbols and rituals, and high and popular culture.[49]

Three major influences are identified: the publication, both in 1973, of Hayden White's *Metahistory: The Historical Imagination in Nineteenth-Century Europe* and Clifford Geertz's *The Interpretation of Cultures*, and in 1977 of the English translation of Foucault's *Discipline and Punish: The Birth of the Prison*. The relevance of White, with his claim that 'empirically concrete' history is an impossibility,[50] escapes me. Geertz did at least offer fairly precise definitions of 'culture', which he perceived as the system of ideas that animates social structure; culture patterns, he said, are ordered clusters of significant symbols by which people make sense of the events through which they live. Linked to his statement that 'I don't believe that society is a mechanical system', his most famous utterance is:

> Believing with Max Weber that man is an animal suspended in webs of significance he himself has spun, I take culture to be those webs and the analysis of it to be therefore not an experimental science in search of law but an interpretative one in search of meaning.[51]

It is thanks to Weber, reinforced by Geertz, that we get endless repetitions of the phrase, or variations upon it, about people 'making sense' of their lives; part of the justification for all of the stuff about 'narratives' and 'stories' is that, allegedly, it is through these that people 'make sense' of their lives. Do people 'make sense' of their lives? I think that is a question which should be examined extremely critically, not simply taken for granted.

It is my conviction that some of the most interesting and valuable history being produced at the end of the twentieth century was that which came under the general rubric of 'The New Cultural History', this being so because of the rigorous methods being applied to a great range of previously unused archive material. It is also my conviction that the elaborate citations of Foucault, Geertz and the rest are quite unnecessary. However, as I promised, I shall leave Olwen Hufton to make the case for the significance of these figures:

> Cultural history achieved a historiographical dominance in the eighties. A new generation of historians fell under the influence of the philosopher Michel Foucault, preoccupied with power relationships and the historical construction of codes of practice which defined right from wrong, normal and abnormal. Equally influential were the anthropologists such as Lévi-Strauss, Clifford Geertz and the sociologist Norbert Elias, whose work on the meaning of ritual within the court society of Versailles and of the essence of the civilizing process – both published before the war – underwent a conspicuous revival . . . Culture was broadly explained as a set of shared meanings,

reflecting ingrained beliefs and determining ritual and practices and the expression of attitudes within a particular group . . . the new cultural historians were quick to insist that the beliefs and attitudes implicit in both high and low culture would necessarily embody assumptions about the essence of manhood and womanhood, the male and the female. Each sex could, for example, be arbitrarily allocated certain attributes and roles: strength and valour belong to men, to make them warriors and hunters; tenderness and frailty to women, to make them nurturers and servants of men. Such attitudes would, furthermore, lay down constraints on what was fitting for each sex. Gender roles, it was argued, were constructed from beliefs, and lay at the core of any culture, determining in the case of each sex what was appropriate and what unfitting, the honourable and the shameful, the acceptable and the forbidden, the possible and that which was to be denied.[52]

That is well and clearly expressed, though it seems to me to say little that a historian who had never heard of Foucault or Geertz could not have arrived at independently. Historians, though, must always be precise and explicit in their language, and must always work out their arguments in logical stages. 'Attitudes' and 'beliefs' are words readily understood; 'meanings', frequently used in the sort of discourse Hufton is talking about, is more problematic. The perception (obvious enough, I would have thought) that custom allocates certain roles to men and different ones to women can very easily slip into denying that there are any biological differences between men and women. If historians are to listen to anthropologists, they must also listen to socio-biologists and evolutionary psychologists, whose theories, too, are often overstated and absurd, but who do present cogent evidence of the biological bases of sexual differences.[53]

The point of all this is that the achievements of such historians as Natalie Zemon Davis, Lynn Hunt, Robert Darnton, and Roger Chartier are to be measured by the (considerable) contributions to historical knowledge made in their research-based works, not by their theorising about history, its nature and intellectual debts.

Natalie Zemon Davis

Some of my puzzlement over the theorising was lifted by a remark made by Natalie Davis herself:

When I was a student, we were ordinarily taught as scientific historians to peel away the fictive elements in our documents so we could get at the real facts.[54]

How appallingly badly she, and the other students, were taught! Since 1970, and the first edition of this book, I have been pointing out that historians are looking for unwitting testimony as much as witting, and that they do not find 'facts' but a whole range of nuances, conditions, states of mind, interconnections, and so on. If we only formalised more rigorously this notion of 'unwitting testimony' we'd have no need of all the anthropological mysticism about 'meanings' and 'making sense', nor the postmodernist mumbo-jumbo about 'deconstruction'. In fact, Davis's statement, and the book in which it appeared, *Fiction in the Archives: Pardon Tales and Their Tellers in Sixteenth-Century France* (Stanford, Calif., 1987), have been much misunderstood. It seems likely that the title, if not the actual book, gave Ludmilla Jordanova the absurd notion about the archives containing complete little stories. Davis was not claiming that the narratives in the royal letters of pardon and remission she was studying were fictitious – her interest was in their 'forming, shaping, crafting': a limited, but legitimate, topic, examining, it should be noted, the human use of language, *not* language's alleged dominance over humans. More important (and on the same page), she noted how many other historians had made use of the rich *unwitting testimony* in these particular archives:

> They have been previous sources for studies of holiday customs, of violence and revenge in different social milieus and age groups, of attitudes towards, and images of the king and other social and cultural norms.

'We can readily see', she concludes, how at least one tale 'provides interesting particulars about wife-beating and small-town prostitution!' Anyway, Davis obviously did come to analyse her sources in a more sophisticated way than her elders had taught her. A series of learned articles illuminated the nature of community protest in sixteenth-century France. Collected together as *Society and Culture in Early Modern France* (Stanford, Calif., 1975), they still form a standard work.

Because of her standing as an authority on sixteenth-century French rural life, Davis became involved in the making of a feature film based on the celebrated story of Martin Guerre. Much of what we know about ordinary people in the past comes from accounts of trials, civil, criminal, or ecclesiastical (it is thanks to the Inquisition that we know so much about the people of Montaillou, and we'll come to another important series of heresy trials in a moment). For legal authorities, it is very important to take *and preserve* accurate records. However, the accounts we have of the two trials of Martin Guerre are exceptional. The parliamentary counsellor (in France, *parlements* were judicial courts), Jean de Coras (no doubt because the case was such a fascinating one), wrote up detailed accounts of the trials, thus, in effect, putting the story into the public domain. Down the centuries the story of 'the return of Martin Guerre' formed the basis for plays, novels, and operettas. *You* probably know the story. In 1549 a rather difficult and unpleasant peasant, Martin Guerre, disappeared from the village of Artigat in the foothills of the Pyrenees. Eight years later Martin Guerre returned to reclaim his wife and property. He had greatly changed, and quickly became highly popular with everyone. Then Guerre fell out with his uncle, who brought a civil case against him charging him with being an imposter.

The film, *Le Retour de Martin Guerre* (1982), was produced and directed by Daniel Vigne, who had already produced a television series about the history of the French countryside (discussed in Chapter 6), with a screenplay by Vigne and Jean-Claude Carrière, who had written screenplays for the comic M. Hulot films as well as illustrated books of an historical nature. Davis was not happy with the anachronisms and inaccurate representations of sixteenth-century peasant life in the film, in which Gérard Depardieu starred as the imposter, and it was agreed that she should write a separate scholarly account, which was translated into French and published in Natalie Zemon Davis, Jean-Claude Carrière, Daniel Vigne, *Le Retour de Martin Guerre* (Paris, 1982), which consisted of two parts: first, the screenplay converted into a kind of novel by the two Frenchmen, and, second, the scholarly account. The English version of the latter, published on its own, did not actually appear until 1983. Davis introduced her account in the following fashion:

> we still know very little about the peasant's hopes and feelings; the way in which they experienced the relation between husband and wife, parent and child ...
>
> But how do historians discover such things about anyone in the past? We look at letters and diaries, autobiographies, memoirs, family histories. We look at literary sources – which, whatever their relation to the real lives of specific people, show us what sentiments and reactions authors considered plausible for a given period.[55]

The point about literary sources (poems, plays, novels) having to be 'plausible' is an excellent one. For later novelists, however, the published account by Jean de Coras had been enough, but not for a scholar like Davis. No victim of the so-called 'cult of the archive', she knew the value of scouring every archive in the district, seeking traces of both Guerre and the imposter, whose real name, almost certainly, was Arnaud du Thil, as well as more general evidence of peasant experiences: she used the records of the different 'jurisdictions', the registers of parliamentary sentences, and contracts of marriage.[56] Her *The Return of Martin Guerre* is a magnificent example of 'New Cultural History' and also of what was coming to be called 'microhistory'.

When not pontificating about how she and her friends have created a new kind of history and are the only ones to have rationally explained the activities of the historian, Lynn Hunt has produced some valuable work, particularly in bringing out the way in which the language used by the French revolutionaries itself became an instrument of political and social change (see her *Politics, Culture and Class in the French Revolution* (1984)).

Best-known, and most perceptive in his understanding of the activities of this trio of brilliant American 'cultural historians', is Robert Darnton (*b.* 1939), graduate of Harvard, sometime journalist, and holder of an Oxford doctorate. Darnton took further (or, more accurately, deeper) the work on 'the history of the book' in pre-revolutionary France pioneered by Furet, Henri-Jean Martin and Roger Chartier, and he did this (I must stress again) first of all by discovering new archives. A large proportion of the books which would have been censored out of existence in France were published in Neuchâtel in Switzerland, so it was to the archives there that Darnton repaired. Then he moved outwards to police records, the archives of Paris printers and of the booksellers' guilds. The fruits of his researches were published in the collection *The Literary Underground of the Old Regime* (Cambridge, Mass., 1982) – while the earlier pioneers had identified the revolutionary ideas in the 'underground press' of the eighteenth century, Darnton came nearer than anyone else to spelling out the connections between revolutionary ideas and revolutionary practice.

In his most famous work, *The Great Cat Massacre and Other Episodes in French Cultural History* (New York, 1984), Darnton demonstrated how a series of microhistories can illuminate cultural history. The eponymous chapter explores the mental world of some harshly treated and disgruntled apprentices, and that of their master and mistress, through an episode in which the apprentices destroy a number of cats, including the beloved and pampered one of the mistress. In introducing this book, Darnton writes that it 'attempts to show not merely what people thought but how they thought – how they *construed* the world'[57] – my italics, since this seems to me an excellent way of expressing what many historians today are trying to do. But he glosses 'construed the world' as 'invested it with meaning, and infused it with emotion', which to me is just fancy Geertzian rhetoric, not actually meaning much; though, of course, Darnton must be free to explain his fascinating and original work in his own way. Finally he makes a point which has been taken up by other cultural historians: 'I have abandoned the usual distinction between elite and popular culture, and have tried to show how intellectuals and common people coped with the same sort of problem.'[58]

The Cambridge Connection

There are further important reflections in the collection *The Forbidden Best Sellers of Pre-Revolutionary France* (New York, 1996). In particular, Darnton goes out of his way to record the importance to 'the new cultural history' of the contributions made by a group of Cambridge political scientists and historians loosely held together by the series of publications on 'Philosophy, Politics, Society' edited from 1956 by the same Peter Laslett who was to become prominent in historical demography.[59] The labels one might reach for here are 'new political history', 'political culture', 'discourse analysis' ('discourse' here not necessarily having the Marxist overtones of Foucauldian usage – a point which could also be made about the use of the word 'narratives' that has become strongly apparent in the most recent work of the group). Key titles are: J. G. A. Pocock (*b.* New Zealand, now an emeritus professor of *history* at Johns Hopkins University in America), *The Ancient Constitution and the Feudal Law* (1957, second edition 1987), *Politics, Language and Time: Essays on Political Thought and History* (1971), *Barbarism and Religion, Vol. 2 Narratives of Civil Government* (1999); Quentin Skinner, *The Foundations of Modern Political Thought* (2 vols, Cambridge, 1978); Keith Michael Baker, *Inventing the French Revolution: Essays on French Political Culture in the Eighteenth Century* (Cambridge, 1990); and Karen O'Brien, *Narratives of Enlightenment: Cosmopolitan History from Voltaire to Gibbon* (Cambridge, 1997). Some of this stuff has become quite markedly Foucauldian, but in essence, it seems to me, the early Cambridge analysts of 'political culture' were talking about 'shared assumptions', that is, 'the unwitting testimony' of primary sources relating to political actions and beliefs.

Microhistory: Menocchio the Miller

The most cited example of microhistory (after, perhaps, *Montaillou*) is *Il formaggio e i vermi: il cosmo di un mugnaio del '500* (1976) by Carlo Ginzburg (*b.* 1939), translated as *The Cheese and the Worms: The Cosmos of a Sixteenth-Century Miller* (1980). Ginzburg makes two points confirming what I have been saying about recent trends in history, the first with regard to scope, the second concerning the inter-relationship between elite and popular culture. 'In the past', he writes:

> historians could be accused of wanting to know only about 'the great deeds of kings', but today this is certainly no longer true. More and more they are turning toward what their predecessors passed over in silence, discarded, or simply ignored.

And he speaks of 'the popular roots of a considerable part of high European culture, both medieval and postmedieval'. The book focuses on a miller of the Friuli in north Italy, 'who was burned at the stake by order of the Holy Office after a life passed in almost complete obscurity'.[60] As Ginzburg remarks, it had become fairly well known among specialist historians that the archives of the archiepiscopal court in the main town of the Friuli region, Udine, contain a rich deposit of inquisitorial papers, but as he admits (this happens), it was by accident that he came across the case of this miller, Domenico Scandella, always called Menocchio.

> The record of his two trials, held fifteen years apart, offer a rich picture of his thoughts and feelings, of his imaginings and aspirations. Other documents give us information about his economic activities and the lives of his children. We even have pages in his own hand and a partial list of what he read (he was, in fact, able to read and write). Though we would like to know more about Menocchio, what we do know permits us to reconstruct a fragment of what is usually called 'the culture of the lower classes'...[61]

Ginzburg recognises that it is not possible to regard a miller who could read and write as a typical peasant figure. The heart of his enterprise lies in comparing what the books Menocchio read actually said (piecing together an entire list of readings was in itself quite a complex job) with the versions Menocchio gave to his judges. The central argument is that the ideas Menocchio expressed, which vary greatly from what was actually in the books he read, must have been drawn from the popular ideas and traditions of the time. Thus, the variation between what Menocchio said, and what he had read, gives us a direct insight into these popular ideas and beliefs.

Chartier

Now I come back to Roger Chartier, for many a hero of both *Annales* and 'new cultural history'. To my taste, Chartier spends too much time on the far side, too much time on obscure Foucauldian metaphysics, and too much time on trying to demonstrate the existence of what he calls 'print culture'. Some of his individual case studies, working from the archives, are brilliant. The opening two sentences to his article on 'From Ritual to the Hearth: Marriage Charters in Seventeenth-Century Lyons' are revealing:

> The archives of the Hospices civils in Lyons contain a collection of 174 wedding charters. This study is founded on the idea that materials of

this sort, which belonged fully to print culture, also had an essential place in the ways in which Christianity was once lived and conceived of.[62]

For Chartier the important point seems to be that these charters belong to this thing called 'print culture'; from the point of view of historical knowledge as usually understood, the important point is 'the ways in which Christianity was once lived and conceived of', which Chartier, however, seems to regard as incidental to his main task. The article on 'The Hanged Woman' in the same collection is essentially a technical disquisition on the nature and format of the *occasionnel*, a one-off printed account, for wide distribution, of some horrific or miraculous event. This particular one, published in Douai in 1589, repeated the story of a woman hanged who, not actually being guilty, miraculously survived:

> The account of the miracle of Montfort, in its two successive versions, bears signs of a tension found in nearly all the *occasionnels* that combined formulas inherited from tradition with current happenings. The story of Anne's miracle is thus partly a new variation on an old hagiographical and pastoral motif, and partly a celebration of a devotional practice closely tied to current events... the *occasionnels* gave printed form to stories that in former times had been told, preached, or recited, and this plurality of possible readings, which was both organised by the text and produced simultaneously by its readers, is doubtless one of the major reasons for their lasting success.[63]

Is this of major *historical* significance?: you judge. The phrase 'organised by the text' takes us into the world of Foucault and Hayden White: do texts 'organise'? – one sees what is meant, but surely the point could be made more precisely and less metaphorically? In a long disquisition on 'print culture' Chartier makes the point that in earlier times (that is, prior to the nineteenth century) reading printed works was not, as in later times, a largely individual and private act, but that it was a shared, communal one, 'those who knew how to read leading those who did not'.[64] To my taste, the pompous, rhetorical, metaphysical way in which he makes this, on the whole fairly simple, point reduces, rather than enhances, his credibility *as a historian*. Chartier is perhaps best seen as a new *érudit*, with *auteur* aspirations, much referred to, but with little influence on the great developments in the teaching and communication of history of the last 20 years.

6   The Start of a New Century: Nothing Ruled Out

In the course of this extended attempt to allow some of the most respected historians at the beginning of the twenty-first century to speak for themselves (and readers, of course, are entirely free to ignore my criticisms), I have picked out the perception that 'elite culture' (or '*the* arts') shares common origins with 'popular culture' (or 'the popular arts'). Much has been written on 'popular culture' since the 1960s, a great deal of it being Marxist and/or postmodernist in approach, falling into the realm of cultural studies rather than history. What I want to mention here is the way in which historians have at last been venturing into the realm of the elite arts (classical music, painting and sculpture, and so on), a realm which still seems to terrify historians and their students alike. This is by way of returning to the fundamental point that in historical writing today no area of human experience is ruled out. We are not now concerned with the turning of the wheel of fashion: no one sub-history is in fashion today, rather all types of history are being pursued in a vigorous, sophisticated, and disciplined manner. While I reject the simplistic implications of the notions of 'a dialogue between past and present' or of 'each age having to rewrite its history', I do insist that history is a social activity, and that, in the end, it must serve the needs of society, imaginatively conceived.

One cannot explain the evolving preoccupations and techniques of historians entirely by some alleged succession of 'cultures', nor even by reference to current events (though these *may* be influential). However, I would hazard the suggestion that three main variables affect the kind of history now being written, or at least the kind of history which receives most attention both within the profession and among the wider public:

1 I unrepentantly give primacy to **sources and archives**. That so much of the recent highly respected work is on French topics is because of the richness of the French national and local archives going far back into the Middle Ages. The discovery and exploitation of new archaeological sites is part of the explanation behind the wonderful growth of 'classical' or 'ancient' history in recent times. The events of 1989 led to the opening of archives, not just in Russia but throughout eastern Europe – with obvious results.

2 But that point in itself links to my second variable, **the way historical events do impinge on the kind of history being produced**. As well as making primary sources available, the fall of the Soviet Empire directed attention back on previous assumptions about the Russian revolution and about the legitimacy of Soviet rule. A particularly powerful example of the way in which developments in the recent

past and in the present affect the writing of history can be found in contemporary Germany: from the middle 1970s there has been an obsession in all corners of the intellectual and artistic world – affecting playwrights, painters, novelists, philosophers, as well as historians – with the Nazi period, the Holocaust, the Second World War, the apparent continuation of some Nazi ideas, the terrorist period of the 1970s, the new feminism (two of the most notorious terrorist leaders were women), unification. Turning from the West, there has been, for obvious reasons, a strong preoccupation with postcolonial history, and with the writing of the history of former colonial territories from the point of view of the indigenous peoples rather than the colonisers.[65]

3 The third variable (and, obviously, it is not a completely independent one either) is what I shall call the **'internal' or 'intellectual'** one. As this chapter, in particular, has made clear, historians have, in recent years, thought deeply about what they are doing, and have made claims for their particular approaches as against those of others. By the end of the twentieth century historians had become more self-aware, more *reflexive* than ever before. This could mean exaggerated claims being made for one particular approach, for example that of 'the new cultural history'. But, all in all, the result has been an expansion in both the scope and the sophistication of history: everything ruled in has meant nothing ruled out, and, importantly, has led to a strong swing in emphasis towards comparative history, history covering several countries, societies, cultures.

The computer has not been nearly as commanding as might have been thought. Computers are vital for data analysis, for the preparation of spreadsheets, and so on. From the 1970s onwards their main potential has been steadily absorbed. My central point about the importance of archives has been reinforced since computers facilitate access to catalogues (where they exist), but not yet, of course, to the actual content of the archives. Massive changes continue to be made in the retrieval and storage of information, and also in modes of communication (CD-Rom, the web, and so on). But all of this does not *fundamentally* affect the production of history, the research and the writing-up of research. More relevant here to concentrate on the ruling everything in/not ruling anything out. Enhanced quantitative techniques, once restricted to economic and demographic history, now affect all types, including political history and cultural history (in all senses of that term). Biography no longer need be narrow, literary, hagiographical (or, alternatively, deliberately reputation-destroying). The two volumes of Ian Kershaw's *Hitler* (1998, 2000) show a fine balance between contextual circumstances, the psychology of the man, and, along a different axis, between the latest secondary work, particularly by German historians, and the use of primary materials.

The study of war, in all its dimensions, has returned as a subject which, given the state of humanity, simply cannot be ignored. It can be seen at its best in the articles published in the new Anglo-American journal *War in History* (founded in 1993). That full professionalism can be attained by an 'amateur' historian, given the new documents and the linguistic and interpretative skills needed, is demonstrated by the account of that monstrous battle *Stalingrad* (1998) by Anthony Beevor. Renewed interest in the two cataclysmic twentieth-century wars has partly been responsible for the fashion for work allegedly about 'memory', most of which, in fact, demonstrates the worst failings of the rhetorical, metaphorical approach to history. Memory is, if one is to preserve the precision essential in historical writing, a faculty belonging to individuals. There is no such thing as 'collective memory'. If what is meant is 'collective beliefs about things that happened in the past' it is best to say so: the abuse of metaphor, here as in so many other instances related to post-modernist attitudes, just produces dubious history.[66] Remembrance, certainly, is a precise and, therefore, legitimate topic. The study of it reinforces the growing consensus that an understanding of the twentieth century requires meticulous analysis of all aspects of the two total wars.[67]

At the beginning of the twenty-first century, historians were re-emphasising the importance of analysing events, as distinct from 'structures' and 'webs of meaning'. This development was symbolised in 1994 when the sub-title of *Annales* was changed again – to *Histoire, Sciences Sociales*. A culminating point came in the March/April issue of 1999, when a major topic was that most *évènementielle* of events, the Fronde. Professor Robert Descimon wrote:

> The return of events, generally represented as incompatible with Fernand Braudel's total history, is opening explanatory perspectives, including that of the bounded rationality of human action.[68]

The leading figure in non-postmodernist scientific history was Yves-Marie Bercé of the École des Chartes, an expert on peasant risings during the medieval and early modern periods.

The advent of postcolonial history has not meant the abolition of what might seem the outmoded tradition of imperial history. Just as A. J. P. Taylor had opened up a challenge in the forties and fifties to then generally accepted views of the origins of the Second World War, so J. Gallagher, R. Robinson and Alice Denny in *Africa and the Victorians: The Official Mind of Imperialism* (1961) challenged the then widely accepted view that there was a sharp break in British imperial policy in the 1870s, anti-imperialist sentiment being strong before that point, overt imperialism coming in after it. The book stressed continuity, and argued that expansion in Africa was driven by forces in Africa rather than in Britain. A great debate was opened up again with the publication in 1993 of the two volumes by P. J. Cain and A. G. Hopkins, *British Imperialism: Crisis and Deconstruction* (1993), which, in general, argued the case that finance was much more important to Britain than industry, and specifically that finance, directed by 'gentlemanly' interests, was primarily responsible for the expansion of the British Empire. For the issues themselves, and for the professional matter of controversy in history, there is the fine collection edited by R. E. Dumett, *Gentlemanly Capitalism and British Imperialism: The New Debate on Empire* (1999). I single out this topic to make it clear that what is correct in history today is not confined to that which is politically correct, and that what may seem like 'old' topics are still being addressed, with the full benefit of all the advances in history as a discipline which I have been identifying in this chapter.

Notes

1 Turner is quoted in G. R. Taylor (ed.), *The Turner Thesis* (London, 1956).
2 Ernest Breisach, *Historiography: Ancient, Medieval, and Modern* (Chicago, 1983), p. 314. See John Higham, *History: Professional Scholarship in America* (Cambridge, Mass., 1983), Chapters II, III, IV and V.
3 See A. M. Schlesinger Sr, *In Retrospect: The History of a Historian* (New York, 1963).
4 See chapter on Febvre by Palmer A. Throop in S. William Halperin (ed.), *Some 20th Century Historians* (Chicago, 1961). There is a brilliant chapter on Febvre and Bloch in Peter Burke, *The French Historical Revolution: The Annales School 1929–89* (Cambridge, 1990), pp. 12–31.
5 Burke, *The Annales School*, p. 17.
6 See chapter by James L. Cate in Halperin, *Some 20th Century Historians*.
7 *Annales d'Histoire Économique et Social*, I (Jan. 1929).
8 Burke, *The Annales School*, p. 22.
9 For an up-to-date account of Lefebvre, see ibid., pp. 12–15, 19–22, 27–31.
10 Ibid., p. 22.
11 Marc Bloch, *The Historian's Craft* (Manchester and New York, 1954; pb edn, 1976), 1976 edn, p. 27.
12 Federico Chabod, *Machiavelli and the Renaissance* (New York, 1958), p. xiii.
13 Quoted by G. N. Clark, *Sir John Harold Clapham* (London, 1946), p. 6.
14 See Richard Pares and A. J. P. Taylor, *Essays Presented to Sir Lewis Namier* (London, 1956).
15 Lewis Namier, *The Structure of Politics at the Accession of George III* (London, 1929), vol. 1, p. iii. For an assessment of Namier, see Linda Colley, *Lewis Namier* (London, 1989).

16 Richard Pares, *George III and the Politicians* (Oxford, 1953; pb edn, 1968), p. 64.

17 Lewis Namier and John Brooke, *Charles Townshend* (London, 1964), p. 2.

18 G. R. Elton, *England Under the Tudors* (2nd edn, 1974), p. vi.

19 See the critical discussion of the Elton thesis by Penry Williams and G. L. Harris in *Past and Present*, 25 (July 1963). The most recent commentary is G. W. Bernard, 'Elton's Cromwell', *History* (October 1998), pp. 587–607. Bernard concludes 'that, far from holding the government of the country in his hands alone, Cromwell was rather the king's hard-working servant'.

20 E. H. Carr, *What is History?* (London, 1961; pb edn, 1964), p. 123.

21 For example, see Colin Jones, *The Charitable Imperative* (London, 1989), p. 8, where Jones agrees with Foucault (though surely Foucault was not the first to point this out) that the regime in pre-modern French 'hospitals' was 'a primitive mix of enforced piety and labour', before going on to point out that (contrary to Foucault) these institutions did 'devote less of their energies to repression than to relief'.

22 E. P. Thompson, 'The Poverty of Theory', in *The Poverty of Theory and Other Essays* (London, 1978), pp. 1–25.

23 Gwynne Lewis, *The French Revolution: Rethinking the Debate* (London, 1993), pp. 123, 124.

24 David Cannadine, *Class in Britain* (London, 1998), pp. 51–2.

25 The distinction comes out very clearly in Eric Hobsbawn, *Uncommon People: Resistance, Rebellion and Jazz* (London, 1998), the collection of both journalism and learned articles which forms a fine introduction to the breadth and depth of Hobsbawm's talents.

26 E. Genovese, *The Political Economy of Slavery: Studies in the Economy and Society of the Slave South* (New York, 1965), pp. 10–11.

27 E. Genovese, *Roll Jordan Roll: The World the Slaves Made* (New York, 1974), p. xv.

28 In *Visions of History* (Manchester, 1983), ed. Henry Ableove, Betsy Blackmar, Peter Dimock, and Jonathan Schneer, p. 2.

29 Burke, *The Annales School*, p. 33.

30 Ibid.

31 Ibid., p. 39.

32 Fernand Braudel, *The Mediterranean and the Mediterranean World in the Age of Philip II* (London, 1973), vol. 1, pp. 20–1.

33 Burke, *The Annales School*, is my guide, though the general comments are naturally my own. For a collection of French views on what has been happening in France, see François Bédarida (ed.), *L'Histoire et le métier d'historien en France 1945–1995* (Paris, 1995).

34 Fernand Braudel, *Civilisation matérielle, économie et capitalisme, XV–XVIII siècles*, vol. II, *Les jeux de l'échange* (Paris, 1979), pp. 535–6.

35 Jean Duvernoy, *Le Registre d'Inquisition de Jacques Fournier, évêque de Pamiers (1318–1325)*, 3 vols (Toulouse, 1965). The original is Latin MS 4030, in the Vatican Library, Rome (an invaluable archive, particularly for medieval history).

36 Michael Kammen (ed.), *The Past Before Us: Contemporary Historical Writing in the United States* (Ithaca, NY, 1980).

37 Lynn Hunt (ed.), *The New Cultural History* (Berkeley, Calif., 1989); Victoria I. Bonnell and Lynn Hunt (eds), *Beyond the Cultural Turn: New Directions in the Study of Society and Culture* (Berkeley, Calif., 1999).
38 E. H. Hunt, 'The New Economic History', *History*, 55 (1968), pp. 3–13.
39 Ibid., p. 12.
40 Niall Ferguson, *Virtual History: Alternatives and Counterfactuals* (London, 1997).
41 P. A. David, H. G. Gutmann, R. Sutch, P. Temin and G. Wright, *Reckoning with Slavery: A Critical Study in the Quantitative History of American Negro Slavery* (1976), pp. 339–40.
42 Asa Briggs, in H. J. Dyos (ed.), *The Study of Urban History* (London, 1968), pp. v–xi.
43 See Michael Shortland and Richard Yeo (eds), *Telling Lives in Science: Essays in Scientific Biography* (Cambridge, 1996).
44 Albrecht Fölsing, *Albert Einstein: A Biography* (New York, 1997), p. xiii.
45 Robert S. Westfall, *Never at Rest: A Biography of Isaac Newton* (Cambridge, 1980), p. x.
46 Ibid.
47 See, for example, Mary Chamberlain and Paul Thompson (eds), *Narrative and Genre* (London, 1998).
48 Robert Darnton, *The Great Cat Massacre and Other Episodes in French Cultural History* (London, 1984), p. 11.
49 Bonnell and Hunt, *Beyond the Cultural Turn*, p. ix.
50 Ibid., p. 2.
51 Clifford Geertz, *The Interpretation of Cultures* (New York, 1973), p. 5.
52 Olwen Hufton, *The Prospect Before Her: A History of Women in Western Europe Volume 1, 1500–1800* (London, 1995), p. 3.
53 See, for example, David M. Buss, *Evolutionary Psychology: The New Science of the Mind* (Boston, Mass., 1999).
54 Natalie Zemon Davis, *Fiction in the Archives: Pardon Tales and Their Tellers in Sixteenth-Century France* (Stanford, Calif., 1987), p. 3.
55 Natalie Zemon Davis, *The Return of Martin Guerre* (Cambridge, Mass., 1983), pp. 1–2.
56 Ibid., p. 5.
57 Darnton, *Cat Massacre*, p. 11.
58 Ibid., p. 14.
59 R. Darnton, *The Forbidden Best Sellers of Pre-Revolutionary France* (New York, 1996), p. 176.
60 Carlo Ginzburg, *The Cheese and the Worms: The Cosmos of a Sixteenth-Century Miller* (London, 1980), p. xiii.
61 Ibid.
62 Roger Chartier, 'From Ritual to the Hearth: Marriage Charters in Seventeenth-Century Lyon', in Roger Chartier (ed.), *The Culture of Print: Power and the Uses of Print in Early Modern France* (Cambridge, 1987), p. 175.
63 Chartier, 'The Hanged Woman', in ibid., p. 88.
64 Chartier, 'General Introduction: Print Culture', in ibid., p. 1.
65 See, for example, Arnold Temu and Bonaventure Swai, *Historians and Africanist History: A Critique* (London, 1981).

66 One cannot but admire the massive seven-volume series edited by Pierre Nora, *Les lieux de mémoire* (Paris, 1984–92). For starters try reading the Preface and Introduction to the first volume of the English translation, *Realms of Memory: Rethinking the French Past: Vol 1. Conflicts and Divisions* (1996). Simon Schama's *Landscape and Memory* (London, 1995) is heavily influenced by Nora – *c'est magnifique, mais ce n'est pas l'histoire*.

67 Much of the most fatuous work on 'memory' is in French; however, a strong contender is Martin Evans and Ken Lunn (eds), *War and Memory in the Twentieth Century* (Oxford, 1997). *Sites of Memory, Sites of Mourning: The Great War in European Cultural History* (Cambridge, 1995) by Jay Winter is sensible and scholarly.

68 *Annales: Histoire, Sciences Sociales*, 54/2 (March/April 1999), p. 319.

5 | The Historian at Work: Forget 'Facts', Foreground Sources

1 'Facts'

That last chapter, and perhaps even parts of the one before, will have provided information on the sorts of matters historians are concerned with, on the kinds of things they are trying to find out. Burckhardt wanted to demonstrate the existence of something which could legitimately be called a Renaissance and its conclusive effects on the subsequent development of western Europe; dozens of historians since have fretted over it, what it was, when it began. Namier wanted to establish exactly how politics worked in eighteenth-century Britain. Historians have argued over the standard of living in the Industrial Revolution, over the motivations and interests behind British imperial expansion, values and attitudes ('mentalities') in eighteenth-century France. One could say that, with regard to each of these very variegated topics, the historians involved were concerned to 'establish the facts'. Critics of history would object to that formulation, preferring to speak of these historians as 'selecting and arranging ("narrativising") the facts in order to present a particular interpretation'. In both cases the use of the phrase 'the facts' is highly unsatisfactory: what are 'the facts' when we are talking about the significance of the Renaissance, or mentalities in eighteenth-century France? I want to suggest that if we want to get to the bottom of what historians at work actually do, we do best to forget the ridiculously simplistic phrase 'the facts'.

What exactly are 'the facts'? Can they be reduced to some basic unit, analogous say to a chemical element, or to an atom, or to a molecule? They can't: the matters which historians deal with, and about which they have a duty not to get it wrong, vary considerably in nature and complexity. There are the simple public facts (date and place of the Battle of Hastings), the complex private facts (the psychological state of a particular individual at a particular point in time). Are 'the Renaissance', 'the Reformation', 'the First World War' facts? If they are clusters of facts, what are the basic individual facts (the 'atoms' or 'molecules')

which make them up? Where do 'the facts' come from? In the last
analysis, as I've already said, they come from the traces that have been
left by past societies, that is, the primary sources. But, of course, historians do not go back to the primary sources to reassure themselves that
the First World War is 'a fact', or even to establish the different dates on
which hostilities broke out between the different countries. Much of
what, in popular speech, we may describe as 'the facts' are already
well known, that is to say can be readily found in the secondary sources.
Rather than fussing over 'the facts', we perhaps do better to remember
two of my key words, 'knowledge' and 'evidence' – knowledge must
ultimately be based on evidence.

When historians embark on a particular research topic, they will
already have considerable knowledge, if not of that precise topic, certainly of matters surrounding and relating to it. To produce new knowledge they will, as we know, have to go to work in the archives, in the
primary sources. What, actually, are they looking for in the primary
sources? Certainly, in the less familiar domains, historians may well be
looking for events, great and small, their dates and chronology, but they
will also be looking for interconnections between them, and between
them and other 'facts' – the working out of interconnections is not
necessarily (as those who, in ignorance, write about 'facts' and 'narrativising' assume) something done during the writing-up stage, since the
interconnections may actually be embedded in the primary sources.
More generally, historians are looking for material conditions, and
changes in them; states of mind; the working of institutions; motivations,
mentalities, values; the balances between intention and accomplishment
– all of these things may *eventually* be worked out, not, of course, from
single sources, but from the great range of sources historians analyse.
Historians will go into the archives conscious of a great number of 'facts'
derived from the secondary sources: they will then be involved in
processes of corroboration, qualification, correction; working in the primary sources, they are continually accumulating details, refining
nuances. I hope all this makes clear just how woefully inadequate any
perception is of historians discovering '*the* facts', or (to turn to the
postmodernist fantasy) of '*the* facts' being ready to hand. The point is
reinforced if we recall the fallible and intractable nature of the sources,
numbingly copious in some areas, scarce and fragmentary in others.
Much has to be garnered indirectly and by inference: attitudes to
spouses from wills, responses to crime, not from the letter of the law,
but from the extent and manner of its enforcement; the nature of social
hierarchy in everything from wage rates to novels. No one but the
historian knows the exciting promise of the most unpromising source;
no one but the historian knows the frustrating opacity and sheer unin-
formativeness of many of the most seductive ones.

One of the most astonishing statements I have ever read from a historian is that of Natalie Zemon Davis quoted in the previous chapter, that, in common with other American historians, she was taught 'to peel away the fictive elements in our documents so that we could get at the real facts'.[1] If only Davis and her fellow Americans had read the very first edition of *The Nature of History*, published in 1970! The idea that 'documents' (that is, primary sources) can be handled in this way in order to yield '*the* real facts' is absurd, as properly educated historians have long known (and have had no need of anthropologists or cultural theorists to tell them about the assumptions and customs revealed in the unwitting testimony). The other great generator of absurd statements about both facts and sources was E. H. Carr. 'The belief', Carr wrote,

> in a hard core of historical facts existing objectively and independently of the interpretation of the historian is a preposterous fallacy, but one which it is very hard to eradicate.[2]

What is preposterous is the insinuation that any historian seriously believes in this 'hard core of historical facts'. In fact, the responsibility for perpetuating fallacy lies with critics who assume the existence of a core of facts which historians then arrange to suit their own purposes. What historians believe in is the need to study and analyse *the sources* as objectively as is humanly possible. Carr, giving a course of lectures to a Cambridge audience, urbane, witty, full of anecdote, metaphor, elegant phrases and occasional cracks at the expense of Oxford philosophers and historians, then continued:

> At Stalybridge Wakes in 1850, a vendor of gingerbread, as the result of some petty dispute, was deliberately kicked to death by an angry mob. Is this a fact of history? A year ago I should unhesitatingly have said 'no'. It was recorded by an eye-witness in some little-known memoirs; but I had never seen it judged worthy of mention by any historian. A year ago Dr. Kitson Clark cited it in his Ford lectures in Oxford. Does this make it into a historical fact? Not, I think, yet. Its present status, I suggest, is that it has been proposed for membership of the select club of historical facts. It now awaits a seconder and sponsors. It may be that in the course of the next few years we shall see this fact appearing first in footnotes, then in the text, of articles and books about nineteenth-century England, and that in twenty or thirty years' time it may be a well-established historical fact. Alternatively, nobody may take it up, in which case it will relapse into the limbo of unhistorical facts about the past from which Dr. Kitson Clark has gallantly attempted to rescue it. What will decide which of

these two things will happen? It will depend, I think, on whether the thesis is accepted by other historians as valid and significant. Its status as a historical fact will turn on a question of interpretation. This element of interpretation enters into every fact of history.[3]

This is amusing, rhetorically satisfying, but complete rubbish. Let us look at the story of the vendor of gingerbread. 'Is this a fact of history?' asks Carr. The answer given is highly eccentric. The proper answer of a trained historian would be that this depends upon a critical analysis of the evidence. How reliable is the eye-witness? Is there corroborating testimony? Perhaps in fact the poor chap wasn't kicked to death at all; perhaps the alleged eye-witness account was an inflated piece of hearsay. That a distinguished professional historian such as Kitson Clark (1900–79) vouches for the reliability of the evidence is impressive, but it is reliability that is, or should be, the issue, not a lot of junk about being proposed and seconded for a club.

2   Primary and Secondary Sources

Vive la différence!

The distinction between primary sources and secondary sources is so important that I have already introduced it; the remainder of this chapter repeats and develops points touched on in my Introduction. Since history's critics feel a constant compulsion to scratch at this distinction, manifestly finding it the equivalent of a particularly irritating itchy spot, both misrepresenting and mocking the distinction, it is necessary to say more about it here. The critics attack the distinction partly because they are secretly embarrassed that they themselves actually have no experience of what it is like to work among primary sources in the archives, and partly because many of them subscribe to the view that everything, primary or secondary, belongs to the single category 'text' and shares in the (invented and nonsensical) quality of 'textuality'. The usual tactic is to dig out some highly untypical example of a 'text' which could, depending upon the topic being investigated, serve as either a primary or a secondary source; then a highly eccentric research topic has to be invented – thus the published books, obviously secondary sources, which I discussed in the previous chapter *could* be primary sources for a study of 'Twentieth-Century Attitudes to the Study of History'; though perhaps just worthy of that one chapter in this modest introductory work of mine, what an excruciatingly tedious monograph that would be! The genius behind this approach is Ludmilla Jordanova,[4] who declares that 'the very terminology "primary" and "secondary" can be misleading' and that 'the division between primary and secondary sources can be treacherous': apparently primary sources evoke in historians 'emotional responses' (dangerous, one gathers) and are possessed of 'persistent historical perfumes, which elicit quite individual responses', but, she continues generously, 'are not to be understood as good or bad'.[5] Jordanova claims to be worried about undergraduates who are being misled – those who have worked with the successive editions of *The Nature of History* will have no problems – but she is the one who is being misleading (what, for God's sake, are 'historical perfumes'?).

Let me be utterly unambiguous about this. The distinction between primary and secondary sources is absolutely explicit, and is not the least bit treacherous or misleading. No magical necromancy attaches to primary sources, but the ultimate truth is that it is only through the primary sources, the relics and traces left by past societies, that we can have any knowledge of them. The discovery and analysis of primary sources alone does not make history; but without the study of primary sources there is no history. Primary sources are sources which were generated within the period being studied. Self-evidently, a book which was a secondary source in the nineteenth century will normally not remain a useful secondary source for students in the twenty-first century, but may, if they are studying certain rather narrow aspects of the nineteenth century, become a primary source for them. There is nothing very difficult about that: the contortions of Jordanova and her like are utterly unnecessary. The distinction is one of nature – primary sources were created within the period studied, secondary sources are produced *later*, by historians studying that earlier period and making use of the primary sources created within it. There are also differences of function. A general reader or student wanting quickly to acquire knowledge about, say, the French Revolution, would go immediately to one or more reliable secondary sources on the French Revolution (it is a purpose of this book of mine to give guidance on how to separate out reliable secondary works from unreliable ones). The young researcher, or the old historian, setting out to do research leading to new contributions to historical knowledge would first of all have to read all of the relevant secondary materials, to be fully abreast of current knowledge and to be aware of the areas particularly needing investigation. But, that done, there would need to be substantial research in the primary sources. Any PhD student following Jordanova's guidance would quickly come a cropper: for obvious reasons, it is a fundamental requirement that a PhD dissertation be very largely based on primary sources.

Behind all the confusion lies the misapprehension that historians are claiming that primary sources contain a higher quality of 'truth' than secondary sources. This is manifestly not so. Primary sources are intractable, opaque, and fragmentary. At best, they shed light from one particular direction; usually you need quite a lot of them before any light is shed at all. Obviously, for a comprehensive view of any particular historical topic, a good secondary source relating to that topic is far more useful than any single primary source. *All* primary sources have to be treated with great care, and require the skills of the historian in their analysis and interpretation. Many primary sources contain secondary information, as when a diarist includes references to, or quotations from, that morning's newspaper. This does not stop the diary from being a primary source, but it does mean that the historian would be best to go back and check the original newspaper. This kind of checking and cross-referencing, this general scepticism, is a normal part of the historian's activities in using primary sources.

The problems are most acute when it comes to dealing with autobiographies (or memoirs) and 'contemporary histories'. If the author of the autobiography (or memoir) belongs to the period being studied, then, the human lifespan being what it is, the autobiography clearly must belong to that period too, and therefore is a primary source. It will be subject to the fallibility of memory (but then that is often true of other primary sources as well), and it may well contain much secondary material; the historian (who, after all, is professionally very preoccupied by this distinction between primary and secondary) will be thoroughly on guard and ready to discount, or cross-check, the secondary material. Some contemporary histories – histories written about a period through which the historian has lived or is living – can have the character of elaborated memoirs and so serve as potentially useful primary sources: striking examples are Clarendon's volumes on the Civil Wars and Churchill's on the twentieth-century ones. The comment of the Tory elder statesman A. J. Balfour on Churchill's account of the First World War was apposite: he called it 'Winston's brilliant autobiography disguised as a history of the universe'.[6] Dated and unreliable as a general (secondary) account of the war, this book has primary value for students of Churchill himself. Contemporary histories deliberately written as secondary (and not personal) accounts – for example, Kenneth O. Morgan, *The People's Peace: Britain Since 1945* – though it might contain primary insights for the sort of obscure topic conjured up by Jordanova, will continue to be treated as a secondary source as long as it serves that function usefully, then will meet the oblivion to which all outdated secondary sources are eventually consigned.

The Hierarchy of Primary Sources; Bibliographies

I mentioned the PhD dissertation. This book is directed towards beginning students and general readers; none the less some of the points made should be useful to PhD students and to others embarking on the writing of history. The clear and vital distinction between primary and secondary sources is embodied in the rules that all writers of PhD dissertations or of scholarly monographs must obey, particularly with regard to the presentation of the bibliography. This must be divided into two parts: the first part, usually by far the most extensive, must list all of the archives and other repositories and collections of primary sources used (and, within the broader headings, the individual classes, or even items, used), the second must list the secondary sources.

The primary sources will be divided up into sub-sections according to a certain implied hierarchy. No thoughtful historian actually believes (as Jordanova repeatedly insists that they do) that archive, handwritten sources are in all cases superior to printed primary sources. In some areas of research printed pamphlets, or, say, published guides to etiquette and conduct, can be of unsurpassed significance. The practical difference between archive sources and published documents is that the former are absolutely unique and exist in sole copies, whereas published documents, in their origins at least, existed in multiple copies – though often rare printed pamphlets or treatises have only survived in single copies, often contained within archive collections. Too much, then, need not be read into the implied hierarchy embedded in the way the primary sources part of a scholarly bibliography is set out. The principle of starting with the rarest, single-copy, usually handwritten documents and proceeding steadily through to the ones in multiple copies and most widely available is a sensible one, but no more than that. The bibliography exists to display systematically the raw materials upon which the scholarly work is based, and it is more quickly grasped and digested if it is set out in accordance with the established conventions. The vital point is that the raw materials should be set out clearly separated into different categories. The main distinctions are between:

1 archive collections, with, sometimes, private collections being listed before, and separately from, public (or government) collections;

2 rare printed materials (usually originating from private individuals or bodies);

3 government printed materials;

4 newspapers and periodicals.

Radical historians are usually as eager to observe the conventions (which are fully flexible enough to accommodate new types of sources as these are discovered and exploited) as conservative ones. Let me take the example of the bibliography to E. P. Thompson's *The Making of the English Working Class* (1965). First the archive materials: Thompson actually takes Public Record Office collections along with, and before, private collections, starting with the relatively well-sorted Home Office papers, of which he made special use of those catalogued as series 40 and 42; then he lists miscellaneous bundles of papers relating to the London Corresponding Society, food riots and other working-class topics found among the less well-sorted Privy Council papers; and lastly the Treasury Solicitor's papers which, among a mass of material of no direct use to Thompson, contain some of the evidence, such as informers' reports, depositions, intercepted letters, from which the Crown briefs against state prisoners were prepared. In the Manuscripts Room of the British Museum, Thompson consulted the much-worked-over Place Collection, which includes minute books and letter books of the London Corresponding Society. In the Sheffield Reference Library Thompson used the Fitzwilliam Papers, where the relevant material for his study included part of the correspondence on public affairs of Earl Fitzwilliam and reports from the Yorkshire justices of the peace and other informants during the time when Fitzwilliam was Lord Lieutenant of the West Riding of Yorkshire. At a private country mansion, Rudding Park, Harrogate, Thompson consulted the Radcliffe Papers and made use of the correspondence of Sir Joseph Radcliffe, a Huddersfield magistrate responsible for bringing Luddite agitators to trial. In the Nottingham City Archives, Thompson consulted the papers of the Framework-Knitter Committee.

Thompson then proceeds to the next level of the primary hierarchy: contemporary pamphlets and periodicals, discovered mainly in the British Museum Reading Room and the John Rylands Library, Manchester. A historian concerned with similar problems in a slightly later period (Thompson is concerned with the late eighteenth century and early nineteenth century, when the governmental system was pretty rudimentary) would then have moved on to another category of (published) primary sources: government reports and reports of parliamentary debates. The bound volumes of Acts of Parliament could also be included here.

Relationship Between Primary and Secondary Sources: Footnotes

The bibliography of a scholarly work will give a broad impression of the relationship between primary and secondary sources. A more detailed impression can be derived from noting the way in which quotations from and references to primary materials are woven into a secondary account, it being the function of the footnote to reveal the precise nature of the particular primary sources involved. Here is an extract, complete with footnote, from another important secondary work, published at around the same time, and by a completely different historian also called Thompson, this time about the nineteenth-century English landed aristocracy – F. M. L. Thompson's *English Landed Society in the Nineteenth Century* (1965):

> Behind all these changes in the balance of forces within the community lay the fact that in the 1880s the landed interest still possessed an influence altogether out of proportion to their numbers. This they owed to the great social consequences which continued to attach to the owners of landed estates, a feeling of respect which had not been greatly affected by half a century's experience of adjustments to the new forces and new necessities thrown up by the industrial revolution. Several landowners had appreciated, by the middle of the century, that land was a luxury which gave very poor financial returns to its owners, and had wondered whether the time had not arrived to put their wealth to more remunerative uses. Sir James Graham in 1845 contemplated retreat from the position of a great landowner. Evelyn Denison expatiated to Lord Fitzwilliam in 1847 'about that "expensive luxury" Land. It is about to become infinitely more expensive than ever', he wrote, 'so great a luxury that many now in possession of it will be obliged to resign it'. This was because, he felt, interest rates on mortgages were about to be pushed to unprecedentedly high levels by the competition of railway debentures, 'which will put pressure on encumbered estates (that is, speaking generally, on half or two thirds of the land of England) to which they have never before been subjected'. He himself, however, was going to sell land 'not because I am of the class of encumbered landlords, for I have luckily extracted myself from that, but because I do not think it worthwhile to keep a security paying 2 percent, when I can get an equally good one paying 5.' Lord Monson put the matter more succinctly when he burst out in 1851: 'What an infernal bore is landed property. No certain income can be reckoned upon. I hope your future wife will have Consols or some such ballast, I think it is worth half as much again as what land is reckoned at.'[1]
>
> [1] D. Spring, 'A Great Agricultural Estate', p. 81. Wentworth Woodhouse MSS, G. 20, J. E. Denison to Lord Fitzwilliam, 18 Aug. 1847. Monson MSS, 25/10/3/1, no. 19, 22 Nov. 1851.

Thompson is making a statement about the landed aristocracy turning to new sources of income, supporting it with two references to manuscript letters, one in the archives of the City Library, Sheffield, the other in the County Record Office in Lincoln, and one reference to a secondary source, an article by another historian, David Spring, which contains yet more evidence, based on *his* primary researches (as Thompson has given full details relating to this article and the learned journal in which it was presented in a previous footnote he does not repeat that information here). I'll explore these questions of relationships between research and secondary sources, and between sources, footnotes, and the writing of a secondary book, in the next chapter.

What I am demonstrating here is both how primary sources differ from secondary ones, and how primary sources are used, how they are integrated into secondary ones. The purpose of those who deny the significance of the difference is to cast doubt on the value of historical *research* and maintain that what is really important is the way in which history books are *written*. Jordanova, as we have noted, speaks scathingly of 'the cult of the archive', while Carr contemptuously dismissed what he termed a 'fetishism of documents':

> The documents were the ark of the Covenant in the temple of facts. The reverent historian approached them with bowed head and spoke of them in awed tones. If you find it in the documents, it is so.[7]

That this is complete drivel, all readers by this time will be fully aware. But it gets worse. Carr then posed a famous question, following it with an extremely silly answer:

> But what when we get down to it, do these documents – the decrees, the treaties, the rent-rolls, the blue books, the official correspondence, the private letters and diaries – tell us?

The answer:

> No document can tell us more than what the author of the document thought – what he thought had happened, what he thought ought to happen or would happen, or perhaps only what he wanted others to think he thought or even only what he himself thought he thought.[8]

No doubt Carr was rewarded with a few dutiful guffaws.

But let us go through the highly fruitful exercise of examining the types of document specified by Carr. A decree records a definite decision by a ruler or government. Whether the decree was actually implemented would be a matter for further investigation, and, like all sources, the decree would have to be set within a context of other relevant documents, but a decree certainly tells us far more than what its author (supposing one single author can be completely and persuasively identified – a large supposition) thought. Consider the Edict of Nantes *signed* by Henry IV of France on 30 April 1598 (though it was not necessarily the pristine expression of the unassisted regal thought processes), which (roughly) gave Protestants and Catholics parity of status. What Henry, whose earlier 'conversion' from Protestantism to

Catholicism had brought him considerable political advantages, really 'thought', or even 'thought he thought', about religion has been a matter of considerable debate and speculation. Henry at the time was simultaneously embroiled in war with Spain and threatened with civil war by his former Protestant supporters (the 'Huguenots'). The Edict reflects the dangers of Henry's situation, the claims advanced by the Protestants, the advice given by his advisers, and the balance between whatever predilections he may have had himself and political calculation, in what he almost certainly intended as a temporary expedient. A many-layered document indeed, yielding riches far beyond Carr's footling foolery – to, that is, the trained historian: master also of the Edicts of Mantes and Poitiers, utterly familiar with the peculiar nature of the claim to public worship made by the Protestants, with the technicalities of *bailliages*, *sénéchaussées*, *parlements* and their special chambers, and so on.

Treaties record what has been agreed between two or more powers; again, a treaty may not be fully carried out, but it will certainly indicate the balance of power and aspirations between the principals, the best bargain each can obtain. As it happens, just two days after the Edict of Nantes was signed Henry (or, more accurately, the advisers who were concentrating on this issue) concluded the treaty of Vervins with Spain. Is it, then, perhaps what Philip II of Spain 'thought he thought' that we learn from this treaty? To anyone not intoxicated with his own rhetoric, as Carr was, it is obvious that these two documents of record will tell the historian with the necessary skills a great deal about the nature and assumptions of both politics and religion and their interrelationships at the end of the sixteenth century. Quite obviously, they are indispensable to the study of both. And without all the other sources turned up by the systematic and imaginative work of historians, we wouldn't have a *clue* (for once, the everyday cliché is completely appropriate) as to, say, who or what the Huguenots were, or even about the basic sequence of events.

Or, for a moment, reflect on the treaty of Versailles, the ideals it enshrined (political equality for women among them), the follies it propagated – Carr's feeble trivialisation is but a passing of wind. Decrees, treaties, as also official correspondence, and (in published form) private letters and diaries were what Carr himself, in the historical studies he came to relatively late in life, was most used to. Even an official letter usually amounts to rather more than the personal thought of one person, though, of course, as ever, the professional historian will check it against, and collate it with, the other relevant sources (a fundamental procedure which Carr ignores). Carr was unfamiliar with the sorts of letters and diaries used by social historians to piece together, say, structures of belief and patterns of family life. Again his comments reveal only his own ignorance, but – and this is the point of taking a sledgehammer to what may seem like a peanut – that same ignorance pervades the work of the cultural theorists who denigrate source-based history without having any understanding of how historians actually use their sources. If we come back to rent-rolls, we are again in the domain of the document of record: since it is certainly not in the interests of a landowner to enter the rents due to him incorrectly, this kind of document is a valuable source of statistical information, offering clear evidence for social and economic relationships into which the element of thought stressed by Carr scarcely enters. 'Blue Books' are the reports of the commissions and committees of investigation which figured prominently in nineteenth-century British politics: a report on the conditions of women and children in the mining industry might well be inflected by the opinions of the investigators (as indeed we know *from the studies made by historians of related documents*) but quite patently has a significance for historians far beyond what Carr allows. With all of these documents, historians find much of value in the assumptions that lie behind what is written, as well as in the overt thought being expressed. Carr, it may be noted, says nothing of archaeology, place names, the landscape, physical artefacts, visual sources, film, and all the other non-traditional sources which historians use: but then, it's rather difficult to indulge in the joke that the field plan of a medieval village shows only what someone 'thought he thought'.

Integrating Primary and Secondary Sources: Strategy

Those commentators who talk about 'the fetishism of documents' and 'the cult of the archive' present an image of historians plunging into collections of primary sources like four-year-olds excitedly rushing into the sea without pausing to change into their swimming costumes first. In fact, it cannot be stressed too much that before embarking on primary research, historians have to develop a *strategy*. A strategy is essential for ensuring that research is systematic, and that time is not wasted on random investigation or duplicating the work of others. Having a strategy is very different from having a predetermined thesis, or some *a priori* theory or ideology. We all have preconceptions and preliminary ideas – and these may, indeed, have come from our readings in the secondary sources. Most historians are familiar with that point in the archives, or perhaps when one is reflecting later on what one has discovered in the archives, when early misconceptions begin to be replaced and new and more convincing interpretations begin to take their place.

The point I want to make here is that, with respect to the relative functions of primary and secondary sources, though distinctively different, they are integrated: study of the secondary sources is absolutely essential in evolving a strategy. A strategy entails a mastery of the existing secondary sources, and identification of the questions that require answering and the problems that need solving (though, as often as not, as research progresses a whole set of new questions and problems will be thrown up), and at least a provisional inventory of the types of sources to be examined (one set of sources, as all historians know, will often throw up problems which then require the study of another set). The strategy is open, not predetermined; but it is not haphazard.

3   The Immense Variety of Primary Sources

Strengths and Weaknesses of Different Types of Primary Sources

As I said in Chapter 1, primary sources did not come into existence to satisfy the curiosity of historians. They derive 'naturally', 'organically', as it were, or, more straightforwardly, 'in the ordinary course of events', from human beings and groups of human beings living their lives, worshipping, making decisions, adjudicating, fornicating, going about their business or fulfilling their vocations, recording, noting, communicating as they go, very occasionally, perhaps, with an eye on the future, but generally in accordance with immediate needs and purposes. The technical skills of the historian lie in sorting these matters out, in understanding how and why a particular source came into existence, how relevant it is to the topic under investigation, and, obviously, the particular codes or language in accordance with which the particular source comes into being as a concrete artefact.[9] The sort of bibliography I have just been discussing is not very adequate for organising and categorising *all* the sources there are dating from *all* periods of history, and *relevant to all* types of historical problem. I invite you, my reader, to try your hand at noting down on a piece of paper as many kinds of primary source as you can think of. A rather more difficult task would be to try to group the different sources that actually exist into 'families' or groups of similar sources. In a moment, I am going to do that, but first I want to make some general points about the different types of sources, and the different strengths and weaknesses they have, depending upon what particular topic is being studied.

1 *The contrast between public and private sources.* The simple contrast here is between sources which were intended to be seen or read by substantial numbers of people (such as Roman Imperial inscriptions, acts of parliament, newspapers) and sources generated purely for the use

of one person or certain specified persons (such as diaries, letters, secret diplomatic documents). We cannot say that one sort is automatically more reliable than the other. We could make the initial presumption that someone writing in their own diary or to a close friend would be unlikely to tell deliberate lies. Conversely, some types of public document may be deliberately designed to mislead. On the other hand, the fact that a document is public and 'open' may create pressures for it to be accurate (I'd say that, for example, of a report by a reputable journalist in a reputable newspaper).

2 *The contrast between 'documents of record' and what I shall call 'discursive sources'.* A 'document of record' is one which by its very existence records that some event took place – it is not someone else's account, but, as it were, it embodies the event itself. Prime examples are acts of parliament, peace treaties, charters (like Magna Carta), and minutes of meetings. An act of parliament itself embodies the event of a law being passed, as a peace treaty embodies the event of a peace treaty being concluded: both may be full of waffle and hypocrisy, and they may indeed never be implemented, but they still record something that definitely happened. The actual existence of Magna Carta (in several copies) does tell us that the issuing of Magna Carta really did take place. Minutes (of Cabinet meetings or, say, the local marriage council annual general meetings) can be uninformative or even misleading, but provided they are not fakes (and that goes for everything) they are records that the meetings did take place. Important documents of record that have recently been much used by historians are wills. Wills record a definite transaction. They may well be the best way of establishing how rich a person was. They can also be used to infer how much, or how little, affection existed between married couples and between parents and children. Much work with primary sources – this is a general point – is done by indirect inference. Discursive sources – somebody else's report that a meeting took place or description of the signing of a treaty – will have their own uses, but are not the best and most direct sources for the events themselves. Other discursive sources which have come into great use in recent times are books advising on social behaviour and etiquette, sometimes known as 'conduct books', studies of customs and folklore, and guides, handbooks, directories and other works of reference. The last category can be given a high rating for potential accuracy, since customers wouldn't buy them if they weren't reliable. The second one should be accurate, though there is always the danger of the enthusiast being tempted to romanticise. The first category offers most problems – are the authors writing about behaviour as it actually is, or are they describing some ideal?

A Taxonomy of Primary Sources

Now, have you written down your list of the many types of primary source? Here is mine:[10]

1   *Documents of record.* As we have seen from the examples of the edict and treaties already mentioned, these, taken in conjunction with other sources, offer an enormous variety of insights and perceptions, but they do also record something that actually happened; they record a 'fact' or 'event', the very edict or treaty itself, and in that specific and limited sense they cannot be 'ideology' (they are 'fact', not 'opinion') – though of course, as historians know better than anyone, minutes, reports of meetings, and so on, recording what a body as a whole *agreed* its decisions to be, can be incomplete and slanted. They may, as with, say, parish registers or rent-rolls, record hard, factual information – the 'facts' will be subject to human error in the original entries, though scarcely to ideology, and will require specialist skills to extract.

   Documents of record have a range and variety that the mockers of 'a fetishism of documents' have never dreamed of. E. P. Thompson, and other historians of the working class, have made great use of police records; in reconstructing the life of Montaillou, Le Roy Ladurie used the records of the Inquisition; one of the most illuminating sets of sources for sexual behaviour in *ancien régime* France are the *déclarations de grossesse*, statements required by law from unwed mothers. These, it need scarcely be said, are *records*, subject to the accuracy and honesty of the scribes, of what the women *said*, not necessarily of what actually happened. No one but the historian can comprehend the fascinating variousness of sources, and what can be done with them; no one better than the historian knows their dreadful fallibility.

2   *Surveys and reports.* These will always have a point of view, as with Carr's Blue Books, but then it is one of the historian's first tasks to be sure that he or she has fully grasped what that point of view is; the task is not to pin down an ideology (rather easy when there seem to be so few on offer, of which, of course, much the most popular is 'bourgeois') or identify a type of discourse, but to penetrate far more deeply in order to isolate such bits of hard evidence as the source does contain.

3   *Chronicles and histories.* Historians who, for a couple of hundred years or more, have been used to the mishmash of superstition and myth, mixed with the occasional recording of fact or attempt at assessment, to be found in monastic and chivalric chronicles and town histories, are entitled to feel some weary resentment at latter-day preachers on the problems of 'deconstructing' texts; medieval historians try as far

as they can to avoid undue dependence on such sources (yet how glad we are to have them for such places as Tajikistan or Vilnius); a few authentic chronicles, difficult though they will be to interpret, are worth any amount of specious theory.

4 *Family and personal sources.* Diaries and memoirs intended for publication will obviously be assessed differently from letters written solely with the purpose of, say, begging for a job, or informing a husband of how the household is faring in his absence; all diaries will have to be treated as the products of rather untypical human beings: but when purpose, social background, personal peculiarities, immediate context, literary conventions – as relevant – are taken into account, how much information there often is for those skilled enough to perceive it!

5 *Polemical, hortatory and prescriptive documents.* Pamphlets, treatises, sermons, political manifestos are among the most used of historical sources: the naïve may think that these are simply conflicting discourses, Catholic against Protestant, Tory against socialist. In fact, apparently competing discourses often reveal shared assumptions about the nature of social structure. Conduct books, advising or prescribing on etiquette and behaviour – often for women! – are much used by historians these days, fully aware that they have to pin down who wrote them, who read them, and how far, if at all, they corresponded to actual behaviour.

6 *Studies of customs and folklore and other academic works; textbooks, works of sociology, etc.* Some important recent books have made considerable use of contemporary studies of folklore and customs – folklorists have their prejudices and blindspots like everyone else, but, on the whole, their driving force tends to be a dedication to their subject, so that again the historian, employing the appropriate wariness and crosschecks, can learn much. The writings of neither Max Weber, nor of Talcott Parsons, tell us how class actually is or was; but they give insights into perceptions of class in, respectively, the late-nineteenth century and the mid-twentieth century. Works of contemporary cultural theorists don't tell us much about either culture or history, but they will tell future historians much about the strange ideas put forward at the beginning of the twenty-first century.

7 *Guides, handbooks, directories, and other works of reference.* I am deliberately making a distinction between these and the conduct books and other sources included under heading 5: guides to social customs, etiquette, and fashion, as perhaps also guides to the contemporary social scene, may straddle the divide – the historian will have to work out whether the intention is to prescribe a desired behaviour, or whether it is simply to report on actual behaviour (often something of

both), but codifications of the law, guides on parliamentary procedure, directories, handbooks, and educational manuals will (rather like a guide to home computing today) have to be accurate, or they will be of no value to their potential customers. Guides to 'Ladies of the Town' are an interesting sub-category; of course they inscribe prevailing values, a slightly more complex matter than those whose unvarying response to the practices of the past is outrage would have us believe.

8 *Media of communication and artefacts of popular culture.* With newspapers, cartoons, etchings, and other illustrative material, posters and advertisements, films, radio tapes, television tapes (none, of course, mentioned by Carr), we move into fields where the cultural theorists also like to trample: no harm done, and perhaps something for historians to learn, provided always the fundamental purposes and achievements of history are kept firmly in mind – not to illustrate predetermined generalisations about competing discourses, or dominant ideologies, but to illuminate the past. These sources are very rich for attitudes, assumptions, mentalities, and values.

9 *Archaeology, industrial archaeology, history on the ground, and physical artefacts.* It has to be recognised that these are sources not directly used by the majority of working historians; yet most would consider it at least an ancillary part of their job to be knowledgeable about the built environment of whatever period or society they are studying and to be familiar with surviving physical relics. The area most affected by archaeological discoveries, obviously, is that traditionally termed 'ancient' or 'classical' history. A major point is confirmed: discovery or application of new sources alters interpretations – in other words, history *depends* on sources. We can learn a lot about the more modern period too, particularly about lifestyles and living conditions, from, for example, household utensils, furniture, and surviving buildings. Large and elaborate inn signs dating from the early seventeenth century indicate that in that period literacy was still not widespread: an ideographic (that is, visual) and easily recognised sign was of more use to the majority than a written one. Such sources may often be of use for rather specialised history, such as, for instance, the history of costume and fashion. But they can play their part too in the study of the wider questions of attitudes and mentalities. Coins have all sorts of subtle uses. Sometimes the actual illustrations and inscriptions on them tell us something about what matters seemed significant to the particular society which used the coins. The Roman emperors used coins for disseminating propaganda. More often coins serve as a basic source of precise information which can help to illuminate the significance of a whole host of other archaeological finds by, for example, giving an exact dating.

The argument can be further sustained from contemplation of one of the most evocative settings in the City of London: standing at a particular point near the Museum of London in the Barbican, one can take in (1) a high-rise block of modern flats, part of the Barbican development itself; (2) in front, to the right, the square tower of the medieval church of St Giles, Cripplegate; and (3) low down to the left, an impressive section of the wall originally built round London by the Romans. At one very fundamental level (not to be scoffed at), this little scene gives the spectator a very potent impression of three different eras in London's history. But, alas, these three magnificent pieces of 'history on the ground' cannot be taken at face value. From a wealth of other sources (including engravings and photographs, as well as written documents) historians know that while St Giles Cripplegate actually survived the Great Fire of London, it had in fact been burnt down over a century before, in 1545, that it was punitively 'restored' by the Victorians, and that it was practically destroyed in the blitz of December 1940 – much of what we see today is a restoration completed in the 1960s; we know also that the wall was in continuous existence until the seventeenth century, constantly reconstructed and rebuilt, and has been subject to deliberate conservation since then: we see the Roman contours, but mainly seventeenth-century materials. As it happens, historians don't actually know when St Giles was originally built: without corroboration from other sources they are disinclined to believe John Stow, whose *A Survey of London* of 1598 (like all the 'histories' in category 3, both a delight and a delusion) claims that it was founded in 1090. As well as demonstrating what is known (all knowledge, inevitably, being in some sense provisional), the scrupulous citation of sources also reveals candidly what is not known: sources are salient both positively and negatively.

10 *Literary and artistic sources.* Many of those who are in the van of condemning what they perceive as the fetishism of documents would maintain that 'art' and 'literature' are meaningless terms; but then they would also maintain that all of the other sources studied by the historian – like novels, plays, paintings, and so on – are merely 'texts' or forms of discourse. The historian who wishes *to produce results* (as distinct from merely elaborating on predetermined conclusions) does best to stick to categories based partly on the physical nature of the source, but mainly on its fundamental contemporary purpose. Paintings are not painted to serve the same purpose as acts of parliament, nor novels drafted to bring wars to a close. Indeed, a criticism which could legitimately be made of an earlier generation of historians who generalised about age of

marriage from the plays of Shakespeare, and about Victorian living conditions from the novels of Dickens, is that they forgot that plays and novels are *deliberately* works of the imagination. There are important bodies of literary and artistic theory which the historian would be extremely foolish to ignore. Every historian, for instance, should be aware of the conventions within which an artist of any particular period or style operates in representing reality, the *schemata* he employs, as Gombrich puts it.[11] But historians will also adhere to their own proven methods: not reading the text in isolation, but studying all the other sources which indicate the origins of the work of literature or art, the intentions of the artist or writer, the conditions under which it was produced, the way it was marketed, and how it was received. If information is to be taken from the text it will, in the usual way, be checked against other relevant sources. In the study of values, attitudes, and assumptions, artistic and literary sources can be invaluable to historians, who, however, neither forget that they are fiction, nor exempt them from the critical caution applied to every other source.

11 *Processed sources.* This inelegant title, redolent of down-market food-stuffs, points to some of the most up-market activities indulged in by historians today: palaeontology, serology, aerial photography, the study of place names, and, of course, the application of advanced computer technology to statistical material. To take the last first, the actual raw data will have to be collected from the various other categories of sources listed here: in origin, it is indisputably primary source material, but it only becomes usable through being processed through a computer. Aerial photographs are not in themselves sources left by the past; rather, the taking of an aerial photograph is a *process* through which the contours of a medieval village, say, or of old field plans, not apparent to someone standing on the ground, become clear. To be absolutely accurate, one should probably say that the actual configurations of the landscape, invisible though they may be to the unaided human eye, form the true primary source. Likewise, the true primary sources for the study of place names are surviving towns, villages, and geographical features and their names, together with all the other categories of sources from which place names may be extracted (old maps, chronicles, and so forth). The study of place names is a process or technique for making use of the data assembled from many sources. As is well known, English towns ending in *-by* or *-thorpe* have been used to plot the extent of Viking settlement. But place-name evidence is no more free-standing or infallible than any other. The date we first *hear* of a place name may not be the same as the date at which it first *came into existence*.

P. H. Sawyer made considerable use of this discrepancy in arguing that the basic pattern of English settlement had already established itself by the seventh century, and not, as usually thought, only in the eleventh century.[12] Palaeontology is the study of pollen cores from peat bog and lake sediments, giving knowledge of vegetational (and therefore cultivational) change. Serology uses the distribution of different blood groups in societies of today to indicate settlement patterns of, say (in Africa), different tribal groups or (in early England) of different nationalities (Anglo-Saxons, Norsemen, and so on). In both of these cases, process and basic source are inextricably intertwined. Historians, I hope it is now clear, exploit every possibility, go to every last resort in the naked pursuit of hard information – how very different is that pursuit from the facile manipulation of so-called 'ideologies' and discourses, and the conjuration of 'textuality'.

12 *'Oral history' and oral traditions.* I put 'oral history' in quotation marks because this phrase, though now absorbed into the language shared by historians and the general public, can be misleading. What is usually meant is 'oral testimony' (that is to say, 'oral sources'), the recording, whether on tape, or in shorthand, or by any other means, of personal recollections (though sometimes what is meant is a fully written-up history based almost exclusively on such sources). For some areas of historical study, including much recent Third World history, such source material is absolutely invaluable. Naturally, it takes great skill, and a mastery of whatever other knowledge is available, to make effective use of what is inherently (given the fallibility of human memory) a highly problematic source. Oral traditions (which take us back far beyond living memory) are especially valuable for societies where the written word is little used. Folk songs and folk sayings can give insights into the attitudes and mentalities of ordinary people in the past. It is in this category of source that we really do encounter the 'stories' which the linguistic materialists tell us are the only sources out of which we construct our lives. It is, on the contrary, fundamental to systematic historical study that realistic distinctions are made between 'stories' properly so-called and the many very different kinds of evidence I have itemised here.

13 *Observed behaviour, surviving customs, technical processes, etc.* Regrettably, there is still a considerable market in the United States for handguns individually crafted as they were in the late eighteenth and early nineteenth centuries before the mass production of fully interchangeable parts: for economic and military historians alike the study of a contemporary craftsman at work in the old manner provides a peculiar, but unique, kind of source. When Marc Bloch was alive, it was still perfectly reasonable for him to believe that, in

studying the French peasants of his day, he would learn about their past. In our day, the focus of such approaches has had to switch to the Third World, where medieval historians can still reasonably hope that the study of practices current there now will throw light on behaviour in the Europe of earlier times. I don't wish to exaggerate the importance of sources and techniques not widely used in mainstream history; I am simply concerned to drive home the point that those who wish to mock the historian's concern with sources should be careful first to be clear that they really do understand what these sources comprise, and should certainly not remain under the illusion that E. H. Carr had anything like the last word on the subject.

Well, I don't suppose you got nearly as many examples as that, and I'm sure you didn't group them in the way I have done. Pause to reflect for a moment: the range of raw materials historians have at their disposal is immense, but all of them contain within them, as well as definite uses to the historian, many difficulties and problems.

4   Witting and Unwitting Testimony

This distinction is now fairly widely accepted in the teaching of history at sixth-form level in Britain. It is a distinction which had, more or less overtly, lain behind the practice of history for several generations. If historians (notoriously reticent about their assumptions and methods) had publicised it more openly there might have been less nonsense talked about historians' naïve belief in the transparency of 'documents', of their need to pay heed to the anthropologists and their 'webs of meaning', and take lessons from the postmodernists and their theories of deconstruction and discourse analysis. We would not have had the nonsense about sources containing 'fictive' elements, which if stripped away will reveal 'real facts'. Historians have always sensed, even if they have not explicitly acknowledged, that sources, as well as containing many kinds of imperfection, also contain many types and many layers of evidence. The crucial, though never absolutely rigid, distinction is between the 'witting' testimony and the 'unwitting'.

My codification of the phrase was prompted by some fairly casual words by the distinguished American historian of science Henry Guerlac, who had spoken of a distinction between the 'intentional record' and the 'unwitting testimony' of official records and private correspondence.[13] 'Witting' means 'deliberate' or 'intentional'; 'unwitting' means 'unaware' or 'unintentional'. 'Testimony' means 'evidence'. Thus, 'witting testimony' is the deliberate or intentional message (often more than merely 'intentional record') of a document or other source; the 'unwitting testimony' is the unintentional evidence (about, for example, the attitudes and values of the author, or about the 'culture' to which he/she belongs) that it also contains. Actually, it is the writer, creator, or creators of the document or source who is, or are, intentional or unintentional, not the testimony itself, so these phrases are examples of a figure of speech, the transferred epithet, where the adjective, which strictly speaking should be applied to a person, is transferred to what the person produced – the phrase is all the more effective for that. Witting testimony, then, is the information or impression that the person or persons who originally compiled or created the source intended to convey, or in some cases to record.

Domesday Book came into existence because William the Conqueror wanted to know exactly how much the land he had conquered was worth: thus he sent his investigators to every part of England to collect details of every village from the sworn testimony (a good example of the normal usage of this word) of local men, details about who held what land and about the value of each holding and its stock. The witting testimony of Domesday Book, then, consists of these factual details of who owned what, how much cattle, how many sheep, what fields, and so on. But, though this was no part of William the Conqueror's intention, Domesday Book also gives historians fascinating insight into the structure, attitudes and life of the various communities of eleventh-century England. This is its unwitting testimony, which may well be more important to historians than the witting testimony. Magna Carta, in intention, was a record of the bargain imposed by the barons on King John in 1215. The nature of that bargain, the witting testimony, is of great interest to historians, but Magna Carta also unwittingly reveals much about social relationships and social assumptions in early thirteenth-century England. Neither Magna Carta nor Domesday Book was drawn up in order to enlighten historians about conditions in medieval English society; but in fact their unwitting testimony has proved invaluable for historians with the knowledge and skills to winnow it out. In Canterbury Cathedral the tomb of the Black Prince with his imposing effigy and surrounding paraphernalia wittingly intimates what an important personage he was; the representation of the dog nestling at his feet unwittingly indicates that the notion of 'man's best friend' was prevalent among the then nobility, an impression confirmed in several of the surrounding tombs.

Hansard's published volumes of Victorian parliamentary debates were intended to inform all interested of exactly what different ministers, and ordinary MPs, had said in the House of Commons: that is their witting testimony and it is of profound interest to political historians. But this publication also tells us something about the way in which

parliamentary debates were conducted, about the procedures and conventions of the Victorian parliament. This is unwitting testimony, interesting, though perhaps in this case not as important as the witting
testimony. However, where the basic assumptions of Members of Parliament are also revealed – for example, their almost automatic acceptance
of the forms and beliefs of revealed religion, taken for granted by them,
but very striking to *us* – then such unwitting testimony can be of great
importance. Victorian political documents do not usually say much
about women, the clear understanding being (and this is supported
wherever there are casual references to women) that women occupied
an inferior place in society and were excluded from public life. The
Victorians did not usually feel the need to express this openly (though
sometimes they did); they took it for granted. But we, 'reading between
the lines' as it were, that is to say reading the unwitting testimony, the
unspoken assumptions, can derive a very clear impression of the role
and status of women in Victorian society (incidentally, 'reading between
the lines' is a good example of the kind of vague colloquialism that is best
avoided: 'extracting the unwitting testimony' is a much more precise
statement). Witting testimony, then, is the message a source deliberately
sets out to convey to contemporaries; the unwitting testimony is the
evidence which historians find very useful, but which the originator of
the document is not conscious might be conveyed to later historians, for
it would be known anyway, or taken for granted, by contemporaries.

The notion of 'unwitting testimony' has, to give one example, been
taken up usefully by Danish film historian Karsten Fledelius:

> Often the most interesting evidence is the 'unwitting testimony' or the
> cinematographic recordings, all those incidental aspects of reality
> which have just 'slipped' into the camera without being consciously
> recorded by the cameraman. The 'evidence by accident' may be ex-
> tremely valuable to the historian.[14]

Evidence also 'slips' into written documents 'by accident' – that is to say
without the writer of the document being aware that matters he/she
unconsciously includes will be of great value to historians.

One can break unwitting testimony down into three sub-sets, three
slightly different types of evidence or information: (i) of which the
creators of the source are simply not conscious; (ii) of which they are
partially conscious but of whose wider significance (and, therefore,
significance to the historian) they are quite unaware; and (iii) which is
so obvious to them that they just mention it in passing. Now, I should
make it clear that a historian working with a large number of primary
sources, comparing, contrasting, collating them, while fully aware of the
different types of evidence that is being accumulated, modified, and

rejected, will not consciously go through these finicky procedures. In this part of the book I am moving from general principles of history applicable at all levels, to discussing specific teaching devices. I am very strongly of the view that in teaching history one should give students a sense of what it is like to be a practising historian. The exercises one devises to try to ensure this inevitably have a strong element of artificiality about them: historians do not study single, pre-selected, preprinted, and often abbreviated documents. But it is only, I believe, by applying a detailed catechism to individual documents that one can develop a sense of the strengths and weaknesses of different sources, always, in turn, dependent upon the actual topic being studied. That is another key phrase, 'strengths and weaknesses': all primary sources, as I have said repeatedly, have their weaknesses; with luck, one also finds their strengths for the particular topic being investigated. I will return to strengths and weaknesses in the next section when I turn to my 'catechism'. Here I want to invite you to participate in a couple of exercises designed to illuminate further the distinction between witting and unwitting testimony.

Try to imagine that you are writing a book or an article on English society in the middle of the nineteenth century, and you are making use of the document which I am about to quote in a moment, a brief extract from a commentary by a leading figure in the Church of England, Horace Mann, which he wrote on the results of a religious census conducted by the Church of England in 1851. See if you can distinguish between the main witting testimony and the most important unwitting testimony (no need to break things down into the three sub-sets).

The most important fact which this investigation as to attendance brings before us is, unquestionably, the alarming number of the non-attendants. Even in the least unfavourable aspect of the figures, just presented, and assuming (as no doubt is right) that the 5,288,294 absent every Sunday are not always the same individuals, it must be apparent that a sadly formidable portion of the English people are habitual neglecters of the public ordinances of religion. Nor is it difficult to indicate to what particular class of the community this portion in the main belongs. The middle classes have augmented rather than diminished that devotional sentiment and strictness of attention to religious services by which, for several centuries, they have so eminently been distinguished. With the upper classes, too, the subject of religion has obtained of late a marked degree of notice, and a regular church-attendance is now ranked among the recognised proprieties of life. It is to satisfy the wants of these two classes that the number of religious structures had of late years so increased. But while the *labouring* myriads of our country have been multiplying with our multiplied material prosperity, it cannot, it is feared, be stated that a corresponding increase has occurred in the attendance of this class in our religious edifices. More especially in cities and large towns it is observable how absolutely insignificant a portion of the congregations is composed of artizans ... the masses of our working population ... are never or but seldom seen in our religious congregations; and the melancholy fact is thus impressed upon our notice that the classes which are most in need of the restraints and consolations of religion are the classes which are most without them ...[15]

The witting testimony, the message which comes through with complete clarity, the one which Mann is obviously striving to put over, is that the alarming (as he sees it) problem of non-attendance is concentrated in the working masses: they, he passionately feels, need religion most, yet heed it least. That is the problem *he* wants *his* readers to give their attention to. He is unconscious of the fact that he is conveying to later readers (the first type of unwitting testimony) the very profound belief in the importance of religion held by himself and those to whom he is addressing this commentary; he does wittingly tell us that religious observance is not a problem with the middle class, and, if it once was one, has now ceased to be one with the upper classes – but the evident belief in the significance of religion goes beyond this factual, witting, information. Mann is consciously concerned about one aspect of the condition of the workers, but he is not, of course, conscious of the historical significance of what he is giving away: it is, for other than religious reasons, important for historians to know how little the workers were affected by religion, and even more to know that what Mann and his like thought the workers needed were 'restraints' and 'consolations'. But for the historian of mid-Victorian society perhaps the most important piece of unwitting testimony (of the third type) is that to do with class structure: Mann takes it for granted that society at that time is divided into the upper classes, the middle classes, and the labouring masses. He is not intending to tell his Victorian contemporaries, who would know the situation very well for themselves, still less future historians, anything about class structure, but, unwittingly, his mapping of it emerges. Now this is only one man's mapping, though if it were wildly wrong, or eccentric, he could hardly expect his deeply felt appeal to be heeded by his readers – so (thinking of the document's strengths and weaknesses) one would have strong grounds for presuming that his mapping was shared by his readers. For a complete account (historians do not rely on single sources, remember), it would have to be put with other perceptions of class structure at the time and, more important, would have, if the historian is to get beyond mere perceptions to the actual realities of the mid-Victorian class structure, to be integrated with statistical evidence (of incomes, housing types, education, the extent of inter-class marriage, etc., etc.).

I would now like us to look together at a letter sent by the French Count de Germiny to the (revolutionary) National Assembly on 20 August 1789, in the early days of the French Revolution. Imagine you are researching on 'Nobles and Peasants in the French Revolution': read the document and see if you can distinguish between the witting and unwitting testimony.

> On 29 July 1789, a group of brigands from elsewhere, together with my vassals and those of Vrigni, the next parish to mine, two hundred in all, came to my *château* at Sassy, parish of Saint Christopher, near Argentan, and, after breaking the locks on the cupboards containing my title deeds, they seized the registers which could be so necessary to me, took them away, or burned them in the woods near my *château*; my guard was unable to offer any resistance, being the only warden in this area, where I myself do not reside. These wretched people had the tocsin rung in neighbouring parishes in order to swell their numbers. I am all the more sad about this loss because I have never let my vassals feel the odious weight of ancient feudalism, of which I am sure they could be redeemed in present circumstances; but who will ever be able to certify and prove the damage they have inflicted on my property? I appeal to your discretion to bring in some law whereby the National Assembly can reimburse me for my loss, above all for the use of common land, as useful to my parishioners as to my own estate, whose title deeds they burned. I will not take steps against those whom I know to have been with the brigands who, not content with burning my papers, have killed my pigeons. But I expect full justice in the spirit of equity which guides you, and which gives me the greatest confidence.[16]

The testimony the Count de Germiny wishes to convey (that is, the witting testimony) is that he has suffered at the hands of brigands and peasants and that he hopes to gain compensation through the National Assembly. He refers specifically to the breaking of locks on cupboards, and the seizing and burning of registers of title deeds. His earlier point that there were brigands and vassals from another parish is amplified when he refers to the tocsin (peal of bells) being rung in several parishes in order to produce much larger numbers than would have been pro-vided by his vassals alone. He specifically mentions that the title deeds expressing his own claims upon common land have been burned. Finally, not only have his papers been burned, but all his pigeons have been killed. The other deliberate (witting) message in the document is that he is not a wicked upholder of ancient feudalism, but indeed is a believer in such feudalism being abolished. The Count also seems to be trying to emphasise his decency by bringing in the question of common land, relevant to the vassals as well as to himself. And he says he is not going to take direct action against his peasants even though they were acting with brigands. That, then, is a summary of the witting testimony: very important but really not much more than a paraphrase of the text itself (we *know* what de Germiny is saying; how far we can *believe* him is a question for the next section).

Now to the unwitting testimony. Quite unconsciously (the first type), de Germiny gives away the fact that he is a non-resident landlord or that, at the very least, he has two residences. Equally, since he gives this away unthinkingly, there was obviously not thought to be anything unusual or reprehensible about a noble living in this relatively lavish way. See how you can keep digging deeper into a document to bring out things about prevailing values and assumptions. In his opening sentence (this is an example of the second type), the Count is not intending to make the historical point about whom the brigands were collaborating with; but he would seem, without deliberately intending it, to be giving evidence against the view (which – you won't know this – was widespread among the peasants at the time) that the brigands were actually working on behalf of the nobility against the peasants. It is also clear – and this is perhaps one of the single most important historical points in the document – that the Count has absolute confidence the National Assembly will listen to him sympathetically. In other words, he does not see any clash of interest (personal or class) between himself as a member of the nobility and the National Assembly (traditionally represented as 'bourgeois'). He clearly feels that it will value property rights just as much as he does.

The most obvious example of the third kind of unwitting testimony lies in the reference to 'my vassals and those of Vrigni'. If you are not a student of history, you may not be aware that 'vassal' is a technical term within the medieval system of land tenure which came to be known as 'feudalism' (a good example of the sort of technical term historians have to understand fully): the 'vassal' holds his land, *owned* by his lord, in return owing allegiance and various services and payments (probably in kind) to that lord. Unwittingly, de Germiny is revealing to us that the 'medieval' system was still in operation at the time of the French Revolution. In practice, of course, historians already know this from a plenitude of sources – as I've said, this is a slightly artificial exercise. Another good example is the reference to title deeds and registers. We as historians learn how important these are to him (he takes that for granted). Evidently these written documents are essential for him to back up his feudal claims (he cannot do this just on the basis of power and prestige alone), and, what is more, the vassals themselves know this. So we have clear (though *unwitting*) testimony to the importance in this society of certain types of legal documentation. We also learn how important to him his pigeon shooting is (and, by implication, how hated by the peasants – the pigeons destroy their crops).

I hope, then, you can see how potentially important unwitting testimony can be, and I hope you can see that in analysing and interpreting primary sources it very definitely is not a matter of stripping away the 'fictive elements' and getting at 'the hardcore of facts'. If the point is still not clear, here is a simple little invented example which ought to drive it home. Imagine that a king in some medieval society wishes to get rid of a courtier who has displeased him. He sends the courtier to a neighbouring kingdom with a sealed message which asks its king to put the bearer of the message to death (a plot device which, it may be remembered, is used in Shakespeare's *Hamlet*). If by chance that message fell into the hands of a present-day historian, its witting testimony would be that, for whatever reason, the courtier had so displeased his king that the king wished him put to death. Unless the courtier was someone of importance, that piece of witting information might not be of great significance. But the historian might wish to go beyond this and say that this piece of evidence revealed the absence of due legal processes in these medieval societies. Now that would be unwitting testimony, going beyond what was actually written in the message itself, since the king did not actually write: 'I being, as is the custom in our societies, a callous and autocratic king, with no respect for due legal processes, hereby ask you ...'

5   A Catechism for the Analysis, Evaluation and Use of Primary Sources

I say 'catechism' because what I am setting out here is very, very basic, and, because the teaching of history has improved greatly since the first edition of *The Nature of History* was published in 1970, it may already be familiar to many readers. Let me just say that, before 1970, no such catechism was published anywhere: my point remains that anyone interested in studying history needs to think, step by step, about the problems involved in making use of primary sources, about, in particular, their strengths and their weaknesses. I do not for a moment claim that professional historians, in their own researches, explicitly and systematically go through these questions; in very many cases they will be able to take the answers for granted. But here, when we get to the bottom of it, is a numbered list of the points which have to be established, or the questions which have to be answered, before a historian can use, interpret, derive information or meanings from, a particular primary source.

The Catechism

1 *Is the source authentic, is it what it purports to be?* Now, in any exercise one might set in a teaching situation, one would be sure that the pre-selected source used was authentic, so in ordinary teaching situations we could ignore this question. However, it is important to be aware of the issue. Take, for example, a medieval charter apparently dated early in the eleventh century and purporting to make a grant of land from the king to a monastery. It is always possible that the charter was actually forged by the monks late in the twelfth century (say) in order to establish a right to the land. The document will still be of value to historians as a genuine twelfth-century forgery which may tell them a good deal about that century, but they will have to be very circumspect in its use if their subject of study lies early in the eleventh century. To establish authenticity the historian will have to deploy the techniques of palaeography and diplomatics. An interesting case in point is provided by *The Life of Thomas Hardy*, the biography of the Victorian novelist Thomas Hardy by his second wife. Scholars subsequently established that the biography had in fact been written by Hardy himself, which, of course, changes its whole nature as evidence. As a relatively objective, factual account by a woman who knew him only in later life it is not *authentic*; in fact it contains the modified version of events which Hardy wished to convey to posterity. On the other hand, as an autobiography by Hardy himself it *is* authentic, and when compared with the real facts as we know them, gives interesting insights into Hardy's thought processes.

Authenticity is often established through the *provenance* of the source (its place of origin). This is particularly important in regard to physical artefacts or archaeological sources. The fact is that the vast majority of written sources used by working historians do not have serious problems of authenticity. Often it is known that a particular document has been safely housed in a particular collection from the very moment it was created, and sometimes there were actual witnesses to its creation; there are many obvious checks on the authenticity of published documents. Still, the issue can crop up, as it did rather spectacularly in 1985 when a British Sunday newspaper published as authentic the quite cleverly faked 'Hitler Diaries'.[17]

2 *When exactly was the source produced? What is its date? How close is its date to the date of the events to which it relates, or to dates relevant to the topic being investigated? How does this particular source relate chronologically to other relevant sources? How does it relate to other significant dates?* For example, there is a famous charter (in the Museum of London) from King John to the citizens of London whose date, May 1215, is shortly before that of Magna Carta itself, so that the grant of this

charter can be related to King John's need to find supporters in the City of London against the barons; the date of the Horace Mann commentary already studied might be related to those of other significant events and developments: for instance, while its tone is extremely pessimistic, 1851 is often seen as a time of gathering optimism among the middle and upper classes, represented by the Great Exhibition of that year. *What, in short, is the significance of the date of the particular source being studied?* In some cases precisely dating a document or, more particularly, a building or physical artefact is an extremely difficult task in itself. But if the historian cannot date the source, it is very difficult indeed for him/her to make much use of it. The more he/she knows about its date, and other related dates, the more use he/she will be able to make of it.

3 *What type of source is it? A private letter? Or an official report, a public document of record, or what?* Usually the answers will be obvious, but it is important to be clear about the type. An official letter sent by a foreign secretary will contain different kinds of information, and will need different types of analysis, from a private letter sent by the same foreign secretary to his wife, which may, in some circumstances, actually contain more frank, and more usable, information. Historians come to recognise the conventions, the codes, if you like, of particular types of sources, and these will have to be taken into account.

4 *How did the source come into existence in the first place, and for what purpose? What person, or group of persons, created the source? What basic attitudes, prejudices, vested interests would he, she or they be likely to have? Who was it written for or addressed to?* An ambassador's report on conditions in the country in which he is stationed may be biased in various directions: if he is a Catholic in a Protestant country he may tend to exaggerate the evidence of a Catholic upsurge; he may send home the kind of information he knows the home government wants to hear; he may, as for instance Neville Henderson, British ambassador to Hitler's Germany, was, be over-anxious to maintain peaceful relations between the two countries; on reporting on a potential enemy he may give a hopelessly optimistic account, say, of the likelihood of unrest among the general populace. If we are dealing with a private letter, was it written with the genuine intention of conveying reliable information, or maybe to curry favour with the recipient? Here knowledge of the respective social positions of writer and recipient will be useful. If we are dealing with some kind of report or investigation, what were the sympathies of the writers of the report? And so on.

5 *How far is the author of the source really in a good position to provide firsthand information on the particular topic the historian is interested in? Is the*

writer dependent, perhaps, on hearsay? How far is Horace Walpole, a Whig aristocrat, reliable in describing the mainsprings of the eighteenth-century 'Wilkes and Liberty' movement? Can middle-class writers really understand the feelings of the poor? John Reed's *Ten Days That Shook the World* (1919) is an exciting on-the-spot account of the Bolshevik Revolution: but, in using it as a primary source, can we be absolutely certain that in fact he ever left his hotel bedroom?

6   *How exactly was the document understood by contemporaries? What, precisely, does it say?* Certain branches of historical investigation require the skills of palaeography, diplomatics and philology. There may be problems of deciphering inscriptions, hieroglyphics and certain types of handwriting. There can be problems arising from archaic or obscure languages. Some of the controversies in medieval history centre on the shade of meaning to be allotted to a specific passage in dog-Latin or medieval French. Any technical phrases, esoteric allusions, or references to individuals or institutions will have to be fully elucidated in order that the full meaning of the document can come through. Thus when an Elizabethan document refers to the Star Chamber, whoever is interpreting the document has to know exactly what the Star Chamber was. Sums of money have to be explicated: no point reading that something cost 1000 *livres* if you have no idea of what that sum meant in terms, say, of the average weekly earnings of an ordinary worker. Statistics will have to be set in contexts (a town of 1000 inhabitants – is that large or small?). Events referred to in the source may have to be elucidated. Allusions to the Bible can be frequent, and a Renaissance letter will usually be loaded with references to classical mythology. All allusions and references and quantities have to be sorted out so that we can be sure that we have got the full meaning of the source as contemporaries would have understood it, before we can go on to make use of the document.

7   Then, finally, we have the question of *how the source relates to knowledge obtained from other sources, both primary and secondary.* In elementary teaching exercises students may well be very short on contextual knowledge. But it cannot be stressed too strongly that in the real practice of history, one can do very little with primary sources unless one already has a very considerable contextual knowledge.

Practising on One Example

Now let us work together once more through the Count de Germiny's letter of complaint to the National Assembly: imagining once more that you are researching on 'Nobles and Peasants in the French Revolution', see if you can apply each of the seven questions in the catechism, commenting where appropriate on what you think are strengths and weaknesses in the document, as a source for your project.

1 *Authenticity*. You have no means of establishing this, though you might assume that I would not waste your time on a document that is not authentic. Actually this document is well vouched for, and has been printed (and translated) by a number of historians.

2 *What date is it? What relevance and significance does the date have?* Well, it's in the first summer of the Revolution, just over a month after the fall of the Bastille, and, if you remember my discussion of Lucien Febvre in Chapter 4, it is during the summer of the 'Great Fear' when the peasants thought they were being attacked by the nobles.

3 *What type of source is it?* As a formal letter of complaint to an official body it is a document of record which definitely records both the fact and the content of the complaint. In this respect, the document is a 'strong' one with regard to our project. How accurate it is with regard to the matters it is reporting is a separate issue, and to decide on that we need to move to question 4, though I would conjecture that in formally complaining to an official body, de Germiny would be careful not to risk distorting the facts too much.

4 *Who created the source? For what purpose? What biases might we expect?* The author is a nobleman whose purpose is to persuade the National Assembly to pass a law enabling him to be reimbursed for the damage he claims he has suffered. Despite the point I have just made about not taking too big a risk, one would none the less expect the Count to express as persuasive a case as possible in his search for compensation. There is a potential 'weakness' in the document here. Furthermore, it might be in his own interest to try to make out that it was not really his own vassals who were causing the trouble, so we might doubt this, and we might also want to look sceptically at his claims about 'brigands' in particular, and also about the participation of vassals from the next parish.

5 *Is the author of the source in a good position to provide reliable information?* It's his property, so in general he ought to be able to give an accurate account. But he does reveal that he himself is not a resident in the area where the trouble took place, so he must be relying to some extent on another source of information, presumably his warden. As the warden was not able to put up any effective defence, he might have been inclined to exaggerate about the numbers, or about their being 'brigands', for example. There are further 'weaknesses' in the source under this heading – but I am inclined to refer back again to point 2,

which would lead me to expect the Count to be pretty punctilious in what he says (one would expect him to have cross-examined the warden pretty rigorously).

6 *What did the document mean to contemporaries? What particular problems of allusion and elucidation are there?* Let me work through the document identifying phrases which need explaining. The use of the word 'brigands' implies that we are here concerned with professional criminals, not just ordinary peasants. 'Vassals' (as I have explained) are peasants who are not completely free but owe feudal duties to their lord. We have a number of place names in the first sentence, and it is a good basic rule always to find out what exact geographical location we are concerned with. '*Château*' is not necessarily a fortified castle, but can simply mean something like a manor house. 'Title deeds' and 'registers': these are the written documents which prove the Count has a legal right to certain lands and to certain feudal duties (including payments, taxes and services). 'Tocsin' is a peal of church bells used to raise the alarm – it had already become a regular symbol of the revolutionary mobs in Paris and elsewhere. 'Odious weight of ancient feudalism' is an important and rich phrase. Over time feudal duties had changed and in some places were more onerous than others – de Germiny is claiming that he is relatively generous in what he demands from his vassals, and he is indicating that he is in favour of ancient dues being abolished ('redeemed'). 'Present circumstances' are the current conditions of revolutionary upheaval. 'Common land' was land to which everyone in the parish, not just the lord, had equal rights (for grazing, gathering wood, and so on). 'Killed all my pigeons': the keeping of pigeons in order to conduct pigeon shoots was common among the nobility, and much hated by the peasants since the pigeons fed on their crops.

7 *How does this source fit into the contextual knowledge we already have?* Obviously, you will have seen for yourself that if you do not already know much about the French Revolution, this document will not mean a lot to you, though I have already brought out what it contains in the way of both witting and unwitting testimony. Clearly it is illuminating of relationships between a lord and his peasants on the one hand, and between the lord and the National Assembly on the other. Further significance accrues to the document if we know that very shortly pressure from the peasant activism during the 'Great Fear' forced the National Assembly before the end of the month to abolish all feudal privileges. The Count was asking for a law to be passed which would gain him reimbursement: no such law in fact was passed. In the document we can only sense the balance of power moving from the nobility to the peasants; in fact, if we have the

contextual knowledge, we can see that the document signifies an important stage in that development.

6   The Arts as Sources

Use and Abuse of the Arts

Historians encounter the arts (the generic term I shall use for literature, painting and sculpture, music, and film, using 'artists' to designate practitioners in any one of these) in three distinct ways: first, in common with all other artefacts produced by past societies, the arts can be used as primary sources in the study of these societies; second, just as the arts can contribute to the study of history, so history, by providing 'context', detail on the past society which produced the particular art form being studied, can help in the study of the arts; finally, the arts may be studied by historians as a measure of the achievements of a particular past society, or historians may be concerned with the production, organisation, patronage or subsidisation, and 'consumption' of the arts in particular past societies. This section concentrates on the first of these ways. Novels and films, and less obviously painting, sculpture and music, can have a special potency as sources in comparative historical studies: when you get down to examining novels and films in every detail it becomes clear that they are very strongly marked by the societies within which they were produced – French films and novels turn out to be uniquely French, American ones uniquely American, and so on, so that, treated as sources, novels and films can tell us something important about the differences between different countries. Accordingly, after discussing novels, I shall move immediately to films, even though those are relevant only to the recent period, before then going back in time to cover painting and sculpture.

Despite my reservations about the adjective, I shall, for convenience, refer to all paintings, novels, symphonies, films, works of popular art and popular music as 'cultural artefacts'. Basically, one applies to cultural artefacts the same catechism as is applicable to all other primary sources, and one seeks out the unwitting testimony as well as the witting. One is concerned, first of all, with what is always referred to technically as (regrettably, in my view) 'meaning', in cruder terms 'the message', in the elite arts usually complex and often oblique. It is always necessary to get that thoroughly worked out; instant impressions (of, say, a painting or piece of music) are of little use. But, in novels and films in particular, the unwitting testimony, the implicit attitudes and values (about gender, for instance), the assumptions (about class, or, say, national characteristics), can be enormously important. That artists during the high Renaissance strove for ever greater 'realism' or (better words, I think) 'naturalism', 'representationalism', 'mimesis', can tell us much about the assumptions and aspirations of the elites in the societies of the time. That some composers at the end of the nineteenth century abandoned tonality is a complex issue: but whether subsequent composers remained traditional, or allied themselves with the avant garde, can tell us much about their intentions. Similarly: is a novel resolutely modernist, or postmodernist, or is it deliberately traditional?

My final general point here is a very important one. If we are to make use of a cultural artefact as a primary source, we need to gather as much relevant contextual information as we can. It is seldom a good idea to take any one primary source in isolation. Works of music are particularly difficult to use as historical sources: but if we take into account letters written by the composers themselves, comments made by critics, and so on, often the significance of a particular work for historical investigation does begin to stand out quite clearly. A single letter, or a single piece or reminiscence, obviously, is not enough, but I believe something of the value of following up other primary sources relating to (in this case) music emerges from this paragraph from the reminiscences of German avant-garde composer Paul Hindemith:

> During my time as a soldier in the First World War, I was a member of a string quartet which served our commanding officer as a means of escape from the miseries of war. He was a great music-lover, and a connoisseur and admirer of French art. It was no wonder, then, that his dearest wish was to hear Debussy's String Quartet. We rehearsed the work and played it to him with much feeling at a private concert. Just after we had finished the slow movement, the signals officer burst in and reported in great consternation that the news of Debussy's death [on 25 March 1918] had just come through on the radio. We did not continue our performance. It was as if the spirit had been removed from our playing. But now we felt for the first time how much more music is than just style, technique and an expression of personal feeling. Here music transcended all political barriers, national hatred and the horrors of war. Never before or since have I felt so clearly in which direction music must be made to go.[18]

Elsewhere, I have discussed a number of musical works together with the contextual information about them, with a view to exploring the less considered ramifications of total war: Elgar's *The Spirit of England* (1916–17) as speaking of the heroism of war, but in an elegiac manner, not at all triumphalist; Benjamin Britten's *War Requiem* (1962) as referring to both wars and speaking of the need for reconciliation; the extreme avant-garde music of Pierre Boulez as emphatically expressing the caesura of the Second World War, and the break with the decadent 1920s and 1930s.[19]

Perhaps it is necessary to repeat, especially with reference to novels and films, that a cultural artefact, like any other primary source, is a source for the period in which it was produced, not for the period to which it refers. Let us be clear also that novels and films are *never* to be accounted secondary sources; silly non-problems are created if we do not reserve the term secondary source for historical works deliberately aimed, without fictional characters or fictional devices, at making contributions to knowledge about the past. *A Tale of Two Cities* (1859) by Charles Dickens, therefore, is a primary source for attitudes and values in the mid-nineteenth century, particularly with respect to fear of revolution or the power of the mob; the fictional events that take place are set within the French Revolution but the novel simply is not *any kind of* source for the French Revolution. Novels are always primary sources, though in many cases they may be thoroughly useless ones. Or when they do provide information, they may well not be the *best* source for that information, a point I elaborate at the end of this sub-section.

Anthony Trollope's *The Prime Minister* (1856) gives clear suggestions of the changing attitudes at mid-century of aristocratic political figures towards the rights of the electors; it also indicates the changing nature of relationships between fathers and daughters. But all such suggestions have to be verified from more conventional sources. Historians once made much of the fact that the Eatonswill election, in *The Pickwick Papers* by Dickens, was set in the pre-1832 era, and used it as an example of what electoral politics were like before the Great Reform Act. Actually, the Great Reform Act had little effect on the conduct of elections, and, in any case, the expert, Norman Gash, tells us: 'the traditional Eatonswill picture of early Victorian elections is in fact not so much exaggerated as a pale and euphemistic version of the contemporary scene!'[20]

The unprecedentedly shocking and explicit treatment of sex in such novels as *Rabbit, Run* (1960) by John Updike, *Les Petites Enfants du Siècle* (1961) by Christiane Rochefort, *Another Country* (1962) by James Baldwin, *Love and Friendship* (1962) by Alison Lurie, and *The Group* (1963) by Mary McCarthy provides powerful primary testimony in arguing that a 'cultural revolution' was beginning to take place in the early 1960s. A similar point could be made in regard to such films as *Room at the Top* (1959) and *Saturday Night and Sunday Morning* (1961).

While the fact is that much of a film's meaning is carried verbally, one does have to be alert to the different types of symbolism: films (as well, obviously, as painting) can be very rich in visual symbolism. The lone horseman outlined on the horizon is a recurrent image in American westerns: such visual symbolism reinforces the presentation of the main protagonist as representing an assumed American ideal of rugged individualism. With regard to style, ranging from the matter of opening credits to the open portrayal of violence and squalor and bodily functions, to the light-hearted cynicism, a Hollywood film of the sixties is almost always instantly recognisable. Then the adoption, in the early seventies, of many of the modernist techniques of European cinema tells us much, both about the velocity of cultural transmission, and about changing self-perceptions in America. Films relating to the immediate or recent past often stimulate controversy (and this, in itself, if it stimulates further historical discussion and investigation, is a good thing). But it must always be remembered that a film is a film is a film. American director Oliver Stone claimed that his *JFK* (1991) was an authentic historical account of President John F. Kennedy. But we don't have to believe him. In fact, from the point of view of serious study, the film is useless as a source on the assassinated president. However, insofar as in the film, Kennedy, and his supporters, are represented as symbolising what is best in America, whereas the (alleged) organisers of his assassination are taken as representing all that is reactionary, racist and repressive, this does illuminate a strand of thinking, strong in certain circles at the time the film was made.

It is fun, and it is becoming fashionable, to work with novels, films, and paintings. Doing this is not evidence of some superior virtue, or sensibility; in fact, most of what we know about most periods in the past will continue to come from the more conventional sources. Historians have had a habit of quoting odd lines from novels, as if these, in themselves, somehow provided some extra illumination. Worse, historians sometimes refer to characters in novels (or even films) as if they were real people. If cultural artefacts are to be used at all in serious historical writing, they have to be used seriously. In my view, if one is going to refer to a novel or a film one must provide sufficient information about the artefact itself, and its production and reception, to make the reference a genuine contribution to knowledge: one must provide a 'quintessential summary' (nature of the artefact, authorial intentions, and so on). When the temptation comes to make use of some cultural artefact the crucial questions to ask are 'does it tell us anything we didn't know already?', and, more probingly, 'does it tell us anything we couldn't discover more readily from a different source?' Novels have sometimes been used as sources for living conditions and standards, as paintings of domestic scenes have sometimes been used as sources for what people ate. But it is far better to go directly to the actual statistics of wage rates and to social investigations for the first topic, and to household accounts, statistics of retail sales and so on for the latter one. A painting of eighteenth-century French peasants consuming bread, garlic and wine may be evidence of their regular diet, but there is always the quite strong possibility that the artist might have been more concerned with infusing his painting with the religious symbolism of the Last Supper than with accurate sociological observation.

Art as a Source

Discussing art as a source, in fact, is an excellent way of bringing out both the use and abuse of cultural artefacts as source materials. It is perfectly legitimate for editors and publishers to wish to brighten up articles and books by including reproductions of various works of art. But, with rare exceptions, such art works will, at best, be no more than illustrations; at worst they may have little real relevance to what is being said in the article or book. The key questions are: did the author him or herself actually make use of the work of art in composing the article or book?; does he or she actually refer to them as would be the case with extracts from diaries or acts of parliament?; or have the illustrations simply been stuck on as decoration, probably by someone else?

Even the most austere political works sometimes contain portraits of the principal characters whose achievements and failings are being discussed, often boldly captioned 'Mary, Queen of Scots', 'Chatham', or whoever. Actually, of course, such portraits are merely representations of the sitters, more or less accurate likenesses depending upon the skill and the aims of the artist (was he a flatterer, did he have some idealised image of monarchy or of women?). In some cases the sitter may not actually have been the person identified in the caption; there used to be dozens of paintings labelled Madame de Pompadour – now all the really good-looking ones are recognised as not being of La Pompadour at all. So: if we are to use portraits as sources for what historical personages really looked like, we have to analyse them, and the purposes of their creators, just as carefully as we would any other historical source, and likewise take into account all the other (mainly written) evidence.

As I keep stressing, an absolutely vital procedure with any source is establishing its date. A nineteenth-century painting of the compiling of a Domesday Book entry is quite worthless as a source for the study of Domesday Book, though it might well tell us much about nineteenth-century romanticisation of the Middle Ages. Some years ago in the Boston Museum of Fine Arts I was renewing acquaintanceship with Turner's *Slave Ship (Slavers Throwing Overboard the Dead and Dying, Typhoon Coming On)* of 1842, when I noticed in the caption the claim that this painting demonstrated Turner's active involvement in the anti-slavery campaign. Here dating is utterly crucial: the slave trade (which is what the picture relates to) was abolished in the British Empire in 1807 (and the institution of slavery in 1833), and, indeed, the incident on which Turner's painting was based took place in the late eighteenth century. Thus, though the painting may be taken as an example of what might be called 'retrospective radicalism' it cannot be an item in the active campaign against the slave trade. (The museum, I may say, responded promptly and courteously to my communication on this point.)

Subsequently, at a conference in the Netherlands, I heard a speaker fantasising about what popular and commercial art says about foreign perceptions of the Dutch. His naïve wafflings about the Dutch being seen as a carefree, bucolic nation were crushed by an expert critic who demonstrated from a great range of other sources that the overwhelming perception foreigners have is of a scrupulously clean and intensely industrious people. The speaker had been trying to fit his artistic sources to the wrong topic; what they did reveal, if analysed properly, were assumptions behind the marketing of biscuits, cocoa, cheeses, and other commodities. It is, alas, all too easy to impose propagandist meanings on artistic sources: this rural landscape represents the ruling class expropriating the peasantry (or, alternatively, the benign harmony of the perfectly integrated society), that domestic interior represents the suppression of women; they may do, but the points have to be argued with evidence external to the paintings themselves, not simply asserted.

But with these negative comments behind me let me pick up again my references to the Last Supper and to nineteenth-century romanticism. The presence of strong religious symbolism in a painting (requiring, naturally, experience and expertise to decode) will tell us a great deal about the belief system of an artist and his patrons. And with the 'isms' of history, we really are in business. It would be quite impossible to give a thorough account of English romanticism at the end of the eighteenth century without analysing the paintings of Constable, Turner, Cotman and the watercolourists. It would be quite absurd to assess the strength of modernism in Britain before the First World War without reference to the paintings of Wyndham Lewis and C. R. W. Nevinson.

Here I am talking of elite art and cultural movements affecting the elite. But popular art (cartoons, woodcuts, etchings and other reproductions, posters) can tell us much about the attitudes and values of wider sections of society, about mentalities, about ordinary folk and popular culture. R. W. Scribner's 'attempt to combine print and picture' in 'a study of visual propaganda, and of its role in the dissemination of the evangelical movement during the first half-century of the Reformation of Germany',[21] entitled *For the Sake of the Simple Folk* (Cambridge, 1981), triumphantly vindicates his argument 'that through a study of visual propaganda we may gain a wider understanding of how the Reformation appealed to common folk than by concentrating attention more narrowly on printed propaganda alone'. On the lower quarters of the two facing pages 60–61 Scribner prints reproductions of two woodcuts (illustrations 43 and 44 respectively in the book); across the same two pages Scribner provides an absolutely precise analysis of these artistic sources, bringing out his main point that in the religious propaganda of the day great use was made of popular games:

> A good example can be found in the title page to the pamphlet *The Lutheran Strebkatz* (ill. 43). The Strebkatz was a popular game in which two opponents engaged in a tug-of-war by gripping between their teeth two rods which were connected by chords. This contraption itself was called the Strebkatz and the players contended for its sole possession. In this version, the chords pass around the contestants' necks. The original form of the game is depicted in the title page of a 1522 pamphlet (ill. 44), where two monks contend for the prize, a wreath held by a watching damsel. In the first instance, the contestants are Luther and the Pope, who is helped by a crowd of supporters representing some of Luther's main opponents – Eck, Emser, Cochleus, Murner, Hochstraten, Lemp and Alfeld. Although the contest seems unequal, Luther has dragged the Pope to his knees so violently that his tiara has fallen off and his money purse has burst.

You can see just how much detailed knowledge Scribner has to have in order to make use of the rich examples of popular art.

Evidently, great movements of ideas, such as the Reformation or the Renaissance, are areas for which artistic sources are bound to be extremely helpful. The distinguished Reformation scholar A. G. Dickens, taking care to have the appropriate reproductions included in his book *The Age of Humanism and Reformation* (1972), used the evidence of the art and architecture of the time to contest the theory that seventeenth-century Baroque art and architecture was a product of the Catholic Reformation, 'a hymn of joy raised by the triumphant Church', closely associated with the Jesuits. The Baroque, he argued, using the artistic sources themselves, 'soon became a multi-purpose style contributing as much to the glorification of monarchs as to the triumph of the Church'.[22]

In his *Italian Renaissance: Culture and Society in Italy* (1986), Peter Burke takes care to place his reproductions of the artistic sources exactly where he is analysing and discussing them in the text: thus they contribute to his argument in exactly the same way that quotations from written sources do. Another celebrated example of the use of art to give breathtaking insights into the mentalities of a particular society in a particular age is *The Embarrassment of Riches: An Interpretation of Dutch Culture in the Golden Age* (New York, 1987) by Simon Schama. Here is part of the analysis which runs beside and underneath the Jan Steen painting *Tavern Scene* (p. 205):

As a source of bawdy innuendo, the pipe seems to have been inexhaustibly ribald...One of the many tavern paintings to include a guffawing self-portrait is virtually an anthology of Dutch smut, no lewd reference to the condition of the girl or to the act which brought it about has been omitted. Broken egg shells, mussels, an open flapkan tankard, a gaping bunghole, a scrutinised chamber pot and no fewer than three pointing handles and stems provide rib-nudging visual counterparts for the cruel prurience of the cacophonous laughter.

Manifestly, for a historian studying an entire period, the art of the period may well be a vital source. Apart from the obvious example of the Renaissance, this is true of, say, the 'Belle Époque' (1890–1914) or the 1960s. Though Aubrey Beardsley, Bonnard and Vuillard, the early Balla, each had his own artistic purposes, the common denominators, once they have been deciphered, speak volumes on the characteristic contradictions of the era: innovation and decadence, complacency and uncertainty, the arrogance of unconstrained wealth and the degradation of unmitigated poverty. In their use of discarded objects and materials, both Nouveau Realisme and Arte Povera are joined to Pop Art in an intimate and revealing relationship to the exploding consumerism of the 1960s and reactions to it.

If we are interested in the way that science, technology and industrialisation came increasingly to dominate life in all of its aspects, certain painters, from Joseph Wright of Derby (his *An Experiment on a Bird in an Air Pump*, *c.* 1767, in the Tate is well known) in the late eighteenth century to Fernand Léger in the twentieth, are helpful witnesses. Portraits, carefully analysed, can be psychologically very penetrating. Certain landscapes and townscapes can be very useful for topography, for what places used to look like; one can practically plot the geographical expansion and transformation of Paris from the remarkable series of paintings now collected in the new extension to the Musée Carnavalet. Other genres can be helpful on questions of dress and fashion, and if read carefully, and in conjunction with the other evidence, on the matter of social distinctions – some of the early eighteenth-century French painters, and many of the Victorian, are useful here.

When discussing history of science, medicine and technology in Chapter 4 I mentioned the need in that sub-history for some scientific knowledge. When it comes to using cultural artefacts the specialist skills of the musicologist, literary scholar, art historian or film critic may well be helpful. When it comes to establishing the meanings of cultural artefacts, I would certainly be all in favour of borrowing from the insights of these different experts. But above all what is needed is the meticulous techniques and profound scepticism of the historian: no source is transparent, and that goes for a painting and a film as well. Too much can be made of the need for theory: 'theory' in the arts, in fact, is the same nonsense as is so-called 'theory' in history, the same neo-Marxist, post-modernist stuff that I have been challenging throughout this book.

One question we always have to ask of artefacts of popular culture, be they woodcuts or novels or popular stories in some form or another, is whether they are of a type that would have to have credibility with readers as representing accurately conditions and attitudes in their society, that would have to be congruent with the experiences of their readers. Such works, obviously, are very useful to historians.

To analyse a film, it is necessary to break it down into sequences, and sometimes into scenes, and shots. It is necessary to recognise the different types of shot and the use of different lenses, understand the language of dissolves, fades, mixes and cuts, and to be sensitive to the way a soundtrack is dubbed and to the deployment of music. With cartoons it is necessary to understand, among other things, the idiom within which they are conceived. With paintings it is necessary to understand the objectives of the artist (artistic and historical), the conventions within which the artist was operating, and the reception accorded to the paintings by patrons and audiences. But behind all that are the fundamental imperatives of history as an autonomous discipline, as set out in my 'catechism'.

Notes

1 See Chapter 4, note 53.
2 E. H. Carr, *What is History?* (London, 1961; pb edn, 1964), pp. 10–11.
3 Ibid., p. 12.
4 Ludmilla Jordanova, *History in Practice* (London, 2000), p. 32.
5 Ibid., pp. 33–4.
6 Quoted in Frances C. Locker (ed.), *Contemporary Authors*, vols 97–100 (Detroit, Mich., 1981), p. 109.
7 Carr, *What is History?*, p. 16.
8 Ibid.
9 Again, these points were developed in my article 'Two Approaches to Historical Study' in *Journal of Contemporary History*, 30/1 (January 1995).
10 The first version of this 'taxonomy' appeared in the old *The Nature of History*, and was developed in my chapter on '"A Fetishism of Documents"?: The Salience of Source-Based History', in Henry Kozicki (ed.), *Developments in Modern Historiography* (New York and London, 1993), pp. 121–7.
11 E. H. Gombrich, *Art and Illusion: A Study in the Psychology of Pictorial Representation* (London, 1960), passim.
12 P. H. Sawyer in P. H. Sawyer (ed.), *Medieval Settlement: Continuity and Change* (London, 1976), p. 2.

13 Henry Guerlac, 'Some Historical Assumptions of the History of Science', in A. C. Crombie (ed.), *Scientific Change* (New York, 1963), p. 799.

14 Karsten Fledelius, 'Film and History – An Introduction to the Theme', in Comité International des Sciences Historiques: XVIᵉ Congrès International des Sciences Historiques, *Rapports, I: Grands Thèmes, Methodologie, Sections Chronologiques*, (i) (Stuttgart, 1985), p. 186.

15 The document is served up in convenient format in John Golby (ed.), *Culture and Society in Britain 1850–1890: A Source Book of Contemporary Writings* (London, 1986), p. 40.

16 This (translated) document can be conveniently found in D. J. Wright, *Revolution and Terror in France 1789–1795* (London, 1974), p. 107.

17 For the full scenario refer to Robert Harris, *Selling Hitler: The Story of the Hitler Diaries* (London, 1986).

18 Paul Hindemith, *Zeugnis in Bildern* (Mainz, 1961), quoted in Geoffrey Skelton, *Paul Hindemith: The Man Behind the Music* (London, 1966), p. 49. See Arthur Marwick, 'Painting and Music During and After the Great War: The Art of Total War', in Roger Chickering and Stig Förster (eds), *Great War, Total War* (Cambridge, 2000), pp. 501–17.

19 In audiotape 2, Open University Course AA312, *Total War and Social Change: Europe 1914–1955* (2001). See Pierre Boulez, lecture entitled 'Where are we now?', 13 May 1968, quoted in Pierre Boulez (trans. Martin Cooper), *Orientations: Collected Writings* (London, 1986), p. 445.

20 Norman Gash, *Politics in the Age of Peel* (London, 1953), p. 147.

21 R. W. Scribner, *For the Sake of Simple Folk* (Cambridge, 1981), pp. 1–2.

22 A. G. Dickens, *The Age of Humanism and Reformation* (Englewood Cliffs, NJ, 1972), pp. 190–2.

6 The Historian at Work: The Communication of Historical Knowledge

1 The Fundamentals of Good Writing

Different Levels of Communication and the Basic Skill of Writing

One of the most important learning outcomes from doing a properly run university degree in history is the ability to collect material *relevant* to a particular topic, and to analyse, collate, and organise it, preparatory to communicating it in clear and precise language. This is what is referred to as a 'transferable skill', a skill of immense value in a wide range of jobs. It is, of course, a skill central to communicating history at a whole range of different levels, though the writing of history (as I shall shortly demonstrate) has special requirements of its own. Whether you are an ordinary citizen interested in writing a piece of local history, a history undergraduate with essays to write, a postgraduate student with a dissertation to produce, or just an avid reader of history books, you need to understand all of this. I flatter myself that even some of my fellow professionals may find what I have to say valuable, particularly with respect to their teaching duties. As a supervisor of postgraduate students, the first great difficulty I have found is that of students who simply cannot write acceptable English at all; the second great difficulty is that of those who feel that for writing history they must adopt some pompous, elaborate, polysyllabic, contorted style, when what is needed in history is explicitness and precision. Many published books on historical topics – not all of them by non-historians – are both sloppily written with respect to individual phrases and sentences, and poorly and confusingly organised overall. All history should be written clearly and unambiguously (a very taxing task requiring training and experience). To single out certain works as being exceptionally well written is appropriate to Grub Street, not to the academy; to call a work of history a work of art is to show a poor understanding of the nature of works of art; a work of history is to be judged by its quality as history; a direct, uncluttered style is not an added extra, but is intrinsic to proper historical communication.

In this section, I start with some of the most fundamental problems in the writing of even quite short pieces. For those tied up in the problems of writing sixth-form or undergraduate essays (and marking them!) I have provided Appendix C on essay-writing. I conclude this section with some general reflections on the relationships between writing and research, and on how writing history differs from writing in other disciplines. In the following sections I work through the techniques which have to be mastered and the problems which have to be addressed in producing finished works of history, concluding with a discussion of the different levels of historical communication, from scholarly monograph to film or television programme, and the various forms of public history (museums, 'heritage', and so forth).[1]

Writing a Paragraph

The problems of writing were addressed in an old, but still important, American work, *The Modern Researcher* by Jacques Barzun and Henry F. Graff (New York, 1957; revised edition 1977). The authors made some pertinent comments on the necessity for *form* and orderliness in writing:

> Facts and ideas in disorder cannot be conveyed to another's mind without loss and are hardly likely to carry much meaning even for the possessor. This is because the mind is so constituted that it demands a minimum of regularity and symmetry, even in the arrangements of toilet articles on top of a bureau.

In written matter, Barzun and Graff continue, 'the most frequent and visible failure of *form* is that which comes from wrong emphasis':

> Organisation distributes emphasis in the right places. The mind cannot give equal attention to every part; it must be guided to those parts – of a sentence or a book – which it should attend to for a correct understanding.[2]

Barzun and Graff quote a passage from a real book (*History of the Elizabethan Stage*, 1930, by E. K. Chambers) in order to show what a piece of writing lacking in form reads like. Again you the reader might like to comment yourself on what is wrong with the passage and (if you are particularly enthusiastic and energetic) make an attempt at rewriting it in a more satisfactory way.

> The great spectacles of [Elizabeth's] reign were liturgies, undertaken by the gallants, or by the nobles whose country houses she visited in

the course of her annual progresses. The most famous of all, the 'Princely Pleasure of Kenilworth' in 1575, was at the expense of Dudley, to whom the ancient royal castle had long been alienated. Gradually, no doubt, the financial stringency was relaxed. Camden notes a growing tendency to luxury about 1574; others trace the change to the coming of the Duke of Alençon in 1581. Elizabeth had found the way to evoke a national spirit, and at the same time to fill her coffers, by the encouragement of piratical enterprise, and the sumptuous entertainments prepared for the welcome of Monsieur were paid for out of the spoils brought back by Drake in the *Golden Hind*. The Alençon negotiations, whether seriously intended or not, represent Elizabeth's last dalliance with the idea of matrimony. They gave way to that historical part of unapproachable virginity, whereby an elderly Cynthia, without complete loss of dignity, was enabled to the end to maintain a sentimental claim upon the attentions, and the purses of her youthful servants. The strenuous years, which led up to the final triumph over the Armada in 1588, spared but little room for revels and for progresses. They left Elizabeth an old woman. But with the removal of the strain, the spirit of gaiety awoke.[3]

What is wrong with this passage is that it is totally disorganised. Facts and ideas tumble out in a very disorderly way. Thus, although it obviously contains a good deal of valuable information, that information is almost impossible to grasp since the presentation is so bad. Clearly the author has done what writers of all levels of experience are sometimes tempted to do, that is to say, simply serve up their notes as they stand, without any attempt to organise them in a manner which will communicate successfully with the readers.

Here now is my attempt at rewriting the passage, which (if you have been diligent) you might like to compare with your own:

As rich men in classical Athens paid for the tragedies and comedies, so the great spectacles of Elizabeth's reign were paid for by her gallants, or by the nobles whose country houses she visited in the course of her annual progresses. The most famous spectacle of all, the 'Princely Pleasure of Kenilworth' in 1575, was provided by Dudley, who had long had possession of the ancient royal castle of Kenilworth. Although depending at first on the pockets of her nobles, Elizabeth gradually began to spend money more freely herself, especially as she found that the encouragement of piratical enterprise not only evoked a national spirit, but also filled her coffers. While Camden [a contemporary writer and historian] notes a growing tendency to luxury about 1574, others have traced it to the coming of the Duke of Alençon in 1581; certainly the sumptuous entertainments prepared for the welcome of Monsieur were paid for out of the spoils brought back by Drake in the *Golden Hind*. However, the Alençon negotiations, whether seriously intended or not, represent Elizabeth's last dalliance with the idea of matrimony. Thereafter, she assumed the part of unapproachable virginity which enabled her, as an elderly Cynthia [this is a somewhat pedantic classical allusion, not altogether unexpected in someone who is writing about Renaissance theatre], to maintain a sentimental claim upon the attentions, and the purses, of youthful servants, without complete loss of dignity. At the same time these later years, which led up to the final triumph over the Armada in 1588, were too strenuous to leave much room for revels and for progresses. Elizabeth was an old woman by the time they were over; yet now with the removal of the strain, the spirit of gaiety could break out in full flood.

Rewriting the passage is not nearly as easy as saying what is wrong with it. The secret (as with all writing) is breaking the material down into separate single ideas. Though one cannot be absolutely sure, through the obscure haze of the passage, just what exactly was in the author's mind, it seems to contain at least twelve separate ideas. In many cases Chambers has run separate ideas together in one phrase; failed to distribute correct emphasis between important ideas and less important ones; and failed to establish a logical sequence between different ideas showing the manner in which they are related to each other. Apart from his failings in *form*, Chambers uses obscure words ('liturgies') and vague, elaborate phrases ('financial stringency') which serve to hide his meaning rather than clarify it.

In the revised passage the first sentence is allowed to stand, save for the obscure word 'liturgy'. Liturgy is a technical term from ancient Greece meaning 'a public service undertaken by private citizens at their own expense'. It referred, among other things, to financing the great tragedies and comedies. Chambers means (1) that the spectacles were paid for by private individuals and (2) that the Elizabethan age was comparable to the great age of Athens. The next sentence, apart from slight rephrasing of possible obscurities, is allowed to stand. There is a main idea: (3) that the most famous spectacle was provided by Dudley at Kenilworth; and a minor one (4) (almost an aside in fact) that the former royal castle at Kenilworth had long been in the hands of Dudley. The next sentence has been drastically altered. In the original the idea about financial stringency being relaxed (5) seems to be incomplete and isolated. In the revised version it is related back to idea (1) and linked with idea (6) (which comes in rather later in the original) which explains how, through encouraging piracy, Elizabeth was herself able to afford more lavish spectacles. The next idea (7) concerns the two different views as to when the new tendency to lavish expenditure began: in the revised version the use of 'while' introduces the idea of two different views; in the original they are simply set down bluntly without any attempt to fit them in with the rest of the passage. In the revised version we then proceed, without starting a new sentence, to link the luxurious spectacle provided for Alençon with the piracy (in this case of Drake and the *Golden Hind*) already mentioned (this is 8)). In the original it comes in rather clumsily, the second reference to the Duke (Monsieur) being separated from the first by a rather different general idea (6) about piracy.

The sentence which follows is practically unchanged save for the addition of the very helpful 'however', which softens the transition from the previous idea and brings out that, having raised the question of luxury, we are now turning back to something different, because (9) this is Elizabeth's 'last dalliance'. The idea (10) of Elizabeth's new part, 'unapproachable virginity', is slightly rephrased in order to keep the flow going. For we now move to the idea (also rephrased for the same reason) that we are back again to a period unfavourable to revels and progresses (11). The final idea (12), badly expressed in two separate disjointed sentences in the original, is that although Elizabeth herself is now an old women, gaiety could again break out: we have already been talking of luxury (and, by implication, gaiety) earlier in the reign so the phrase about how 'the spirit of gaiety awoke' (implying that it now appeared *for the first time*) is confusing; the point, apparently, is that it is bigger and better gaiety than before, gaiety 'in full flood'.

Writing a Thesis or Book

Obviously, if getting one paragraph right is difficult, how much more difficult it is to get a whole dissertation or book right. Two commands govern the marcher lands between research and writing: 'select' and 'sort'. You can't just bung everything down, and you can't just bung it down any old how. You have to select significant bits of information and evidence and reject the insignificant. You have to group like bits of information together so that a clear point is made, rather than have bits and pieces dispersed ineffectually throughout an essay, dissertation, or book. The beginner has much learning in front of him/her here: it is an historian who is expert in the particular period or topic who will have the most secure sense of what is significant and what is not. Filling up pages with miscellaneous information which the writer thinks is somehow potentially relevant without himself/herself being clear what precisely that relevance is, is a waste of space. Information provided for the sake of information is not really information at all. The writer must be fully aware of its significance and *make that significance clear to readers*. The great give-away phrases are ones like 'it is important to note that...', 'perhaps this is the place to remark that...', which warn that the writer has a piece of information which he/she wants to unload, but about the importance of which he/she is not really at all clear, or a piece of information about whose proper place (if any) in the unfolding of the argument he/she has no idea. We all of us, old as well as young, do well to heed the lapidary words of English historian Kitson Clark: 'One of the earliest and most painful lessons which a young researcher must master is that much that he has discovered with difficulty, and with some exaltation, will prove in due course to be of no significance and of no imaginable interest, and in the end will have to be left out.'[4]

During and after the writing process itself, two commands are paramount: 'reflect' and 'revise'. There are always times when we cannot find the words to express the information, ideas, conclusions, connections or whatever we think we wish to express. I say 'think' because it is sometimes not that the words are lacking, but that what we want to express isn't really properly thought out. At moments of difficulty, we have to stop and reflect, but that does not mean bringing writing to a stop. Usually the best thing is to try out various formulations in writing. Either we sort things out, or we find that we have to go back and do some more research, or some more reading. The facility we have for trying out our thoughts in writing (or, perhaps, in speech) with colleagues and friends is to me one of the most convincing demonstrations that language is indeed a tool which we human beings can use to our advantage (and not an alien, independent system which dominates us, as the postmodernists claim). It is those who are unpractised in writing who think that just because they have managed to string a hundred or so sentences together, they have already achieved something. Those of us who have written many books know how much every sentence, paragraph, chapter, and collection of chapters has to be pondered and reflected upon; and, of course, revised, revised, revised. But even the most experienced of us have that enormous moment of relief when we have completed a substantial book, and we, too, for a time are blinded by the knowledge of our own excruciating endeavours, and by our conviction that we really do have something significant to say. Then the gaps, the infelicities, the inconsistencies begin to become apparent.

All would-be writers of history, and above all PhD students, need to be warned that, entirely apart from the reflection and rewriting of individual sentences and paragraphs I have mentioned, three or four drafts of a completed work may not be enough, and that one certainly will not be. One absolutely vital procedure must be followed with both sixth-form and undergraduate essays, and with larger works at higher levels: every phrase, every sentence, every paragraph, every chapter must be checked rigorously to establish that it really is contributing to the overall account, interpretation, or thesis being presented – each phrase, each sentence, each chapter, must in some completely explicit way lead logically onto the next one. If there are sentences which, on reflection, seem to you rather odd or out of place, delete them or rewrite them. If you have gone off at a tangent, or even suspect that you may have, do something about it. If you have got into a muddle, don't leave it to the reader to try to sort things out.

2   Explanation, Periodisation, and Structure

Analysis

A piece of historical writing which simply makes available new information is not to be scoffed at (given the intractability of primary sources, new information is often won only through sweat and tears, if not actually blood), but in a substantial historical work one expects more than just straightforward narrative or description, one looks for analysis and explanation. It is probably fair to say that in almost all of their work historians are, in some way or another, addressing 'why?' or 'how?' questions. Most readers, I suspect, will more readily think of 'why?' questions – that is, questions about causes – than 'how?' ones. What were the causes of the American Revolution, the French Revolution, the Industrial Revolution, the Thirty Years War, the First World War? Sometimes 'origins' seems a better word than 'causes'. What were the origins of the Renaissance, the Reformation, the Enlightenment? These, like questions such as 'Why did the ancient Greek ascendancy give way to the Roman?', 'Why did the Roman empire collapse?', 'Why did a united English kingdom come into existence?', 'Why did the British empire become so powerful?', are all questions of explanation. There are also questions about the consequences of the fall of Rome, of the French Revolution, of the First World War. Again these are questions of explanation – explaining the connections, say, between what happened during the French Revolution and what happened after. The explanation I am concerned with here is to do with cause and effect, origins and consequences, interconnections, chains of causation.

The sort of 'how?' questions historians address are: 'How did medieval peasants perceive the world in which they lived?', 'How did the medieval monarchy work?', 'How did the Catholic Church regulate manners and morals?' These questions involve explanation in a slightly different sense, explication, perhaps, being a better word. I shall treat such questions as coming under the general heading 'analysis'. Analysis comes about whenever we probe beneath mere narrative or description, not just setting out, for instance, the main events or achievements of the Renaissance, but explicating their nature, how they came about, and, above all, their significance. Analysis and explanation are overlapping terms entailing the addressing of the very difficult questions 'what exactly?', 'how exactly?', and 'why exactly?' But I want now to focus on matters of causes and outcomes.

Causes and Outcomes: The Elton Model

Again, I must remind myself that while a main purpose of this book is to involve students and general readers in a feeling for how practising historians think and go about their business, there are obvious differences between writing scholarly, research-based history and writing essays at school and university. Once again, it is a matter of certain common principles, applied, however, at different levels of sophistication. I'll start off with some obvious points relating to any attempt to write serious history, before moving on to some more problematic areas. In explaining some event, or series of events, a mere undifferentiated list of causes will not do: there needs to be some sense of the relationship between the different causes, an indication of which are more important, which less. At the very least there should be the distinction between, on the one hand, 'long-term' causes, and, on the other, 'immediate' or 'direct' causes. Geoffrey Elton, in his *Political History: Principles and Practice* (1970), produced a model, using the word 'situational' rather than 'long-term', which he then elaborated with respect to the causes of the English Reformation. To my taste the model is rather too narrowly orientated towards political history, his direct causes being confined to the actions of the main political actors, whether intentional or unintentional:

> Historical causes (events, actions, thought, and situations) divide into two distinct categories: (1) those providing conditions for the production of a given event which I will call situational causes, and (2) those directly productive of it. The latter again sub-divide into (a) intentional causes (when the producer willed the product) and (b) unintentional causes; these latter further subdivide into (i) those where an act of will produced unintended results, and (ii) those in which no active will was involved.[5]

One could try applying the two-stage model of long-term or situational causes and immediate or direct causes to the French Revolution (to which I referred several times during the course of Chapter 4). One could say that the long-term causes were matters like the chronic inefficiency of the monarchical government in raising the revenues it needed, the criticisms of existing government being mounted by the *philosophes* and diffused through the enormous expansion in publishing, and the hardships and grievances endured by the many for so long. For immediate causes one might mention: the actual bankruptcy of the monarchical government in 1786; the dismissal of the popular minister Necker; the refusal of the Assembly of Notables and of the parliaments to co-operate in bringing in the necessary reform programme; the famine of 1787 and 1788; the summoning of the Estates General for May 1789.

However, one might note that what I have just set out only takes us as far as the early summer of 1789 and the beginnings of what looked like a constitutional revolution which would retain the monarchy. If we want to explain the Revolution as a complex series of interrelating events, spread over several years, getting ever more extreme, and involving more and more people, then we have to look at the way in which the Revolution became, as it were, self-fuelling, at how some of the consequences of the early causes themselves became causes of further developments and change. Such developments as the storming of the Bastille and the 'Great Fear' are both events of the early Revolution itself, and the causes of further developments. All this is simply by way of showing that in history we can't have simple, mechanistic cause-and-effect models. You can't put all the causes on one side of an equation (even if you do divide them up into the two types) and say that they equal a certain consequence on the other side of the equation. The past is constantly in flux: we are constantly getting what might be crudely described as 'knock-on effects', as well as 'feedback', 'cross-currents', and reactions stimulating further action.

How we resolve these problems depends on just exactly what it is we are trying to explain: is it, say, the first outbreak of revolution and the first challenges to absolute monarchy in 1789, or is it the whole massive phenomenon of the French Revolution? Is it why European war broke out in September 1939, or is it why, from 1941, there was a world war involving Russia and America on one side, and Japan and Germany on the other? The timescale one decides to adopt will also be crucial: is one trying to explain why a particular event took place at the precise moment it did, or why such an event should take place at all? Taking a long perspective and aiming to explain why the First World War should have happened at all, one would tend to stress the longer-term causes; but one might prefer to concentrate on the early twentieth century and why exactly war came in late July and early August 1914.

If one is trying to identify the consequences of, say, the French Revolution or the First World War one cannot, it should go without saying, rely on *post hoc propter hoc* – that because certain changes follow the

French Revolution or the First World War they were, therefore, *caused* by these events. Again, we have to take longer-term factors into account, assessing how far they themselves would have brought about the changes irrespective of the revolution or the war. It is, I hope, unnecessary to say that no historians, in trying to explain causes or consequences, look towards general laws: 'it was the result of capitalist exploitation or of imperialist expansion' is little more persuasive than 'it was God's will'.

Hierarchy of Explanatory Factors

My own starting point, then, is that one cannot make mechanistic distinctions between 'causes' and 'effects' (or 'consequences'), because 'effects' immediately start becoming 'causes' of further effects; if we prefer the route of seeking for 'origins', we very quickly find that the 'origins' are products of some antecedent 'causes'. This means that there are problems relating to the very concept of 'events', taken to embrace wars, revolutions, sudden deaths, assassinations, *coups d'état*, famines, election results: events have traditionally been seen as something requiring explanation, but events, of course, can also have consequences. In my view, we cannot go beyond a broad hierarchy of explanatory factors, which is then almost infinitely adaptable to the particular topic being discussed. That hierarchy is: (1) structural, ideological, and institutional circumstances; (2) events; (3) human agencies; and (4) convergence and contingency.

1 *Structural, ideological, and institutional circumstances* both establish the possibilities that there are for change, and set the constraints which will inhibit that change.

   (a) *Structural* (geographical, demographic, economic, and technological): favourable trends in any of these will promote change; a low level of technology or a backward economy will be likely to inhibit change, as will a declining population, though over-population and extreme pressure on scarce resources is also likely to be a negative factor. Geographical factors may in one period be favourable to change (as with Britain at the time of the Industrial Revolution) and at other times unfavourable to change (with the possible exceptions of North Sea oil and gas, Britain has no special geographical advantages today).

   (b) *Ideological* (what is believed and is possible to be believed, religious faiths, existing political and social philosophies): ideas, beliefs and values are very important. Religious faith, pride in the nation, political principles, can be powerful motivators; belief in the powers of monarchy and a hierarchical structure, religious faiths which teach resignation to life as it is, can be great obstacles to change. Ideas cannot be fully acted upon until they have been fully formulated. There can be no democracy until someone has thought up the idea of democracy; nor equality for women until the belief that women are inherently inferior to men has been destroyed. Without a concept of change itself, there is very little change.

(c) *Institutions* (systems of government, justice, policing, voting and education, religious organisations, working-class organisations, the family). The nature and extent of change, or the lack of it, is often determined by institutions. Absolutist empires and monarchies tend to be very resistant to change; systems incorporating some kind of parliamentary institutions are generally more flexible.

2 *Events*. As I have said, there was a tendency to perceive events (wars, revolutions, and economic crises being the principal ones) as requiring attention more to their causes than to their consequences. For some time it has been more clearly seen that events themselves (including plagues, famines, sudden deaths, the late and unexpected birth of an heir, to give further examples) can, operating within the circumstances I have just defined, and reacting with the agencies I have still to come to, have significant outcomes. Events themselves, of course, are not really independent variables, they have their own causes.

3 *Human agencies*. Braudel thought that human will and human action counted for little or nothing. He was followed in this by the structuralists, post-structuralists, and postmodernists. As I have already said, how precisely one handles the issues of explanation will depend on the time perspective one is taking. It may be that in the ultimate scheme of things human volition and human action may really count for nothing, but for the manageable topics and necessarily limited time periods historians deal with it is usually possible to show, with evidence, where human actions have been influential, if not decisive (and, of course, also where they have been ineffectual, or have produced results opposite to those intended). Much depends on the topic being studied: a detailed study of politics, or of international diplomacy, within a limited period will both be likely to stress human agency; a broader study of social change will be less likely to do so. Politicians, presidents, prime ministers and, in certain periods, bishops and popes, all aspire, by direct intervention, to alter the course of events; philanthropists and pressure groups, and some philosophers at least, all hope to influence them. None know better

than historians the folly of human aspiration and ambition; but none the less there are few historians today who would declare that there are no circumstances in which human agencies, be they trade unions, employers' confederations, or fanatical religious sects, cannot have any effects at all. The precise balance between the different variables I have mentioned will be for the individual historian to work out depending on the precise topic.

4 *Convergence and contingency.* Sheer accident is only likely to be of any significance if the other variables are so aligned that a certain type of accident will have a special impact (quite a chapter of accidents, or bungles, attended the assassination in June 1914 of the Archduke Franz-Ferdinand in Sarajevo – the assassin, Gavrilo Princip, was lucky to make it to Sarajevo in the first place, then he missed his first chance to commit the deed, then a wrong turning on the part of the imperial entourage presented him with the fatal opportunity; added to this the international situation and, in particular, the determination of the Austrian Empire, backed by Germany, to seize the opportunity offered to crush her troublesome neighbour Serbia provided the occasion for the outbreak of European war). Of course, the shooting itself was not accidental, in that it was a deliberate political assassination. In earlier times accidental deaths of kings or popes or emperors, depending upon the alignment of the other variables, could have serious consequences. What, however, is really crucial is the way in which circumstances, events, human actions *accumulate*, or converge: it is critical *convergence* which so often produces serious outcomes, changes, or events.

Structure

In writing their articles and books historians, depending on how they have read the evidence of their primary sources, and guided by the relevant secondary sources, have to keep these matters in mind. They have to do that while also providing a clear sense of the sequence of developments and events, that is to say, the order in which they happened (*narrative*), while, as and where necessary, providing *description*, of, say, what a medieval fair or a prison was like, or an aerial dog-fight high above the front line in the First World War, *and*, most important, *analysis* of all the types I have already mentioned (how was trade organised in the Middle Ages, what was the basis of penal policy, how did strategy and tactics interrelate during the First World War?). Unfortunately, it is not possible to fulfil all of these functions simultaneously. It is not possible to write simultaneously about the causes of certain events and about their significance and consequences. Putting it rather crudely and imperfectly, but none the less identifying a very real problem: historians often have to cover what may conventionally, if inadequately, be defined as the political, economic, and social aspects of their topic. Once more, it is usually not possible to write simultaneously about political developments (who was in power, what laws were passed, and so on) and about the state of the economy (fluctuations in prices, and so on).

There may also be the problem of periodisation. Let me repeat that periodisation is purely an analytical device of historians, with no external, immanent existence. Periodisation is simply a means of chopping up the past into manageable chunks of time. Of course, it will seem to the historian, with good reason based on the evidence derived from the sources, that a particular period, or chunk of time, contains a certain unity, in that events, attitudes, values, social hierarchies, seem to be closely integrated with each other, to share common features, and that there are identifiable points of change when a 'period' defined in this way gives place to a 'new period'. A period which suits the political historian may well not suit an economic or social one, as one which suits the study of western Europe will certainly not suit the study of Africa or Japan. Many historical books and articles will be situated firmly within what the author considers to be one unified period. But a book focusing on one particular topic, the family, say, might cover several periods – so here is another complication: it would be hard to deal simultaneously with the economic aspects of the family in Roman times and economic aspects of the family in the seventeenth century. In other cases, even in a relatively sharply focused study, it might be necessary for analytical purposes to break even the short period covered down into separate sub-periods: it would be difficult to make sense of the Renaissance, or the French Revolution, without dividing them up in this way. Once more, then, as well as having different themes and topics to deal with, the historian may well have different time periods, and will certainly, as I have already said, have to give a sense of the passing of time. Because of all this, historians have to devise a structure which, in an organised, comprehensible fashion, will do justice to all the different aspects that have to be dealt with.

Devising such a structure, and carrying it through successfully, is one of the most difficult tasks of the historian. This structure – finally represented in the table of contents, the organisation of chapters and sections of chapters – determines the special form that a piece of historical writing takes. It is a form governed by the fruits of work done in the primary and secondary sources, and by the peculiar demands, as I have just explained them, of historical communication. It has absolutely nothing to do with the nonsense about the need for 'emplotment' or 'narrative' (in the imagined sense of the postmodernists). The fundamental point is that any substantial piece of historical writing will have to have – more than just organisation or a plan – a 'structure'. This is not simply imposed arbitrarily by the historian in order to find some way of resolving all the problems I have mentioned, or to give some beautiful harmony or symmetry to the work. The historian, as a result of his or her researches, and of long reflection on these researches, will begin to perceive a logical order, a series of connections and interrelationships (in short, a 'structure'), which will be as true to the actual aspects of the past the historian is concerned with as it is possible for a historian producing knowledge about these aspects of the past to make it.

Two Examples of Structures

Since structures arise from the full inwardness of the work done by the historian, it is not easy to give examples which can be immediately grasped, when we have not been through all the activities and agonising of the historian. However, I propose here to give two examples, one from a scholarly monograph based entirely on original research in the primary sources, and the other a highly superior hybrid of textbook and interpretative synthesis (see the final section of this chapter), incorporating some fascinating primary research by the author – *The Age of Extremes: The Short Twentieth Century 1914–1991* (1994) by Eric Hobsbawm.

My first example is Ruth Richardson's *Death, Dissection and the Destitute* (1988). To understand how she arrived at the structure for this book, I need to explain that she was seeking to resolve a number of problems. Working on Mary Shelley's *Frankenstein* she had become interested in the eminently non-fictional Burke and Hare, infamous grave robbers and murderers. The standard medical histories told her that body snatching (to provide bodies for anatomical study) came suddenly to an end in 1832, which seemed surprising, particularly when no clear reasons were given. At the same time, at another, and perhaps deeper, level of interest, Richardson was very aware of the deep fear which the poor had had, all through the nineteenth century and well into the twentieth century, of dying in a poor house, and in the obsession to be found among all members of the working class with having a proper funeral. She became preoccupied with the status in popular culture of the newly dead corpse, and with popular attitudes towards it. Wider issues which seemed worth further exploration related to the development of medical science, and to the reordering of society in the early nineteenth century along utilitarian lines. She quickly became aware that the Anatomy Act of 1832, though touched on occasionally by other writers, had never been systematically studied.

The Anatomy Act was passed during the crisis over the 'Great Reform Bill' of 1832, and within the longer period of 'utilitarian reform' whose most famous (or notorious) achievement was the Poor Law Amendment Act of 1834. The Anatomy Act made it lawful for the corpses of those whose bodies were unclaimed at death, and particularly those who had been living 'at public expense' in hospitals (or, subsequently, in the new poor houses established by the 1834 Act), to be handed over for medical dissection. Already one or two advanced figures among the richer classes had, in the interests of medical science, bequeathed their bodies for this purpose; but among the rich and poor alike there was a general horror of the whole idea. The Act made sure that the horror would fall exclusively on the poor. In the years before the Act, the legal supply of corpses for dissection had come from the hangman: for murderers dissection was an explicit part of the sentence, deliberately designed to terrorise the criminal. The new Anatomy Act, which was deliberately wrapped in ambiguity and deceit, the better to prevent the poor from claiming the corpses of their relatives or friends, became part of nineteenth-century bureaucracy: its scarifying effects on the destitute endured well into the twentieth century.

At first sight, the structure of Dr Richardson's study (on which she spent ten years) seems very simple; but then the best structures, once the author has worked them out, usually do *appear* simple. The centrepiece of the book is the Act itself, but Richardson had to explain both how it came about in relation to (a) medical history and (b) the politics of the time, and why, when it came, it had such enormous significance for the poor. She had also to analyse how the Act actually operated within the Victorian bureaucracy, and to work out the detail of its impact right into the twentieth century. Thus, the book is divided into three parts, the most important being the middle one, entitled 'The Act'. The first part is entitled 'The Body', and in three separate chapters sets up three analytical, and to some extent chronological, themes. First, there is a study of 'The Corpse and Popular Culture', which establishes a long historical perspective and, making effective use, in particular, of the studies of contemporary folklorists, brings out the reverential treatment accorded to the corpse which was believed to have some kind of life still in it immediately after death. The second chapter moves into the realm of medical history, analysing how medical men had to combat popular sentiment in trying to achieve a sense of scientific detachment towards the corpse. The third chapter is entitled 'The Corpse as a Commodity' and traces the way in which, as the growth of medical schools raised the demand for corpses, the supply from hanged felons proved insufficient, and a trade in corpses, usually stolen from graves, grew up.

Part Two is a brilliant weaving together of topics and detailed chronology. In Chapter IV, 'The Sanctity of the Grave Asserted', the three themes of Part One are most effectively built upon to explain the immediate context, in the 1820s, for the arguments and discussions leading to the Act. Chapter V is as good an example of technical source criticism as could be found anywhere, concentrating in particular on the *Proceedings and Report of the Parliamentary Select Committee* appointed in the spring of 1828 to examine the problem, and on the ancillary documentation; a persuasive and lucid analysis justifies the chapter title, 'Foregone Conclusions'. There then follows a complete change of pace and content, perfectly integrated, however, into the overall analysis. It was soon after the Select Committee reported that the Burke and Hare murders reached their climax, the full story becoming known in February 1829. Chapter VI, 'Trading Assassins', is an exciting piece of narrative which at the same time relates the sordid events to the broader themes and to the political manoeuvres leading to the Anatomy Bill itself. Chapter VII discusses alternative means which might have been employed to secure the necessary anatomical specimens, while at the same time demonstrating the interaction between agitation over parliamentary reform and the shaping of the second Anatomy Bill (the first having been withdrawn): the Bill in its final form, Richardson explains, was a product of fear of, and contempt for, the poor. Chapter VIII follows through in detail to the actual enactment of the Act on 1 August 1832.

Part Three is a most impressive attempt, on the basis of particularly fragmentary and intractable evidence, to analyse the effects the Act had on the poor and, in particular, their fear of dying in the workhouse. Chapter IX brings out forcefully the supreme, and apparently deliberate, cruelties of the Act, both for friends and relatives not in a financial position to 'claim' the body as the law required, and for the dead persons themselves, who were well aware in advance of the fate that awaited their corpses. Chapter X, 'The Bureaucrat's Bad Dream', details a story of 'opposition, riot, shortage, maldistribution, speculation, disinterment and noninterment of corpses, indecency, misconduct, collusion, corruption'. The final chapter, coming up to and after the advent of the welfare state, drives home the theme of dissection as punishment for 'the unpardonable offence' of destitution, and explains both the terror inspired by the Act and the fact that hitherto it had been almost completely ignored by historians: 'over the course of Victoria's reign, the fact that the misfortune of poverty could qualify a person for dismemberment after death became too intensely painful for contemplation; became taboo. The memory went underground of a fate literally unspeakable.'[6]

For the Hobsbawm book, I am going to set out his table of contents, which shows immediately how he has divided his book into three subperiods, which actually are, though he doesn't explicitly give the dates, 1914–45, 1945–73, and 1972–91.

Table of Contents for Hobsbawm's Age of Extremes

PART ONE: THE AGE OF CATASTROPHE

Though brief, Hobsbawm's chapter titles give a pretty clear idea of the main topic for each chapter. Accordingly, I am going to attempt, part by part, chapter by chapter, to explain why Hobsbawm has ordered the individual topics in the way he has: in other words, I am going to try to explain the structure of the book, chapter by chapter.

Part One

Chapter 1   Clearly Hobsbawm felt that the two wars of 1914–18 and 1939–45 were the dominating events in his 'Age of Catastrophe' and so therefore this is the topic he starts off with.

Chapter 2   But almost equally important is the Communist revolution set off at the end of the First World War, and having repercussions across the world.

Chapter 3   Then, of course, practically the whole of the inter-war years were dominated by the massive economic depressions. I hope you can see the logical sequence, massive events and circumstances: war, revolution, economic collapse.

Chapter 4   Hobsbawm now turns to ideological (in the non-Marxist sense) aspects: liberalism was essentially a nineteenth-century set of beliefs and values which could scarcely survive the shattering blows of war, revolution, and economic collapse (again, now that I have spelled it out, I hope you can see the logical development).

Chapter 5   The title here may seem puzzling, and perhaps suggestive of some repetition, for the 'common enemy' is indeed Nazism and Fascism. However, what Hobsbawm has done – and this is very typical of the kind of analytical distinctions historians have to make – is to separate out war as a general phenomenon (involving killing, cost, destruction, and so on), and the specific, and again ideological, topic of the alien ideas of Nazism and Fascism, and how they were combated.

Chapter 6   One of Hobsbawm's great strengths is the way in which he integrates discussion of the arts into discussion of other historical developments, but obviously it makes sense to have one concentrated chapter in which the arts can be analysed in some detail.

Chapter 7   Now, as it were, the wheel has come full circle: we began with essentially political and event-based topics (war and revolution); now we come back to the third great series of world-shaking events (partly induced by the wars, so this chapter must come at the end, not at the beginning), the fall of the great European empires.

Part Two

Chapter 8   Again we start with the dominating international political circumstances.

Chapter 9   But immediately we have to come to the question of economic recovery, affluence, and material prosperity which very much determined developments, at least in the Western countries.

Chapter 10   Here, Hobsbawm is working out the consequences for ordinary people of the economic circumstances he has described in the previous chapter.

Chapter 11   He then, in a further example of logical sequence, takes this further by looking at changes in human relationships, sexual behaviour, and so on.

Chapter 12   Most of what he has been talking about so far basically refers to the industrialised world. Therefore, it is logical now to take a concentrated look at the Third World.

Chapter 13   The other parts of the world which need special attention are those which have fallen under Communist regimes, Russia, of course, but now also China.

Part Three

Chapter 14   Hobsbawm has to justify his description of this third period as 'the landslide', so he naturally starts off by identifying the new events which have destroyed his 'golden age'.
They start with the international oil crisis of 1973, and
continue with the severe troubles faced by all of the Western economies, particularly in the face of 'globalisation'
and the challenge of the newly developed Asian countries.

Chapter 15   Again the theme of the Third World is picked up: this is
the area in which revolution is continuing.

Chapter 16   Now we come to another set of crucial events characteris-
ing this third period – however, since they only become
apparent from 1989 onwards they could not have been
dealt with earlier: the collapse of the Russian and the
East European Communist regimes.

Chapter 17   The analogue of Chapter 6.

Chapter 18   Another of Hobsbawm's great strengths is his ability to
discuss the sciences and the technologies, and again to
integrate them into other developments. Clearly a separate
chapter is needed in order to give them their due
weight.

Chapter 19   This is essentially a summing-up chapter.

I am sure you, the reader, will be perfectly clear that I was not trying to give any kind of instant history of the twentieth century there, but just demonstrating the style of thought, determined by the author's actual reading and research, which goes into working out a convincing structure for a massive book of this sort. What I was hoping to convey is a sense of logical sequence, of the analytical separation out into differ-ent topics (not muddling up together matters that need to be separated out) and of how a balance is struck between topics and periodisation.

3   Comparative History

Advances in science, medicine and technology continue to astonish. History cannot compete, yet there is something deeply satisfying about the steady developments in both scope and methods. I have already suggested that one of the most striking areas of progress in recent years is that of comparative history. This is not, to repeat, to say that there is something necessarily better about comparative history. There will still need to be single-country histories, and detailed studies of institutions, events, social conditions within single countries.

The special virtue of comparative history is that by comparing and contrasting analogous developments within different countries additional illumination is cast on all the countries involved by the very process of comparison, while, at the same time, common elements, which might not have been appreciated previously, are brought out. Taking a group of countries as a unity is not comparative history, and taking a variety of points from a variety of different countries in order to support one broad theme or case is not comparative history: for example, a book describing a broad process of changes in sexual attitudes and behaviour across Europe which takes some examples from one country, others from another, and yet more from other different countries is not a comparative history – to be that, we would have to have explicit comparisons and contrasts between, say, Italy and Britain, France and Germany, or whatever. Even in single-country histories, it can be specially valuable to have comparisons brought in from time to time with other countries, particularly ones which are going through broadly similar historical developments.

Comparative history is history which covers similar topics over several different countries, thus bringing out comparisons and contrasts between the different countries, and showing which developments were part of a common movement, and which peculiar to individual countries. Looking at several countries together gives a clearer sense of wider historical movements, changes in economic organisation, changes in class and power structures, the influences of scientific discovery and technological innovation, the changing role and status of women, and so on.

From what I have already said about the complex and time-consuming tasks associated with working with primary sources, it will not seem surprising that so far there have not been a very large number of genuinely comparative works based on the archives of the several different countries involved. Comparative studies are often largely based on the secondary sources existing for different individual countries. Often they belong to specially created series designed to encourage comparative study, and therefore again tend to be based on secondary sources. There is, therefore, a great opportunity for universities to create their own comparative history courses.

4   Concepts and Clichés

Clichés

The writing of history requires the utmost precision in the handling of language. Easily said but very hard work to achieve. Nothing is easier than to slip into a weary cliché ('taken by storm', 'defining moment', 'face value', 'stick to his guns', 'loose cannon', 'jury is out'), flog old metaphors which explain nothing ('wars accelerate – or are catalysts of – change'), use a fancy word because it sounds trendy even if we are not quite clear exactly what it means ('historiography', 'discourse', 'ideology', 'textuality'), or, most common in history, use some vague concept whose scope and meaning is far from clear – the classic instance being 'public opinion' (everybody's opinion, the opinion of a few newspaper proprietors, or what?). It is essential to be as precise and explicit as it is in scientific writing. This is one of the ways in which a work of history differs totally from a novel or a poem: a creative writer may quite deliberately exploit the ambiguities and resonances of language, but a historian should make special efforts to be as clear and explicit as possible, and to separate out unambiguously what is securely established from what is basically speculation. Historians should never try to conceal their own failure to think out exactly what it is they want to say, or their failure to find the straightforward words in which to express it, by creating a smoke-screen of metaphors. Particularly to be avoided is the deadly virus of dead metaphor: spectrum of opinion, spectre of defeat, climate of ideas, tool of analysis, frontiers of knowledge. Worst of all, in my view, is the routine use of 'dramatic' which presumably ought to mean something like 'with the force and emotion of a drama', when usually all that is actually meant is 'big': never a rise in prices, never a fall in stocks, never a religious revival nor a political recovery, but each must be 'dramatic'. Clichés and dead metaphors are dangerous because they come to us so readily that we have ceased to consider whether they really are the best words for what we want to say, and whether indeed they actually do say anything precise.

Concepts

Problems also arise with conceptual terms, collective nouns, and certain complex words which carry several distinct meanings. We need concepts to describe what we perceive as happening in human and social relationships and activities but for which no ordinary words exist, and to bring the intellectual thinking element into our writing of history.

The difficulty with some conceptual terms is that they have been deliberately created in support of some particular theory, and thus carry with them a considerable freight of assumptions and value judgements. Thus, the invented word 'textuality' is inextricably associated with neo-Marxist postmodernist theory about how any piece of writing, or 'text' (in some versions the word is also applied to cultural artefacts), is inevitably contaminated with bourgeois values; to use the term is to accept the assumption that there is no critical distinction between primary and secondary sources. Even more problematic are words which both have a standard, neutral meaning and are also crucial terms in a particular theory. Classic instances are 'ideology', and 'ideological', and 'discourse', and 'discursive'. In expanding my own approach to issues of explanation I have spoken of 'ideological circumstances', as distinct from 'structural' and 'institutional' circumstances, and given examples of what I mean. 'Ideology' in this neutral usage simply means 'set of ideas', usually with the implication that this set of ideas will lead to some kind of action, or at least proselytising. Thus one could speak of 'Nazi ideology', 'Thatcherite ideology', 'feminist ideology', or perhaps even 'public-school ideology'. However, in Marxist and postmodernist discourse, 'ideology' is used in a technical way, directly related to Marxist theory about class. Each class is said to have its own ideology, related, though not necessarily in a simple and direct way, to its basic economic interests. In a period in which the bourgeois class, allegedly, dominates, the 'dominant ideology' is bourgeois ideology, which is represented (wrongly, the implication of the theory is) as being the ideology of the whole nation. Ideology, then, is seen as something false, the mask which conceals the reality of bourgeois dominance and repression.

You will have noted my use of 'discourse' a couple of sentences back: that was neutral usage, simply signifying 'the forms of language in which a particular sort of people customarily express themselves'. One could talk of 'feminist discourse', or one could talk of 'historical discourse' to signify the way in which historians write their books and articles, using footnotes, and being punctilious in certain distinctive ways, for example. Discourse, as used by postmodernists, is specifically related to their theories about the exercise of power in society. While I talked at the beginning of Chapter 5 about the distinction between documents of record and more 'discursive' sources, all I meant by the latter was sources which are prosy, descriptive, talk round a subject, rather than being the embodiments of something that actually happened. In postmodernist theory, discursive signifies being bound in with the alleged power structure of society. It is vitally important to be sure how one is using words of this sort, and, above all, not to slide between different meanings.

'Gender', 'Patriarchy', 'Moral Panics', and so on

The word 'gender' was originally purely a grammatical term. Feminists at the end of the 1960s and the beginning of the 1970s brought the word into intellectual, and then everyday, discourse (again an example of the neutral use of this word) as an alternative to 'sex', to signify what they maintained was culturally constructed rather than biologically given. Since 'sex' has come more and more simply to mean sexual activity, the word 'gender' has been widely adopted, even by people who do not necessarily accept that the major differences in the roles and behaviour of men and women are culturally constructed. There can, therefore, be a dangerous ambiguity here: one may have to clarify the extent of one's own ideological (neutral usage) assumptions. As I keep saying, ambiguity is always to be avoided in historical writing.

'Patriarchy' is another example of an existing word with a limited meaning – the reference is to relatively primitive societies where power was quite explicitly lodged in the hands of male elders – being taken up and given new signification by feminists. That men have often oppressed women is abundantly clear from the sources, but in historical writing one should always think through very carefully the implications of using a term of this sort; the glib use of words which are part of a political ideology is to be discouraged.

Historians themselves sometimes coin conceptual terms in order to drive home the particular point they are trying to make: one example we found in Chapter 4 was Lawrence Stone's concept of 'affective individualism' (sometimes called 'love') as radically changing the nature of marriage in Britain in the 1640s. Historians of the early modern period have also introduced the term 'political nation', which is certainly a great improvement on 'public opinion', to refer to that minority of the population who were interested in political issues. A helpful distinction is often made between 'court' – those who gather round the monarch and his/her government – and 'country' – those who scorn the life of the court and see themselves as upholding the interests of the country as a whole.

From sociology has come the term 'moral panics', taken either as episodes which demonstrate a deep fear and sense of crisis among the bourgeoisie, or, alternatively, episodes deliberately stirred up by the toffs in order to suppress the riff-raff. Personally, I have never been convinced that any of the episodes so designated ever came anywhere near to justifying the term 'panic': the advice is as before – no historian should glibly adopt the term 'moral panic' without scrutinising the particular episode very carefully to make sure that the term really is justified. In discussing the so-called 'new cultural history' in Chapter 4 I mention some of the phrases favoured by anthropologists about people (peasants for example) 'making sense of' or 'giving meaning to' their world. Obviously, a number of distinguished historians have found these phrases helpful. All I can offer is a word of caution: I am uncomfortable with such phrases myself, but for those who feel that they really do have a precise significance, and that significance can be conveyed to readers, fine. Likewise with phrases about meaning, or identity, being 'constructed': my question always is, precisely who is doing the constructing?

'Culture' and 'Cultural'

We have quite a lot of other words, frequently encountered in everyday usage, which also cause difficulties. 'Culture' and 'cultural' are obvious ones. I have already admitted to finding 'cultural artefacts' a useful phrase, for which there seems no ready substitute. If one wrote a history focusing on what in the newspapers are called 'the arts and entertainments' one might well feel justified in calling it a 'cultural history' – 'artistic history' would not sound right. Indeed, to many people the word 'culture' immediately suggests opera, art, poetry, but there is a much wider, anthropological sense, in which 'culture' is used to mean something like 'the network or totality of attitudes, values and practices of a particular group of human beings'. Some recent writers have suggested that the crucial point about culture in this usage is that the focus is on thought, on mental processes. Yet, arising out of the work of Braudel we have had historians talking of 'material culture', while, on the other hand, there is that useful word 'mentalities'.

The word 'culture' is used a lot in everyday conversation, and by politicians, often pejoratively, as in 'culture of dependency', 'blame culture'. In a work of history one might speak of 'aristocratic culture', meaning, perhaps, life in a big house on a landed estate, freed from the need to earn a living, but involving the manipulation of investments, the collection of rent and administration of the estate, the bossing around of tenants and servants, a London 'season', fine paintings and furniture (or is that 'material culture', and something different?), arranged marriages, dressing up differently for different parts of the day, a belief in one's automatic right to participate in government, huntin', shootin', and fishin': all that could be said to make up the 'network' or 'totality' of aristocratic culture. Similarly one might speak of 'youth culture' – the new 'youth culture', involving coffee bars, rock music, special clothes, which began to appear at the end of the 1950s, is often reckoned a crucial factor in the social changes of the 1960s. Sometimes we speak of 'Western culture' embracing 'the Western way of life': all the attitudes and values and practices, springing from the classical tradition, modified by Christian religion, by the eighteenth-century Enlightenment, by the French Revolution, by romanticism, by overseas conquests and colonialism, by the upheavals of the twentieth century. A 'culture', apparently, can be very big, or extremely small, depending upon the context within which the concept is being used. Maybe we just have to recognise the variousness of the word and rely on our readers (listeners) to pick up the meaning from the context. But this is dangerous in historical writing, and leaves too many opportunities for sliding from one meaning to another: 'culture' is a word to be used very self-consciously indeed, alternatives being sought wherever possible.

'Class' and 'State'

'Class' is another word which has to be used with some care. A wealth of evidence indicates that modern societies divide up into a small number (three or four) of aggregates, arranged in a hierarchy and within each of which customs and behaviour seem to be broadly shared, distinguished from each other by wealth, status, access to power, life chances, and so on. This phenomenon we call 'class', and the different aggregates are 'classes'. However, some writers would still maintain that the phenomenon I am here describing as 'class' should be termed 'social stratification' and that the term 'class' should be confined to signifying the dynamic element in historical change identified (allegedly) by Marx and Weber. Then there is the question of what labels to use. In all the developed countries phrases similar to 'upper-class accent', 'middle-class education', 'working-class housing' are in wide use. This could suggest how many classes there are and what labels to give them. However, Marxists insist that there are only two classes, 'the middle class' and 'the working class'. It is easy to use the language of class in a facile way; much more difficult, but very necessary, is to work out clearly in advance the implications of the language one is using. Too many writers switch confusingly between the different connotations of class language.

'State' seems a very straightforward word, yet it, too, can be very confusing. Historians talk frequently about 'the rise of the nation state' or 'the power of the state'. Some writers try to insist that there is a permanent and unalterable distinction between 'the state' on the one side and 'society' on the other. The United States of America is made up of 51 individual states; Germany too is a federal republic made up of individual 'states'. The central connotation within the word is that of 'power, authority, control'. A 'nation state' is formed when the unit over which power, authority and control is exercised coincides with the geographical territory occupied by one 'nation' (German, French, Italian, or whatever); a rough opposite is the old Austro-Hungarian Empire which might be defined as a multi-national state. Sometimes the word is used to mean something like 'the government and all its apparatus of power and control' (thus being distinguished from 'society'), sometimes it applies to the whole country over which power and control is exercised. Within federal systems a certain designated amount of power and control is allocated to the individual states, but overall they are subordinate to the federal government: if one talks, in the singular, of 'the German state' or 'the American state' then one is referring to the federal government and all its apparatus of control. The point here is to accept, and engage with, the different meanings, not to insist that the word 'state' must be used in only one way – quite manifestly, it isn't.

Revisionism

Another pair of words to be used with caution is 'revisionism' and 'revisionist'. While one can, for instance, speak of a recognisable, and consistent, group of 'medieval historians', or of 'economic historians', there is no consistent, recognisable group of 'revisionist historians'. The word has that pompous ring which attracts many historians (and then their students). Unless the context and meaning is absolutely clear it is best avoided. The word arises from the way in which a broad consensus sometimes arises over some particular historical topic. For example, there was a time when Namier's views about eighteenth-century British politics (discussed in Chapter 4) exercised an almost complete hegemony in that domain; those who began to argue that he had been wrong to empty eighteenth-century politics totally of ideological commitment could be termed 'revisionist' – but the trouble is that historians continually criticise and qualify the work of others, and there is always the danger that we will have re-revisionists and re-re-revisionists. Often critics of a particular thesis criticise it on a variety of different grounds, thus speaking of *the* revisionists can be misleading.

Another area where something of a consensus arose was over the question of the origins of the Second World War. Right through to the late 1950s it seemed overwhelmingly obvious that the Second World War had one overriding cause: Hitler and his evil intentions. Although he wasn't quite the only one, A. J. P. Taylor was the most effective and best-known critic of this view, arguing (I summarise drastically) that the war came about through miscalculation and accident, rather than Hitler's deliberate intention. One can speak of Taylor as leading a re-visionist school, though again I'm not sure that the phrase is particularly helpful. We don't on the whole speak of the re-revisionists, though in fact Taylor's views have been pretty thoroughly discredited, the new emphasis being placed not just on Hitler himself but on the whole dynamic of Nazism. The whole thing is made complicated, and perhaps ridiculous, by the fact that within study of the very same subject the phrase 'revisionists' is also used to refer to those politicians and commentators who at the time supported revising the terms of the Treaty of Versailles.

The release of hitherto secret Russian documents since 1989 has led to the revising of standard views about the Soviet Union held in the West. It is now seen that Stalin and the Soviet Communist Party did not have such an absolutely total grip on Russian society as was widely believed by those who used the term 'totalitarian' to describe that society. Obviously history based on primary sources is to be preferred to history based on guesswork and external perceptions of the Soviet regime, but whether in its *conclusions* (as distinct from the wealth of evidence deployed) the new history differs so much from the old, and is itself sufficiently unified, to justify the deployment of the label 'revisionist', I personally rather doubt.

5   Quotations and Scholarly Apparatus

Use of Quotation

Because of the relationship between 'history', 'the past', and 'sources' almost every piece of historical writing will contain direct quotations from source material. According to Barzun and Graff, in their advice to researchers, quotations 'must as far as possible be merged into the text'.[7] Insofar as they are speaking of quotations from *secondary* works this is quite sound advice. There are few more tiresome, or less persuasive, confections than assemblages of direct quotations from other writers. With regard to primary sources it is broadly true, as Barzun and Graff say with all the force of the italics at their disposal, that *'quotations are illustrations not proofs'*,[8] yet, given the special difficulties of 'proof' in historical study, this is by no means always so. Quite often the whole brunt of a particular phase of a historian's argument depends upon the text of a new document which he or she has discovered, or upon a new significance which he or she has seen in certain sentences in a well-known document. In such cases the quotations must be given a distinctive prominence, usually through indentation and separate type (if the quotation is more than a phrase or two), otherwise by placing them in inverted commas: the last thing the historian wants to do is to merge this vital material with his or her own commentary (of course, the historian has selected the quotation in the first place, but at least by setting it out clearly he or she does enter into a dialogue with the reader – nothing irritates more than those over-confident historians of an earlier generation who wrote their books as, in essence, a paraphrase of what they conceived to be the basic documents for their topic, 'merging' reliable authorities, dubious authorities, and their own errors and prejudices into one undifferentiated whole). Frequently, furthermore, an unadulterated direct quotation from a contemporary source can be a most effective and economical means of conveying a sense of period, a sense of understanding from the inside. Even where the quotation is simply illustrative, its illustrative value will stand out all the more clearly for being properly presented.

Still, Barzun and Graff do have a point. Clearly a technique of presentation that is necessary in an academic monograph may be much less suitable for other levels of historical writing; and of course it is open to abuse by the writer of an alleged scholarly monograph. There is all the difference in the world between the deliberate full-dress citation of a long quotation for some definite historical purpose, and the mere stringing together of a miscellaneous collection of such quotations in the hope that the end product will pass for a kind of history. When one comes to the undergraduate essay, or the work of historical popularisation drawing exclusively upon secondary authorities, there will often be little justification for the indented quotation, save perhaps in the case of a particularly striking and important passage with which the writer does not agree but around which he or she wishes to build up an argument, or in the case of a crucial piece of primary material (even if actually procured from a secondary source). On the whole, quotations should be kept to an absolute minimum in both popularisations and undergraduate essays. The opinion that a case is somehow clinched by citing the direct speech of one or two authorities is as erroneous as it seems to be widespread: a silly, un-historical judgement is no less silly because it happens to have been once uttered by a once-eminent authority. The writer who embarks upon that dialogue with the reader which I have several times stressed as integral to historical writing must be sure that it is his/her side of the dialogue that is being expressed and not an assortment of ill-digested and misunderstood items culled from other people. 'Scissors-and-paste' is the contemptuous phrase we rightly apply to a piece of would-be historical writing which in practice amounts to little more than such an assortment.

Undoubtedly one of the most common errors beginning PhD students fall into is the overuse of over-long direct quotations. Partly this is because inexperienced researchers, having, perhaps with some effort, discovered some apparently juicy sources, are desperately keen to show them off; partly it is because, quite frankly, it is simpler to copy out and reproduce large chunks of material than to think very carefully about which particular phrases one needs to quote and why. On the whole, while I maintain my general defence of the importance, for clearly identified purposes, of direct quotation, I would agree with Barzun and Graff that what one wants is the shortest piece of quotation compatible with making the point the historian wishes to make – the provisos always being that the quotations are not so brief, so 'out of context', as to be misleading, and that they are sufficiently clearly identified that readers can, if they wish, check the full original. Here, in a brief passage about the Jacobite rebellion of 1715 taken from *Eighteenth-Century England* (1974) by Dorothy Marshall, is an excellent example of the incorporation of two brief quotations, one from a song, the other from a diary, into the general argument:

> *There's some say that we wan; and some say that they wan,*
> *And some say that nane wan at a', man*

At all events the stalemate continued, so that the Pretender [the Jacobite claimant to the throne] when he finally reached Scotland at the end of the year wrote to Bolingbroke, 'I find things in a prosperous way'. It was wishful thinking based on inadequate knowledge, for by then English preparations had been made for the kill.

G. R. Elton's textbook *England Under the Tudors* offers a good example of the use of quotation to illustrate and drive home a specific point about what he calls the 'Tudor revolution in government'. Elton doesn't simply leave the quotation lying, as it were, inert, but picks up and discusses a key word in it:

> The essential ingredient of the Tudor revolution was the concept of national sovereignty. The philosophy underlying Cromwell's [Thomas Cromwell, the powerful Secretary of State] work was summarised brilliantly in his preamble to the Act of Appeals (1533), the operative clause of which reads as follows: 'This realm of England is an Empire, and so hath been accepted in the world, governed by one Supreme Head and King having the dignity and royal estate of the Imperial Crown of the same, unto whom a body politic, compact of all sorts and degrees of people divided in terms and by names of Spirituality and Temporalty, be bounden and owe to bear next to God a natural and humble obedience.'
>
> The critical term is 'empire'. Kings of England had before this claimed to be emperors – the title occurs in Anglo-Saxon times and was taken by Edward I, Richard II, and Henry V – but the meaning here is different. Those earlier 'emperors' had so called themselves because they ruled, or claimed to rule, more than one kingdom, as Edward I claimed Scotland and Henry V France. In the Act of Appeals, on the other hand, England by herself is described as an empire, and it is clear both from the passage cited and from what follows that the word here denoted a political unit, a self-governing state free from (as they put it) 'the authority of any foreign potentates'. We call this sort of thing a sovereign national state.[9]

Identifying Quotations: Footnotes

When readers pick up a book they usually note the name of the author: even if they don't, they have only, should they be outraged by something in the book, to turn back to the title-page to detect the perpetrator. When apprised by quotation marks or indentation that a certain passage is a quotation from some different source, the reader has an equal right to have that source identified. Above all where the entire thesis of a scholarly work is built up on primary materials, these materials, and the sources for any specific pieces of information whether contained in direct quotation or referred to indirectly, must be fully identified for readers so that they have some check on the reliability of what is being said. The easiest way to provide this necessary identification of both primary and secondary sources is a note at the foot of the page, or, less desirably, at the end of the chapter or of the book. Only fools scoff at the historian's footnotes and references. Significantly, it was the planners of the old *Cambridge Modern History* (those 'over-confident historians of an earlier generation') who thought they could do without footnotes – nobody could doubt *their* experts. We are wiser today: no work which claims serious scholarly attention deserves that attention unless it is equipped with the full apparatus of references, provided to enable readers, if they wish, to participate to the full in their side of the dialogue, and as a guide to future researchers in the same field.

And here we have the only true rationale for the rules governing this technical branch of scholarship: references are for use, not show; and they must be furnished in such a way that they are genuinely useful. Almost always there is some good reason for the finicky styles of presentation evolved by scholars: for example, if it has come to be accepted that a certain source is cited in a certain way, it is obviously sensible for all researchers to follow the same practice rather than introduce possibly confusing styles or abbreviations of their own. From the point of view of detailed scholarship it is often important to know whether a particular document cited – holograph, manuscript, or perhaps typescript – is published or unpublished: scholars therefore have adopted the convention of italicising (or underscoring) titles of published materials, while printing titles or citations of unpublished ones in ordinary roman. Agreed conventions enable economies of space in setting out references (hence the various Latin abbreviations, loc. cit., ibid., and so on, which we need not bother with here); but what is essential is that enough information be provided for another researcher without undue difficulty to track down the same reference. It is a *sine qua non* of the scholarly reference that it be honest. This is why some historians insist upon a golden rule that before any work is published all references must be checked. But there is, of course, a difference between the inaccuracy that is human, and wilful dishonesty (also, alas, all too human). If I confess that I do not myself go in for the systematic checking of all my own references, I can add that I have had occasion to regret my own carelessness when endeavouring to follow up and take further some of my own previous researches, finding certain materials much harder to retrace than my own footnotes would suggest. The historian does well to remember that his most dedicated reader may turn out to be himself.

Earlier in this section I mentioned the case of the undergraduate essayist or popular writer citing a piece of primary material which he or she had in fact taken from a secondary authority; this is a practice which sometimes is forced upon even the most rigorous scholars. What is called for in the appropriate footnote is a statement both of the primary source involved, and of the secondary source where in fact it was found. If the remarks quoted are those of a foreign secretary or ambassador there is little point in citing as the reference, say, 'W. L. Langer, *The Franco-Russian Alliance 1890–1894* (1929), p. 277' – the reader wants to know *which* foreign secretary or ambassador made the remark, and, of course, *where* and *when*; 1929, needed in the full reference, is *not* the *critical* date. But, on the other hand, to blandly give as the reference 'Aerenthal, Austrian First Secretary in St Petersburg to Kàlnoky of the Russian Foreign Office, 10 November 1892' would be to give the dishonest and misleading impression that the dispatch itself (as distinct from Langer's quotation of it) had been studied. The reference required by honesty and common sense would be something along the lines of 'Aerenthal's dispatch...etc...as quoted by W. L. Langer...etc.'[10] The need for a footnote reference arises in cases other than where a direct quotation has been made. Most of the time historians take from their sources, primary and secondary, not whole phrases for quotation, but single ideas, or single pieces of information, such as a wage rate, a price increase, or a decision made in some court or council; again, obviously, an appropriate reference is called for.

Valuable historical works have been written with much less in the way of scholarly apparatus than the foregoing paragraphs would seem to call for; they remain good books, but to the extent that they irritate the serious reader who asks (as serious readers of any historical work must constantly ask) 'How does he know *that*?' they are less good than they might be. Since scholarly apparatus is there for use, in the end only the specific circumstances can determine how elaborate an apparatus any particular piece of writing requires. Where absurdity marches in is when secondary authorities without pretence to original scholarship attempt to masquerade behind the trappings of scholarship.

Bibliographies

The bibliography provides an overview. As I have already indicated, in discussing E. P. Thompson's most famous work, the first part will be concerned with primary sources, and will indicate the range of archives consulted (and also, of course, negatively, will show if some really important archive has been ignored); it will also demonstrate the variety of primary sources consulted, including the printed ones such as newspapers, guides to etiquette, and so on. The second part of the bibliography will consist of secondary sources, enabling the reader to check if the historian has taken into account the views of historians who have pioneered this subject area, or who have presented different or contrary interpretations to this historian's own. In the preface to volume three of his *Economic History of Modern Britain*, J. H. Clapham went on record against 'What in my heart I regard as the rather pedantic and ostentatious tradition of the formal bibliography in a book which contains footnotes'. Nothing could be more disingenuous: the compilation of a bibliography is certainly a tedious chore and one which, a book finally finished, any author can be excused for shrinking from; but often, sad though the thought might be, it is sometimes the single most useful service the author performs. Clapham and his generation rode high in the supreme confidence that if they wrote a book, that book would be read. They were probably wrong even then: Clapham's *magnum opus* is now much more used as a work of reference than read cover to cover. Increasingly in a busy age one 'savours' books, even good ones – reads carefully passages directly relevant to one's own immediate interest, skiffs through the rest. But what one certainly does want is a bibliography (not as a sign of the author's worthiness as a historian, but as an aid to one's own further reading and research), and one does not want to have to scan through footnotes to compile one – a labour which properly rests with the author. There are few sights more incongruous than the converted PhD dissertation which some publisher has been prevailed upon to bring out with the minimum of alteration save that, in the interests of economy, the one portion that might conceivably be of use to others, the bibliography, has been chopped off. At its best, as with the E. P. Thompson bibliography, a bibliography is a significant guide to the raw materials on which the work of history is based. I speak here of the scholarly bibliography appended to a work of original scholarship. In a textbook, or general study, it may well be appropriate for the bibliography to take the rather different form of a guide to further reading.

As I have said before, arguments over the status of history very much depend upon one's basic assumptions. If you *assume* that historians operate in good faith and with integrity, and are not bourgeois stooges, or unwitting victims of their cultural context, and, accordingly, that it is worthwhile reading what they write if you want to find out about the past, then you will accept the view I am putting forward here that it is through scholarly apparatus that the historian invites the reader to share in the evidence upon which the historian's account is based. Historical communication, I have consistently maintained, should always involve a dialogue between reader and historian. In their minds, readers should always be raising comments like the following: 'That's interesting – where did he/she get that from?'; 'Come on now, I don't believe *that*: what on earth are the sources?'; 'Interesting idea, but I bet there's no hard evidence for it'. Readers of history should be sceptical, doubts at the ready. Doubts are most quickly resolved, or confirmed, by looking at the appropriate footnote. Readers should always have a basis on which to disagree with the interpretations and conclusions being presented by the author. Good history should be authoritative, but it should never be authoritarian.

6   Types of Historical Communication: From Scholarly Monograph to Museums, Films and Television

Levels of Historical Communication: 'Public History'

During the period when I was writing this book, the spring of 2000, I was invited by the *Sunday Times* to write an article comparing the 'anti-capitalist' protests that had broken out on May Day with the protests of 1968. Thirty years ago I might have termed this piece of journalism, with a firm historical basis, 'applied history'. The term never caught on, and has been superseded by an American coinage, 'public history'. Having always maintained that history is a social necessity, the provision of an essential service to society, I am not sure how necessary this term is, though certainly the task of making special studies of the way in which history is communicated to wider audiences is a worthwhile one. History has always been communicated at different levels and to different audiences. Here I shall consider in turn: the postgraduate dissertation; the scholarly monograph; the learned article; the scholarly synthesis (a non-technical and rather elastic term which I use to cover a range of the most exciting works produced by historians); and the textbook (which can range from being close to the scholarly synthesis in incorporating original work to the most straightforward communication of basic information). These are all conceived within the academic and educational context, though some may be quite widely read by the general public. I then come to popular history (books deliberately designed to sell well), museums, films, and television programmes: all of these, I suppose, could be called public history. I have written extensively about all of them without feeling any need to invoke that term: what is important is that 'public history' must not be allowed to become just another slogan or some kind of patented monopoly ('our MA in Public History is the only genuine article').

The PhD Thesis or Dissertation

The first major piece of serious historical research which most would-be members of the historical profession undertake is in the form of a dissertation directed in the UK and the USA towards the degree of Doctor of Philosophy (curious name, but let it pass) or for one of the major European distinctions (which may carry an automatic entitlement to a particular job within the profession). In Britain, the PhD should, as well as being an apprenticeship exercise, make some clearly defined contribution to historical knowledge; for dissertations of less real historical significance there are the lesser degrees of MPhil and BPhil. The principle is a good one: all historians should, at an early stage, wrestle with the problems of producing a substantial, sustained, well-structured piece of work. Candidates are expected to have conducted research in depth over a very narrow and specific field, the bulk of their work being in primary sources, preferably ones which have not been too thoroughly explored by others. The completed dissertation must display, in full, or even pedantic degree, the proper apparatus of scholarship. For generations theses were typed, though now, of course, they are usually word-processed. They are then specially bound, usually in not more than three or four copies, with one copy being available for consultation by other researchers in the university where the degree was taken. It is now possible to consult some PhD dissertations in electronic form on the web. Because a thesis is not published, its title will not be underlined or italicised when being cited in scholarly apparatus. Since the topic will always be rather narrow, a PhD thesis will not automatically be suitable for publication.

Monographs and Learned Articles

However, the scope of the PhD thesis may be extended (more research, wider reading) so that it can be published as an academic monograph; or it may serve as the basis for one or more learned articles. Many monographs and many articles, naturally, originate elsewhere than in a postgraduate dissertation. Sometimes historians have ideas which they reckon, if followed up, will yield interesting articles; as the research proceeds they find they have a full-length monograph on their hands. Sometimes they write a monograph and find there are certain fragments left over, interesting in themselves, but of a nature to disrupt the thematic unity of the monograph: so these are worked up into learned articles. The essence of both the learned article and the monograph is that they deal with one single, clearly defined topic, and they are based on the relevant primary source materials.

The learned article, in particular, will usually scrutinise (and often criticise!) any secondary sources in which other historians may have dealt with the same topic, and it will be printed and published in one of the learned journals – for example, *The English Historical Review*, *Past and Present*, *History*, or *Contemporary European History*. Usually 20–30 pages in length (10 000–15 000 words), this is the most characteristic product of the ordinary working historian, and the one in which the historian's activities most obviously resemble those of the scientist, at the same time strikingly demonstrating the point that historians are generally concerned with limited, precise topics, not with the grand problems of human existence. Let us consider the three articles published in the February 1993 issue of *History*: 'The Domesday Survey: Context and Purpose'; 'The Problems of Literacy in Early Modern England'; 'The Pests of Human Society: Stockbrokers, Jobbers and Speculation in Mid-Eighteenth-Century Britain'.

The author of the first article, noting (as I have done) the enormous use made of Domesday Book as a source for social life in early medieval England, and the extensive application of computer-based techniques, stresses the vital importance of knowing why, and in what circumstances, the survey was set up in the first place: it is to these limited objectives that the article addresses itself.

Several times in this book I have raised the question of how one explains social change. Without question one of the most important agents of change in the development of societies has been the spread of literacy. The nature and extent of literacy in early modern England (roughly the sixteenth and seventeenth centuries) are very hard to establish. The second article concentrates on these very precise issues. The third article starts off by referring to 'present-day concerns' about regulating the 'City of London', going on to say how particularly great that problem was in the mid-eighteenth century, a discussion of which is the specific and limited topic of the article.

When citing a learned article, the title of the published journal will be italicised, and volume number, date, and page references will be given. The actual title of the article will not be italicised but will be put in quotation marks, as I have done above.

The Scholarly Synthesis

Now I move to the range of partially overlapping types, which run from the scholarly monograph to the scholarly synthesis to the partially research-based textbook. It is within this range that we find the most important and distinguished work produced by historians (a tiny number of which may be reviewed in the posh newspapers, or even featured on television – but we should always be very careful to avoid generalising about what historians do on the basis of the proportionately almost infinitesimal number of works that receive this kind of attention). Of books that I have already mentioned, those by Peter Laslett and Lawrence Stone relating to the family, Le Roy Ladurie and Natalie Zemon Davis in 'microhistory', and Ian Kershaw on Hitler, stand near the beginning of this range, while Eric Hobsbawm on the twentieth century and William Doyle on the French Revolution come somewhere in the middle, perhaps tending towards the end of it. By 'scholarly synthesis' I mean a book which both has a substantial amount of original research in the primary sources, and synthesises and interprets the monographs and other secondary works of other historians relevant to what will be a wide-ranging subject. But not that wide-ranging. Even in their most important books historians remain *specialists*, dealing with carefully delimited topics within which they can claim to have a unique expertise. If we return to the same issue of *History*, and move to the book review pages, divided into 'Ancient and Medieval', 'Early Modern' and 'Late Modern', we find that the overwhelming majority of the books reviewed there are also very limited and specific in context, not the sort to be reviewed in the posh Sunday newspapers. Here are four characteristic titles: *Lordship, Knighthood and Locality: A Study in English Society, c.1180 to c.1280*; *Science and the Sciences in the Thirteenth Century*; *The Culture of English Anti-Slavery, 1780–1860* (note *that* word again!); *Rhineland Radicals: The Democratic Movement and the Revolution of 1848–1849.*

Textbooks

Obviously, textbooks can be written for a variety of different age groups and audiences. On the whole, it would be true to say that the more elementary the textbook the more dependent it will be on the books of others, that is, on secondary sources. But writing a high-level textbook on a complex subject, drawing on the vast amount of relevant secondary sources, including dissertations and learned articles, can be a very difficult task, posing most of the basic problems to be found in all forms of historical writing – selection, form, structure, the balance of narrative and description against analysis. Some of the dialogue between writer and reader may go into suspension since what the reader is seeking is authoritative guidance. In highly controversial areas the aim should be a balanced view of competing hypotheses.

I would suggest the following criteria for judging a history textbook. First, it should be informed by an understanding of what the major authorities have said; where there is unresolved controversy, something of this should be reflected in the book. Second, it should be informed by the latest major discoveries by present-day researchers. Some scholarly matters, obviously, are too technical or too detailed to command space in a textbook; but no textbook should present interpretations which run contrary to the considered opinions of the recognised experts. Finally, even a textbook should carry with it some of the stuff and excitement of history. History, we all know, is not a mere succession of dates, of kings and presidents; nor does it divide neatly into three-paragraph sections, each of equal length and each amenable to some encapsulating title, such as 'The New Monarchy', 'The Age of Transition', 'Normalcy', 'Appeasement'. Textbooks aimed at more junior audiences are something of a different case; their writing involves much greater understanding of educational psychology than most professional historians can pretend to. All one can ask is that junior school textbooks, still being the main contact which the majority of people have with history, should not do more violence than is absolutely necessary to the historical accounts given by the best recent academic writers.

Additionally, there is a type of textbook (often for university students and general readers) devoted to the provision of extracts selected from primary sources (known as a 'source book'), or excerpts from a range of secondary sources (known as a 'collection of readings' or 'reader').

Pop History

Ordinary readers who survive their school textbooks and allow themselves in later life to succumb to the intrinsic fascination of history will probably seek works of a more popular character than those discussed so far. In an ideal world, the books selling to the largest numbers of readers would be books written by professional historians, to the highest scholarly standards, but written in a straightforward, accessible style. But the fact is that a few names (for a whole variety of reasons, not all of them unconnected with marketing and the media) sell very well, while most do not. Publishers shrink from anything that hints of the study or scholarly apparatus; they welcome 'fine writing' and purple passages. Some writers of popular history still purport to convey to their readers the thoughts at particular moments of their historical personages: this is a deplorable, totally unhistorical habit, since we can never have any way of knowing what people *thought* (as distinct from what they wrote in diaries, letters, memoirs, and so on). It is only fair, however, to record that the standard of popular history has gone up greatly in the last 20 years or so, partly as a result of the entry into this particular form of communication by professional historians.

The main point I want to make is that a work of history should be judged by what it is setting out to do, by the level it is aiming to operate on. It is as pointless to criticise a PhD thesis for being narrow as it is to expect a work of popular history to present the last word in sophisticated scholarly analysis. One should be suspicious of mere book-making: book-making arises when someone feels that it would be nice to write a book, without having any ideas about, or commitment to, any particular subject, or simply takes on the task as a mechanical job of work; the book in fact might be about anything, and will usually turn out to be the mindless plunder of the labours of others. One would rightly tend to mistrust the work of someone who writes a book about the twentieth-century novel one year, and a book about Magna Carta the next. Good history can be written by non-academics (that is, by journalists, businessmen, or whoever), many of whom may at an earlier stage have had a historical training, and many of whom too are happy to turn to the hard slog of historical research. The biggest advantage, probably, that professional historians have comes from living with their subject day in and day out, from teaching it, and from presenting seminar papers to colleagues: they are constantly forced to examine their thoughts, to organise them coherently, to face the pitfalls of historical explanation, to iron out inconsistencies, to eradicate non-explanations, and to appreciate the difference between flowery rhetoric and genuine historical analysis.

Some Examples of Public History

A well-organised museum can be a good means of communicating certain aspects of the past. Thorough explication of each of the physical artefacts on display is required, together with some account of the historical context congruent with the latest historical research. The danger can sometimes be of trying to do too much. Physical artefacts, though immensely important in helping us grasp the concrete realities of past societies, can never form the basis for a complete historical account. Museum displays should not attempt to say more than they are suited to saying. This principle applies also to film and television programmes: indeed, effective television programmes can often be made by relying largely on the artefacts displayed in a museum.

As I move to film and television, it is probably best if I say a little bit about my own experiences. My experience with general service television programmes has, I should admit at once, been extremely limited. Back in the sixties I was employed as a consultant and, for one programme, scriptwriter on the BBC series *The Lost Peace* (about the inter-war years). From this experience I formed an abiding hostility to the conventional way of making history programmes – writing a script and then finding pieces of visual material to put on the screen while the words were being spoken, with the result that, either, two separate meanings were striking the viewer simultaneously, or that the visual material was simply 'wallpaper'. Much more recently I was commissioned as a consultant for one programme (dealing with the 1960s) in the generally excellent *People's Century*; my job was to help convert a programme originally made for American audiences (and containing some errors) into one suitable for British audiences. During my 32 years at the Open University I have been involved in a large number of television programmes, most, but not all, relating to historical methodology and the use of physical artefacts as primary sources. For my purposes, displays in the Museum of London (physical and, in particular, domestic artefacts from Roman times to the present) and the Musée Carnavalet in Paris (artefacts relating to the French Revolution) were particularly valuable. An early programme which I still believe has educational value was one demonstrating the actual technology that lay behind the invention of printing: here we used the splendid display in the Guthenberg Museum in Mainz, with difficulty persuading the museum attendant responsible for Guthenberg's printing press not to dress up in fifteenth-century costume! – as it happens, I have (see below) become less puritanical about the use of dressing-up and the deployment of brief acted sequences. I have written quite a lot about the uses of the media in teaching history, and have spoken on that subject in a number of countries, most recently at an international conference in Bonn in February 1999.

Television History

Throughout most of my career there has been a rather sharp divide between historical documentaries made on a broadly commercial basis for transmission to relatively large audiences, and videos specially made by historians for their own educational purposes. I do believe that that divide may now be closing up, and that there may be more and more opportunities for historians to become involved in general service programmes. Here, I intend first to survey some of the things that were going wrong throughout most of the period, and which provide salutary lessons, and then to look at some of the more recent, more optimistic developments.

Over many years, the BBC's regular series *Timewatch* has shown genuine concern to bring to an intelligent general audience insights into new research areas being opened up by professional historians. But there have been problems. In May 1984 the *Timewatch* series presented a programme on the Norman Conquest. Though praised by the TV critics, this programme was a classic example of how not to do history on television. Exactly what the programme was trying to do was never made clear, though various devices were used to try to make the viewer feel that there was some exciting controversy over which historians were in passionate conflict and that, in particular, from the application of computer techniques to Domesday Book, breathtaking discoveries were on the way. History *is* an exciting subject but the excitement must, as it were, be allowed to emerge from within, particularly on television where tricks and clichés, unless forcibly restrained, just tumble out one after the other. John Tusa, the presenter, hammed up the fictitious drama, pausing, drawing a deep breath, turning across the camera like a latter-day Kenneth Clark (presenter of the famous art history series *Civilisation*). There were excerpts from interviews with famous and less famous historians edited to convey donnish dedication to a particular cause, but so brief, and so lacking in context, as to be practically incoherent. At the end the various dons were brought together in a kind of brains trust, a highly stereotyped way of ending a TV documentary of any description. Professor J. C. Holt was asked if he thought the Norman Conquest had any real impact on Britain. Yes, of course, he said, one had simply to compare pre-Norman Romanesque churches with post-Conquest churches. What a perfect opportunity for a genuine televisual exploration of a point totally grounded on visual evidence! But, whereas earlier the programme had lost no opportunity to unload the usual old wallpaper (an actor reading from Domesday Book mentions cows, so grazing cows come up on the screen), this time the point passed as a purely verbal one without the viewer being given any opportunity to assess the validity of the evidence upon which it was based. The entire programme had been planned as a series of television clichés, not built outwards from the richness of the available visual evidence.

There have of course been many good *Timewatch* programmes, careful reports on current research rather than attempts to blitz viewers into bemused acquiescence, and, in the early seventies, Thames Television's *World at War*, directed by Jeremy Isaacs, set new standards for prodigious research and integrity of presentation. Even that series, however, did in the end follow the old formula of settling first on an interpretation or storyline, then illustrating it with archive film material and edited 'eye-witness' interviews, rather than working outwards critically from the visual material. The general theme was that all war is dreadful, expressed in the opening sequence of the opening programme where, after the hideous civilian massacre carried out by the Germans at Oradour, the commentator (plummy and sententious Sir Laurence Olivier) remarks that shortly the young German soldiers too will be killed. That a more open approach might have been preferable was driven home strikingly in May 1988 when Isaacs, in a TV lecture on the series, without batting an eyelid expressed a different view: the war *had* been necessary.

The essential consideration, in my view, is as follows: theses, articles, monographs, general histories, and textbooks are made up of paragraphs and sentences and are, despite the enormous variety of non-traditional sources that exists, drawn mainly from written sources, primary and secondary. Film and television programmes are made up of visual images, though they will also contain other elements such as spoken commentary and perhaps even music (just as a book may contain illustrations or diagrams); they should be largely drawn from visual evidence. That contrast is the key to the whole discussion over the value and use of film. However, the opinion is controversial. Some historians, and certainly many film makers and television producers, would argue that a film or television programme can be used to put over exactly the same topic as a book or article might be used for; only, they argue, film, having greater immediacy and emotional potency, particularly in a world when we are all used to the visual media, will put over whatever particular historical interpretation is agreed on with much more force and appeal than a mere book or lecture would. Here, then, is the great divide: between those who wish to use the visual media and all their allied resources to put over a particular interpretation with the greatest possible force, and those who believe in using film and television to explore the complexities of visual evidence. The method of patient reconstruction, combined with the most detailed scholarly analysis of film as source material and exploration of the uses of film for educational purposes, is exemplified in the work of the Institut für den Wissenschaftlichen Film at Göttingen, of Stichting Film in Wetenscap at Utrecht, of Karsten Fledelius and his compatriots in Denmark, and of the British Universities' Film Consortium in Britain. Further developments, always to the highest academic standards, have been fostered by the International Association for Audio Visual Material in Historical Research and Education (IAMHIST).[11]

The argument, then, is that if history film or television programmes are to be made (and they definitely should be made) they should concentrate on those topics where visual evidence is genuinely of significance. It follows that no major historical topic could be exhaustively covered in a film or television programme; and that no complete history course could be given through the medium of television alone. For many major topics, and for most of the conceptual arguments, it will be necessary to have resort to the traditional printed or spoken word. No doubt, the various general broadcasting services will go on presenting historical programmes which attempt to give a comprehensive coverage of their subject. Obviously the major television stations cannot expect their viewers to undertake a heavy course of supplementary reading before viewing such programmes, which, at their best, may be regarded as the equivalent of the very highest quality coffee-table history books. However, they will be better as history, for general audiences as well as students, to the extent to which they adhere to the basic principle that visual programmes should essentially deal with visual evidence, and should not unload vast amounts of conceptual analysis or even factual narrative which can only be presented over either (a) irrelevant 'wall-paper' or (b) interesting unidentified visual material which will, in fact, run in competition with the commentary, making it difficult to concentrate on one or the other.

One stock-in-trade of the conventional film maker is the 'eye-witness interview', too often used without any apparent awareness of the fallibility of eye-witness accounts, particularly of events which may have taken place a generation before. It is always intriguing to see and hear the veterans of old wars or old trade union battles; but whether what they say is actually much of a contribution to historical knowledge is another matter. Usually what they say either fits in with the predetermined interpretation of the film maker, or simply provides a little light relief.

Thus, I come to the fundamental principle that anyone making a historical film or television programme should be as familiar with the visual materials which will provide the basis of that programme as they would be with the written materials which would form the basis of an article or book. They will also have to have a belief in the value of visual evidence, whether it be archaeology, history on the ground, paintings, cartoons, advertisements, or newsreel, documentary, or feature film: I take it that this book has already made out the case for the immense value of all such sources. It is possible to do much with photography, paintings, advertisements, cartoons, provided always that these are treated with respect as documents, just as written documents should be treated respectfully by the serious historian. I say 'just as', but in fact a specially deliberate care has to be taken with visual evidence. One can interleave quotations, direct or indirect, from many written sources into one paragraph. Sleight of hand has been such a regular device of film makers for so long, and anyway visual evidence is not easy to identify separately unless a special effort is made, that it is important to be particularly self-conscious in this respect when putting together a film. It should at all times be clear to the viewer exactly what it is he or she is seeing and where it came from. This of course runs entirely contrary to the basic film maker's craft of montage, of editing tiny clips from here and there into one beautiful smooth compilation. But such very smoothness does violence to the complex problems of historical study.

It is easier, of course, to enunciate such principles than to realise them successfully in practice. Much will depend upon the exact context within which the completed film or television programme is to be used. But the principle that the programme will not in itself be self-contained remains true. Either it will have to be supplemented with the printed word, or it will have to be set within a classroom context in which the lecturer can provide the necessary verbal and conceptual information. Still, there can be no doubt that every programme, however rooted in, and confined to, visual evidence, will need to contain a certain amount of verbal analysis and explanation. Here we run up against one of the most entrenched prejudices of professional producers of film and television programmes: let the continuous flow of visuals never be interrupted by a boring academic talking directly to camera.

There is a second entrenched prejudice of professional producers: never put statistics on the screen. I, on the contrary, believe not only that quantitative evidence is crucial to most aspects of historical study, but that such evidence, presented in a way which invites the audience to participate in discussing its significance, can be absolutely fascinating for viewers. Once again it is all a matter of openness, honesty, of inviting audiences – at whatever level – to participate in the excitement of discovery, of working out conclusions. Academics making historical programmes should not be afraid to use direct 'talking heads', nor to present statistical tables, provided they are left on the screen for as long as is necessary for them to be absorbed, and provided they are fully explicated and discussed. One of the most notable – and I think regrettable – features of the major, and in many ways highly admirable, television series produced in Britain in recent years is that practically the first thing they do is tell us which famous actor is providing the narration – Laurence Olivier, Kenneth Branagh, and others. Actors are an irrelevance, and probably a nuisance, in the presentation of history. Two series presented recently on British television have triumphantly validated what I have been saying for years, that an enthusiastic and knowledgeable academic talking directly to camera is infinitely more effective (and apparently popular) than some hired hand, however prestigious: *The Western Front*, presented by Professor Richard Holmes, and *Elizabeth I*, presented by Dr David Starkey. The latter occasionally uses acted sequences, but on the whole the intellectual, source-related commentary direct to camera by Dr Starkey carries the thing through.

The desirable development towards the historian, rather than to the director, or some theatrical knight, taking the central role continued with BBC2's 16-part *History of Britain* by Simon Schama (launched on 30 September 2000). In addition to Schama commenting and analysing directly in vision, there was an admirable emphasis on 'history on the ground' and even some telling (spoken) quotations from clearly identified written primary sources. Though departing far from his own specialist interests in the eighteenth and nineteenth centuries, and being constrained to speak the less than precise language of everyday, Schama managed to impart something of the quality of what I have termed the interpretative synthesis. On television, at least, the *auteur* is a welcome figure.

The latest production from Jeremy Isaacs was *The Cold War*. Isaacs and his co-worker, Taylor Downing, tell us that in the making of the series, 8500 newsreel and other film items were viewed. The professional historical advisers employed were John Lewis Gaddis, Robert Lovett Professor of Military and Naval History at Yale University, Professor Lawrence Freedman, of the University of London, and Vladislav Zubok, of the National Security Archive, Washington. 'Each', Isaacs and Downing tell us, 'scrutinised every frame and read every syllable of the text of the series.'[12] That leads me to my first criticism of this immensely admirable series: that the role of the historians was only reactive, rather than pro-active, scrutinising work essentially conceived and initiated by the commercial producers, rather than initiating the work themselves. My other criticism of the series, and one which applies to most such series, is that there is an overuse of eye-witnesses. Thirdly, the individual pieces of film evidence are not always identified and evaluated clearly enough. Finally, though we have many eye-witnesses, and we have the rich tones of Kenneth Branagh doing the commentary, we never have historians in person providing direct to camera commentary and explication. Only a much smaller series came very close to my ideal. Peter Hennessy, a professor at London University and author of the authoritative book, based on massive research in the primary sources, *Never Again: Britain 1945–1951* (1992), was responsible for making the television series *What Has Become of Us?*, broadcast on Britain's Channel 4 in late 1994. In this fundamentally visual account of British post-war history we saw Hennessy in vision, frequently in the Public Records Office, discussing and analysing the sources upon which his history is based, and also taking us out to examine relevant examples of history on the ground.

Feature Films

I've been talking here of television programmes or films which, in the trade, would be classified as 'documentaries'; they are the visual analogues of written books that are secondary sources. Feature films, no more than historical novels, are not secondary sources, though they can form the basis for the discussion of historical topics. Indeed, as more and more of the population learn smatterings of history from film and television, historians need to enter further into public discussion of the status of feature films, trying to educate the populace to understand the distinction between fact and fiction. As I was writing this chapter, the whole issue blew up again with respect to the American film *U-571*, based loosely on the true episode in which a British naval officer captured the famous Enigma machine from a German submarine in May 1941, but entirely recast as a tale of American heroism set in April 1942. While the director, Jonathon Mostow, declared that the film was 'entertainment, not information', there were British cries of 'stealing our history' and calls for the film to be prefaced with some statement about the true historical facts. I still incline to the view that a film is a film is a film, and that everyone should be encouraged to understand this; at the same time, historians need to be ready to prepare detailed commentaries which show exactly how films which appear to be based on real events in fact depart very seriously from these events.

There is, of course, no shortage of postmodernist critics to claim that a feature film is just as legitimate a medium for representing something to do with the past as is a documentary one. The most vociferous contemporary exponent of postmodernist approaches to history and film is the American professor Robert A. Rosenstone, who declares that a feature film can provide a 'construction of the past' as legitimate as a book written by an academic historian.[13] Once again I point to the absurdity of the notion of 'constructing' or 'reconstructing' the past. Fortunately, as an exemplary indication of what historians could achieve, we have the brilliant collection by expert professional historians, *Past Imperfect: History According to the Movies* (1995), edited by Mark C. Carnes, which carefully compares some of the major 'historical' films of our time (such as *The Longest Day*, *Mississippi Burning*, *Gandhi*) with the latest knowledge on their alleged subjects as established by historians. In his excellent introduction, Carnes writes:

> Like drama and fiction, movies inspire and entertain. They often teach important truths about the human condition. They do not provide a substitute for history that has been painstakingly assembled from the best available evidence and analysis.[14]

There could be no better quotation with which to end this chapter.

Notes

1 For an early work on 'public history' see Susan Porter Benson, Stephen Brier, Roy Rosenzweig, *Presenting the Past: Essays on History and the Public* (New York, 1980).
2 Jacques Barzun and Henry F. Graff, *The Modern Researcher* (New York, 1957; pb edn, 1962), pp. 229–30 (my references are to this edition). The same important points are made in the revised edition (1977), p. 197.

3 The passage is quoted by ibid., p. 231. The revised edition chooses a different passage, from a different book, but again by poor old E. K. Chambers!
4 G. Kitson Clark, *Guide for Research Students Working in Historical Subjects* (Cambridge, 1960), p. 31.
5 G. R. Elton, *Political History: Principles and Practice* (London, 1970), p. 138.
6 Ruth Richardson, *Death, Dissection and the Destitute* (1988; pb edn, 1989), pb edn p. 281.
7 Barzun and Graff, *The Modern Researcher*, p. 290.
8 Ibid.
9 Dorothy Marshall, *Eighteenth-Century England* (London, 1974), p. 82; G. R. Elton, *England Under the Tudors* (London, 1955), p. 100.
10 W. L. Langer, *The Franco-Russian Alliance 1890–1894* (London, 1929), p. 277. Professor Langer was a distinguished American diplomatic historian.
11 See the section 'Film et Histoire' in Comité International des Sciences historiques, *XVIe Congress International des Sciences Historiques: Rapports* I (Stuttgart, 1985), pp. 180–239, papers by Fledelius, Dolezel and Bodensieck, and Sorlin and Marwick.
12 Jeremy Isaacs and Taylor Downing, *Cold War: For 45 years the World held its Breath* (London, 1998), pp. ix–x.
13 Robert A. Rosenstone, *Visions of the Past: The Challenge of Film to our Idea of History* (Cambridge, Mass., 1995), p. 127.
14 Mark C. Carnes, *Past Imperfect: History According to the Movies* (New York, 1995), p. 10.

7 Theory, the Sciences, the Humanities

1 History, Theory, the Sciences

Sokal and Bricmont

In the spring/summer 1996 issue of *Social Text*, an American post-modernist journal of cultural studies, there was published an article, 'Transgressing the Boundaries: Toward a Transformative Hermeneutics of Quantum Gravity', by Alan D. Sokal, a Professor of Physics at New York University. The fundamental position of postmodernist cultural theorists is that the sciences are culturally constructed, that there are no objective standards to which scientific discoveries or scientific theories can appeal (an argument which, when applied to history, we have already become very familiar with in this book). Certain theorists, mostly French, began to argue that the most recent developments in the sciences themselves undercut all claims to objectivity, and demonstrated that scientific knowledge was entirely relative: Jean-François Lyotard, in his *The Postmodern Condition* (1979), spoke of 'postmodern science' which he said was insecure, open to different interpretations, lacking in absolute standards. These theorists began to incorporate scientific terms and scientific theories into their writings, always with a view to asserting that scientists themselves supported the view of their subject as being culturally constructed. All of this was part of the radical political argument (I cannot stress too often that the postmodernists are not neutral philosophers, they are the inheritors of Marxist radicalism) that science must be made 'democratic', instead of being dominated by an elite (that is, scientists who actually know what they're talking about) and should be open to the influences of ordinary people, feminists, gays, and so on.

As a physicist, Sokal could appreciate that these writings were complete nonsense: the writers did not understand the science they were so glibly citing and were using scientific terms and scientific theories in mistaken and absurd ways. In one of the most magnificent counter-strokes yet against the pernicious rubbish being peddled by the postmodernists (against, as I have said, history as well as the sciences) Sokal wrote what was, in fact, a hoax article. He took genuine quotations from the French writers (Gilles Deleuze, Jacques Derrida, Lyotard, Luce Irigaray, Michel Serres, and others) and some of their leading American acolytes (including Stanley Aronowitz and Valerie Greenberg) and simply stuck them together into an article, as he puts it, 'brimming with absurdities and blatant non sequiturs'.[1] What the editors of the journal liked was that the article was full of obsequious references to themselves and their like, and, still more, it came to the same conclusions that all of their own articles did:

> Finally, postmodern science provides a powerful refutation of the authoritarianism and elitism inherent in traditional science, as well as an empirical basis for a democratic approach to scientific work... The content and methodology of postmodern science thus provide powerful intellectual support for the progressive political project, understood in its broadest sense: the transgressing of boundaries, the breaking down of barriers, the radical democratization of all aspects of social, economic, political and cultural life... The teaching of science and mathematics must be purged of its authoritarian and elitist characteristics, and the content of these subjects enriched by incorporating the insights of the feminist, queer, multi-culturalist, and ecological critiques.[2]

Since most of the articles published by *Social Text* were complete rubbish, one perhaps cannot altogether blame the editors for not realising that this one was a hoax. And that brings me to my first general point: in history (as, of course, in the sciences), learned journals do have standards against which they judge the articles sent to them, and thus are in a strong position to weed out hoaxes and, obviously, articles which, though perfectly genuine, are simply not up to the required quality. To postmodernists, however, the critical question is 'Does this follow the correct political line?' Out of their own words and practices, the postmodernists condemn themselves to ridicule and make clear that the sorts of criticisms they make of serious disciplines are totally unworthy of attention. A key postmodernist aim is the transgressing of boundaries, as Sokal acutely realised. An established discipline with its own principles and established methodologies forms a good preventative against the purveying of nonsense. Those who wish to peddle propaganda naturally wish to break down the disciplines, bring in pretentious, misunderstood lumps of science, deny the validity of the critical distinction in history between primary and secondary source, and so on. Articles in cultural studies (Sokal captures the form perfectly) are simply made up of quotations from and references to other works in cultural studies – to what historians would call secondary sources (no wonder, therefore, that postmodernists don't like the distinction between secondary and primary sources); an article for a historical journal would have to be based overwhelmingly on primary sources, that is, it would have to show signs of serious research, rather than simply being a repetition of the statements of others.

The two debilitating weaknesses of postmodernist epistemology, completely invalidating its criticisms both of the sciences and of history, are, first, that it is ultimately simply radical political propaganda, and second, that it is merely insistent repetition of that propaganda, closed to new ideas, closed to anything that could be called serious research, merely trapped out with ever more elaborate, confused, and misunderstood borrowings from domains in which the authors have themselves never done any serious work. Subsequent to the hoax, Sokal, in collaboration with Jean Bricmont, Professor of Theoretical Physics at the University of Louvain in Belgium, published a devastatingly detailed exposure of the misuse of science by the revered apostles of French postmodernism, remarking of their works 'that if the texts seem incomprehensible, it is for the excellent reason that they mean precisely nothing'.[3] The aim of Sokal and Bricmont was to draw attention to 'the repeated abuse of concepts and terminology coming from mathematics and physics', summarised as:

1. Holding forth at length on scientific theories about which one has at best, an exceedingly hazy idea. The most common tactic is to use scientific (or pseudo-scientific) terminology without bothering much about what the words actually *mean*.
2. Importing concepts from the natural sciences into the humanities or social sciences without giving the slightest conceptual or empirical justification. If a biologist wanted to apply, in her research, elementary notions of mathematical topology, set theory or differential geometry, she would be asked to give some explanation. A vague analogy would not be taken very seriously by her colleagues. Here, by contrast, we learn from Lacan that the structure of the neurotic subject is exactly the taurus (it is no less than reality itself, cf. p. 19), from Kristeva that poetic language can be theorized in terms of the cardinality of the continuum (cf. p. 38), and from Baudrillard that modern war takes place in a non-Euclidean space (cf. p. 137) – all without explanation.
3. Displaying a superficial erudition by shamelessly throwing around technical terms in a context where they are completely irrelevant. The goal is, no doubt, to impress and, above all, to intimidate the non-scientist reader. Even some academic and

media commentators fall into the trap: Roland Barthes is impressed by the precision of Julia Kristeva's work (cf. p. 37) and *Le Monde* admires the erudition of Paul Virilio (cf. p. 159).

4. Manipulating phrases and sentences that are, in fact, meaningless. Some of these authors exhibit a veritable intoxication with words, combined with a superb indifference to their meaning.[4]

Sokal's hoax had repercussions beyond the academic community, and was referred to on the front page of the *New York Times*. The subsequent book, initially published in French in 1997, then in English in 1998, was featured in *The Guardian* as having shown that 'modern French philosophy is a load of old tosh'.[5] The reactions of the progenitors and supporters of the 'load of old tosh' were highly revealing. Derrida attempted a mighty, Gallic, putdown, calling him 'le pauvre Sokal' ('poor Sokal'), which only exposed the arrogant authoritarianism of this school of philosophy, its total unwillingness to enter into any kind of debate, and the absolute hypocrisy of its pretensions to being 'democratic'. An article in the French left-wing daily newspaper *Libération* described Sokal and Bricmont as 'humourless scientistic pedants who correct grammatical errors in love letters', while John Sturrock, British apologist for postmodernism and *éminence grise* of the *London Review of Books*, criticised Sokal and Bricmont in that journal, for demanding a 'stultifying rigour'. The equation of postmodernist philosophy with the writing of love letters, and the identifying of rigour as 'stultifying' ('write what you like, oh great philosophers, never mind if it is nonsense' – and they do), almost say all that needs saying. The sciences, and history, are proud of not being analogues of love letters, and equally proud of the rigour of their standards of intellect, logic, and evidence – such rigour is liberating, not stultifying.

The Nature of Scientific Theory

The position of the postmodernists in regard to 'rigour' and 'theory' is also a confusing one. At one time, they (or some of them) actually boasted about their own 'theoretical rigour' (a rather odd phrase, evoking strong echoes of 'rigor mortis'). In fact, what the postmodernists declare over and over again, in their interventions in history and in the other humanities, is that they are the upholders of theory, and that those who disagree with them are outdated exponents of a discredited empiricism. But what is theory? It is abundantly clear that postmodernists, many of them calling themselves cultural *theorists*, whatever attacks they may make on claims to scientific objectivity, are keen to claim the authority and prestige that attach to the natural sciences with their theories and laws. What I, therefore, propose to do is to consider first the nature of theory and laws in the natural sciences. In light of that discussion, I shall then consider the relationship of history to the natural sciences (what I have insisted on so far, remember, is simply that history is bodies of knowledge about the past, in the same way that the sciences are bodies of knowledge about the physical universe and the natural world; I have *not* said that history *is* a natural science – it very definitely is not). Having discussed the *differences* (and the similarities) between history and the natural sciences, I shall then focus on the nature of so-called postmodernist and cultural 'theory', briefly examining the ideas of Saussure, Foucault and the others. This will lead, at the end of this section, to a discussion of the place of theory within history. The second section of the chapter is then concerned with the relationships between history, sociobiology, the social sciences, and the humanities.

'Theory' is one of those difficult words, more complex even than 'culture', 'ideology', or 'class'. There is the obvious, everyday usage of 'a mere hypothesis, speculation, conjecture', as when one might say 'that's OK in theory, but the facts are...' (note that word 'fact' again!). However (I turn now to the definitions to be found in the second edition of the *Oxford English Dictionary*), theory in the natural sciences is:

A scheme or system of ideas or statements held as an explanation or account of a group of facts or phenomena; a hypothesis which has been confirmed or established by observation or experiment, and is propounded or accepted as accounting for the known facts; a statement of what are held to be the general laws, principles or causes of something known or observed.

In mathematics, the definition varies slightly:

A systematic statement of the general principles or laws of some branch of mathematics, a set of theorems forming a connected system: as *the theory of equations, of functions, of numbers, of probabilities.*

In the twentieth century one hears more of theory (as, obviously, in 'the theory of relativity') than of laws, the scientific laws formulated in earlier centuries now being understood as being true, not absolutely, but under certain conditions and within certain ranges, a law being 'a generalised record of nature, not a command which compels nature'.[6] None the less, these qualifications made, a scientific law remains a scientific law, and a law is itself theoretical, in the sense of the definition just given. A scientific law, then, is

a theoretical principle deduced from particular facts, applicable to a defined group or class of phenomena, and expressible by the statement that a particular phenomenon always occurs if certain conditions be present.

Among the most famous examples are Newton's laws of motion. Most readers will know of Boyle's Law, known to the French as Mariotte's Law, because, characteristic French chauvinism apart, the law that for a gas at a given temperature, pressure varies inversely to volume, propounded by Boyle in 1662, was subsequently confirmed by Mariotte (1620–84). The law always known as Bode's Law was popularised by Johann Bode, though actually first announced by Johann Titius (1729–96). It is what it says, of course, which is important:

The distances of the planets from the sun in astronomical units is found by adding 4 to the series 0, 3, 6, 12, 24, . . . and dividing the number so obtained by 10.

As we have seen, the postmodernists insist that there is a postmodernist science which supports their ideas about the relativity of all knowledge and the way in which all knowledge is culturally constructed. This results from the mistaken platitude that relativity has overthrown the certainties of Newtonian physics and rather crude misunderstandings of the implications of chaos theory and Gödel's theorem.[7] Albert Einstein himself stated in 1948:

No one must think that Newton's great creation can be overthrown by Relativity or any other theory. His clear and wide ideas will forever retain their significance as the foundation on which our modern conceptions of physics have been built.[8]

The sciences, and mathematics, do depend on theories and laws (the specific conditions under which they are operable always being specified). Central to the massive work on the smashing apart of sub-atomic particles going on at CERN (whose official name in English is the European Organization for Nuclear Research), and the conclusions being drawn from it, are the laws of energy and momentum conservation. The physicists there cannot directly observe the reactions, but, using giant projectors, study their traces ('tyre marks', one of the scientists likened these to); not altogether dissimilar, I would say, to the 'traces' of the past, the primary sources, which historians study. The work proceeds within what are openly recognised as the 'laws' of relativity and quantum theory, but it is also recognised that it could eventually disprove them. Historians do not have laws of this sort because there is no way in which they could be tested – and while all of the all-encompassing laws and theories which have been put forward (such as those of the Marxists or the postmodernists) can be seen to have little salience in the detailed investigations carried out by historians, they cannot quite be disproved in the way a scientific law could be disproved.

Back in the seventeenth century Francis Bacon stated, rather simplistically, obviously, the basics of the scientific method:

> make observations and record the facts
> perform many experiments and tabulate the results
> extract rules and laws by induction[9]

A more sophisticated twentieth-century version was provided by American philosopher of science Ernest Nagel:

> if there is a single scientific method it lies in the way in which scientists check and counter-check their knowledge by experiment and reasoning from several angles, so that they feel that their knowledge is warranted, that its validity is assured.[10]

History and the Sciences

Now I want to look at the implications of these definitions with respect to bringing out the differences and similarities between history and the sciences. In Francis Bacon's three simple points, the differences stand out very starkly. Historians seek for information of all kinds in the sources, and they record what they have found: if in spirit that is akin to making observations and recording the facts, it is very far from the same in practice. Historians simply do not 'perform many experiments and tabulate the results', nor do they extract rules and laws by induction, though the accounts and interpretations they give certainly are 'by induction', that is to say, from the evidence, empirically. Ernest Nagel's description of scientific method offers stronger analogies with what historians do, but then also points up the differences. The phrase I'd like to single out is 'from several angles': we have seen that, on the whole, historical knowledge advances as historians bring in new methods, new approaches, and new sources. The more historians do this the more they, too, 'feel that their knowledge is warranted, that its validity is assured'. Certainly reasoning comes prominently into the historian's activities, but the checking and counter-checking is very definitely not 'by experiment'. Historians do not go in for the sort of statement 'that a particular phenomenon always occurs if certain conditions be present'; there are absolutely no equivalents in history to Boyle's Law or Bode's Law. Scientific laws can often be expressed in the form of mathematical formulae; that is simply not true in history. There are no equivalents in history of the theory of equations, of functions, of numbers, of probabilities, and there are no statements of 'what are held to be the general laws, principles or causes of something known or observed'. My contention, then, is, not that history is a natural science, which obviously it is not, but that historians operate in the same *spirit* as natural scientists, always working from the evidence, always basing their generalisations, interpretations, or theses on the evidence (not on metaphysical speculation). It is noteworthy that the distinguished biologist Lewis Wolpert has said that he sees his activities as resembling those of historians.[11]

I have already (in Chapter 2) discussed the question of subjectivity in history. Events in the past carry intense emotional charges and inevitably involve value judgements of some sort: describing certain events as 'massacres', for instance, or analysing the motives of a particular politician. Historians should still approach these matters in the spirit of scientific objectivity, but clearly the scope for value judgements, for subjectivity, is much greater in history than in the natural sciences. This point is inexorably entailed in the first of the fundamental differences between history and the sciences, which I am now going to list:

1 There is a fundamental difference in the subject of study: the natural sciences are concerned with the phenomena of the natural world and the physical universe, while history is concerned with human beings and human societies in the past. There is a difference in the phenomena studied, and these phenomena are very different in character.

2 Historians do not carry out controlled experiments of the sort typically conducted in a science laboratory.

3 While historians may very properly develop theories and theses, they are not concerned with developing laws and theories in the way that scientists are.

4 While scientific laws and theory have powers of prediction, history (though it should equip us to cope more intelligently with the world in which we live) does not have such powers.

5 While the relations and interactions studied by scientists are almost always best expressed mathematically, this is not generally so of those studied by historians.

6 The contributions to knowledge produced by historians come in the form of extended pieces of prose (articles or books), while major scientific discoveries are often best reported in very terse articles, sometimes in a page or two of mathematical equations.

Historians and scientists are both affected by career pressures and the normal human fallibilities and vanities. J. D. Watson's exuberant, unbuttoned account of the hunt for DNA in *The Double Helix* (1968) has been a classic for years: Steven Rose's wickedly witty memoir of a brain biologist is in the process of becoming one. To keep the grants rolling in, as Rose explains, scientists have to keep churning out the research papers, sometimes contrived, often trivial, produced at break-neck speed in order to achieve publication ahead of the opposition, bland, and sometimes obsequious, in order to avoid offence to potential referees. Sudden revelations, sudden solutions to problems which have been producing deadlock for days or weeks, come mysteriously to scientists, as they also come to historians.[12] Scientists are at great pains to point out that scientific discoveries do not conform to 'common sense'.[13] The same is actually true of history. The case being made in this book is certainly not that, while the theories of the postmodernists deny common sense (they can be criticised on more thorough grounds than that), history is based on common sense. No, history is based on the primary sources, and the primary sources left by past societies can reveal beliefs and actions which totally defy what would today be considered 'common sense'. Common sense might tell us that when misery, and oppression, and injustice are heaped on subordinate peoples, they will rise up in revolt; but this is by no means necessarily the case. Common sense might tell us that permissiveness in the 1960s followed upon the invention and distribution of the contraceptive pill. In fact the statistical, and all kinds of other, evidence demonstrate that sexual attitudes and behaviour changed immensely even while only a tiny minority of women were taking the pill. What did contribute to permissiveness was the way in which the advent of the pill, as a highly newsworthy item, stimulated open discussion about sexual matters. Human beings in the past have not always, or even usually, behaved completely rationally (the concept of 'bounded', or limited, rationality is a useful one): so common sense is a poor guide to how, and why, people behaved in the past.

History as an Autonomous Discipline

My purpose in associating history with the natural sciences is not to gain some kind of spurious respectability for history; it is to insist that history should be judged as a scientific activity, not as a literary one. My intention also is to explode any silly metaphors about history being 'a craft', or muddled platitudes about history being 'both art and science'. What I do say about history is that it is an autonomous discipline: it is, if one has a liking for Latin tags, *sui generis*, it has its own distinctive and well-tried methods.

You cannot just do history any way you want, you cannot suddenly dream up some stunning explanation of the fall of the Roman Empire, or of the origins of the First World War, without a secure basis in both the latest secondary sources and, more importantly, in the primary sources. But apart from the rigorous insistence on certain methods and standards, history is not an authoritarian subject. Do the research, produce the arguments, and you can challenge the works of the most eminent authorities. Indeed, as we have seen, this is often the way in which historical knowledge increases. The biggest postmodernist lie is that it is not authoritarian, that it is destructive of all 'grand narratives'. In fact, the postmodernist fantasy is the grandest narrative of all, laying down the law about the nature and imperatives of language, narrative, discourse, epistemes, and the rest, about the wickedness of 'bourgeois society', the necessity for 'transcending boundaries', and for supporting (in academic discourse – such causes may well command our support as citizens) feminism, gay liberation, and all radical causes.

Postmodernist Metaphysics

Let us look now at the various assertions which go to make up postmodernist metaphysics. I have already discussed (and dismissed) postmodernist criticisms of historical writing: basically that, while the postmodernists themselves have access to undisputed truth as to how language and 'the discursive' work, historians can only tell a variety of stories, none with objective validity. However, some historians have argued that certain postmodernist assertions can actually be incorporated into the writing of history, particularly that concerning the nature of language and the alleged imperatives governing its use, and that relating to the many, often hidden, ways in which power operates in society.

'Credit' for the first is usually allocated to the Swiss linguist Ferdinand de Saussure, who died in 1913, and whose ideas were then developed in the 1960s and after by Roland Barthes, Jacques Derrida, and Foucault. The second is very largely associated with Foucault. Saussure's *Cours de linguistique générale* (*Course in General Linguistics*), published three years after his death, has always seemed to me a particularly feeble branch on which to hang a ponderous theory, though I suppose that even if Saussure had never existed somebody else could always have been made responsible for it. The book was actually put together by two colleagues of Saussure's, Charles Bally and Albert Sechehaye. Saussure had presented his thoughts in courses of lectures given in 1906–7, 1908–9 and 1910–11, but Bally and Sechehaye had been unable to find any of Saussure's own notes. Certainly Saussure never himself set out his theories in consolidated form; as every historian knows, you can get away with murder in a course of lectures, nemesis striking only when you have to produce a book. Bally and Sechehaye relied on notes taken by former students, not a method I would myself feel comfortable with. The simple point made by Saussure was that there is no intrinsic relationship between the *signifier* (the word) and the *signified* (what the word 'means'). Saussure went on to insist that since words have no inherent meaning, they could only derive their meaning from within the entire system of language, and that that system is external to human beings, arising instead from the power structure of society.[14] For myself, I cannot imagine what a word which did have an intrinsic relationship with the signified would actually look like. Words, after all, are only words, and presumably derive their meanings from the way in which human beings (*not* something external to them) agree to use them. Postmodernists like to give the impression that Saussurian ideas are a central and accepted part of linguistics as a discipline: it is only necessary to consult the standard works by such authorities as Chomsky, Lyons, Lepschy, and Pinker to discover that this is simply not so.[15]

Barthes was obsessed with the impossibility of expressing anything straightforwardly (at 'degree zero', as he put it), unencumbered by the sediments of bourgeois society and custom. Speaking dramatically of 'the death of the author', he went on to argue that it is readers who give the meanings to texts. With Derrida, and others, there has developed the idea of 'textuality', the hidden characteristics derived from the bourgeois power structure alleged to be inherent in all texts ('textuality' is held to destroy the validity of the distinction between primary and secondary sources), and of everything being 'constructed within language' as distinct from having an external reality. Historians following these precepts have to accept that it is impossible to get any firm witting testimony from their primary sources – postmodernists do not allow for the all-important concept of unwitting testimony – and that it is impossible for the historian himself/herself to convey his/her accounts and analyses clearly and unambiguously (readers will always be free to extract meanings of their own). There is something to this emphasis on language, of course. As I have already pointed out, it is all too easy for historians to write sloppily, to reach for the easy cliché or metaphor. But from one's own reading of, say, Braudel or Hobsbawm, or Darnton, one knows that historians can write lucidly and unambiguously. One also knows that with hard work, and constant revision, one can change one's own faltering and clumsy first efforts into prose which expresses precisely what one wants to say.

It is also true that much of what we think we know about current events does not come from direct observation, but is communicated to us in language, principally through television and newspapers. But just as one can establish that there is a relationship between primary sources and the past events they relate to, it is very easy to show that there is a correspondence, though, obviously, far from a complete and exact one, between events and accounts of them. Most of us have, at some time or another, been at demonstrations, election meetings, football matches, theatrical events, and then subsequently been able to match these to newspaper or television accounts. That language dominates us, that we are entangled helplessly in its coils, and that everything is constructed within language, is quite simply, and demonstrably, nonsense.

Foucault

Much of Foucault's work had a historical character to it, in that it dealt with events and attitudes in past societies, which is probably why some historians have felt bound to take account of it, though I believe Foucault's influence has been grossly exaggerated, and is now definitely on the wane. The main historical topics he preoccupied himself with were: medicine and hospitals; madness and asylums; crime, punishment and prisons; sexuality. The insistent themes are that what may to the innocent look like desirable reforms are in fact further cunning means of exercising control (by the bourgeois ruling class, obviously – need you ask?!), that the rise of rational thought (which historians, including myself, have seen as one of the desirable features of modern society) has actually been a means of legitimising power rather than a means of challenging it, and that the very labels (language) applied to, say, 'illness', 'madness', 'crime', 'homosexual', do not signify objective categories, but are instruments of power. Similarly, hospitals, asylums, and so on are not there to help the poor, but to exercise power over them. In his *History of Sexuality*, Foucault did not celebrate any growing emancipation in sexual matters, but rather maintained that what others perceived as advances were really impositions of new controls. Foucault brought a new concentration upon 'the body', though it is not always very clear whether he is referring to something of corporeal existence, or something 'constructed within language'; indeed it is not always clear (to me at least) what he means at all. He seems, characteristically, to be arguing that while there was the façade of parliamentary institutions and new political liberties, new controls were directed at the body. He wrote:

> What was being formed was a policy of coercions that act upon the body, a calculated manipulation of its elements, its gestures, its behaviour. The human body was entering a machinery of power that explores it, breaks it down and rearranges it... This discipline produces subjected and practised bodies, 'docile bodies'.[16]

Historians (for career reasons, if no other) are always looking for new (and sometimes trendy) subjects to take up, and towards the end of the twentieth century 'the body', interpreted in various ways, did become the subject of a number of historical works, sometimes proving a useful organising principle, as, say, in the work of Joanna Bourke.[17] There was an obvious appeal to feminist historians, who felt that the female body was forced to contort itself and bedeck itself in unnatural ways (not that feminist postmodernists believed that there *were* 'natural ways').

Compromising with Postmodernism

I want to look at historians writing *about* history, and then at historians actually writing history (of a sort), who have attempted to justify and/or assimilate postmodernist ideas. Let me make my own position clear. I do not believe there can be any accommodation between postmodernist ideas and the approaches of serious professional historians. Working historians realise that there can be no compromising on their basic methodology, but too many want to appear to be trendy and up-to-the-minute (though the minute has now probably passed, and the trends are looking distinctly tatty), wish to appease powerful academic figures who do espouse postmodernism and cultural theory, wish to be seen as supporters of feminism and radicalism, wish to show a gentlemanly or maidenly restraint and inclusiveness, refuse to face up to the fact that, as philosopher John Searle puts it, 'the most famous and admired philosophers are often the ones with the most preposterous theories',[18] in short, refuse to denounce rubbish when they see it.

The most egregious example is *Telling the Truth about History*, by Joyce Appleby, Lynn Hunt, and Margaret Jacob. This combines a pathetic attempt at reconciling the irreconcilable with a distinctively American academic pomposity, compounded by frequent slides into cliché and indeed slang: debates rage; courses are navigated; conceptual fault-lines are explored; the nature of reality is 'up for grabs'; cultural and linguistic approaches 'help in the ongoing task of puncturing the shield of science behind which reductionism often hid'.[19] The usual exaggerated claims are made for cultural, or anthropological, approaches:

> The historian of culture sought to dig beneath the formal production of law, literature, science, and art to the codes, clues, hints, signs, gestures, and artefacts through which people communicate their values and their truths.[20]

Historians had actually been doing this for a long time, but this fact is swamped in fashionable nonsense about 'narratives' and 'stories'. Historians, the authors say, have chosen narratives 'as others have chosen comedy, romance, or irony for their writings'. Are these categories really mutually exclusive? – I have already explained how historians have to (at least) combine the modes of narrative, analysis and description. Failing to recognise that a vital skill of the historian (acquired only with great difficulty) involves the deliberate eschewal of the carelessness of everyday speech, and the development of very precise and explicit language, they declare:

> Everyone uses language largely unaware of the cultural specificity of words, the rules and protocols of expression, the evasions in their euphemisms, the nuances from group associations, or the verbal detours imposed by social taboos.[21]

'We are not, therefore', the authors tell us grandly, 'rejecting out of hand everything put forward by the postmodernists', particularly since, they continue, 'the text analogy aspects of postmodernist theories have some real political and epistemological attractions'.[22] On epistemology I'll pass, but *political* attractions should have no place in determining scholarly method.

The authors finally claim to have arrived at 'A New Theory of Objectivity'. This is very persuasive, but it is certainly not the least bit new, and it could have been simply stated without all the prior contorted efforts at inclusiveness:

> history-writing and history-reading are a shared enterprise in which the community of practitioners acts as a check on the historian just as Newton's experiments on moving objects and Darwin's observations of fossils constrained what they could say.[23]

The very arguments of *The Nature of History* (1970, 1981, 1989), in fact.

We proceed to a jingoistic 'Summing Up' advocating 'a democratic, and hence American, creed' whose

> myth-dispelling disclosures...point to the power of a revitalised public, when operating in a pluralistic democracy... [mediating] ...intelligently between society and the individual, knowledge and passion, clarity and obfuscation, hope and doubt. Telling the truth takes a collective effort.[24]

Collective among historians, yes, but the collectivity is better without the inclusion of postmodernists.

The other book I wish to consider in this context is the latest edition (2000) of John Tosh's elegant and persuasive *The Pursuit of History*. In earlier editions, Tosh argued that to be a respectable discipline history must have theory, and, he continued, the only theory there is is that provided by Marxism.[25] The latest edition is rather more sophisticated, and slightly more pluralistic, though, if anything, Tosh's deep emotional commitment to Marxism comes through even more strongly. He goes on at inordinate length about what Marx really said, as distinct from the way in which his views have been simplified and misrepresented. This is really of no more than scholastic importance: what matters is the Marxist or Marxisant influences which dominate certain approaches to history today, including postmodernist ones. Tosh's own slightly more restrained formulation now is: 'for as long as historians recognise the need for theory, they will be drawn to the Marxist tradition'.[26] Much depends, as I have explained earlier in this chapter, on what one means by 'theory'.

No longer backing Marxism as the sole theory – though he does continue to assert that: 'Through the base/superstructure model Marxism offers a particularly useful way of conceiving the totality of social relations in any given society'[27] (an assertion which is actually highly dubious) – he argues for the importance of 'gender theory'. This he defines as embodying the assumption that 'most of what passes for natural (or God-given) sexual difference is in fact socially and culturally constructed, and must therefore be understood as the outcome of historical process'.[28] The 'most' is surely wrong, while the phrase 'historical process' is, for someone making his stand on the salience of theory, an astonishingly vague one.

Tosh's endorsement of postmodernism is now much less wholehearted than it had been when he first introduced that topic in the 1991 edition of *The Pursuit of History* – perhaps he had been reading postmodernism's critics, possibly myself, or Richard Evans.[29] Tosh seeks an accommodation between postmodernism and professional history, but the claims he makes on behalf of the influence of the former are scarcely persuasive. The 'postmodernist reappraisal', he says, 'has major implications for how we understand the activity of being a historian'.[30] Actually, most historians, including me, have perfectly well understood the activity of being a historian without the assistance of the postmodernist 'reappraisal'. That 'reappraisal', as retailed by Tosh, is a most peculiar one.

> the historian is seen as the vector of a range of political positions rooted in the here-and-now. Because the documentary residue of the past is open to so many readings, and because historians employ language which is ideologically tainted, history-writing is never innocent. There being no shape to history, historians cannot reconstruct and delineate it from outside. The stories they tell, and the human subjects they write about, are merely subjective preference, drawn from an infinity of possible strategies. . . . Historians, it is said, do not uncover the past; they invent it. And the time-honoured distinction between fact and fiction is blurred . . .[31]

Throughout this book I have given many instances of the distinctions between history and fiction.

Or try this:

> Historians are ... sympathetic to the notion that texts embody more than one level of meaning, and that the implicit or unconscious meaning may be what gives the text its power ... Determining the discourse to which a particular text belongs, and its relation to other relevant discourses, is a task that goes beyond the procedures of source criticism as traditionally understood. As a result, historians now tend to be more sensitive to the counter-currents of meaning in their sources, pushing Mark Bloch's well-known aphorism about 'witnesses in spite of themselves' in a new and rewarding direction.[32]

I am not the only historian who is utterly unsympathetic to the notion that 'texts' have 'power', or to the suggestion that primary sources can be readily related to 'relevant discourses', or who wonders what is meant by 'levels of meaning', 'counter-currents of meaning', or – another of Tosh's choice phrases – 'dimensions of textual meaning'. Marc Bloch's 'witnesses in spite of themselves' was simply a poetic anticipation of my prosaic, but more systematic, 'unwitting testimony'.

Tosh claims that, in face of this postmodernist wisdom, the 'Rankean project of re-creating the past collapses'.[33] But then, as I have stated over and over again in this book, professional historians do not 'recreate' the past, they produce knowledge about it. It transpires, however, that postmodernism is not a superior form of analysis, it merely belongs, as many of us have always thought, and said, to a 'particular cultural moment': its 'appeal is best explained by its resonance with some of the defining tendencies in contemporary thought'[34] – 'defining tendencies' is another of those soggy, meaningless phrases to put along with 'dimensions of textual meaning'. Finally, Tosh disposes most effectively (as, of course, others have already done) with postmodernist claims about the impossibility of either primary sources, or the writings of historians, being expressed in clear, unambiguous language:

> daily life tells us that language works extremely well in many situations where meaning is clearly communicated and correctly inferred. On any other assumption human interaction would break down completely. If language demonstrably serves these practical functions in the present, there is no reason why it should not be understood in a similar spirit when preserved in documents dating from the past.[35]

Tosh came to praise postmodernism; he ends up burying it.

If I have spent a lot of time on Tosh, that is in many ways a compliment to him. In the last edition of the old *Nature of History* I referred to the original 1984 edition of his book in the following terms: 'admirably achieves the objectives set out in the sub-title; strongly Marxist and therefore a useful antidote to my own book'. My position now would be that all students should be familiar with the approaches that Tosh expounds: but I do have to say for those seeking a practical guide to how history actually is written, and ought to be written, I believe my book to be more valuable than his. For his part, Tosh, in referring to an article of mine which made many of the criticisms of postmodernism that he now repeats, links me to Geoffrey Elton, and describes both of us as seeking 'refuge in an untenable empiricism'.[36] Against that, Tosh is arguing for the paramountcy of 'theory' (actually fanciful metaphysical speculation): but, as I have shown, his own advocacy collapses into self-contradiction and incoherence. I would say that the empiricism of both Elton and myself is highly 'tenable' in that it has enabled both of us to make greater and lesser (though of course contestable) contributions to historical knowledge. And theory in science, as I have already demonstrated, is actually based on empiricism, and should indeed be distinguished from 'fanciful metaphysical speculation' and mere radical propaganda.

The achievements of those who have tried to bring to their own historical writing the postmodernist approaches advocated by Tosh (though not too strongly!) have not been very impressive. The essays in *Dead Certainties: Unwarranted Speculation* (1991) by the ultra-famous Simon Schama (he is, one should note, as anti-Marxist as I am myself) are intended to demonstrate that there is little difference between history and fiction. Low-grade fiction they certainly are – history they ain't. Patrick Joyce examines (and re-examines!) working-class experience and working-class language in an extremely tiny arena, Lancashire.[37] Alun Munslow's *Discourse and Culture: The Creation of America 1870–1920* (1992) is a series of biographical essays, not a structured monograph. Keith Jenkins, before abandoning Christianity for postmodernism, wrote a British Council of Churches pamphlet, *The Closed Door: A Christian Critique of Britain's Immigration Policies* (1984). Historians of the compromising tendency lard their writings with the fashionable phrases 'discourse', 'narrative', and 'culturally constructed'. A number of feminist works wrap their genuine contributions to knowledge in thick blankets of postmodernist jargon – I shall discuss three. Among British historians, Kevin Sharpe has attracted respectful attention (I remain an unbeliever) for applying techniques of discourse analysis (rather in the vein of the Cambridge school discussed in Chapter 5) to seventeenth-century politics.[38]

First of my three feminist books is *City of Dreadful Delight: Narratives of Sexual Danger in Late-Victorian London* (1992) by Judith R. Walkowitz. This is non-metaphysical and, indeed, empiricist, being based on an impressive range of primary sources; but it is above all political, explicitly a contribution (quite an original one) to radical feminist discussion. It studies the 1880s London of Jack the Ripper, the new population influx, the stories of dreadful danger to women that circulated: 'the new entrants to the urban scene produced new stories of the city that competed, intersected with, appropriated, and revised the dominant imaginative mappings of London'.[39] Couldn't what is being said here be expressed more precisely and correctly? Readers must judge for themselves:

> Today as in the past, feminists struggle to devise an effective strategy to combat sexual violence and humiliation in our society, where violent misogyny seems so deeply rooted. Similarly, the media continues to amplify the terror of male violence, as it did during the sexual scandals of the 1880s, persuading women that they are helpless victims. In this cultural milieu, we feminists have to come to grips with the painful historic contradictions of feminist sexual strategies, not only for the sex workers who still regard commercialised sex as the 'best-paid industry', but also for ourselves...But feminists also need to recognise the degree to which we participate in and help to circulate cultural scripts that represent male violence or female victimisation as the products of single causes and effects. Reliance on an iconography of female victimisation can undercut the political impact of feminists' own public initiatives...[40]

'Cultural scripts' – do they exist? Isn't 'script' just another vague metaphor?

Another American scholar, Kathleen Canning, has done a massive study of female textile workers in nineteenth-century Germany, entitled *Languages of Labor and Gender: Female Factory Work in Germany 1850–1914* (1996), based on an enormous amount of primary research, and expressing some genuinely interesting ideas. But the deliberate adoption of postmodernist modes and jargon seems to me to simply inhibit the expression of anything concrete and precise, and to pose a barrier between author and reader:

> Cast as a study of both the discourse and experiences of work, this book seeks to resolve the opposition between these terms, to untangle their relationships, and to resist a fixed notion by which one of the pair (discourse) always seems to determine or construct the other (experience). Despite the uneasiness of many historians with the term 'discourse', as with any other historical method, the specific uses and effectiveness of discursive analysis are determined by the nature of the enquiry. In the case of the history of gender – as a symbolic system or as a signifier of relations of power in which men and women are positioned differently – discursive analysis is a

significant, even essential, conceptual tool. Indeed, when the voices of historical actors (female textile workers, for example) resound only rarely in archival sources and are generally difficult to 'retrieve', the painstaking work of reconstructing discursive domains, of appraising the power of rhetoric and images to construct gender, becomes a necessary prerequisite for the analysis of 'lived experience', especially when the history of experience is defined as a process of making, assigning, or contesting meanings.[41]

At the end of the book Canning claims that 'inherent in' the distinction between men at work and women in the home

> were particular perceptions of the female body. Depicting the expansion of female factory employment as a 'temporary pathological symptom of the social body', the narratives of social reform implicated the female body centrally in the making of the social and identified the 'female organism' as a key site of intervention for both the regulatory and tutelary regimes of state social policy.[42]

Again readers must judge for themselves. Many of you, I suspect, will need a translation, and I would say to any of you endeavouring to write history at any level, that you should not write history which does require translation. I believe that the important things Canning wants to say could be expressed without the metaphysical verbiage. I don't believe there is any sound evidence for believing in such abstract categories as 'discursive domains'; I believe the introduction of the concept of the 'body' is merely trendy, and serves no genuine analytical purpose; the quick switch to the 'social body' is simply a bit of verbal trickery, meriting the contempt that most puns deserve.

Making Peace: The Reconstruction of Gender in Inter-War Britain (1993) sounds promising. How promising, I will leave you to decide when you have read this paragraph from the end of the opening chapter:

> It will be evident that I am drawing on poststructuralist theories of language in my analysis of war, gender, sexuality, and feminism. Such an approach starts with the assumption that every language act produces meanings that exceed the author's intention; that all texts create multiple meanings; that these meanings may contradict one another; and that interpretation of the text does not recover a 'true' or original meaning but is itself a part of the play of signification that produces textuality. I do not wish to imply that the meanings I have attributed to the texts, particularly the literary ones, quoted throughout this book, are the only ones, but rather to argue that the texts produce at least the meanings I identify. For the purposes of

my analysis, the more complex work of textuality has been left un-addressed.[43]

Let me just say that I believe the two main contentions here are, at least with respect to the study of history, false. If you are very careful and precise in your use of language (a fiendish task, as I keep saying) you will say exactly what you mean, no more, no less: you will not 'exceed' your 'intention'. When you analyse a text, or a primary source, as I prefer to say, you will, provided you have a precise topic in mind, and provided you follow the techniques described in Chapter 5, be able to extract firmly definable testimony, both witting and unwitting, relevant to that topic.

2   History, Sociobiology, Social Sciences and Humanities

Evolutionary Psychology

I don't think that gender studies (let alone gender theory) have anything like the significance in the study of history that Tosh attributes to them: this is a specialist area as valid as the manifold other specialist areas favoured by historians, no less, no more. However, the scientific principle of counter-checking from several angles is particularly to be heeded in these new areas where speculation is rife. Just as I am sceptical about the application of postmodernist theory to history, so also I am sceptical about the theories of sociobiology and evolutionary psychology. However, I am absolutely clear that if historians are to go out of their way to make a fuss about the study of 'gender' then they have an obligation to pay attention to what is said about gender by sociobiology and evolutionary psychology. There is empirical work of importance which does draw attention to basic biological differences, beyond the obvious primary and secondary sexual characteristics: differences in brain size, and in the functioning of the brain, for instance. I am not for a moment saying that this is reading for the generality of historians, but I am saying that if historians are making a specialism of sex and gender, then they must consider all the options.

Much sociobiology and evolutionary psychology shares the same faults as are to be found in Marxism, feminism, and postmodernism: gross exaggeration of points which are basically correct, anthropomorphism and resort to metaphor. Most famously, *The Selfish Gene* (1990) by Richard Dawkins ludicrously anthropomorphises (that is to say, attributes human characteristics to) the gene itself. Generally, the conditions of genetic inheritance are grossly simplified, and its significance vastly exaggerated.

Economics, Political Science, Social Psychology

Much of the brilliance of Sokal's hoax is missed by those of us who do not really understand the correct use of the scientific terms whose misuse he so cleverly exposes. But we can fix the main part of his title in our minds, 'The Transgression of Boundaries'. Rather in the same mechanical way in which the phrase 'culturally constructed' is tossed around, it has become fashionable to laud 'interdisciplinarity' and 'holistic approaches' while decrying boundaries between subject areas and disciplines. This book is a book in praise of boundaries, a book insisting on the autonomy of history, a book which deplores the so-called interdisciplinarity from which in fact all semblance of disciplines has departed. At the same time, it follows from everything that I have said about the development of historical studies that historians, depending on their particular specialism, do find it useful, and sometimes essential, to have a sound knowledge of other disciplines. The most obvious one is economics: every historian needs a basic knowledge of economics, and every history degree should introduce students to basic economics. Second to economics as a necessary complementary discipline I would put political science – historians can't help coming across theories of monarchy, sovereignty, liberalism, democracy, and so on. More generally, it is helpful if historians, given that they are dealing with human actions and human societies, have some knowledge of psychology, particularly social psychology. It is self-evident that historians require knowledge of certain aspects of geography. The case for anthropology has already been discussed: the claims that anthropology revealed to historians new ways of analysing their sources have only been entertained by those unaware that historians have long been tapping the rich potential of unwitting testimony.

The strongest single characteristic, as we have seen, of the *Annales* school was the desire to integrate the social sciences with history. To any kind of integration or fusion I am utterly opposed. Historians must *borrow* where they may and where they must, but the core of history, and its claim to being able to produce balanced, evidence-based judgements, rest on its autonomy. Critical and cultural theory stand at the opposite extreme to the empirical methods of the historian: there can certainly be no merger between history and cultural studies. The links to other disciplines, really, are obvious. Historians of science need knowledge of the relevant sciences; historians of film need some understanding of how films come into existence; historians of literature need an understanding of literary forms and conventions, an understanding for instance of the structure of the sonnet. Historians of ideas will need some philosophy, and, of course, history becomes entangled with philosophy whenever there are discussions (as in this book) of methodology and epistemology; I have no more to say here on that matter. I have not mentioned sociology: that is because the superficial similarities between history and sociology are so great that it is most important to insist on the distinction between the two. Once again, there are many borrowings historians can make from sociology, particularly where sociology borders on political science and social psychology; some sociologists in fact do a kind of history, but the distinctions between the two disciplines have to be maintained, lest the paramountcy of the correct handling of primary sources be lost sight of.

History's Place in the University

Where, then, when it comes to university administration, do we place history? I have given my definitions of the discipline, have insisted that it is not 'a craft', not 'both art and science', I have pointed out analogies with (but also differences from) the natural sciences. I have made it clear that professional history is very different from the writing of novels, and therefore is not literature in that sense of the term. But 'literature' (or 'comparative literature', or, simply, 'English') in the academic sense is not usually concerned directly with the writing of novels, as 'art history' is not usually concerned with the painting of paintings, nor 'musicology' with the composing of symphonies. Insofar as these academic disciplines are concerned with research and analysis and the writing up of research, they make reasonably satisfactory companions for history in a faculty of arts or humanities, though, depending on size and resources, there is, in my view, a strong case for history forming a faculty, or at least a school, of its own. Another option is to place history in a faculty of social sciences, or perhaps to put 'general' history among the arts, with economic history in the social sciences. My preference is for keeping all the sub-histories together, and using the device of administrative division to make history's distinctiveness from the social sciences as clear as possible. But then most of the arts subjects these days are even more riddled with dubious theory than the social sciences. Whatever the administrative arrangements, the point is that history must assert its own autonomous, rigorous methodology, and its immunity to metaphysical speculation.

History is NOT Literature

What does have to be driven home here is the absolutely fundamental distinction between history (a scholarly matter) and the writing of novels, plays, poetry, and other forms of fiction (a creative matter), the fallacies and conceits of what I have called the *auteur* theory of history, and the total misunderstandings of such philosophers as Paul Ricoeur, who first insists that history is essentially the same as novel-writing, and then draws absurd conclusions from this illegitimate contention.[44] Novelist after novelist has testified to the way in which, once writing commences, characters and plot begin to take over, so that very often the finished novel is very different from the author's original plans for it. The very opposite is the case with historians. Historians *must* develop a structure before they begin serious writing. Often the structure will prove inadequate, but the answer is to revise the structure, not to keep writing in the hope of writing one's way out of trouble. The structure is devised, and revised, by the historian in order to produce an account, incorporating narrative, analysis and description, different topics and themes, different aspects of the past (economic, cultural, and so on), which best conveys to the reader what actually was happening, what interactions there were, what changed, and what did not, as perceived by the historian. This is not the way novelists work.

Historians should not even dream of thinking of themselves as possessing 'creative genius'. Some readers may read history books as they would read novels, but the fundamental duties of historians, to make contributions to knowledge about the past in as accurate and well-substantiated a way as they possibly can, are very different from those of novelists. 'Accurate', 'well-substantiated' and, indeed, 'duties' are really not words that one would apply to novelists.

Notes

1 Alan Sokal and Jean Bricmont, *Intellectual Impostures: Postmodern Philosophy's Abuse of Science* (London, 1998), p. 1.
2 Alan Sokal, 'Transgressing the Boundaries: Towards a Transformative Hermeneutics of Quantum Gravity', reprinted in ibid. as Appendix A, pp. 223–6.
3 Sokal and Bricmont, *Intellectual Impostures*, p. 5.
4 Ibid., p. 4.
5 This, and other reactions to the original French publication of the Sokal and Bricmont book, are printed on the cover of, and in the Preface to, the English edition.
6 Eric M. Rogers, *Astronomy for the Inquiring Mind: The Growth and Use of Theory in Science* (Princeton, NJ, 1982), p. 156.
7 Sokal and Bricmont, *Intellectual Impostures*, esp. Chapters 7 and 11.
8 Rogers, *Astronomy*, frontispiece.
9 Ibid., p. 162.

10 Ibid.
11 Lewis Wolpert, 'A Passion for Science', in Lewis Wolpert and Alison Richards (eds), *A Passion for Science* (Oxford, 1988), p. 6.
12 Steven Rose, *The Making of Memory: From Molecules to Mind* (London, 1992), pp. 297–306.
13 Lewis Wolpert, *The Unnatural Nature of Science* (London, 1992), passim.
14 I develop these points in Arthur Marwick, 'Two Approaches to Historical Study: The Metaphysical (including "Postmodernism") and the Historical', *Journal of Contemporary History*, 30/1 (1995), p. 14.
15 See Noam Chomsky, *Language and the Problem of Knowledge* (Cambridge, Mass., 1988); John Lyons, *Language and Linguistics* (Cambridge, 1981); Giulio Lepschy, *A Survey of Structural Linguistics* (London, 1982); Stephen Pinker, *The Language Instinct* (London, 1995).
16 Michel Foucault, *Discipline and Punish* (London, 1979), p. 138. See Katie Conboy, Nadia Medina, and Sarah Stanbury, *Writing on the Body: Female Embodiment and Feminist Theory* (New York, 1997), esp. pp. 7, 128, 132.
17 See esp. Joanna Bourke, *Dismembering the Male: Men's Bodies, Britain and the Great War* (London, 1996).
18 See Chapter 1, n. 5.
19 Joyce Appleby, Lynn Hunt, Margaret Jacob, *Telling the Truth about History* (New York, 1994), pp. 10, 202, 235.
20 Ibid., p. 217.
21 Ibid., p. 267.
22 Ibid., pp. 230–1.
23 Ibid., p. 261.
24 Ibid., pp. 307–9.
25 John Tosh, *The Pursuit of History: Aims, Methods and New Directions in the Study of Modern History* (London, 1984), Chapter 8, esp. pp. 143, 149.
26 Ibid. (2000 edn), p. 154.
27 Ibid., p. 149.
28 Ibid., p. 156.
29 Ibid. (1991 edn), pp. 86–90, 178–83; Richard J. Evans, *In Defence of History* (London, 1997).
30 Tosh, *The Pursuit of History* (2000 edn), p. 125.
31 Ibid., p. 126.
32 Ibid., p. 128.
33 Ibid., p. 125.
34 Ibid., p. 126.
35 Ibid., p. 129.
36 Ibid., p. 131.
37 Patrick Joyce, *Work, Society and Politics* (London, 1980), *Visions of the People: Industrial England and the Question of Class 1848–1914* (Cambridge, 1991), *Democratic Subjects: The Self and the Social in Nineteenth-Century England* (Cambridge, 1994).
38 Kevin Sharpe, *Politics and Ideas in Early Stuart England* (London, 1989).
39 Judith R. Walkowitz, *City of Dreadful Delight: Narratives of Sexual Danger in Late-Victorian London* (London, 1992), p. 18.
40 Ibid., p. 244.

41 Kathleen Canning, *Languages of Labor and Gender: Female Factory Work in Germany 1850–1914* (1996), pp. 10, 326.

42 Ibid., p. 326.

43 Susan Kingsley Kent, *Making Peace: The Reconstruction of Gender in Inter-war Britain* (New Haven, NJ, 1993), p. 11.

44 Paul Ricoeur, *The Contribution of French Historiography to the Theory of History* (Oxford, 1980).

8 | Conclusion: Crisis, What Crisis?

When I gave what was jokingly referred to as my 'Inaugural Lecture' (I had actually been in post for almost a quarter of a century) at the Open University in October 1993, 'Metahistory is Bunk – History is Essential', I invited a number of scholars who I knew would be very critical of my talk to discuss it at a seminar the following day. At the end of the published version, a totally different artefact, 'Two Approaches to History: The Metaphysical (including "Postmodernism") and the Historical', I added this acknowledgement:

> For helping me to clarify my thoughts, I would like to thank my critics: Professors Hayden White, Ludmilla Jordanova, Stuart Hall, Steven Rose and Anthony Easthope; Sir Kenneth Dover, Drs John Tosh and Alan Bassindale (Dean of Science at the University).

When I arranged for publication of this article (after it had been refereed by a Cambridge professor) in the January 1995 issue of the *Journal of Contemporary History* I stipulated that it should be followed by a 'Response' from Hayden White. After a highly critical (perhaps even intemperate) summary of my article as he understood it, White continued:

> Marwick affects to perceive behind all this nothing less than a Marxist or at least a 'materialist' and possibly a Maoist plot, which would alarm him were he not certain that the hated Marxism had been thoroughly discredited by the course of recent 'events'.
> But I am less interested in documenting Marwick's paranoia than in registering what I take to be a few of the reasons why he has good cause to fear for the future of the profession whose practices he wishes to defend.

Principal among the reasons why I should 'fear for the future', it transpires towards the end of White's 'Response', is this:

266

Most historians are not only incapable of analysing the discursive dimensions of their writing, they positively repress the idea that there might be such a dimension. In the professional training of historians, there is much talk of the 'historical method' (although this remains a largely untheorized concept), but not even talk of how to *write* a historical work, whether of a narrative or an argumentative kind.[1]

Fascinating pieces of discourse: I am proud to have been instrumental in securing their publication. Actually I have talked rather a lot about how to write historical works, and certainly a great deal about historical method (though I would not myself use the ugly verb 'to theorise'). But what is most notable here is the authoritarian use of the phrase 'discursive dimensions', meaning the alleged way in which historical writing is implicated in the alleged power structure of society. What a weight of assumptions are contained within these two words (the high-falutin' analogue of 'With one bound Jack was free'!); clearly White has never given any thought to the possibility that there might *not* be such a dimension.

Going back to the first quotation, I am not clear whether I am being accused of real paranoia (actually perceiving plots), or of 'affecting' paranoia (only affecting to perceive them). In fact, the 'paranoia' would seem to belong to White, whose commitment to Marxism is such that he reacts to my critical approach to it as a Catholic would to anyone casting doubt on the Virgin Birth, or a Muslim to anyone seeming to cast aspersions on Mahomet. Indeed, out of their mouths the postmodernists reveal that, far from being a scholarly discipline, or super-discipline, postmodernism is really just a belief system ('religion', if you like) based on the assertions of such 'authorities' as Marx, Saussure and Foucault. This comes through with almost endearing transparency in the entries on 'critical theory' and 'theory' in David Macey's *The Penguin Dictionary of Critical Theory* (London, 2000), where, himself a true believer, he admits that both are 'unlike a scientific theory' and aim openly at 'guiding human action' and 'transforming the present social order'; 'theory', in fact, refers to 'a blend of Marxism, psychoanalysis and structuralism'. As citizens we are entitled to our own deeply held political and religious beliefs, but such beliefs have no place in education and the pursuit of knowledge. The criticisms of history made by the postmodernists, heavily based on faith alone, are worthless. Returning to White, I don't 'hate' Marxism. In Chapter 4 I acknowledged the achievements of such Marxist historians as Hobsbawm, Thompson, Gutmann, Kocka, and Lefebvre, just as I acknowledged the achievements of such conservatives as Elton and Namier (with whose politics I strongly disagree). The only problem with Marxism is that it is wrong, that's all.

Most illuminating is White's phrase about my having 'good cause to fear for the future of the profession' whose 'practices I wish to defend'. Here we come to the point singled out in my title for this chapter. From the time of the crash of the British firm Overend and Gurney in 1868 Marx and his followers predicted the imminent collapse of British capitalism, and the followers have gone on doing so ever since. Over and over again in the recent twentieth century, we were told that history, in the sense of 'the profession whose practices I wish to defend', being no more than an expression of capitalist ideology, was in a state of crisis. It's probably not worth citing now all the idiotic statements, of which White's is paradigmatic, since the tone has changed considerably in recent years.[2] History's critics are now beginning to realise that history is indeed a social necessity, as I have long argued, that people are fascinated by the past, understand its importance, and want reliable history, the kind that is produced by professional historians. The cry used to be that there is no way of actually knowing the past, and that all we can do is study the different versions of the past put forward by historians, in order to demonstrate the validity of statements about language, about bourgeois hegemony and control of knowledge. Suddenly there is an awareness of how much interest there is in the history of the historians, and how pathetic and irrelevant the attacks of Hayden White and his acolytes really are. The battle now is to try to influence the way in which knowledge about the past is taught.

This is why Tosh and Jordanova are abandoning their categorical pronouncements, and quietly jettisoning Foucault, Barthes, and White. They can't beat the 'empirical' professional historians, so they want to join us. What Jordanova's book[3] recognises – something I have been declaring since 1970 – is that history is of central importance to society. She goes on insisting that history is essentially 'political' because she wants to preserve a niche for the kind of history that propagates her radical feminist programme. But my case that history can, subject to the reservations about its concern with human values and human passions, be just as disinterested as the sciences, no less, no more, is rapidly winning acceptance. Jordanova, in her ignorance, claims that, in the universities, historians do not teach about the handling of sources and the writing of history. Of course, she would like to see people with her political views control training in the principles and methods of history. You see, history taught in accordance with the methods and principles set out in this book does not support the wild speculations of radicals. History is the enemy of absolutists, totalitarians, and ideologists, whether of left or right. The Turkish government to this day continues to prevent its own historians from undertaking scholarly research into the Armenian massacres which took place during the First World War. It is those who have guilty secrets to hide, or ludicrous theories to propagate, who fear professional history, and hope, either to take it over, or to threaten it with some non-existent crisis.

Having said all that, I make no special claims for history. The creative arts are of fundamental importance; so are the sciences and technologies. A central theme of this book has been that we must not confuse these different human activities, as the ideologists and the holists would wish us to do. History is one important specialism among many. Let us take a final close look at it, giving special attention, as I have done throughout my career, to the way in which it should be taught, and the way in which it should be communicated.

The notion that the sciences are products of the scientists is almost a commonplace. Because the influences of the past are more immediate, more all-pervasive, and, so to speak, more accessible, than the implications of the sciences, it is less readily perceived that our knowledge of the past is not something we are born with or acquire as we absorb drawing-room behaviour and gain street wisdom, but derives from historians. There is a natural, and continuing, confusion between 'history' and 'the past', there being no such confusion between 'the natural world and the physical universe' on one side and 'the sciences' on the other. But we cannot address epistemological and methodological problems if we do not accept a definition of history as 'bodies of knowledge about the past and all that is involved in producing this knowledge, communicating it, and teaching about it'.

These bodies of knowledge are enormous. There is no way, within manageable time and resource, of communicating it all, or teaching about it all. But to deal with only a tiny limited sector is not to deal with history at all. I sometimes encounter students, particularly mature students, with a passion for some particular period in history. While genuine enthusiasm and commitment to a particular area of study is an important element in doing history, I feel myself bound to point out that just studying one period you are already fascinated by is not really enough if you want to become a historian. You couldn't do a degree in medicine and study only the big toe of the right foot. Any proper education in history, or any serious preparation for advanced work in history, must involve the study of a range of periods and topics. There will always be enormous gaps, of course – an ancillary reason for stressing the importance of the study of the what, why, and how of history (students then have some qualifications for studying new periods, new countries, on their own). It is particularly important that a history syllabus should not be confined to the contemporary period (though, as it happens, my own main specialism lies in that area). The past which governs our lives in so many ways is not confined to the recent past. Nowhere is this more true than with the vexed issue of nationalism. It can be argued that those who have seen nationalism as purely political (rather than having genuine ethnic roots) or in some way 'imagined' or 'constructed' have been misled by concentrating largely on nineteenth-century history. As I have said, one must consider all the options, one must look at things from different angles: it is thus necessary to consider the claims of medieval historians that nationalism does indeed have deep and authentic roots.[4] Ponder for a moment the defiant statement of the Scots in the Declaration of Arbroath of 1320:

> So long as a mere hundred of us stand, we will never surrender to the dominion of England. What we fight for is not glory nor wealth nor honour, but freedom, that no good man yields, save with his life.[5]

Not too long ago history was taught very unsystematically, with little emphasis on how to write it, or how to analyse primary sources. That simply is no longer true. Not everyone, certainly, has gone as far as the Open University History Department, so I propose here to set out a few points in relation to undergraduate history teaching as it developed in the department I was appointed to set up in 1969. We place, naturally, a considerable emphasis on the handling of primary sources of all types. We have abolished the notion of 'gobbets' (very short extracts from primary sources on which students are asked to comment). All teaching exercises on primary sources are in some sense artificial, but commenting on gobbets was particularly far from the real activities of historians. Were they merely exercises in memory, requiring recall of the content of the whole document from which the gobbet had been extracted? Were the gobbets to be regarded as fundamental evidence or simply illustration? Were they to be analysed critically? Probably gobbets exercises worked best in constitutional history and perhaps diplomatic history, where the few lines quoted could be represented as stages in constitutional development or on the road to war. But that could entail merely parroting back pre-learned statements about the 'significance' of these few lines. Gobbets were an inheritance from the traditional study of classics, itself based on the notion of their being a corpus of basic texts. In historical study there is no basic core of texts: the scope of history expands as new types of primary source are brought into use. The continuing reliance on gobbets questions did indeed give some support to the misconceptions of E. H. Carr and others about historians simply interpreting and reinterpreting the same basic material in accordance with their own fancies.

My policy is to set a fairly lengthy extract, half a page or more, then require the student to say what type of document is being examined (with the opportunity to comment on its strengths or weaknesses for the subject matter of the particular course being studied), to set the extract within its historical context, to comment in detail on matters referred to in the text, on the language used, and so on, and then to give an assessment of the historical significance of the extract with regard to the events and issues being studied in the particular course.

Writing a detailed commentary on a substantial extract from a primary source is thus one form of written work. We then distinguish between four other types: the standard essay addressing a specific and fairly limited topic (my advice always is to break the question set down into its component parts, then address these directly, producing an answer which genuinely considers the various options, before coming to a definite conclusion – see Appendix C); the 'thematic' essay, concerning a wide-ranging general topic, such as the relationship (if any) between war and revolution in the twentieth century; the 'double essay', involving a rather specialised topic and a greater amount of reading than in the first type of essay; finally, the advanced-level undergraduate dissertation, involving some genuine primary research. As will have become apparent from Chapter 6, I put great emphasis on the way in which any piece of historical writing, given the requirement to provide narrative, analysis, and description, to balance chronology against topic, to bring in, as appropriate to the particular question being addressed, political, economic, or other factors, requires a persuasive and defensible structure. This structure must arise from reflection on the evidence. One of the many problems with left-wing theory, or just sentiment, is that too often inexperienced writers, having accumulated various bits of evidence, simply force them into a structure determined by the theory or sentiment.

In studying history it is vital to understand the distinction between 'history' and 'the past', and that 'history' is a form of knowledge, just as the sciences are forms of knowledge. I have detailed the differences, as well as the similarities, between history and the sciences. For the individual doing it, history may be a personal indulgence, but the pursuit of history by the academic community of scholars, teachers and students is vital to society. Having said that, I have to make it clear that I am not claiming for history the kind of immediate 'pay-offs' that one can expect from substantial areas of science and technology. The study of history (evidently!) does not lead directly to universal peace, or even to providing solutions to, say, the Palestine, Balkan, or Irish problems. What can be claimed is that the systematic study of history leads to a general, and necessary, understanding of the past, without which it would be impossible to even begin to address these problems.

We have no need to import pseudo-science into historical study. I have described the processes of historical research in some detail: for most projects it simply is not helpful to state a hypothesis in advance; genuine research, genuinely pursued, will often lead in directions not originally envisaged. History is a specialist discipline, with methods of its own. It is *not* simply based on common sense, and it is not a branch of literature. It is not a craft, and historians do not attempt to reconstruct the past. Keith Jenkins (with some justice) attacks the flabby notion of history as 'a craft', presented by historians who have not thought things through; he shirks engaging with my definition of history as 'bodies of knowledge about the past'.[6] History is based fundamentally on the evidence squeezed out from the primary sources by those with the requisite skills, though historians also depend heavily on the evidence provided by the secondary works of other historians. An understanding of the way in which historians have long been concerned with the unwitting testimony of primary sources, for codes, values, customs, unspoken assumptions, obviates any need to resort to cultural anthropology, though I would certainly not wish to deny that knowledge of ancillary subjects, social sciences, literary criticism, art theory, as well as anthropology, can help in bringing a deeper and fuller understanding of unwitting testimony.

No one is more familiar than the historian with the problems of language to be encountered in primary sources, which abound in obscure technical terms, words and phrases which have changed their meanings over the centuries, attitudes and concepts which no longer exist today, and may be scarcely expressible in the language of today. However, in writing up their researches, historians, if they put in the immense and taxing efforts required, if they revise, revise, revise, can be explicit and precise. Everyday language is sloppy and frequently ambiguous: historians have to work hard to avoid everyday clichés, everyday metaphors, everyday sloppiness. Historians do not seek the allusiveness and resonances of language which are fundamental to novels, plays, and poetry. And they should strive to avoid the fancy jargon of the postmodernists and cultural theorists: they should think very carefully before they talk about 'webs of meaning', 'cultural scripts', or 'discursive domains'.

In concluding the original, 1970, *The Nature of History*, I wrote: 'History belongs to every man. That is a strength not a weakness.' In the second edition (1981) the statement was amended to include 'and every woman', then dropped altogether from the third edition (1989). The broad sentiment was right, but, as with so much in that distant, pioneering work, crudely expressed. A lesson for all apprentice historians is that sentiment is not enough; the quality required is thought. The problem with pop history, public history, applied history (choose your own label) is that it can quickly become, if it did not start out as such, myth rather than history. In the publicising of public history and the need for universal participation there is some confusion. Governments these days demand that history departments demonstrate the utility of their teaching with respect to the finding of jobs. This does not embarrass me: I have from the start (without using the jargon) boasted of the 'transferable skills' provided by a training in history. Through the media, through the various activities associated with 'heritage', history is highly marketable. History is necessary, history is useful; but I take the perhaps rather austere view that it would be a pity if history became implicated in the notion of making loads of money.

At its very core history must be a scholarly discipline, based on thorough analysis of the evidence, and in the writing up of which language is deployed with the utmost precision. There must be constant awareness of the methods and principles of that discipline, constant attention to how it is taught, and how, at different levels, it is communicated to wider audiences. I believe *The New Nature of History: Knowledge, Evidence, Language* to be a necessary book, but I now eagerly return to serious research and, I hope, the production of history, rather than mere historiography and historical epistemology.

Notes

1   Hayden White, 'Response to Arthur Marwick', *Journal of Contemporary History*, 30/2 (April 1995), pp. 245, 248.
2   However, Keith Jenkins, who exists within his own little time bubble, revives the issue in *Why History?: Ethics and Postmodernity* (London, 1999), pp. 103ff.
3   Ludmilla Jordanova, *History in Practice* (London, 2000).
4   A good starting point is Adrian Hastings, *The Construction of Nationhood: Ethnicity, Religion and Nationalism* (Cambridge, 1997). For a judicious balance between the Middle Ages and 'the pivotal years' of the eighteenth and nineteenth centuries, see Hagen Schulze, *States, Nations and Nationalism: From the Middle Ages to the Present* (Munich, 1994; Oxford, 1996).
5   Quoted in W. C. Dickinson, Gordon Donaldson and Isobel Milne, *Source Book of Scottish History*, vol. 1 (Edinburgh, 1955), p. 98.
6   Jenkins, *Why History?*, p. 9.

Appendix A: An Example of Learning Outcomes for a History Degree

1 Knowledge and Understanding

(i)   An understanding that history is a scientific discipline producing bodies of knowledge about the past, these being constantly subject, as in the sciences, to controversy, debate, refinement and correction; but that further, while precise quantification is vital in many aspects of history, relationships and discoveries in history cannot be expressed in mathematical formulae as they are so often in the sciences.

(ii)   An understanding of the problems of language as embodied in such critical historical concepts as 'economy', 'legitimacy', 'culture', 'democracy', 'industrialisation', 'urbanisation', and 'class', and a familiarity with the ways such terms are used in historical discourse.

(iii)   An ability to explicate the value of the comparative method in history and to be able to apply that method in the study of Britain, America, and the countries of Europe in the seventeenth, eighteenth, nineteenth, and twentieth centuries.

(iv)   An ability to explain the significance of developments in France and the British Isles in the seventeenth century, Britain and America since the eighteenth century, and Europe in the nineteenth century, in the subsequent development of all of these societies.

(v)   The ability to expound the basic principles of economic history and political science, specifically with reference to nineteenth-century Europe and the historical development of Britain and America.

(vi)   A knowledge of crucial features of twentieth-century European history, essential to the informed citizen wishing to take part in contemporary debates, and, therefore, a quality of general value in any occupation.

(vii)   An ability to argue knowledgeably over the historical significance of the two major wars which took place in the first half of the twentieth century, discussing their causes and consequences, both short- and long-term, and discussing how far, and in what senses, the label 'total war' is justifiable.

(viii)   An appreciation that everything written pertaining to history is not of equal value and that much that is written is written for reasons other than the advancement of historical knowledge (for personal, political, or ideological reasons, for instance); everything, secondary or primary, should be approached with scepticism and caution.

(ix)   The ability to carry out a private research project in primary sources right through to the production of a short thesis in which the evidence is marshalled and the arguments advanced at a standard appropriate to Level Four, with references and bibliography conforming to the style of the *English Historical Review*.

2   Key Skills

(i)   The ability to evaluate and analyse evidence of all kinds, secondary and primary, the latter including written documents of all kinds, history on the ground, a variety of cultural artefacts, and film and radio broadcasts, and to extract relevant information and ideas from it.

(ii)   The ability to write coherent and well-organised reports (or 'essays') of various types, addressing precise problems and developing balanced and well-substantiated arguments.

(iii)   The ability to use computers for the compilation of spreadsheets and the elementary analysis of data.

(iv)   A grasp of how historical knowledge is acquired and communicated, which will facilitate continuous development in learning how to learn history, and thus a steady enhancement of historical knowledge.

(v)   An understanding of cliometrics and counter-factual econometrics, their advantages and disadvantages.

3   Cognitive Skills

(i)   The skill of seeking out, collecting, and *selecting* relevant information – a training in finding out.

(ii)   The ability to explicate and evaluate theories and concepts, and an understanding of their use and abuse.

(iii)   The verbal skills necessary for intelligent participation in argument and debate and for the presentation of a position on, or interpretation of, a particular historical topic.

(iv)   The facility of using experience and opportunity continually to develop your own communication skills.

4   Professional and Practical Skills

(i)   Verified competence in the presentation of five different types of written communication: evaluation, analysis, and assessment of the historical significance of one or more primary sources; a standard Level Three historical essay, addressing one specific topic or problem; a double-length essay drawing upon reading done in a range of books obtained in a university library; a 'thematic' essay ranging over one or more of the major issues raised in the study of a particular theme or topic in history; a Level Four research-based dissertation, with references and bibliography in the style of the *English Historical Review*.

(ii) A professional facility in coping with the information explosion that is a facet of all occupations today and in assessing and filtering the messages constantly battering against us, and in the interpretation of sources of all kinds – professional documentation, electronic communication and data, newspapers, magazines, television, advertisements, political statements, expert announcements, graphs, histograms, and graphic visual imagery of all types.

(iii) An understanding of the problems and concepts involved in historical explanation and an awareness that there is some relationship (however hard to define in specific instances) between structural, ideological, and institutional circumstances and events, contingency, and human agency.

(iv) An understanding of the nature of historical change and a personal adaptability to change and flexibility of response.

(v) An understanding of past modes of thought and behaviour, with an appreciation that present attitudes may themselves be ephemeral, and an ability to avoid anachronism; an understanding of, and empathy with, attitudes and ideas different from our own.

Appendix B: Examples of Aims and Objectives

1 Aims of the Open University Course *Total War and Social Change: Europe 1914–1955*

(i)   To enable you to argue in an informed way over the nature, extent and causes of social change within and across the main European countries 1914–55, which are defined for the purposes of this course as Russia, Austria–Hungary (up to the aftermath of the First World War only), France, Germany, Italy and the United Kingdom; other European countries will feature only with regard to specific events and topics.

(ii)   To help you to understand the nature of total war and how it differs from other kinds of war, and to help you to discuss in an informed way the relationship (if any) between total war and revolution, and total war and genocide.

(iii)   To enable you to discuss the causes of the two wars, evaluating 'structural' (that is to say 'concerning economic and demographic imperatives') forces against ideological and institutional ones and those of geopolitics, ideology, nationalism, human agency and contingency.

(iv)   To enable you to argue in an informed way about the role of total war with respect to social change, and in particular to evaluate the significance of the two total wars relative to structural, ideological and institutional forces and to enable you to discuss the relationship of the wars to the major geopolitical changes.

(v)   To assist you in developing skills learned at Level One and Level Two in:

(a) the critical analysis and interpretation of primary source materials, including written documents as well as literary and artistic materials, film, radio, and the artefacts of popular culture.

(b) understanding the differences between the 'professional', 'source-based' approach to historical study and the more theoretical approaches of Marxists, Weberians, postmodernists, and some (by no means all) feminist historians.

(c) dealing with such problems as periodisation and historical semantics; and

(d) writing history essays of Level Three, or BA (Honours), standard.

(vi)   To take further your understanding of the nature of historiographical controversy (a matter first raised in the Level One course, dealt with further at

Level Two), and to enable you to arrive at informed judgements on the issues and debates presented within the framework of the course.

2   Objectives for Unit 13, 'Challenges to Central Government, 1660s to 1714', from the Open University course *Princes and Peoples: The British Isles and France c. 1630–1714*

(i)   You should be able to expound the contrast between the turbulent political history of the British Isles and the events preceding, including and succeeding the 'Glorious Revolution' and the relatively stable progress of centralised monarchy in France.

(ii)   You should be in a position to analyse and compare the nature and extent of the political changes to central government in the different countries and how they were dealt with, being able, in particular, to discuss knowledgeably the notion that in this period the French monarchy won its struggle with the nobility and the English monarchy lost.

(iii)   You should be able to assess the character and significance of the different kinds of religious opposition manifested in the different countries.

(iv)   You should be able to itemise the main outbreaks of popular protest in the various countries, analysing their causes and significance, and identifying the main differences between events in France and events in the British Isles.

(v)   You should be able to demonstrate an understanding of the way in which political, religious and popular protest were often intertwined.

(vi)   You should have further advanced your skills in historical methodology and comparative historical study.

Appendix C: Writing History

1 Planning a History Essay

Imagine you are writing an essay on 'In what ways, if any, did the experiences of the First World War increase the political rights and raise the consciousness of women in Britain and France?' The first thing to do is break the essay question down into its basic components.

1 There are actually four components to this question, which immediately give rise to four separate questions which need to be answered. Try to identify for yourself (a) the four 'components', then (b) the four questions.

2 Work out what matters of definition have to be settled and what other issues, implicit in the question as a whole, have to be discussed before you can attack the essay question satisfactorily as a whole.

Here are my thoughts:

1(a) The four components are: women in Britain, women in France, political rights and consciousness.

1(b) The questions are:
What effects, if any, did the war have on the political rights of British women?
What effects, if any, did the war have on the political rights of French women?
What effects, if any, did the war have on the consciousness of British women?
What effects, if any, did the war have on the consciousness of French women?

2 You need to explain 'political rights' – the right to vote, and the right to be elected to parliament or national assembly. You also need to explain 'consciousness' – which means self-confidence, women's belief in their own capacities, and a willingness to speak up for themselves.
Before it is possible to answer the question as a whole, you would need to establish whether political rights *were* increased (a) in Britain, (b) in France,

and in the same way whether consciousness *was* raised. Where you did feel that you could detect changes you'd have to ask how far they came about for other reasons (structural, political, and so on) rather than because of the war. All this has to be sorted out if you are to give a clear, balanced answer to the question 'In what ways, if any . . . '. In this essay it would be difficult to avoid the disagreements between different historians and you would certainly have to explain clearly where you stood in relation to the different views.

3   Now here are some plans:

Example I (This is the very barest of plans, arising out of the discussion above)
1   POLITICAL RIGHTS IN BRITAIN
    Definition, then account of what happened with evaluation of the significance of war as against other factors.
2   POLITICAL RIGHTS IN FRANCE
    Definition, then account of what happened with evaluation of the significance of war as against other factors.
3   CONSCIOUSNESS IN BRITAIN
    Definition, then account of what happened with evaluation of the significance of war as against other factors.
4   CONSCIOUSNESS IN FRANCE
    Definition, then account of what happened with evaluation of the significance of war as against other factors.
5   CONCLUSION

Example II (This is a more elaborate version of Example I which reserves space for the other issues raised in the discussion)
1   INTRODUCTION
1(a)   Explanations of political rights and consciousness.
1(b)   What actually happened and the historians' debate. (Significant political rights in Britain, effectively none at national level in France. Some debate among historians over raising of consciousness – you'd have to offer some firm conclusions for each of Britain and France.)
2   LONG-TERM FORCES TENDING TOWARDS POLITICAL RIGHTS AND HIGHER CONSCIOUSNESS IN BOTH BRITAIN AND FRANCE
2(a)   Long-term change in women's role in the economy.
2(b)   Ideological forces and the women's movement.
3   POLITICAL RIGHTS IN BRITAIN
3(a)   Discussion of the significance of the women's suffrage movement.
3(b)   Discussion of actual course of events during war, evaluating contribution of war experience as against other factors. Firm conclusion stated. (Did war actually obstruct women's rights?)
4   POLITICAL RIGHTS IN FRANCE
       Depending on what line you'd established in 1(b) you'd say: (i) war had no effect; (ii) war obstructed women's rights; (iii) war had some effects (that is, removing prejudice in national assembly). Again state a firm conclusion.
5   CONSCIOUSNESS IN BRITAIN AND FRANCE

5(a)   Discuss arguments of the various historians who have written on this topic. Your conclusions here will depend on your evaluations of each of these, but remember also to refer as necessary to points made in 2, in order to offer a careful evaluation.

5(b)   Similar discussions for France, bringing out any comparisons and contrasts if there are any.

6   CONCLUSION
        Can be very brief since you will have been producing arguments and conclusions as you worked your way through.

Example III (This example puts heavy emphasis on the questions raised by the essay being matters of historical debate)

1   THE HISTORICAL DEBATE
1(a)   The various views on the war and political rights in Britain and France.
1(b)   The various views on the war and consciousness in Britain and France.
2   DEVELOPMENTS IN BRITAIN, 1914–c. 1921 (RIGHTS AND CON-SCIOUSNESS)
        Discussion of different factors; your conclusions.
3   DEVELOPMENTS IN FRANCE, 1914–c. 1921
        Discussion of different factors; your conclusions.
4   CONCLUSION

Example IV (This is a variation on Example III)

1   THE ARGUMENT THAT WAR DID NOT HAVE ANY EFFECTS OR WAS NEGATIVE IN ITS EFFECTS
1(a)   Political rights in France.
1(b)   Political rights in Britain.
1(c)   Consciousness in Britain.
1(d)   Consciousness in France.
2   THE ARGUMENT THAT WAR DID HAVE POSITIVE EFFECTS
2(a)   Political rights in France.
2(b)   Political rights in Britain.
2(c)   Consciousness in Britain.
2(d)   Consciousness in France.
3   CONCLUSION

Example V

1   LONG-TERM FORCES POSSIBLY AFFECTING POLITICAL RIGHTS AND CONSCIOUSNESS (BRITAIN AND FRANCE)
2   POLITICAL FORCES POSSIBLY AFFECTING POLITICAL RIGHTS AND CONSCIOUSNESS (BRITAIN AND FRANCE)
3   EFFECTS OF WAR EXPERIENCES POSSIBLY AFFECTING POLIT-ICAL RIGHTS AND CONSCIOUSNESS (BRITAIN AND FRANCE)
4   CONCLUSION

Of my five plans, I think Example II is best, in that it leaves room to explore all the different issues involved in the question sufficiently. It would be perfectly possible to write good essays based on the other plans (provided that the various ramifications were gone into along the way), but insofar as they are rather basic and simple, I'd see them as plans for exam answers rather than for the more expansive and detailed format of an essay.

2   Guidance on Writing an Essay

(i)   You must demonstrate the ability to find and select relevant material (thus, the inclusion of irrelevant material will result in a reduction in your grade).

(ii)   And the ability to address precise problems: this is very important, and, indeed, expresses the essence of what I want to return to at the end – you must be clear about exactly what problem or problems you're being asked to address, and you must go straight into doing that. You are not invited to indulge in broad philosophising or speculation, and doing this is likely to result in a reduction in your grade.

(iii)   And an ability to develop balanced arguments: you must show that, before settling on your own line of argument and conclusion, you have considered other possible lines of argument.

(iv)   Your argument must be well substantiated: it must be based on precise pieces of information ('facts', in a slightly unsatisfactory shorthand) and evidence, drawn from secondary or primary sources.

(v)   Your essay must be coherent and well organised: that is to say that it must be based on a plan, along the lines of the examples given above. You do not submit the plan with your essay, but it will be immediately clear to your tutor whether or not you have taken the trouble to prepare a serious plan, *and follow* it. Sometimes students produce plans which are merely a convenient way of dividing up the material, without any reference to the requirement for developing a balanced and well- substantiated argument. Sometimes they do develop such a plan, and then quite simply fail to follow it.

(vi)   The essay has to be written in English prose of an acceptable standard: we do not wish to make an obstacle of this, but obviously you cannot receive the highest grades if your grammar and spelling are incorrect; for those who have basic difficulties we do expect to see a real effort to improve over the year; we do not want fancy rhetoric, and elaborate words should certainly not be used unless you're absolutely clear that you know their meaning; in a first draft of an essay it is almost impossible to avoid loose, and even slang, phrases, but you should try to improve upon these in the version actually submitted to your tutor.

(vii)   Quotations, references and bibliography should be set out in the approved manner: quotations should either be in quotation marks or set out in indented form without quotation marks, and should have a reference footnote or endnote, as should important statements of fact upon which your argument depends; a bibliography is simply a list of the books you have used.

(viii)   You must show that you have read the question carefully and understood exactly what is being asked.

(ix)   You should resolve any problems of definition (as with 'political rights' and 'consciousness' in the example just given).

(x)   If within the question there are in fact several questions, or several issues needing to be resolved, you have to show that you have understood this. You may need to break the question down into separate components – your grade will in part depend on how well you have worked out the complexities of the question.

(xi)   Your essay must make clear what line or conclusion you are opting for.

(xii)   Every single sentence in your essay must in some way or another be contributing to your overall argument (even if, in the interests of balance, it is identifying a counter-argument which overall you are rejecting).

(xiii)   Show that you realise that sometimes it is necessary in your final draft to insert another sentence or phrase bringing out how what you are saying contributes to the development of your overall argument.

(xiv)   Avoid 'scissors and paste' (a large number of quotations simply 'pasted' together); that is to say, avoid over-quotation and do not leave quotations to 'speak for themselves'.

(xv)   Be sure that you're supplying answers to the question 'How do you know that?' whenever it would occur to your tutor to ask it.

(xvi)   Do not use references or bibliography simply for show – they are there for use.

3   A Brief Guide to Referencing for Historians (by my colleague Annika Mombauer)

When writing a history essay, it is essential that you indicate your sources of information. To indicate your sources, you will need to provide references, usually in footnotes or endnotes, as well as a bibliography of the books, essays and articles that you have read to compile your work. This is important information for the reader, indicating where your information came from, and helping him/her to find out more about a certain topic if they wish. In handwritten essays it is easier to compile endnotes; if you are word-processing your document, footnotes are preferable. Whichever you choose, your notes should be numbered consecutively.

As students of a history course, you need to acquire the tools of a historian: for example, how to do a literature search on a chosen subject and find recent publications, how to evaluate the reading that you are doing, and how to communicate your findings in an appropriate form. Skills you should acquire and practise include proper referencing.

There are serious reasons for getting this right. A student who displays competence in using the tools of a historian is more likely to get a good mark than one who doesn't. More importantly, however, all historians have to be concerned with the issue of plagiarism, which is, simply put, pretending that someone else's research, thoughts or arguments are your own. Plagiarism is not always a conscious or deliberate attempt at cheating, but can happen almost inadvertently if you fail to provide references. This is why it is important to get into the habit of proper referencing. By providing clear, precise references to your reading you will not run the risk of being accused of plagiarism.

Forms of Reference

A variety of systems of referencing are in use, such as the 'author–date system' (or 'Harvard system'), which is used, for example, in the social sciences. You may have encountered this system in some courses, and you may want to continue using it, although the system we recommend here is more appropriate for history. You need to make sure that whichever system you adopt you apply it consistently. Don't adopt two different systems in one essay, but stick to one way of referencing. For historians, that way should be as follows:

To cite a book (monograph, essay collection, work of one or more authors), list

- Author or editor
- Title, including sub-titles, in italics (if word-processed) or underlined (if handwritten or typed)
- Publication details: publisher (optional), place and date of publication (essential)
- Page number(s) that you are referring to or quoting from.

Example: A. J. P. Taylor, *The Origins of the Second World War* (London, 1961), p. 79.

To cite an essay in a collection of essays, list:

- Author of essay
- Title of the essay in inverted commas
- Editor of the volume
- Title of the volume in italics (if word-processed) or underlined (if handwritten or typed)
- Publication details: publisher (optional), place and date of publication (essential)
- Page number(s) that you are referring to or quoting from.

Example: Mark Roseman, 'National Socialism and Modernisation', in R. Bessel (ed.), *Fascist Italy Nazi Germany* (Cambridge University Press, Cambridge, 1996), pp. xx–xxv, p. xxi.

To cite an article in a scholarly journal, list:

- Author of the article
- Title of the article in inverted commas
- Title of the journal in italics (if word-processed) or underlined (if handwritten or typed)
- Publication details: volume number, date of publication, page numbers in journal
- Page number(s) that you are referring to or quoting from.

Example: Richard Overy, 'Germany, "Domestic Crisis" and War in 1939', *Past and Present*, 116 (August 1987), pp. x–xx, p. xi.

When listing your sources in your bibliography, don't forget to list *all* works that you have consulted, whether you cite them in the text or not. Arrange your bibliography alphabetically, and put surnames before first names.

Example: Overy, Richard, 'Germany, "Domestic Crisis" and War in 1939', *Past and Present*, 116 (August 1987), pp. x–xx, p. xi.

Taylor, A. J. P., *The Origins of the Second World War* (London, 1961).

When Do You Need to Provide References?

Knowing how and when to include citations, and how to reference them, takes practice and may require advice from your tutor. There are two main reasons for providing references in an essay:

1   Including a citation from another source in your own argument. You may want to do this to quote a striking phrase, or a particular point that you encounter in your reading. If you do so, you have to indicate the citation by using inverted commas at the beginning and end, and by providing a footnote reference.

Example: According to A. J. P. Taylor, the Second World War was to a large extent 'a repeat performance of the first'.[1]

Short citations like this one, and up to about three lines in length, should be incorporated into the text. Longer citations should be indented and visibly set apart from the rest of your text. If you indicate a citation in this way, you do not use inverted commas. As a general rule, it is better to paraphrase your reading and give arguments in your own words (with an appropriate reference, as demonstrated in Example 2 below), rather than to include lots of long citations.

Example: Although Gregor Schöllgen is critical of Fritz Fischer's work, he admits that Fischer's great merit was his use of an exceptionally large number of primary sources:

> It is beyond doubt that Fritz Fischer's research, based on intensive study of the sources, has had a profound effect on German historical writing. Whether one accepts his main theses or not, the results of his work now form an integral part of any analysis of the foreign policy of Imperial Germany.[2]

2   You may want to refer to a general argument that you encounter in your reading. Rather than a specific citation, you would only refer to a particular chapter or a few pages. This is how you might do it:

> As Fritz Fellner explains, the escalation of the crisis between Austria-Hungary and Serbia into a large-scale war was due to Germany's determination to test the willingness of the Entente powers to go to war. All

---

[1] A. J. P. Taylor, *The Origins of the Second World War* (London, 1961), p. 18.
[2] Gregor Schöllgen (ed.), *Escape into War* (London, 1991), p. 4.

important decisions were, according to Fellner, taken in Berlin with little regard for Vienna.[3]

[Your footnote would then be at the foot of this page.]

Finally, once you have provided a complete citation (that is, the author's first and second names, and full title of the book, or of the article and journal title, the place and date of publication), you can then use a shorter reference when you refer to the same book or article again. We have already cited Taylor. If we were to mention his book *The Origins of the Second World War* again, we would give this shortened reference in the footnote as shown at the foot of this page.[4] And, finally, if a little later your next reference is to the same text and no reference to a different publication has been made in the meantime, you can make it even easier for yourself with this short footnote.[5] 'Ibid.' indicates a citation from the same place.

This information may seem dull and overly complicated, but if you try to get it right from the beginning, referencing will become second nature, rather than a difficult task. If in doubt, look at the way other historians cite their sources. Most will use the same system described here, and knowing how to write references yourself will also help you to follow up the references you encounter in other historians' writings.

---

[3] Fritz Fellner, 'Austria-Hungary', in Keith Wilson (ed.), *Decisions for War, 1914* (London, 1995), pp. 9–25.
[4] Taylor, *Origins*, p. x.
[5] Ibid.

Appendix D: Glossary

(A version of this glossary first appeared in the 1989 edition of *The Nature of History*; readers may find it illuminating to compare my list with that provided by Ludmilla Jordanova in her *History in Practice* (2000).)

ANNALES, ANNALES 'SCHOOL': *Annales* is the historical journal founded in 1929 by Lucien Febvre and Marc Bloch, and given a new lease of life after 1945 when it was associated with the prestigious École des Hautes Études en Sciences Sociales (to give the institution its most recent name). *Annales*, the journal, and the 'school' loosely associated with it, and the École, are characterised above all by an insistence that history should make use of the discoveries of the social sciences and incorporate social science methods. The approach (which in fact is far more diverse than usually assumed) has been described as structural-functionalist, and certainly *Annales* historians, strongly influenced by structuralism in anthropology, place great emphasis on what they perceive to be the underlying structures in history.

ARTS: in British universities a Faculty of Arts usually includes such subjects as English (or Literature), Philosophy, Art History, and also History. Sometimes 'The Arts' connotes these various disciplines; on other occasions it means the 'creative' arts – that is to say, painting, poetry, sculpture, and so on.

ASSIMILATIONIST: the view that history should be assimilated to the methods of the natural sciences.

AUTONOMOUS: when applied to history means that history is not a part of literature, or of the sciences, or of cultural studies, but has its own specialist methodology.

CAPITALISM: used in a general way by historians to describe the kind of economic system that has existed for at least the last 100 or 200 years in 'the West', very definitely from the time of industrialisation, and with respect to important elements, since the commercial developments of the sixteenth, seventeenth, and eighteenth centuries. In Marxist discourse there is a more precise meaning, Marxism postulating that capitalism is the social order which succeeded feudalism, having overthrown it, and is now, in the contemporary period, subject to overthrow by working-class or socialist revolution.

CHARISMA: a term coined by the famous German sociologist Max Weber meaning the almost magical qualities of attractiveness possessed by certain political leaders.

CLASS: as generally used by historians it means the broad aggregations of families and individuals into which modern societies divide, these aggregations falling into a rough hierarchy according to the wealth, influence, power or whatever possessed by individuals within each aggregation, and generally characterised by common lifestyles, patterns of behaviour, and so on. Such historians would see classes as coming into existence only in, say, the later eighteenth century, under the impetus of industrialisation and the political upheavals of the time. Marxists, however, apply the term to all periods of history, and in a precise technical way. According to Marxism a person's class is determined by their relationship to the dominant mode of production, and in every 'stage' of history one class will dominate – for example the bourgeois, or capitalist, class in the age of capitalism.

CLASS AWARENESS: an awareness of belonging to a particular class without necessarily feeling that this involves conflict or a need to take action.

CLASS CONSCIOUSNESS: this is a specifically Marxist term and occurs, or is alleged to occur, when members of a class become aware of the way in which their interests are in conflict with those of another class and are prepared to take action in pursuit of their interests.

CLIO: in Greek mythology, the goddess or Muse of history. Best avoided as pretentious and inevitably metaphorical and rhetorical. Cliometrics is a pretentious synonym for econometric history.

COMPARATIVE HISTORY: history which, by fixing on like or analogous institutions or practices in different countries, produces comparisons and contrasts between these countries.

CONDITIONS OF CULTURAL CONSUMPTION: the market conditions within which novels are purchased and read, paintings are bought and exhibited, plays are watched, music listened to, and so on.

CONDITIONS OF CULTURAL PRODUCTION: the social, economic, political and ideological context within which cultural artefacts are produced.

CONJONCTURE: favoured term of *Annales* historians meaning a trend or cycle (for example of prices), much shorter than the *longue durée*, but operating within the constraints and structure of it.

COUNTER-FACTUAL HISTORY: a form of history in which the historian works out what would have happened if one particular factor or decision had been different – at its most impressive in econometric history where, for instance, one economic development is removed (for example, the building of railways in the United States).

CULTURAL THEORY: an approach to the study of the arts which stresses the importance of the social and historical context and, in particular, the power structure, and is based on Marxist assumptions about class, ideology, and the dialectic.

CULTURALLY CONSTRUCTED (as in, say, sexual practices or notions of beauty): created by the society, or 'culture', to which they belong – as distinct from having any natural or universal existence.

CULTURE: (a) ('anthropological' meaning) the entire network of activities, practices and institutions within a given society; (b) ('aesthetic' meaning) the artistic and leisure activities and products of a given society (better, in my view, to say 'the arts, entertainments, media and books').

DIALECTIC: originating with Plato, developed by Hegel and then by Marx, a concept postulating that within every society there is 'thesis' and 'antithesis', dominant idea and countervailing idea, existing mode of production and emerging mode of production, dominant ideology and alternative ideology. This concept lies at the heart of even the most sophisticated contemporary Marxist thinking, though it has no basis in empirical observation.

DIPLOMATICS: the ancillary technique of the study of charters, decrees, and so on, and of the style and language in which they are written.

DISCOURSE THEORY: an approach which posits language as the central (and in some cases only) subject for academic study. All primary sources, it is alleged, embody one or more *discourses* which are seen as expressing the structure of power in a particular society; rather than divide sources into different categories, the crucial task is to identify different discourses. Heavily dependent on Marxist assumptions about dominance and ideology. 'Discourse' also has a neutral meaning as the distinctive mode of communicating and expressing the ideas of a particular group, as in, say, postmodernist discourse – embracing the fancy jargon, rhetoric, and so on – or feminist discourse.

DISENCHANTMENT: the usual sociological, though rather inaccurate, translation of Max Weber's German word *Entzauberung*. A better translation would be 'demagnification'. Weber, and many historians following him, have seen this as a characteristic of modernisation, the rejection of old authorities, superstitions, and so on.

DISSERTATION: the typed, or word-processed, book-length product which a scholar submits for a degree (for example a PhD) or other academic honour or status. In Britain sometimes also described as a 'thesis'.

ENTZAUBERUNG: see DISENCHANTMENT.

EXEMPLAR HISTORY: history designed to teach potential members of the ruling elite how to govern.

FEUDALISM (adjective FEUDAL): the term was invented in the seventeenth century to describe the legal and social order prevailing in most European countries in the Middle Ages: originally, its essential feature was that men held land from their superiors by virtue of performing for them some designated service (for example, military service). In Marxist discourse the term has a more precise connotation as defining the 'stage' in the 'unfolding of history' which preceded capitalism.

HEGEMONY: in traditional history this simply meant the power or influence exercised over several countries by one country: for instance, in pre-1914 European history one might talk of German hegemony over eastern Europe. However, in contemporary Marxist cultural theory (developed from the work of Gramsci) hegemony refers to the cultural monopoly allegedly exercised by the dominant class: thus it is alleged that working-class cultural practices (such as reading books by right-wing authors) are not really 'genuinely' working-class at all, but simply a part of bourgeois hegemony.

HERMENEUTIC: pertaining to the understanding of texts.

HERMENEUTICS: the study of the understanding of texts; however, a special Marxist version has developed in the last quarter of a century, associated in particular with the German Marxist scholar Jürgen Habermas.

HISTORICISM (adjective HISTORICIST): an approach which sees history as an absolutely central discipline because it postulates that everything is explained by its past development, while at the same time insisting that each age has unique characteristics, and a unique value of its own (the word was incorrectly used by Karl Popper to refer to grand-scale theorising about history – what I call metahistory – particularly Marxism).

HISTORIOGRAPHY: the systematic study of historians' writings about the past.

HISTORY: the most concise definition is:

> The bodies of knowledge about the past produced by historians, together with everything that is involved in the production, communication of, and teaching about that knowledge.

HOLISTIC: this is one of the most fashionable adjectives of our day, creating a satisfying glow over the implication that one is taking a broad, unified view, 'seeing things whole', not being 'narrowly' specialised. Often its usage is merely meaningless rhetoric, but in the hands of postmodernists and those of a Marxisant persuasion it means being in conformity with the unified, totalising assumptions of Marxism and postmodernism. Like so many similar words, it has a perfectly reputable, and indeed admirable, usage, when it means seeing the interconnectedness of things, the essential unity and indivisibility of nature and the environment, the profound insights of a world religion (even if one may utterly disagree with it).

HUMANITIES: sometimes an alternative for 'Arts' as in the first definition given above; sometimes taken to include both the arts in that sense and the social sciences.

IBID. (as used in footnote references): means that the source is exactly the same as the one given in the previous footnote.

IDEAL TYPE: another concept coined by Max Weber, meaning an abstract, average, or 'model' type, not something that actually exists, but a composite of all the basic characteristics: for instance, one could create the 'ideal type' of the medieval peasant, which would have all the characteristics agreed upon by historians, but would not be any actual peasant who really lived (note that 'ideal' here means 'pertaining to an idea', or 'in the mind', it does not mean 'perfect').

IDEOGRAPHIC: represented entirely visually (as in a picture) and without the use of words: for example as in an inn sign.

IDEOLOGY: (1) cluster or system of ideas, values and beliefs (of, for example, an entire society, a social group, a political party); (2) (in Marxism, cultural theory, and discourse theory) the system of ideas, values and beliefs through which the ruling class preserves its dominance.

IDIOGRAPHIC: the approach to history which argues that history is entirely different from the sciences and should follow purely pragmatic approaches of its own.

IMPERIALISM: the system of thought and action pertaining to the support of the idea of empire, that is to say one country ruling over, and exploiting, others. In Marxist thought imperialism is seen as an advanced stage of capitalism, and as belonging specifically to the period after 1880. Other historians would argue that imperialism can happen in many different ages.

INTERDISCIPLINARY: There are many problems in the sciences, in the humanities, in social life and politics, which cannot be solved by one discipline alone; sometimes interdisciplinary approaches, combining several disciplines, are required. Most academic and educational institutions nowadays offer some 'interdisciplinary' courses which bring together several disciplines: chemistry, biology and physics, for instance, or history, politics and sociology, or philosophy, literature, art history, music and history. The idea is to show where certain disciplines overlap with, and reinforce, each other. But if taught rigorously, these courses will also bring out the distinctive differences between different disciplines. 'Interdisciplinary' is a modish adjective for those who espouse postmodernism and Marxisant approaches, and for those who like to be modish for the sake of being modish. To them, 'interdisciplinary' usually means study conducted in accordance with the assumptions of postmodernism and Marxism. It must always be remembered that the knowledges that are essential to the survival and development of human societies, and the achievement of universal human freedom, are inevitably highly specialised. Those who resist specialisation on ideological grounds only do damage.

LOC. CIT.: technical term used in footnotes, meaning the same place (page, etc.) as has already been cited.

LONGUE DURÉE: basic term of Annales school: the almost unchanging long-term structures of everyday life which act as a constraint upon shorter-term trends (conjonctures).

MARXISM: the approach to history developed by Karl Marx and refined by his followers, stressing that 'history', conceived of as process, unfolds in a series of stages which, after the current phase of bourgeois capitalism, will lead to the triumph of the proletariat and the classless society, that the dialectic (the existing mode of production coming into conflict with an emergent mode of production) is central to this process of unfolding, and that class conflict is the motor of history, classes being determined by their relationship to the dominant mode of production (see also CLASS CONSCIOUSNESS and IDEOLOGY).

MENTALITIES: the mental sets, attitudes and outlook of particular groups or even of whole societies.

METAHISTORY: grand-scale theorising in history, as in Marxism, or the writings of Spengler or A. J. Toynbee.

MIDDLE AGES: the term originates in the Renaissance and applies to the period of history between classical times and the Renaissance: it is important to note that the phrase can only be applied to European history, and has no meaning for most of the rest of the world.

MODERNISATION: used to describe the whole complex network of developments which are held to be characteristic of the modern world, e.g. 'disenchantment', exploitation of technology, economic growth, mass society, etc., etc.

MONOGRAPH: published scholarly work which goes in great depth into one topic, usually wider than a PhD dissertation, but narrower than an 'interpretative synthesis'.

MYTH: a version of the past which usually has some element of truth in it, but which distorts what actually happened in support of some vested interest.

NEGOTIATION: has an obvious and straightforward meaning in political history, but as used in Marxist cultural theory refers to the way in which, allegedly, the dominant ideology 'negotiates' with alternative ideologies in order to maintain the hegemony of the ruling class.

NOMINALISM: originally the doctrine that concepts have no realities corresponding to them, used in historical study to apply to an approach to history which denies any value to conceptual approaches or generalisation.

NOMOTHETIC: the approach to history which tries to assimilate it to the natural sciences by postulating general laws and the need for theory.

OP. CIT.: technical term used in footnotes, meaning the work already cited.

PALAEOBOTANY: the scientific study of the traces of old vegetation, making it possible, for instance, to trace older patterns of cultivation in, say, medieval society.

PALAEOGRAPHY: the ancillary technique of studying archaic forms of handwriting.

PARADIGM (in historiography): the (alleged) dominant approach to historical study in any particular period or society, hence, for example, the exemplar paradigm, the *Annales*, or, say, the Progressive paradigm, or the New Left paradigm, etc., etc.

PASSIM: technical term in footnotes meaning that the point being cited can be found in many places throughout the book being referred to.

PAST, THE: what has actually happened, what has actually existed: always, at any point in time, gone for good, it is the basic subject area of the historian (or, more accurately, the *human* past is the basic subject area of the historian).

PHILOLOGY: the study of the structure and devices of language – an important ancillary technique in the development of the discipline of history.

POSITIVISM: the approach to the study of the past developed by Auguste Comte which tried to make history a science with regularities and general laws. However, Marxists often use the word to criticise the kind of history I have been explicating in this book, that is to say, history which above all stresses the importance of the systematic criticism of primary sources. Though confusing, this usage can be legitimated because of the phrase coined by the French scholar Fustel de Coulanges, 'positivism of the document', which in effect was an extreme statement of the source-based, non-metaphysical position.

POSTMODERNISM: according to its protagonists, a completely new way of looking at the world, academic study, philosophy, artistic production, etc., arising from the 'discoveries' of Foucault, Barthes, Derrida, Lyotard, Baudrillard (in France) and Jameson (in America), and the so-called 'linguistic turn', supposed to have happened in the late 1960s or early 1970s, and maintaining in essence that 'everything is constructed within language', that is to say that outside of language there is no reality. Postmodernism derives its view of the world from Marxism and maintains that the societies we live in, being bourgeois, are evil; while some postmodernists take up an entirely nihilistic position, most support radical political action and aim at the destruction of all traditional or modern modes of thought and study (dismissed as 'grand narratives'). In reality, postmodernism is a totalising belief system based on faith alone. It is distinguished by elaborate rhetoric and a specialised jargon which fails to conceal the essential naïvety of its basic ideas, derived from a discredited Marxism. If it often sounds like nonsense, that is because it is nonsense.

PROSOPOGRAPHY: multiple biography, the building up of an interpretation of the past by detailed biographical studies of individuals.

PROTESTANT ETHIC: the attitude of hard work and saving associated (by Weber in the first place) with the Protestant religion.

PUBLIC HISTORY: the phrase was invented in America to apply to the public, and usually commercial, use of history, as in journalism, or tracing family trees, or providing histories for business corporations; now applied also to history in the media, 'heritage', etc.

RADICAL: literally 'from the roots': i.e. an extreme reformer; but the word has taken on various inflections of meaning, and in late nineteenth-century usage, for example, actually meant a rather moderate liberal reformer. The extreme connotation returned from the 1960s onwards.

REGRESSION: a method of studying the past by starting with phenomena in the present which may in one way or another be survivals from the past.

RELATIVISM (as applied to history): the view that there are no objective standards: in each age and culture history will be written differently, and, indeed, even within one culture different groups and different individuals will produce different types of history. To relativists this is all perfectly normal and nothing can be done about it. Marxists and postmodernists are relativists. Against them, this book argues that there are consistent professional standards against which all history can be measured.

RENAISSANCE: literally 'rebirth'; usually applied to the period of change (perhaps lasting several centuries) in which, to express matters in a rather unsatisfactory cliché, the medieval or feudal world in Europe came to an end. The essential original characteristic was the revival or rebirth of classical learning.

REVOLUTION: overthrowing of existing system or set of ideas: in political history means more than a simple *coup d'état* or change of ruler, and always implies some change affecting more groups in society than simply the ruling family.

SCHOLARLY SYNTHESIS: a useful way of describing a book which ranges more widely than a monograph and which, though based to a considerable extent on the secondary works of others, which it interprets and synthesises, also contains much more original work than would be found in a textbook.

SEMIOLOGY: branch of linguistics concerned with signs and symbols.

SEMIOTICS: study of the signs which (allegedly) represent human behaviour in all its modes.

SERIAL HISTORY: history based on the premise that statistical series (of landholding, prices, and so on) provide a firm structural base to which other social phenomena can be related.

SEROLOGY: the study of blood groups; can be useful for tracing population movements in the past for societies for which there is little other evidence.

SOCIAL CONTROL: used by right-wing sociologists to explain the way in which stability is maintained in societies, and by left-wing sociologists and historians to explain the way in which the dominant class, allegedly, maintains its hegemony.

SOCIOLOGY OF KNOWLEDGE: an approach to academic study which maintains that everything is socially or culturally constructed.

SOURCE, PRIMARY: a relic of a past age (document, artefact, etc.) which originated in that age.

SOURCE, SECONDARY: a contribution to knowledge about a past age written up later, using (if a serious historical work) primary sources.

STATUS: Weber made a distinction between a person's class, which he held to be an entirely economic category, and their status group, which referred to their position on the prestige hierarchy. Historians often use the word 'class' to include prestige as well as economic elements.

STRUCTURAL: Like many similar words this one is used in a variety of slightly different ways. In my own preferred usage, it refers to that group of circumstances or 'forces' which usually have a critical, if not determining, influence on outcomes (events, social developments, etc.): economic, geographic, demographic and technological. In some recent work (particularly American) 'structural' is used to describe an approach which stresses the wider circumstances as distinct from the effects of deliberate human actions, the latter (rather unsatisfactorily, in my view) being described as the 'voluntarist' approach.

STRUCTURALISM: an approach to academic study which originated in linguistics, but which was also developed in social anthropology. It is the structuralism of social anthropology that has affected some historical writing, particularly that associated with *Annales*. Structuralism seeks to find basic structures in human behaviour and human societies and stresses the key significance of language, signs and codes. Structuralism became readily linked to Marxism and cultural and linguistic theory insofar as it 'seeks its structures not on the surface, at the level of the observed, but below or behind empirical reality' (Michael Lane, 1970), and led, via post-structuralism, into postmodernism.

THEORY: in the sciences a general proposition (perhaps in the form of a 'law', often in the form of a mathematical formula) relating to some branch of the study of the natural world or physical universe and based on controlled experiments and/or empirical observation. Scientific theories (there is no one totalising theory) are of proven use in the investigations and experiments which advance scientific knowledge, though they are not always operable in extreme conditions; a scientific theory will always be abandoned if the overwhelming weight of empirical evidence is against it. Specific theories are used by historians, often ones borrowed from other disciplines, such as economics or social psychology. The basic theories upon which historical study as described in this book is founded (nature of primary sources and the analysis of them, etc.) are better described as 'assumptions'. The theories that historians themselves produce (such as Elton's 'Tudor revolution in government') are better described as theses – thus we have 'the Fischer thesis' or 'the Taylor thesis'. Postmodernists speak of 'critical theory', 'cultural theory', and sometimes just 'theory'. Really, they are speaking only of 'assumptions', or 'faith'. What they call theory bears no relation to the term as understood in the sciences, and as it should be used by historians. The same strictures apply to 'Marxist theory', though I would be the first to admit that Marxist political ideas have often been the stimulus towards producing impressive *contributions* to historical knowledge (*not* comprehensive, unchallengeable statements). Postmodernists like to use the ugly verb 'to theorise', which means to place some idea or piece of information into the context of Marxist or postmodernist theory, thought by postmodernists to be an admirable thing to do. I should add that along with 'economic theory' such phrases as 'literary theory', 'film theory', 'sociological theory', 'linguistic theory' are both legitimate and useful, being drawn from empirical study within the *separate* subject areas. Some knowledge of all of these can be valuable for historians.

THESIS: can be used in two very different ways: (a) the hypothesis, or theory, or interpretation put forward by a particular historian, as in Turner's 'frontier thesis'; (b) as a synonym for dissertation (for a PhD, etc.).

TOTAL HISTORY: history which endeavours to integrate together all aspects of human society, aesthetic and cultural, as well as social, economic and political, private as well as public.

VOLUNTARIST: This word can have many meanings but has recently been used by American historians to define an approach which, as distinct from the so-called 'structural' approach, stresses the importance of human agency. There is absolutely no reason, of course, why any historian should feel bound to opt for one approach or the other. One used to talk of historians considering both 'unguided' forces (structural, ideological, institutional) and 'guided' forces (those produced by deliberate human actions).

WHIG INTERPRETATION OF HISTORY: the view, prevalent in nineteenth-century Britain, that history was the record of steady progress towards liberal ideas and institutions.

Further Reading

I believe in making a distinction between a 'Bibliography' and 'Further Reading'. A work of scholarly research requires a bibliography, listing all sources, primary and secondary, used. This is a different kind of book. I suppose the 'primary sources' are the writings of Fernand Braudel, A. J. P. Taylor, and others, but the listing of these would be tedious and pointless. This Further Reading is simply aimed at utility, that utility being enhanced, I hope, by the annotations. I have dropped many of the older books listed in the three editions of *The Nature of History*.

Two useful compilations from the 1980s are R. C. Richardson, *The Study of History: A Bibliographical Guide* (Manchester, 1988), and the bibliography in Ernst Breisach, *Historiography: Ancient, Medieval, Modern* (Chicago, 1983), a comprehensive and authoritative work. Michael Bentley (ed.), *Companion to Historiography* (London, 1997), is a reliable collection of essays. Kelly Boyd, *Encyclopædia of Historians and Historical Writing*, 2 vols (London, 1999), is massive, the trouble being the bigger the book, the more the omissions stand out. The emphasis is almost entirely on historians, rather than on what they produce, in John Cannon (ed.), *The Blackwell Dictionary of Historians* (1988). There was quite a flurry of historiographical and epistemological books towards the end of the old century and at the beginning of the new: these are probably best accessed through the internet.

My Further Reading is divided into two sections:

A   Historiography (history of history)
B   Epistemology (i.e. the 'What?', 'Why?' and 'How?' of history)

A   Historiography

Ausubel, Herman, *Historians and their Craft: A Study of Presidential Addresses to the American Historical Association 1884–1945* (New York, 1950): the silly things they said.

Barnes, H. Elmer, *A History of Historical Writing* (Norman, Okla., 1936; revised pb edn, New York, 1962): encyclopaedic; too often reads like an encyclopaedia.

Beasley, W. G. and Pulleybank, Edwin, *Historians of China and Japan* (London and New York, 1961): necessary corrective to my concentration on the Western tradition.

Bell, Henry E., *Maitland: A Critical Examination and Assessment* (London, 1965).

Bendix, Reinhard, *Max Weber: An Intellectual Portrait* (Garden City, NY, and London, 1960).

Black, J. B., *The Art of History* (London, 1926): a study of the Enlightenment historians.

Burk, Kathleen, *Troublemaker: The Life and History of A.J.P. Taylor* (London, 2000): three biographies and an autobiography (see below) exaggerate Taylor's significance as a historian: his career was peculiar and peculiarly British.

Burke, Peter (ed.), *Economy and Society in Early Modern Europe* (London, 1972): essays from *Annales*, brilliantly introduced – a good starting point.

Burke, Peter, *The French Historical Revolution: The Annales School 1929–1989* (Cambridge, 1990): clear and authoritative, by far the best introduction to *Annales*.

Burke, Peter, *Varieties of Cultural History* (Cambridge, 1997): collection of readings from historians discussed towards the end of Chapter 5.

Butterfield, Herbert, *The Whig Interpretation of History* (London, 1931).

Butterfield, Herbert, *Man on his Past: The Study of the History of Historical Writing* (Cambridge, 1955; Boston, Mass., 1966): classics in their way, but scarcely of pressing relevance for today.

Cannon, John (ed.), *The Historian at Work* (1980): authoritative essays on individual historians with an excellent editor's introduction.

Cole, Robert, *A. J. P. Taylor: The Traitor within the Gates* (London, 1993): see comments on Burk biography.

Finley, M. I., *The Greek Historians: The Essence of Herodotus, Thucydides, Xenophon, Polybius* (New York, 1959; London, 1960).

Fisher, H. A. L., *Frederick William Maitland* (London, 1910): interesting for what it tells about Fisher and his generation, as well as for what it says about Maitland.

Hale, J. R., *The Evolution of British Historiography: From Bacon to Namier* (London and New York, 1967).

Halperin, S. William (ed.), *Some 20th Century Historians* (Chicago, 1961): contains illuminating essays by James L. Cate on Pirenne, Henry R. Winkler on Trevelyan, Gordon H. McNeil on Lefebvre, S. William Halperin on Renouvin, and Palmer A. Throop on Febvre.

Hay, Denys, *Annalists and Historians: Western Historiography from the VIIIth to the XVIIIth Century* (London, 1977).

Higham, John, *History: Professional Scholarship in America* (new edn, Baltimore, 1983): authoritative for American developments in the earlier part of the twentieth century.

Hobsbawm, Eric, *Uncommon People: Resistance, Rebellion and Jazz* (London, 1998): good introduction to the great man's range, from impeccable scholarship to challenging Marxist journalism.

Hughes, H. Stuart, *Consciousness and Society: The Reorientation of European Social Thought 1890–1930* (New York, 1958; London, 1959): intellectual history at its finest, specially relevant here for Chapter 6 on Dilthey, Croce and Meinecke.

Hughes-Warrington, Marnie, *Fifty Key Thinkers on History* (London, 2000): not everybody's top 50, but the potted biographies are competently done.

Hunt, Lynn (ed.), *The New Cultural History* (Berkeley, Calif., 1989): essays authoritatively introducing this genre of history.

Iggers, George, *New Directions in European Historiography* (rev. edn, London, Methuen, 1985): absolutely indispensable.

Iggers, George C. and Powell, James M. (eds), *Leopold von Ranke and the Shaping of the Historical Discipline* (Syracuse, NY, 1990): powerful essays give the great German a good going-over.

Kenyon, John, *The History Men: The Historical Profession in England since the Renaissance* (1983): very strong on the earlier periods, very brief on the twentieth century.

Porter, Roy, *Gibbon: Making History* (new edn, London, 1995).

Powicke, F. M., *Historical Study in Oxford* (London, 1929): a primary source!

Schuyler, R. L. (ed.), *Frederick William Maitland, Historian: Selections from his Writings . . . with an Introduction . . .* (Berkeley, Calif., 1960).

Sisman, Adam, *A.J.P. Taylor: A Biography* (1994): see previous note on Taylor.

Smith Fussner, F., *The Historical Revolution: English Historical Writing and Thought, 1580–1640* (London and New York, 1962).

Stedman Jones, Gareth, 'History: The Poverty of Empiricism', in R. Blackburn (ed.), *Ideology in Social Science* (1972), pp. 96–115: fine knockabout attack on the alleged 'conceptual poverty' of British history.

Stern, Friz (ed.), *The Varieties of History: Voltaire to the Present* (New York, 1956; 2nd edn, London, 1970): valuable collection of readings, though I am not keen on this idea of 'varieties' of history.

Stone, Lawrence, *The Past and the Present Revisited* (London, 1987): survey of (then) recent trends.

Taylor, A. J. P., *A Personal History* (London, 1983): see previous comment on Taylor.

Thompson, James Westfall, *A History of Historical Writing*, 2 vols (New York, 1942): still an important work of reference, though there are many inaccuracies, and the judgements are trite.

Woodman, A. J., *Rhetoric in Classical Historiography* (1988).

B   Epistemology

Abrams, Philip, *Historical Sociology* (Shepton Mallet, 1982): pleads for a merging of history and sociology, but on Marxist terms.

Ankersmit, Frank and Kellner, Hans (eds), *A New Philosophy of History* (London, 1995): a collection which, according to Kellner's Introduction, has 'A shared vision that history can be re-described as a discourse that is fundamentally rhetorical, and that representing the past takes place through the creation of powerful, persuasive images which can best be understood as created objects, models, metaphors or proposals about reality' – you have been warned!

Appleby, Joyce, Hunt, Lynn and Jacob, Margaret, *Telling the Truth about History* (New York, 1994): wastes far too much time trying to incorporate postmodernism before working through to what we all knew anyway; appallingly American mix of grovelling and slang.

Ashley-Montague, M. F. (ed.), *Toynbee and History* (Boston, Mass., 1956).

Atkinson, R. E., *Knowledge and Explanation in History* (London, 1978): a philosopher who really understands historians.

Ballard, Martin (ed.), *New Movements in the Study and Teaching of History* (1970): a primary source!

Barraclough, Geoffrey, *Main Trends in History* (London, 1979): still a useful and wide-ranging study.

Barzun, Jacques, *Clio and the Doctors* (Chicago, 1974): ultra-conservative.

Barzun, Jacques and Graff, Henry F., *The Modern Researcher* (New York, 1957; rev. edn, 1977): wise advice on how to go about writing history at all levels.

Bédarida, François (ed.), *L'Histoire et le métier d'historien en France 1945–1995* (Paris, 1995): there is plenty in English on recent developments in France, but for specialists this is essential reading.

Benson, Susan Porter, Brier, Stephen and Rosenzweig, Roy, *Presenting the Past: Essays on History and the Public* (New York, 1980): pioneering essays in support of public history.

Beresford, M. W. and St Joseph, J. K. S., *Medieval England: An Aerial Survey* (Cambridge, 1958): very useful for this type of 'processed source'.

Berkhofer, Robert, *Beyond the Great Story: History as Text and Discourse* (Cambridge, Mass., 1995): the title gives fair warning.

Black, Jeremy and McRaild, Donald M., *Studying History* (2nd edn, 2000): English gentleman's vade-mecum, nice to everyone; the importance of Marxism is grossly overstated, but the new edition has some neat critical comments on postmodernism.

Bloch, Marc, *The Historian's Craft* (Manchester and New York, 1954; pb edn, 1976): classic by one of the two founders of the first generation of the *Annales* school (though the translated title is misleading – it should be *The Historian's Profession*).

Bottomore, T. B. and Rubel, M., *Karl Marx: Selected Writings in Sociology and Social Philosophy* (London, 1956; pb edn, 1967).

Braudel, Fernand, *On History* (London, 1980): essays by the famous French historian.

British Universities Film Council, *Film and the Historian* (London, 1968): things have progressed greatly since the sixties.

Burke, Peter, *History and Social Theory* (Cambridge, 1992): inevitably, as an enthusiast for social science and anthropological approaches, Burke overdoes it, but well worth reading all the same.

Canary, Robert H. and Kozicki, Henry, *The Writing of History: Literary Form and Historical Understanding* (Madison, Wis., 1978): leans to the 'history as literature' position.

Carnes, Mark C., *Past Imperfect: History According to the Movies* (New York, 1995): brilliant introduction and outstanding essays on feature films dealing with historical topics – a film is a film is a film, and *never* history.

Carr, E. H., *What is History?* (London, 1961; pb edn, 1964): still stimulating in many ways, but ought to have been titled *What E. H. Carr Thought History Ought To Be*; strongly Marxist, it contains many misconceptions.

Clark, G. Kitson, *Guide for Research Students Working in Historical Subjects* (Cambridge, 1960): advice which is still well worth heeding.

Cohen, David William, *The Combing of History* (Chicago, 1994): an endearingly personalised book trying to bring together anthropology and postmodernism with particular reference to African history.

Collingwood, R. G., *The Philosophy of History* (London, 1930).

Collingwood, R. G., *An Autobiography* (London, 1939).

Collingwood, R. G., *The Idea of History* (London, 1946): re-reading these works for this book, I was struck by how positively archaic they are.

Collingwood, R. G., *The Principles of History and Other Writings in Philosophy of History* (eds. W. H. Dray and W. J. van der Dussen, Oxford, 1999): 'rediscovered' works recently published; do we need them? I couldn't possibly comment.

Conway, David, *A Farewell to Marx: An Outline and Appraisal of his Theories* (London, 1987).

Crombie, A. C. (ed.), *Scientific Change* (New York, 1963): contains important essays on history of science by A. C. Crombie and M. A. Hoskin, and by Henry Guerlac.

Denley, Peter and Hopkin, Deian (eds), *History and Computing* (Manchester, 1987).

Dickinson, A. K., Lee, P. J. and Rogers, P. J., *Learning History* (London, 1984): useful essays.

Donnachie, Ian and Whatley, Christopher, *The Manufacture of Scottish History* (1992): grovels before the A. J. Youngson book mentioned below, and like it shows little awareness of the intellectual issues involved.

Dray, W. H., *Philosophy of History* (Englewood Cliffs, NJ, 1964): ideal encapsulation of the topics which, to a professional philosopher, make up 'philosophy of history'.

Dunne, Tom (ed.), *The Writer as Witness: Literature as Historical Evidence* (Irish Historical Studies 16, Cork, 1987): collection of solid essays with excitable introduction which cites the usual authorities in asserting, unpersuasively, that history 'is a statement as personal in its way as that of the poet or novelist'.

Dyos, H. J. (ed.), *The Study of Urban History* (London, 1968): written at the time when urban history was still in high fashion.

Easthope, Anthony, 'Romancing the Stone: History-writing and Rhetoric', *Social History* (May 1993), pp. 235–49: the childish pun in this attack on Lawrence Stone is a sufficient guide to the quality of the article.

Elton, G. R., *The Practice of History* (Sydney, Australia, 1967): Elton performed an enormous service to history by taking on the philosophers and ideologists on their own ground, and thoroughly vanquishing them; still a most important book.

Elton, G. R., *Political History: Principles and Practice* (London, 1970): also an important book, though Elton was blind to the importance of social and cultural history.

Elton, G. R., *Return to Essentials: Some Reflections on the Present State of Historical Study* (Cambridge, 1991): three fittingly pugnacious lectures delivered in 1990, together with some older material.

Evans, Richard, *In Defence of History* (London, 1997): excellent, though Evans treats me as if I were the only historian ever to have written a less than perfect sentence.

Fay, Brian, Pomper, Philip and Vann, Richard T., *History and Theory: Contemporary Readings* (Oxford, 1998): a very good and varied collection, if you are interested in that sort of thing.

Ferguson, Niall (ed.), *Virtual History: Alternatives and Counterfactuals* (London, 1997): 'counterfactuals' in econometric history deserve serious attention; Ferguson's Introduction is a magnificent demolition of determinism (Marxism, structuralism, etc.), but he and his contributors fail to make the case that historians should always consider possible alternative outcomes.

Ferro, Marc, *The Use and Abuse of History: or, How the Past is Taught* (London, 1984): fabulously informative, provides the essential justification for the systematic study of history.

Ferro, Marc, *L'Histoire sous surveillance* (Paris, 1985): stimulating, naturally, but rather assertive on behalf of the *Annales* school.

'Film et Histoire', in *XVIe Congrès Internationale de Science Historique: Rapport*, vol. 1 (Stuttgart, 1985), pp. 180–239: with essays by Fledelius, two Germans, a Russian, Sorlin and Marwick, this is still a good guide within a short space to both methods and literature.

Floud, Roderick, *An Introduction to Quantitative Methods for Historians* (London, 1973): early work in the field.

Fox-Genovese, Elizabeth and Lasch-Quinn, Elisabeth (eds), *Reconstructing History: The Emergence of a New Historical Society* (New York, 1999): rich, up-to-date collection by many distinguished American historians, containing much wisdom.

Furet, François, *In the Workshop of History* (Chicago, 1984): almost jingoistic assertion of the case for the *Annales* approach.

Galbraith, V. H., *An Introduction to the Study of History* (London, 1964): classic statement of the approaches to history which I was rebelling against in the sixties, and in the first *The Nature of History*.

Gardiner, Patrick, *The Nature of Historical Explanation* (London, 1952): historical explanation as most historians themselves understand it (if and when they think about it at all).

Gay, Peter, *Style in History* (New York, 1974): studies Gibbon, Ranke, Macaulay and Burckhardt; says history is art and science.

Gay, Peter, *Art and Act: On Causes in History – Manet, Gropius, Mondrian* (New York, 1976): studies three artists; says causation is complex.

Gay, Peter, *Freud for Historians* (New York, 1985): since Gay has magnificently practised what he preaches in the series of books beginning with *The Bourgeois Experience: Victoria to Freud*, this guide is fully worthy of attention.

Geyl, Pieter, *Napoleon: For and Against* (1949): based on textbooks and popular accounts, this never gets to grips with its alleged subject.

Geyl, Pieter, *The Use and Abuse of History* (1955): this book came out when I was a student and is eloquent testimony to the superficial nonsense which then passed for a guide to the historian's activities.

Hamerow, Theodore S., *Reflections on History and Historians* (Madison, Wis., 1987): original study of the nature of the historical profession.

Hancock, W. K., *Professing History* (Sidney, 1974): first-hand testimony from a major historian of his day.

Haskell, Thomas L., *Objectivity is not Neutrality: Explanatory Schemes in History* (Baltimore, Mass., 1998): a rag-bag; the excellent essay of the title also appears in Fay, Pomper and Vann.

Haslam, Jonathan, *The Vices of Integrity: E. H. Carr, 1892–1982* (London, 1999): written in the belief that there is intrinsic interest in the squabbles of dead Cambridge dons and in the inability of Carr to make up his mind over what he believed about history; does not shake my view that the *What is History?* of 1961 is fundamentally Marxist.

Hayden, Dolores, *The Power of Place, Urban Landscapes and Public History* (Cambridge, Mass., 1995): fashionable mix of fashionable interests.

Himmelfarb, Gertrude, 'Postmodernist History', in her *On Looking into the Abyss: Unkindly Thoughts on Culture and Society* (New York, 1994), pp. 131–61: powerful argument that postmodernism is not only unconvincing, it's not even new.

Hoskins, W. G., *Field Work in Local History* (London, 1967): useful.

Howard, Michael, *The Lessons of History: An Inaugural Lecture* (Oxford, 1981): magisterial.

Hughes, H. Stuart, *History as Art and as Science* (New York, 1964): historians used to believe this, rather than seeing history as bodies of knowledge.

Iggers, George C. and Parker, Harold T., *International Handbook of Historical Studies: Contemporary Research and Theory* (Westport, Conn., 1979): for its time, comprehensive.

Jenkins, Keith, *Rethinking History* (London, 1991): simplistic, clumsy, inaccurate; because they already know the truth, postmodernists see no need for correct quotation or precise citation.

Jenkins, Keith, *On 'What is History?': From Carr and Elton to Rorty and White* (London, 1995): no great improvement; though there are many references to, there is no reading by, me, since the editor was unwilling to submit his edited extracts for my approval, or to pay the standard fee.

Jenkins, Keith, *Why History?: Ethics and Postmodernity* (London, 1999): essays on the usual suspects (Derrida, White, etc.) with a characteristically feeble attack on Richard Evans's *In Defence of History*.

Jenkins, Keith (ed.), *The Postmodern History Reader* (London, 1997): definitely a useful collection.

Jordanova, Ludmilla, *History in Practice* (London, 2000): former Foucauldian warlady begins to recant, but remains confused about the distinction between primary and secondary sources, and the nature of archives; good on public history.

Joyce, Patrick, 'History and Post-Modernism', *Past and Present*, 133 (November 1991): 'A recognition of the irreducibly discursive character of the social undermines the idea of social totality', so said Joyce in his sharp response to Stone (see below).

Joyce, Patrick, 'The End of Social History?', *Social History*, 20 (1995), pp. 73–91: Planet Joyce is a strange world inhabited by such abstractions as 'the social' and 'the discursive'.

Joyce, Patrick, 'The Return of History: Postmodernism and the Politics of Academic History in Britain', *Past and Present*, 158 (Feb. 1998): the return to Planet Joyce is as baffling as ever – full of jargon, cliché, and unfocused rage.

Kellner, Hans, *Language and Historical Representation: Getting the Story Crooked* (Madison, Wis., 1989): low-octane Hayden White.

Kelly, Catrina, 'History and Post-Modernism', *Past and Present*, 133 (November 1991), pp. 209–13: an avowed feminist joins in.

Ladurie, E. Le Roy, *The Territory of the Historian* (London, 1979): essays by a major French historian.

Lambert, Sir Henry C. M., *The Nature of History* (London, 1933): a rather slim essay.

Lane, Michael (ed.), *Structuralism: A Reader* (London, 1970): an excellent introduction; includes an essay on 'Historical Discourse' by Roland Barthes himself.

Langlois, C. V. and Seignobos, C., *Introduction to the Study of History* (London, 1898; new edn, London and New York, 1966): classic work from a time of critical change in historical study.

Laslett, Barbara *et al.* (eds), *History and Theory: Feminist Research, Debates, Contestations* (Chicago, 1997): covers everything mentioned in the capacious title.

Leff, Gordon, *History and Social Theory* (London, 1969): particularly strong on 'contingency', on the fragmentary nature of sources, and on the significance of periodisation.

Le Goff, Jacques and Nora, Pierre (eds), *Constructing the Past: Essays in Historical Methodology* (Cambridge, 1985): more wisdom from the French.

Lemon, Michael, *The Discipline of History and the History of Thought* (London, 1995): no Marwick – well, OK – but no Elton, Carr, Tosh, Stone either; a plethora of philosophers, and nothing for genuine students of history to latch onto.

Lloyd, Christopher, *Explanation in Social History* (Oxford, 1986): comprehensive survey of almost everybody (Marx, Hempel, Habermas, Foucault, etc.) except those who actually write history, concluding, as it starts out, in favour of a theory-based, unified, sociological history.

Lowenthal, David, *The Past is a Foreign Country* (Cambridge, 1985): massive account of the romantic appeal of the past by distinguished American historian, rhetorical and imprecise; Lowenthal's claims that we 'change' the past and that it is 'increasingly suffused by the present' indicate a total confusion between 'history' and 'the past'.

MacLennan, Gregor, *Marxism and the Methodologies of History* (1981): insists that those who place great emphasis on the methodology of empirical history (as I do) are as ideologically motivated as any Marxist, but, revealingly, nowhere engages with any of my own arguments on the matter.

Mandlebaum, Maurice, *The Anatomy of Historical Knowledge* (Baltimore, 1977): pioneering philosopher in the field gives mature reflections on what constitutes explanation in history and whether historical knowledge is as reliable as other forms of knowledge, and concludes (I agree) that historical explanations are adequate and historical knowledge securely based.

Marho, *Visions of History* (Manchester, 1983): radical historians speak, with some illuminating confessions from Eric Hobsbawm.

Marwick, Arthur, *The Nature of History* (1970, 1981, 1989): what I was trying to say was right, but the first and second editions were often naïve, and the third edition had too much stuff that was ponderous and boring.

Marwick, Arthur, 'Art as Historical Source', *Modern History Review*, 4/2 (Nov. 1992), pp. 9–10.

Marwick, Arthur, '"A Fetishism of Documents?" The Salience of Source-Based History', in Henry Kozicki (ed.), *Developments in Modern Historiography* (New York and London, 1993), pp. 107–38.

Marwick, Arthur, 'Explicitness and Precision in the Use of Sources, Concepts and Signifiers in Producing *Contributions* to Historical Knowledge: In Explication of Non-metaphysical History', in *Social History Society Bulletin*: brief summary of a paper delivered (without notes) in a three-way debate with Patrick Joyce and Ludmilla Jordanova at a Social History Society Annual Conference, 1994.

Marwick, Arthur, 'Two Approaches to Historical Study: The Metaphysical (including "Postmodernism") and the Historical', *Journal of Contemporary History*, 30/1 (January 1995), pp. 5–34.

Marwick, Arthur, 'Structured Distance Teaching', in Alan Booth and Paul Hyland (eds), *Teaching History in Higher Education* (Oxford, 1995), pp. 487–97.

Marwick, Arthur, 'Concepts and Sources: Seven Modest Rules for the 21st Century', in *Political History on the Eve of the XXI Century: Traditions and Innovations* (Moscow, 1995), pp. 9–22: keynote address to international conference at Moscow Academy of Sciences, May 1994.

Marwick, Arthur, 'History in the Modern Media', in Haus der Geschichte der Bundesrepublik Deutschland (Museum of Contemporary History, Bonn), *The Culture of European History in the 21st Century* (Berlin, 1999), pp. 146–55.

Marwick, Arthur, 'Painting and Music During and After the Great War: The Art of Total War', in Roger Chickering and Stig Förster (eds), *Great War, Total War: Combat and Mobilization on the Western Front, 1914–1918* (Cambridge, 2000), pp. 501–17.

Marwick, Arthur (ed.), *The Arts, Literature and Society* (London, 1989): listing this and the titles above is not simply an exercise in trumpet-blowing; I am anxious to show that I have been addressing major epistemological problems since the late 1980s.

Merriman, Nick, *Beyond the Glass Case: The Past, the Heritage and the Public in Britain* (Leicester, 1991): interesting aspect of public history.

Munslow, Alun, *Deconstructing History* (London, 1997): fair account written from a postmodernist standpoint; Munslow pins labels – 'constructionist', 'reconstructionist', etc. – on different groups of historians, revealing some fundamental misconceptions.

Namier, L. B., *Avenues of History* (London, 1952): includes, in the essay on 'History', a condensed statement of Namier's views on historical writing.

Palmer, Brian D., *Descent into Discourse: The Reification of Language and the Writing of Social History* (Philadelphia, Penn., 1990): an 'old Marxist' critique of postmodernism.

Poster, Mark, *Foucault, Marxism and History: Mode of Production vs Mode of Information* (Cambridge, 1984): lucid and helpful.

Rabb, Theodore K. and Rotberg, Robert I. (eds), *The New History, the 1980s and Beyond: Studies in Interdisciplinary History* (Princeton, NJ, 1982): interesting essays of variable quality.

Reddy, William M., *Money and Liberty in Modern Europe: A Critique of Historical Understanding* (New York, 1986): shows where Marxist analysis of the various allegedly bourgeois revolutions has gone wrong; all the more impressive since Reddy is a Marxist.

Ricoeur, Paul, *The Contribution of French Historiography to the Theory of History* (Oxford, 1980): much nonsense about 'narrative' and 'emplotment'.

Rigby, S. H., *Marxism and History: A Critical Introduction* (2nd edn, Manchester, 1998): specialist study by a specialist.

Rose, Stephen, *The Making of Memory: From Molecules to Mind* (London, 1992): wise and witty memoirs of brain biologist; the rigours of science and the human fallibility of scientists echo those, respectively, of history and historians.

Rosenstone, Robert A., *Visions of the Past: The Challenge of Film to our Idea of History* (Cambridge, Mass., 1995): self-styled pioneer of postmodernist idea that films are just another kind of history pontificates unpersuasively.

Rosenstone, Robert A. (ed.), *Revisioning History: Film and the Construction of the New Past* (Cambridge, Mass., 1995): collection of essays trying to make the same case.

Samuel, Raphael, *Theatres of Memory, Vol. 1: Past and Present in Contemporary Culture* (London, 1994).

Samuel, Raphael, *Theatres of Memory, Vol. 2: Island Stories* (London, 1998): Samuel was an original; the protagonist of one type of public history.

Searle, John, *Mind, Language and Society: Philosophy in the Real World* (London, 1999): this distinguished and authoritative philosopher completely destroys the claims of the speculative philosophers and the postmodernists.

Seldon, Anthony (ed.), *Contemporary History: Practice and Method* (Oxford, 1988): useful collection.

Shoemaker, Robert and Vincent, Mary (eds), *Gender and History in Western Europe* (London, 1998): useful collection.

Smith, B., *The Gender of History: Men, Women and Historical Practice* (Cambridge, Mass., 1998): the title says enough.

Smith, Paul (ed.), *The Historian and Film* (Cambridge, 1976): collection of essays dating from the time when British historians were just beginning to take film seriously.

Sobchack, Vivian (ed.), *The Persistence of History: Cinema, Television and the Modern Event* (New York, 1996): despite leanings towards postmodernism, some very interesting essays.

Sokal, Alan and Bricmont, Jean, *Intellectual Impostures: Postmodern Philosophy's Abuse of Science* (London, 1998): Sokal is, as a citizen, so committed to left-wing causes that he worked as a maths teacher under the Sandinista regime in Nicaragua, something the arrogant charlatans of French postmodernism would never dream of doing; with fellow physicist Bricmont he systematically exposes the attempts of the charlatans to incorporate scientific concepts and scientific language into what is really political propaganda.

Sorlin, Pierre, *The Film in History: Restaging the Past* (Oxford, 1980): the opening section on methodology is particularly useful.

Southgate, Beverley, *History: What and Why?: Ancient, Modern and Post-modern Perspectives* (London, 1996): another of these books which pays little heed to the critics of postmodernism.

Speigel, Gabrielle M., 'History, Historicism and the Social Logic of the Text in the Middle Ages', *Speculum: A Journal of Medieval Studies*, 65 (1990), pp. 59–86: it was a short note on this article by Lawrence Stone that touched off a brief but fiery debate on postmodernism; in fact Speigel, while critical of extreme postmodernist positions, was taking it for granted that history would have to accommodate postmodernism.

Stanford, Michael, *The Nature of Historical Knowledge* (Oxford, 1986): leans towards the metaphysical.

Stanford, Michael, *A Companion to the Study of History* (Oxford, 1994): thoughtful book, with a fair measure of fanciful waffle ('History is a unity...it is like a family...').

Stannard, David E., *Shrinking History: On Freud and the Failure of Psychohistory* (Oxford, 1980): all historians should know some psychology, but the notion of a separate 'psychohistory' was pretentious nonsense: Stannard uses a sledge-hammer to point this out.

Stoianovich, Traian, *French Historical Method: The* Annales *Paradigm* (Ithaca, NY, 1976): thorough study of the *Annales* school.

Stone, Lawrence, *The Past and the Present* (Boston, Mass., 1981): reprint of essays published between 1962 and 1980; Chapter 3, 'The Revival of Narrative: Reflections on a New Old History', is from *Past and Present*, 85 (1979).

Stone, Lawrence, 'Note: History and Post-Modernism', *Past and Present*, 133 (May 1991), pp. 217–18: Stone denounced postmodernism but thought the Speigel article (see above) offered a way out.

Stone, Lawrence, 'History and Post-Modernism', *Past and Present*, 135 (May 1992), pp. 188–93: Stone's urbane winding-up of the *Past and Present* debate – 'historians play with words, words do not play with each other' (I, of course, think historians should not play with words).

Thompson, E. P., *The Poverty of Theory and Other Essays* (London, 1978): the main essay is indispensable reading, with the defence of sound historical method coming over at least as strongly as the Marxist inflections.

Thompson, Paul, *The Voice of the Past: Oral History* (2nd edn, Oxford, 1988): introduction from leading exponent.

Thompson, Willie, *What Happened to History?* (London, 2000): brilliant on the parallels between history and the sciences, but as an only partly reconstructed Marxist grossly overestimates the importance of E. H. Carr.

Tosh, John, *The Pursuit of History: Aims, Methods and New Directions in the Study of Modern History* (London, 1984; 3rd edn, 2000): interesting to follow Tosh's development from vulgar Marxism, to naïvely enthusiastic postmodernism, to maturity; this latest edition is elegant and intelligent, but the continuing passionate emotional commitment to Marxism seems strange in the twenty-first century.

Tosh, John (ed.), *Historians on History: An Anthology* (London, 2000): splendidly wide-ranging collection, a godsend for sixth-form and university students.

Veyne, Paul, *Writing History: Essays on Epistemology* (Manchester, 1984): another Frenchman nattering about narrative and how historical writing is analogous to novel-writing.

Vincent, John, *An Intelligent Person's Guide to History* (London, 1995): idiosyncratic and written as if no one else had ever ventured into this area.

Walsh, W. H., *Introduction to the Philosophy of History* (London and New York, 1951; revised pb edn, 1967): clear, unpretentious, but not very profound.

Warren, John, *The Past and its Presenters: An Introduction to Issues in Historiography* (London, 1998): the slick title cannot protect this naïve defence of postmodernism; this writer of excellent school textbooks with a very unpostmodern emphasis on primary sources is presumably now withdrawing them from the market – at least until the wind changes again.

Watson, James, *The Double Helix: A Personal Account of the Discovery of DNA* (Harmondsworth, 1970): classic memoir of the co-discoverer of the structure of DNA; scientists, like historians, are all too human.

White, Hayden, *Metahistory: The Historical Imagination in Nineteenth-Century Europe* (Baltimore, Md., 1973): a brilliant and pioneering study of five *auteurs* of long ago. White's subsequent work is vitiated by the absurd assumption that historians still write in the mode of Hegel, Michelet, etc.

White, Hayden, *Tropics of Discourse* (Baltimore, Md., 1978).

White, Hayden, *The Content of the Form: Narrative Discourse and Historical Representation* (Baltimore, Md., 1987): White, perhaps *the* leading postmodernist critic of history, is an able linguist and his collections of essays (like most postmodernists he does not write books) ably convey the ideas of continental neo-Marxist and postmodernist thinkers to impressionable Americans (and British acolytes).

White, Hayden, 'Response to Arthur Marwick', *Journal of Contemporary History*, 30/2 (April 1995).

Windschuttle, Keith, *The Killing of History: How Literary Critics and Social Theorists are Murdering our Past* (New York, 1997, published Australia, 1994): good on this Aussie for using 'the work of real historians to combat their theoretical opponents'; clear that history is not fiction, but joins with the *auteurs* in seeing it as literature.

Wolpert, Lewis, *The Unnatural Nature of Science* (London, 1992): science is not based on common sense (neither is history).

Young, Robert, *White Mythologies: Writing History and the West* (1990): critical postmodernist view.

Youngson, A. J., *The Prince and the Pretender: A Study in the Writing of History* (1985): amateurish work by a distinguished professional economic historian; in history, above all, attempts at epistemology must show awareness of other writings on the subject.

Index

Note: Page numbers in **bold** type refer to main entries in the glossary.